Lincoln's Confidant

FIGURE 1. Noah Brooks as Lincoln would have first known him (about 1855). Author's collection.

Lincoln's Confidant

The Life of Noah Brooks

WAYNE C. TEMPLE

Edited by Douglas L. Wilson
and Rodney O. Davis

Introduction by Michael Burlingame

Published by
the Knox College Lincoln Studies Center
and the

**UNIVERSITY OF
ILLINOIS PRESS**
Urbana, Chicago, and Springfield

Library of Congress Control Number: 2018954795
ISBN 978-0-252-04217-1 (hardcover) | ISBN 978-0-252-05091-6 (e-book)

This volume is dedicated to the late J. G. Randall

Contents

Series Editors' Preface

THE KNOX COLLEGE Lincoln Studies Center's Publication Series was established primarily to publish source materials that enhance Lincoln scholarship and has thus far featured four new editorial works that make important sources more accessible and in reliable texts. The fifth volume is, strictly speaking, neither new nor an editorial work, but rather a deeply researched doctoral dissertation published more than sixty years ago. We are pleased to offer it as a valuable, if neglected, source for judging the relationship between President Abraham Lincoln and one of his most forthcoming confidants, Noah Brooks. While serving as a newspaper correspondent in Washington, Brooks renewed an earlier acquaintance with the president and was frequently in his company. After Lincoln's death, Brooks's many published recollections would become a prime biographical resource for glimpses of the personal and private side of the great president's life. Especially in light of Lincoln's reputation for being reserved and uncommunicative in personal matters, even among his friends, Brooks's credentials as a close confidant have often been challenged and the standing of his testimony questioned. In the editors' opinion, Dr. Wayne C. Temple's dissertation, completed in 1956 and reprinted here with a few minor changes and corrections, sheds more light on who Brooks was and the relationship he enjoyed with Abraham Lincoln than any subsequent account.

Introduction

MICHAEL BURLINGAME

WAYNE C. TEMPLE, Lincoln scholar extraordinaire, has made innumerable contributions to the literature about America's sixteenth president, starting with his doctoral dissertation on Noah Brooks, Lincoln's journalist-friend who was slated to become chief White House secretary during the Great Emancipator's second term.

In the Civil War, few people were as close to Lincoln as Brooks, a kind of surrogate son to the president, who was twenty years his senior. Brooks had known Lincoln back in Illinois, where both served in the antislavery ranks, Lincoln as an officer and Brooks as an enlisted man. Between December 1862, when Brooks moved from California to Washington DC, until the day Lincoln was assassinated, the young correspondent for the *Sacramento Union* saw the president "almost daily," as he later recalled.[1] Hours after Lincoln died, Brooks wrote that it "was my good fortune to make his acquaintance years ago, during the early days of Republicanism, in Illinois, and since my sojourn in Washington that early acquaintance has ripened into intimacy near and confiding."[2] Later in 1865, Mary Lincoln told Brooks that her husband had been "so earnest a friend of yours, that we will always remember you with the kindest feelings & will always, be pleased to hear from you."[3] The following year she remembered "the great affection and confidence, my husband, cherished" for Brooks.[4] A mutual friend of the president and Brooks told the Rev. Dr. James A. Reed that the journalist "was so intimate with the president that he visited him socially at times when others were refused admission, took tea with the family, spending evenings with them, reading to him, and conversing with him freely."[5] In 1896, John Conness, who represented California in the US Senate during the Civil War, wrote that "no man living had a better opportunity to know Lincoln's mind than Noah Brooks."[6] Another Californian who served in Congress during Lincoln's administration, Cornelius Cole, testified that the president and Brooks were so close because "Noah Brooks was one of the few men about the president who never asked anything for himself, and Lincoln rewarded him by giving the best gift he had to offer—his friendship."[7]

Lincoln and Brooks shared much in common. Each was amiable, pun-loving, and friendly, and each enjoyed literature, hated slavery, and overcame early hardships to emerge as self-made men.

During the Civil War, Brooks wrote 258 Washington dispatches, many of them full of valuable information about the president's thoughts and actions. He relied on them when he wrote his reminiscences of those days.[8] Excerpts from the dispatches dealing with Lincoln have been published in a scholarly edition.[9] Some historians have expressed skepticism about the intimacy with Lincoln that Brooks described, but Wayne Temple's thorough biography goes far to show that such skepticism is unwarranted.[10]

*　*　*

Born on February 5, 1924, in Delaware County, Ohio, Wayne Temple was named after the Revolutionary War hero Mad Anthony Wayne.[11] He grew up without siblings on his family's small farm, where he performed chores so ably that when he was only nine years old his parents left him alone for more than a week to mind the farm while they attended a fair in Chicago. His mother was a school teacher who taught him to read and do arithmetic before he began his formal education at a one-room schoolhouse. His father, who had only eight years of schooling, would not let young Wayne skip grades, arguing that precocious children who were promoted ahead of their age group seldom turned out very well.

After two years in a country school, Temple entered a consolidated school in nearby Prospect, from which he graduated as valedictorian in 1941. He won a football scholarship to Ohio State University, where he intended to major in chemistry, but halfway through his freshman year he was drafted into the Army Air Corps. Hoping to become a gunner on a B-17 bomber, he was disappointed when he was assigned to study engineering at the University of Illinois. There he took courses not only in the sciences but also the humanities, including history. And so it was that Temple first encountered James G. Randall, then the country's foremost Lincoln authority, who kindled the young Ohioan's curiosity about the sixteenth president.[12]

But Uncle Sam wanted Temple as an engineer, not as a historian, so off he went to Europe as a member of the Army Communication Service. Among other things, his unit put in an airfield and communications for the personal use of General Dwight Eisenhower, whom he befriended. During the war he formed a resolution to finish his college education and earn a PhD in history.

Upon his discharge in 1946, Temple returned to Ohio State but was dismayed to find that most of the friends he had earlier made there had died in the war, so he quit and went home. At the suggestion of his father, he successfully applied for readmission to the University of Illinois, which he entered as a sophomore. One of the first courses he took was Professor Randall's survey of American constitutional history. As Temple recalled, Randall "inspired students and brought out the best in them," and so the professor "became one of my favorite teachers, and I secretly hoped that one day he might ask me to study with him on the graduate level."[13] In turn, Randall came to regard Temple highly; whenever he had to miss a class, he would have Temple act as a substitute, delivering lectures from his Randall's notes. Going a step further, in June 1949, just as Temple completed his undergraduate studies, the newly retired Randall offered him a job as his research assistant. Over the next four years, Temple reported almost every weekday afternoon to Randall's apartment, where both the professor and his wife (Ruth Painter Randall) plugged away on their books. (He was working on the final two volumes of his tetralogy, *Lincoln the President*, and she was writing a biography of Mary Lincoln).[14]

At Randall's suggestion, and under his direction, Temple wrote a master's thesis ("Noah Brooks: Friend of Lincoln," completed in 1951) and a dissertation ("Noah Brooks, 1830–1903," completed in 1956).[15] Some of Randall's graduate students had done biographical studies of Lincoln's contemporaries,[16] and the professor inveigled Temple into choosing Brooks by suggesting that it was really impossible to write his life story because no collection of his personal papers existed. Taking the bait, the headstrong Temple insisted he could do it, and with characteristically dogged persistence, he managed to discover some of Brooks's letters. The result is a thoroughly convincing portrait of a man who knew Lincoln uncommonly well.

Since completing his dissertation, Temple has focused intently on Lincoln, editing *The Lincoln Herald* for several years and writing numerous articles as well as several books, including *By Square and Compasses: The Building of Lincoln's Home and Its Saga* (1984); *Abraham Lincoln, From Skeptic to Prophet* (1995); *The Taste Is in My Mouth a Little: Lincoln's Victuals and Potables* (2004); and *Lincoln's Surgeons at His Assassination* (2015). With his wife, Sunderine, Temple wrote *Abraham Lincoln and Illinois' Fifth Capitol* (2006). His favorite among his books is *Abraham Lincoln, From Skeptic to Prophet*, ostensibly a study of Lincoln's religion but which he describes as "really a biography of the Lincoln family."

It is fitting that in light of his exceptionally long career, Temple's study of Noah Brooks—the work that launched his seventy-plus years of active and productive scholarship—should finally appear in book form, published by the press of the university where it was conceived and produced.

Notes

1. Noah Brooks, *Abraham Lincoln and the Downfall of American Slavery* (New York: Putnam's, 1894), vi.

2. Washington correspondence, April 16, 1865, *Sacramento Daily Union*, May 17, 1865.

3. Mary Todd Lincoln to Noah Brooks, Chicago, December 18, 1865, in *Mary Todd Lincoln: Her Life and Letters*, ed. Justin G. Turner and Linda Levitt Turner (New York: Knopf, 1972), 311.

4. Mary Todd Lincoln to Noah Brooks, Chicago, May 11, 1866; Turner and Turner, *Mary Todd Lincoln*, 363.

5. James Armstrong Reed, "The Later Life and Religious Sentiments of Abraham Lincoln," *Scribner's Monthly*, July 1873, 339–40.

6. John Conness to Charles Hamlin, n.p., February 21, 1896, in Charles Eugene Hamlin, *The Life and Times of Hannibal Hamlin* (1899; Port Washington, N.Y.: Kennikat, 1971), 485.

7. Robert J. Cole, quoting his father, Cornelius Cole, in Noah Brooks, *Abraham Lincoln by Friend and Foe*, ed. Robert J. Cole (New York: Gold Medal Library, 1922), 8–9.

8. The two most important are *Washington in Lincoln's Time* (New York: Century, 1895), and *Abraham Lincoln and the Downfall of American Slavery* (New York: Putnam's, 1894).

9. Michael Burlingame, ed., *Lincoln Observed: Civil War Dispatches of Noah Brooks* (Baltimore: Johns Hopkins University Press, 1998).

10. See *Recollected Words of Abraham Lincoln*, ed. Don E. Fehrenbacher and Virginia Fehrenbacher (Stanford, Calif.: Stanford University Press, 1996), 41, 517–18.

11. Much of the information that follows comes from an interview with Temple, conducted by Steven Rogstad of Racine Wisconsin, on August 6, 1995, in Temple's Springfield home, and from a series of interviews conducted by James Cornelius, Lincoln curator at the Abraham Lincoln Presidential Library in Springfield, at that library in February 2015. Rogstad kindly lent me tapes of his interview with Temple, which were transcribed for the Knox College Lincoln Studies Center by Martha J. Miller. Cornelius's interviews are available online at http://www.illinois.gov/alplm/library/collections/oralhistory/historiansspeak/Pages/TempleDr.Wayne.aspx.

12. Harry E. Pratt, "James Garfield Randall, 1881–1953," *Journal of the Illinois State Historical Society* 46 (1953): 119–31; Wayne C. Temple, "J. G. Randall: Dean of the Lincoln Scholars," *Illinois Libraries* 67 (1985): 498–506; Robert G. Wick, "The Historian and the Poet: James G. Randall, Carl Sandburg and the Life of Abraham Lincoln," *Journal of Illinois History* 13 (2010): 289–304.

13. Temple, "Randall," 500. When Randall died in 1953, Temple described him as "the kindest man whom I've ever known. . . . He knew everyone . . . and they all loved him." Letter to Mrs. Randall's sister-in-law, in Ruth Painter Randall, *I, Ruth: Autobiography of a Marriage; The Self-Told Story of the Woman who Married the Great Lincoln Scholar, James G. Randall, and through Her Interest in His Work Became a Lincoln Author Herself* (Boston: Little, Brown, 1968). 240.

14. J. G. Randall, *Lincoln the President* (4 vols.; New York: Dodd, Mead, 1945–55); Ruth Painter Randall, *Mary Lincoln: Biography of a Marriage* (Boston, Little, Brown, 1953).

15. A slightly altered form of the dissertation appeared serially in *The Lincoln Herald* between 1970 and 1972.

16. Pratt, "Randall," 120.

Noah Brooks, 1830–1903

by
Wayne Calhoun Temple

A.B., University of Illinois, 1949
A.M., University of Illinois, 1951

THESIS
SUBMITTED IN PARTIAL FULFILLMENT OF THE REQUIREMENTS
FOR THE DEGREE OF DOCTOR OF PHILOSOPHY IN HISTORY
IN THE GRADUATE COLLEGE OF THE
UNIVERSITY OF ILLINOIS, 1956

Urbana, Illinois

Table of Contents

Acknowledgments

THE LATE PROFESSOR J. G. Randall suggested the subject of Noah Brooks to me in 1949 and greatly aided me in my study and research. Since his death in 1953, Professors A. E. Bestor and Richard N. Current have guided my study and given me the benefits of their seasoned learning and scholarship. To these men I owe a deep debt of gratitude.

CHAPTER I

From Maine's "Aristocracy of the Sea"

IN HIS OWN DAY Noah Brooks, indefatigable journalist and litterateur, had "more acquaintances than any man of his years not in what is called public life,"[1] though in after years few Americans remembered him, except for specialists in American literature and students of Abraham Lincoln. "No man living had better opportunity to know Lincoln's mind than Noah Brooks," reported John Conness, friend of Lincoln and senator from California, 1863–1869.[2] Another "mutual friend" stated that Brooks "was so intimate with the President that he visited him socially at times when others were refused admission, took tea with the family, spending evenings with him, reading to him, and conversing with him freely on social and religious topics, and in my opinion knows more of the secret inner life and religious views of Mr. Lincoln, at least during the term of his presidency, than any man living."[3]

Lincoln's Springfield law partner, "Billy" Herndon, scoffed at this statement and called Brooks a "would-be keeper of Lincoln's conscience while in Washington."[4] Herndon's choice for presidential confidant was J. G. Nicolay, Lincoln's private secretary, but Herndon did not know the Lincoln of Washington D.C. who struggled with the problems of a civil war, nor did he take into account the fact that Lincoln had actually chosen Brooks to replace Nicolay as his private secretary. Only an assassin's bullet kept him from that position of honor and trust. To clear the way for Brooks, Lincoln finally "induced" Nicolay "to go abroad."[5] On March 11, 1865, he was nominated for the position of consul to Paris, and the Senate confirmed the appointment, which would allow Nicolay to depart without losing face.[6] One major fault of Nicolay and his assistant, John Hay, was their tactless relations with Mrs. Lincoln. Neither Nicolay nor Hay got along with her. And she, with the help of others, apparently succeeded in removing them both[7] since Hay was also conveniently appointed secretary of the legation at Paris. But Brooks never assumed his post because Nicolay stayed on to finish up the affairs of his office, and Lincoln was shot before the secretaries sailed on June 24.[8]

Brooks would have made a good private secretary for Lincoln. He was quiet, could keep confidential matters to himself, and understood the peculiar quirks of Mrs. Lincoln. He was kind to her and she liked him very much. In fact, he was one of the three people she remembered and talked about even in her period of mental instability in 1875. A correspondent obtained an interview with her at Dr. R. J. Patterson's Bellevue Insane Retreat at Batavia, Illinois, and she talked of only three persons: her husband, Noah Brooks, and Judge James B. Bradwell.[9] She knew that Brooks was devoted to Lincoln, and others also shared her feeling of confidence in Brooks. Truman H. Bartlett (1835–1923), a sculptor, wrote on the back of his copy of Brooks's photograph: "Nearer to Lincoln when President than any others, save Nicolay & Hay—from 1862 to the death of L[incoln] & really knew more about L[incoln]."[10]

Lincoln and Brooks had met several times during the Fremont campaign in Illinois, and their friendship was renewed when Brooks went to Washington in 1862 as the correspondent of the Sacramento *Daily Union*. There, Brooks "saw him almost daily until his tragical death."[11] However, there was something special about Brooks. Lincoln had many good friends, but only a very few intimate comrades. "Noah Brooks," a contemporary said, "was one of the few men about the President who never asked anything for himself and Lincoln rewarded him by giving the best gift he had to offer—his friendship."[12] He did ask for things upon occasion, but not for himself. "Often when I would ask a favor for some poor soldier or friendless deserving youth," Brooks confided, "he would give his whole attention to the matter, as though that were his most important business on hand, and would laughingly say: 'It seems to me you have a knack for picking up just such cases that nobody else thinks of.'"[13]

But Brook's claim to fame does not rest only upon the fact that he was an intimate friend of Lincoln. Brooks won "world-wide fame" as a journalist and a man of letters.[14] He was known and respected by the leading writers of his era, and his facility for rapid composition allowed him to hold an editor's post and still write numerous articles and books in his spare moments. "Noah Brooks," declared one of his club friends, "was an example of a peculiarly American and interesting type of man of letters, mingling with the journalism which was his chief occupation, the writing of fiction, narratives of travel and observation, personal sketches in the nature of *memoires pour servir* and serious biography and history."[15] Nearly everything connected with literature or history interested Brooks. For example, when the fate of Poe's Fordham cottage hung in the balance he pleaded for its preservation because of Poe's "great literary importance."[16]

Personal Description

Brooks was somewhat below average height, being about five feet five inches. He walked with a short, quick step, wore size eight shoes, and in his later years weighed in the vicinity of 180 pounds. His complexion was fair, like his father's, and his nose was aquiline. He had a marked New England accent, which he never lost despite his many travels.[17] As to his personality, he was of a "genial and social nature" with rare conversational abilities. Writers who knew Brooks testify to his "personal charm" and sterling qualities.[18] He was always ready to make new friends and relate his large accumulation of interesting incidents or reminiscences. And he possessed many fascinating memories of his association with the leading literary figures of the day, not to mention Lincoln. Among these were Mark Twain and Bret Harte.[19] Needless to say, he was an extrovert, a fluent conversationalist, and a facile writer. Brooks was generally to be found wherever the company was the most interesting, the food supreme, and the camaraderie light and gay.

With such a personality he was the perfect club man. "During his years of unattached literary and journalistic life in New York he knew everybody."[20] He was one of the organizers and founders of the Authors Club as well as a member of the Lotos Club and the famous Century Association. His tastes were most expensive. In his eating habits he was a gourmet "and enjoyed visits hither and yon in search of top eateries in the city." One of his choice delicacies was raw oysters which he always sought whenever available.[21] He was a Bohemian in many ways, and although a practicing orthodox Congregationalist, he enjoyed his glass of port wine with the evening meal.[22] It would seem that this journalist could see little connection between a man's stomach and his soul. Is there? In the Authors Club of New York he was in his element when telling stories or listening to others. Here, he toyed with a fancy pair of *pince-nez* glasses on a cord while he smoked his favorite cigars and exchanged jolly conversation with his friends until the early hours of the morning.[23]

If there was a noticeable flaw in Brooks's nature, it was his total disregard for money. He never had a care for the morrow. Saving money was not one of his attributes; he spent his wages freely and never worried when he did not have money. His friends always came to his rescue with loans or gifts. From his moderate earnings he gave freely to young people who he thought would make good if given an opportunity. He also gave freely of his time and influence "to further the interests of those who were struggling to make a start in life, helping to open them to avenues to success," explained the minister who preached his funeral.[24] Nevertheless, he was always able to dress and live like a gentleman.[25] Many of Brooks's writing friends were noted for their careless dress and their lack of interest in appearance. But in the Eastern circle of authors there were three notable exceptions to this rule: Edmund Clarence Stedman,[26] Bret Harte and Noah Brooks. By studying the many photographs of Brooks which the author assembled, it is easy to see that he followed the yearly fashions more closely than most women. He was a fastidious dresser. The worst insult that he could give to a man was to say that he was "a liar and his clothes don't fit."[27]

One of the best keys to his personality is the set of answers which he penned into Edmund Clarence Stedman's album.[28] These self-appraisals were written about 1878; although obviously some of the answers were written in jest, many of them ring true.

Colour? *Greenback.*
Flower? *Heliotrope.*
Tree? *The brave old oak.*
Object in Nature? *The Sea.*
Hour in the Day? *Dinner-hour.*
Season in the Year? *A California Spring.*
Perfume? *Heliotrope.*
Gem? *Opal.*
Style of Beauty? *I like 'em all.*
Names? *Charlie—Mabel.*
Painters? *Helios, Rubens, Hans Makart, Diaz.*
Musicians? *All but Wagner.*
Piece of Sculpture? *The California Butter Woman.*
Poets? *The Divine Williams, Tennyson, Whittier.*
Poetesses? *Mrs. Browning, Jean Ingelow.*
Prose Authors? *Addison, Goldsmith, Dickens, Irving.*
Character in Romance? *J.S.C. Abbott's Napoleon.*[29]
In History? *Abraham Lincoln.*
Book to take up for an hour? *Never have so much time.*
What book (not religious) would you part with last? *Richardson's Dictionary.*
What epoch would you choose to have lived in? *The present.*
Where would you like to live? *Where SHE is.*[30]

Favorite amusement? *Building castles in Spain.*
Occupation? *Loafing.*
What trait of character do you most admire in man? *Cheeriness.*
In woman? *Sweetness.*
What do you most detest in each? *Insincerity.*
If not yourself, who would you rather be? *Tupper.*[31]
Idea of happiness? *Lots of money and nothing to do.*
Of misery? *Work and poverty.*
Bete noire? *Work.*
Dream? *To find HER.*
Dread? *That I shall not find HER.*
Your distinguishing characteristics? *Laziness and good nature.*
Of your better half? *Patience under tribulations.*
The sublimest passion? *Give it up.*
The Sweetest words? *"I love you."*
Saddest words? *"She's not at home."*
Aim in life? *To have a good time and help others.*
Motto? *Dum vivimus, vivimus.*[32]

When he represented himself as lazy he told something of a truth. Indolence was part of his temperament, and yet he was industrious in that he wrote many articles and books in addition to his newspaper work. But since he had to earn a living, writing was the easiest way because it cost him little effort. Just as he talked fluently, he also wrote easily. Like Lincoln, he tried his hand at many jobs and failed for lack of interest. Journalism was the niche into which he best fitted.

Ancestry

Brooks was descended from pure New England stock which time became members of Maine's "aristocracy of the sea." The pride of the family was Brooks's great-nephew, Frank Brooks Upham (1872–1939), an Annapolis graduate who in 1933 rose to the rank of full admiral in the United States Navy and was the commander of the whole Asiatic Fleet. Today the Uphams still follow the sea or serve in the army.

The earliest American ancestor of Noah Brooks arrived in Plymouth Colony in 1635 on board the *Blessing.* She was a thirty-ton ship, built of locust and launched by John Winthrop on July 4, 1631 (O.S.), and had the honor of being one of the first ships built in the Colonies.[33] This forefather of the Brooks family was William Brooke (the spelling gradually evolved into Brooks), and his former home was Edgerton, County of Kent, England.[34] He cleared the port of London on June 17, 1635, and under this date there appear in the English port record these words: "Theis vnder-written names are to be transported to New-England imbarqued in the *Blessing* JO: LECESTER M[aster] the p[ar]ties having brought Cert[ification] from the Minister [and] Justices of their conformitie being no Subsedy Men, tooke ye oaths of Alleg[iance and] Supremacie."[35]

Among the thirty-four names which follow this caption is that of William Brooke, twenty years of age. Immediately following the entry is that of his brother, Gilbert, who was fourteen. Quite naturally these brothers stayed close during their initial years in Plymouth Colony. William Brooke and his brother left England, no doubt, in order to better their lot. The year 1635 fell in that memorable decade of heavy English migration to the American Colonies. In this period, roughly 1630–1640, many thousands of Englishmen left their homeland to live in America or the West Indies. These emigrants felt that economic conditions could be no worse in the colonies than in depression-riddled England.

Just where the *Blessing* put the Brooke brothers ashore is not certain, but they probably landed at Plymouth. Their next destination was Marshfield, a settlement just north of Plymouth. Here, they commenced their young lives anew—probably both as indentured servants. At least it is certain that Gilbert sold his services, for a period of years, to William Vassell.[36] Gilbert's master was a man of position who had been a patentee of the Massachusetts Bay Colony and was at Boston in 1630. He returned to America on the same ship as the Brooke brothers.

Eight years after settling in Marshfield, William and Gilbert achieved their first major goal; they were made "freemen," a position which entitled them to participate in the affairs of the town and to hold public office.[37] William soon became a leader among his fellow townsmen, and in the following year, 1644, he was named to the grand jury.[38] Two years later, he obtained an official position: surveyor of the highways for Marshfield.[39] And, in 1649, he was again elected to this office.[40]

Sometime after 1649 these brothers left Marshfield and moved farther north to Scituate, a town located approximately twenty miles above Plymouth and founded about 1628. Here, the focus must fall upon William since he was the ancestor of Noah Brooks. William took the "Oath of Fidelity" in 1657[41] and became a "freeman" of Scituate the following year.[42] Evidently, a freeman from one settlement could not transfer his rank to another without first taking new oaths and affiliating with the local church.

William Brooke was now well started on the road to financial independence and personal satisfaction, and even more honors followed. On the 5th of June 1667, he was named one of the two constables of Scituate.[43] This new constable was a "householder," and he earned his living by farming a piece of land which lay south of Till's Creek, known later as Dwelly's Creek.[44] At an unrecorded date, he married Susanna Dunham, a widow from Plymouth,[45] but since William could not write,[46] his name did not long survive the phonetic spelling of the parish clerks. Soon the "e" was dropped from his surname, and in the church records it appears as Brook.[47] It was not long after this change that the pens of clerks, probably for easier pronunciation, added an "s" to his family name. His only surviving son, Nathaniel, was born in 1646 and was the second of eight children.[48]

The descendants of William Brooks (Nathaniel, Nathaniel Jr., Taylor, and Captain Noah Brooks) continued to live in Scituate where they earned their livings either from the sea or its associated industries. Very little specific information is known about the Brooks family until the advent of the sixth generation. In this line of direct descent was Barker Brooks, the second son of Noah Brooks, a sea captain. Barker was born in Scituate on September 10, 1789,[49] but he left the village of his ancestors and went to Boston where he was engaged in the building of ships. The shipwrights of Scituate received the best of training, and their services were in great demand at other yards.[50] Sometime before the War of 1812, however, he terminated his stay there and journeyed north to Castine (Maine), then a part of Massachusetts. Here, the young shipbuilder married Margaret ("Peggy") Perkins, on July 16, 1816. His bride was the daughter of Captain Joseph Perkins who was one of the most prominent citizens of Castine. Perkins was a ship owner and a man of much property; at one time he held eight thousand feet of wharf frontage.[51]

Barker Brooks was also a prominent man in Castine. He was a master shipbuilder, regarded by many as one of the three best craftsmen of his time.[52] He owned his own shipyard and built some of the finest ships in New England. One of the products of his own hands, the *Adams*, was eventually secured by one of his sons, John Holmes Brooks, who became her proud master after having been her second mate for some years.[53] Among the townspeople Barker was respectfully known as "Master Brooks," a muscular man who, according to one of his contemporaries, Joseph L. Stevens, could hit a cricket ball farther than any other boy in Castine.[54] Coupled with this prodigious strength was a genial nature. The older inhabitants of Castine told Frank Kidder Upham that Barker was tall and dignified in appearance, with a light complexion. In his business transactions he was known for his integrity, which gained him "the respect and esteem of the entire community."[55] He evidently was also a well educated man, for he could write a very good letter.

The only known correspondence of his shows good composition with only a few words spelled phonetically.[56]

Youth and Education

Castine in the early Nineteenth Century was, according to Noah Brooks's own description, a "picturesque, old-fashioned, quiet town, situated on a lovely peninsula which slopes gently to two waters of Penobscot Bay; a broad, bright bay, studded with innumerable islands; a sweeping river, which flows past the town on one side and a hilly and woody shore on the other; a bare eminence, crowned with the ruins of an ancient fort, overlooking town, bay, river, forest and a wide panorama."[57] Into this setting Noah was born on October 24, 1830,[58] the youngest of eight children of Barker and Margaret Brooks (two of whom, a set of infant twins, had died nearly five years before). Among his living brothers and sisters were Phebe, born in 1817; Marianne, 1819; Joseph Barker, 1820; James Otis, 1822; and John Holmes, 1828.[59]

Noah was a seven months' baby, but he overcame this handicap and developed into a sturdy youth. He was named after his grandfather and uncle on the paternal side of the family,[60] both of whom were sea captains and one of whom—the uncle—was a prominent citizen and a prosperous shipbuilder of South Boston. This Boston uncle served on the common council in 1823, representing Ward Twelve of the new municipal government, started only the previous year.[61] In his shipyard he trained, as apprentices, some of the finest ship carpenters in New England.[62]

Though ships and canvas as well as swimming and boating were an integral part of his environment, Noah was not destined to follow the sea as his forebears had done and as many of his playmates were to do. The boys in Old Castine spent most of their time out of doors, running, jumping or exploring the "Back P'int and the Block House,"[63] but when the years of childhood were past, "at least half" of them were expected to go to sea. Castine boys, at an early age, quickly learned the name and purpose of every rope or spar and could readily identify ships, brigs, and schooners.[64] With such a salt-water background, it is remarkable that Noah did not follow the sea. Perhaps the early death of both his parents within the short space of a month and a half kept him from becoming the master of a swift trading vessel.

At the age of seven, Noah became an orphan. His mother—not yet forty-eight—died on January 30, 1838,[65] as the result of an internal abscess,[66] leaving the burden of raising the family to a hard-working and busy father. But within a few weeks, on March 16,[67] he too died from internal complications which had been caused by an accidental injury;[68] Barker was only forty-eight and in the prime of life. When Uncle Noah Brooks learned of the death of his brother, he wrote to the orphans telling them to put their trust in the Lord and live a good life. In addition to this solace he offered them any aid or comfort which might be in his power to grant.[69] Uncle Noah, however, was living in Boston and the children were in Maine. The elder sisters solved the problem for the younger children; the oldest one, Phebe, married Benjamin D. Gay on December 26, 1838,[70] and the younger sister, Marianne, became the bride of S. K. Upham the following year. According to Brooks's own statement he "was kept at the homestead by his elder sisters,"[71] which would indicate that these two young ladies maintained the family home before and after their marriages for not only Noah but also John, nearly ten years old at the death of his father; James Otis, fifteen; and Joseph Barker, seventeen. The new mistresses of the old homestead were little more than adolescents themselves. Marianne was just nineteen and Phebe was twenty when their parents died, so they participated in and lent dignity to the play of Noah and his little group who organized themselves into a military company called The Hancock Cadets (Castine being in Hancock County). On one memorable occasion, July 4, 1840, they paraded in honor of William Henry Harrison; Noah was the standard bearer of the company of twelve "cadets," and the older sisters of the group made a flag for the celebration. Since the ship *Canova* was being dismantled at the time, they used the drapery material from her cabin for the ensign. Noah received the flag in a presentation ceremony and replied with a memorized speech one of his sisters had written.[72]

In addition to the happy hours of play, there was the more serious business of school work. Although Noah never received a college education, as many of his fellow literary companions did, he was well versed in the liberal arts. He seems to have liked school very much. The local elementary school gave him his basic education,[73] and then he attended a private school,[74] where his tuition was probably paid from the estate of his parents or by his brother-in-law, S. K. Upham, who was well-to-do. This private school was probably the one taught by Almira A. and Sarah H. Hawes; Castine did not have a free public high school until after Brooks had finished his education and left home.[75]

One of the books he used in public school was *The American First Class Book*, compiled by John Pierpont and published at Boston in 1823. From this work he learned reading, parsing, and public speaking, and since its selections were taken largely from the classics, Brooks acquired a taste for "wholesome literature." He later claimed that it was largely due to this book that he learned to enjoy the classics.[76] Another textbook he enjoyed reading was "Peter Parley's" history of the United States. "Peter Parley" was the pen name of Samuel G. Goodrich, who wrote many tales dealing with colonial or revolutionary history. Goodrich's textbook was exciting, and Brooks recalled it "with solid satisfaction." The question of whether or not it was an authentic history never bothered the eager reader; it was a most interesting book. Brooks, as "a small student," learned geography from one of the many textbooks on this subject written by Jesse Olney. Olney's book fascinated him and he spent many hours poring over the informative pages.

There were few books written especially for children in Brooks's day, but he read what was available: *Robinson Crusoe*, *The Swiss Family Robinson*, *Pilgrim's Progress*, and Charles and Mary Lamb's stories from Shakspere. But he found his chief delight in digesting the works of James Fenimore Cooper, since many of his books revolved about adventures upon the sea. Castine was a seaport, and stories like *The Pilot*, *The Red Rover*, *The Wing-and-Wing*, or *The Two Admirals* were memorized by endless re-reading. Although Brooks also admired and read Cooper's series called the Leatherstocking Tales, these volumes were not so fascinating to him as Cooper's stories of the sea. Cooper had been a midshipman in the Navy and knew this subject better. Another large volume of sea stories which captured Brooks's boyhood fancy was *Captain Riley's Narrative*, which dealt with the adventures of a sailor cast away upon the coast of Africa. Likewise, Dana's *Two Years Before the Mast* was another favorite.

The boys and their families received some books from Boston, but when they had read and re-read this meager number they turned their prying eyes to the shelves of the Castine public library. It was here that Brooks read Frances Burney's *Diary and Letters*, a collection which told of the interesting happenings which she had observed at the English court or heard in the literary circles of London. Perhaps it was this set of volumes which awakened a life-long interest in literature; at least, this work was clearly in his mind years later. Charles Dickens was another of his favorite authors. Besides these books, there were a few journals available. In Brooks's home the family subscribed to a literary newspaper which was issued weekly in New York by Park Benjamin. This was *The New World*. It arrived by mail every Saturday night, and just as regularly it was always carefully hidden to prevent the boys (who remained at home while the older girls went to church) from reading it on Sundays—a mortal sin! However, as is generally the case in such matters, the young Brookses turned the house upside down until it was found. Once discovered, it yielded such spell-binding stories as "Sylvester Sound, the Somnambulist."

When Brooks was about fifteen he was introduced to the reading of poetry.[77] From this time forward he always enjoyed poems, and a few years later he published several passable ones himself. During his school days Brooks acted in several plays and especially enjoyed appearing in Shakspere's *Hamlet.* Likewise, the declamation exercises appealed to his literary nature, and he memorized long orations which were delivered before the school.[78]

In 1847 his formal education was ended when he completed the equivalent of high school at Castine,[79] but he had the gift of an inquiring mind which led him to read and learn as much as time would permit. After graduation, however, young Brooks decided to seek his fortune away from home. Evidently, the sea was not strong enough to absorb his interest, or perhaps he realized that the youngest son among four orphan boys was not very likely to become the master of a ship. Whatever the reason, he turned his attention to the learning of a profession, which later gave him much personal satisfaction but never a steady income.

CHAPTER II

Paint and Printer's Ink

Goes to Boston

Young Brooks was an ambitious lad, but since there was no prospect of his going to college, he determined to learn a profession in Boston. It was his desire to become an artist—a landscape painter.[1] In Boston the eager boy had relatives: he did not go there as a total stranger. When he arrived, probably in April of 1848,[2] his brother-in-law, Sylvanus Kidder Upham,[3] was living on Havre Street in East Boston. Upham had been in the leather business in Castine, but when it proved to be unprofitable he migrated to Boston about 1843 or 1844. There he formed a partnership with Noah's older brother, Joseph Barker Brooks. These two enterprising merchants, located on Long Wharf, dealt in the West India trade and also operated a commission business. With the coming of the gold rush, however, S. K. Upham sailed for California in February of 1849, after having moved his family to Salem.[4]

Noah Brooks did not stay with any of his relatives. Instead, he roomed and boarded with William Sargent, who lived in Chelsea, a suburb lying north of Boston and across the bay. Sargent was a "house, sign, & fancy painter" and in 1850 had a shop on Portland Street in Boston.[5] The following year, however, Sargent moved his place of business to Shurtleff Street (near Central Avenue) in Chelsea, but he lived at No. 39 Maverick, near Shawmut Street. Brooks had a comfortable room—probably over Sargent's shop[6]—and here many of his friends gathered in the evenings, since he was the proud possessor of a private room with a cheery fireplace,[7] where he and his friends could talk or play chess.[8]

It was in Chelsea that Brooks met Charles Tilden Wilder (1831–1897), who was then living with his parents at No. 12 Suffolk Street. This young man became one of Brooks's closest friends. When Brooks first knew him, he was a clerk in the firm of Wilder & Company, which his father, Charles B. Wilder, had founded in 1840. It was a wholesale and retail paper establishment located at the corner of Water and Congress Streets in Boston, and soon after Charles T. became of age, he entered the firm as a full partner with his father and brother, Herbert A. Wilder.[9] "Charlie" Wilder, as Brooks always called him, had lots of money and shared his good fortune with Brooks. Even after he left Boston, Brooks said that if he was ever in need of funds, Charlie Wilder would take care of him.[10] Charlie had been educated in the public schools of Chelsea and at Monson Academy where he obtained an appreciation for art and literature, which also interested Brooks.[11] Sometimes Wilder would stay with Brooks over night, and at such times they did their own cooking. The dishes which they enjoyed most were oyster stew and stewed lobster.[12]

Art and Journalism

Soon after his arrival in Boston, Brooks began to study drawing, applying himself with diligence to "the *fine arts*." On Tuesday and Friday evenings he took drawing lessons from a teacher named J. Wolcott, who lived on Howard Street. Thursday nights were also reserved for practicing the skills which the "drawing master" had taught him.[13] The would-be artist continued his lessons, and by 1850 was studying and sketching the human body in "anatomical and physiological lectures." With these advanced courses he should have been studying harder, yet he confessed that he did not "attend so much to drawing as formerly."[14] There were many reasons why he no longer had so much time for practice. He spent many of his spare moments in reading famous authors, such as Macaulay,[15] or attending the theatre,[16] or serving as librarian of a Chelsea debating society.[17] He also belonged to the Winnissimmet Literary Institute, whose members met every Monday night[18] to read their literary compositions or take parts in dialogues. The Institute maintained a library where members could read many of the best works of the day. Brooks's enthusiasm won him the presidency of the Institute in 1852.[19] As if these many activities did not keep him busy enough, he also held membership in a political group known as the Chelsea Taylor Club, whose slogan was "Oysters we can swallow but Van Buren and Adams we can't." He did not merely attend their social events; he also worked hard to obtain a political office in Chelsea.[20] He was indeed a very ambitious young man.

In spite of these varied diversions, he continued to do some artistic painting. Sometimes he was given commissions by patrons of the arts to paint landscapes for them.[21] The settings and inspirations for some of these paintings he
obtained from the many trips which he took into the picturesque regions of
New England. One such excursion was to the "Switzerland of America" with
Charlie Wilder. They left Boston by train on July 10, 1851, bound for Lowell;
from here their route followed the Merrimack River for some distance and
then swung eastward to Lake Winnipesaukee, New Hampshire. They paused
here to view the placid lake from the deck of a steamer, the *Lady of the Lake*.
Following a brief tour of the countryside, they made a circuit around the
White Mountains, climbing some of the prominent peaks such as Mt. Lafayette. After seven days in New Hampshire they crossed the border into Maine
by coach. The rest of the journey to Castine was by steamer and stagecoach.

Wilder stayed in the Penobscot country with Brooks for a few days but
left on July 24 for the return trip to Boston. Brooks remained to rest, sketch,
and loaf until August 21.[22] He always stayed away from the large cities as long
as possible during hot weather, since personal comfort was of the utmost
importance to him. Once back in Boston, he painted several of the scenes
which he had sketched on his tour through the White Mountains.[23]

From a study of his pencil sketches and oil paintings it is evident that
Brooks had some artistic talents, but he lacked the genius which would have
enabled him to earn a steady livelihood with his pencil and brush. His studies
in art were not wasted, though, for he used his artistic skills throughout his
life. As a diversion from his daily work he sometimes hiked into the country
with a sketch pad and pencil, and at times he supplemented his precarious
income by instructing beginners in drawing.

In an autobiographical sketch, Brooks later stated that in the midst of his
artistic studies "he developed a strong taste for literature, contributing short
sketches, notices, essays and humorous tales to the weekly newspaper and to
magazines of the day, and by the time he was twenty-one, he was able to earn
his living by his pen."[24] Friends have related that he drifted into newspaper
work largely through the influence of Benjamin P. Shillaber (1814–1890),
the prominent creator of the "Mrs. Partington" stories.[25] His most steady
employment was as a reporter on the staff of the Boston *Atlas*, a daily Whig
paper published by Schouler and Brewer at No. 5 Old State House. Its political
affiliations were the same as the ones Brooks had favored since childhood.[26]
In addition to this job he contributed to several weekly publications issued
locally. For the *Yankee Blade* (founded in 1842) he wrote a series entitled
"People I have met—not by N. P. Willis," including such stories as "The Old
Fogie," and "The Apple Woman at the Corner."[27] For the Chelsea *Pioneer*

(published from 1846 until its merger with the Chelsea *Telegraph* in 1851), he contributed rural letters which purported to be from Castine,[28] and he later provided copy for the Chelsea *Telegraph*.[29] He also wrote articles for the *American Union*, his material drawn largely from happenings in Castine, thinly disguised. One of these sketches was recognized by readers in Castine, much to his embarrassment.[30]

Besides writing articles, he may also have set type in a Boston newspaper office. In later years, while commenting upon the handwriting of Horace Greeley he wrote: "In my youth I had some experience with the handwriting of Mr. Rufus Choate, and Mr. Greeley's manuscript was, I think, far more legible than the famous Boston lawyer's."[31] This statement could be interpreted to mean that he had set type in some of Choate's speeches.

Brooks got his first opportunity to write for a publication of more than a local circulation when *The Carpet-Bag* appeared in 1851. This humorous weekly paper was largely the brain child of Benjamin P. Shillaber. Until 1847 Shillaber "had been a manipulator of the stick and rule, with no ambitious aspirations for a literary career." In that year his "Mrs. Partington" stories, in the Boston *Post*, found a ready reading public. In 1850 Shillaber began to work for the *Pathfinder and Railway Guide*, a small periodical which was passed out gratuitously to passengers riding on trains. The profit came from the advertisements with which it was "well buttressed." But "affairs were not looking at their best," and the proprietors and editors decided to inaugurate the publication of a humorous sheet.[32]

The first number of *The Carpet-Bag* appeared on March 29, 1851, and the masthead indicated that Shillaber shared the editorial duties with Silas W. Wilder. The latter was a partner in the firm of George K. Snow & S. W. Wilder, who printed the new periodical in the *Pathfinder* office. An elaborate drawing at the top along the borders of the first page gave the illusion of a carpetbag, and the editors explained that the name was chosen because it expressed "the miscellaneous character of a good paper, into which are crowded a variety of things, necessary for comfort and happiness on the highway of life."

The writers and publisher set out to convince staid Bostonians that they needed a comic paper similar to *Punch* and would find such a paper in *The Carpet-Bag*. One of the talented contributors was John Townsend Trowbridge, known to his public as "Paul Creyton," who was "attracted less by any pecuniary advantage" than by his "very great liking" for Shillaber."[33] "Creyton" was always smiling and had "a merry twinkle in his pleasant blue eyes."[34] Shillaber himself possessed "wit and humor and amiable social qualities," and he was "in the prime of life, a stout, hale, hearty man, considerably above the common stature, with a plain, frank face, a full breast, an honest heart, and a head clear as crystal." He was "as genial as the sunshine, and generous to a fault," but in his dress he was careless and gave the appearance of being a "back-woodsman."[35] Another of the contributors was the "brilliant young Irishman," Charles Graham Halpine, who wrote under the pseudonym of "Charles Broadbent," and later in his literary career won world acclaim as "Private Miles O'Reilly."[36] But the most famous contributor was Samuel Langhorne Clemens, who sent in a little sketch—probably the first he ever published in a widely circulating journal—entitled "The Dandy Frightening the Squatter" and signed simply "S.L.C."[37] "Mark Twain" and his brother, Orion, read *The Carpet-Bag* and often reprinted humorous articles from it. In the Hannibal (Missouri) *Journal* from March 4 to June 3, 1852, no fewer than a dozen of *The Carpet-Bag's* stories were reprinted by the Clemens brothers.[38]

Noah Brooks was also a member of *The Carpet-Bag* staff and several times told of his association with this publication, but he never made public the identity of his work.[39] Since most of the contributors used pen names and none of their printed memoirs revealed Brooks's pseudonym, it seemed impossible to identify Brooks's contributions, but recently a collection of his letters was discovered by Mr. Francis Whiting Hatch of Boston. One of these letters revealed the secret. "I have sent you from time to time," Brooks informed a friend in Castine, "several papers containing some of my articles and have generally marked them. My signature, however, is Jacques, and you may have had papers sent to you and not known for what purpose unless you know the signature. . . ." He went on to say that he had the use of whatever exchanges he needed at the various newspaper offices where he wrote, and at *The Carpet-Bag* office he had a box where he received his mail.[40]

But Brooks apparently contributed a series of articles to *The Carpet-Bag* before he adopted the name "Jacques." In the issue of April 19, 1851—the third number of the first volume—a series of sketches begins bearing the title "Leaves from the Penobscot." Although none of the seven articles is signed, the introduction to the first one and the internal evidence indicate that Noah Brooks wrote them. "We shall give, weekly,"[41] the editors explained, "something under this head, that a queer citizen who resides upon Penobscot Bay pens in, as it floats down from the upper waters of the river, and sends to us. There is a raft more of them up there." Brooks's birthplace—Castine, Maine—is located on Penobscot Bay and he was the only writer on *The Carpet-Bag* from the Penobscot region. He had a deep love for his old home town and chose "Castine" as his pen name when he served as correspondent during the Civil War. It seems logical that he would also identify himself with the Penobscot area while writing for *The Carpet-Bag*. Another clue is found in one of the little stories called "The Legend of the Devil's Track." The locale for this legend is in Hancock County, wherein Castine is located.[42] The style, as well as the subject matter of these sketches, seems to be characteristic of Brooks.

The first of the "Leaves from the Penobscot" deals with the subject of "Ancient and Modern Courtship." It is typical of the early writings which Brooks contributed to *The Carpet-Bag*. He did not try to be extremely funny. Instead, he generally chose a rather serious subject and dealt with it philosophically. The humor is usually there, but manifests itself only in the burlesque manner in which Brooks elevates an insignificant subject to a position of utmost importance. This kind of treatment allowed him to bring into his writings the ideas gleaned from many outstanding authors. It was during these early years in Boston that Brooks was reading Seneca, Shakspere, Spenser, Samuel Johnson, Milton, Thackeray, Emerson, Washington Irving, and a host of others.[43] In this manner, he attempted to gain the literary knowledge which a more fortunate young man would have obtained in college.

In commenting upon courtship, Brooks laments the degeneration of the art to a "modern formula." Matrimony, he explains, "has now come to be solved by the expression of a theorem, or general rule, just as is a question of algebra." Parents teach their children to believe that affection must be hidden or one of the parties will take advantage of this outward manifestation of love and "drive too sharp a bargain." Money is the cause of this degeneration, Brooks says. He ends the sketch with a large dose of irony, suggesting that loves should court by using such expression as, "Madam, I lay my railroad stocks at your feet"; "Deign to accept my hand and my pocket book"; "Your real estate excites in my heart, the most profound emotion"; or "Your stock in trade convinces me that our souls are kindred."[44]

His next article utilizes some philosophy, but draws its origin from an incident which had occurred in Maine when the potato rust struck in 1838. Entitled "Caution Against Vanity," it relates the story of three men who have potato patches adjoining each other. When the rust suddenly strikes, one of the owners (not yet plagued) asks his neighbor why the disease has not bothered his potatoes. "Oh," he replies, "I put up a petition [to God]." To which the questioner says, "Well, if it don't come off fair by morning, I do not know but I shall be in the same fix as Jones; so if you will put a petition for my patch to-morrow morning, I will give you five bushels of potatoes in the fall." The bargain is made, but the following morning the praying farmer finds his own patch black with rust, while the potatoes of the non-practicing Christian are untouched. The more fortunate man goes immediately to his friend who is to pray for the safety of his potatoes and says: "Well, neighbor

Brown, after all I guess you needn't put up that petition; I'm afraid it ain't good for five bushels." This story, says Brooks, shows that one should "not be too confident" of himself.[45]

Next Brooks wrote "The Legend of the Devil's Track." In it Brooks is trying it imitate the introduction of one of the most successful books of this period. The basis for the legend, Brooks declares, is an old manuscript written in Elizabethan verse with a smattering of Indian words which an old Indian deciphered for him. This method of introducing a story is certainly an adaptation of the device used by Nathaniel Hawthorne in *The Scarlet Letter*, published at Boston in the early part of 1850. It is known that Brooks read this book; he received it as a Christmas present in 1850 and carefully studied the plot.[46] Hawthorne was one of Brooks's favorite authors, and when *The Blithedale Romance* appeared in the book shops, Brooks also read this volume.[47] The setting for Brooks's tale is along Penobscot Bay in Hancock County where there are "deep indentures" in the solid rock. They give the appearance of footprints: one in the shape of a man's foot, and the other of such a shape as might have been made by that foot which was cloven by the descent which Milton describes. The Penobscot Indians have a legend about these tracks, Brooks testifies, and he merely repeats it for his readers. This third in the Penobscot series has yet another significance: it is his first attempt at poetry for *The Carpet-Bag*. And it is a rather long poem, having fourteen stanzas of nine lines each.[48]

"Rainy Weather" is another topic which receives a philosophical treatment from Brooks's pen. In this he discusses the different attitudes held by various types of people in regard to rain. Some, he judges, enjoy rainy weather merely because it makes others miserable. As for himself, Brooks agrees with Samuel Johnson that "he could conceive of no more miserable man than one who could not enjoy a book on a rainy day." The solution for rainy weather is "a taste for books," he reasons.[49] Although written with a humorous touch, this article reveals much about the young writer.

Turning from this semi-humorous sketch, Brooks launched off on a subject which is amusingly ridiculous. Using as his theme the editorial expression "it's all moonshine" (which at the time indicted something worthless), he points out some of the great events which have been accomplished at night. "Wasn't Rome burned by moonshine?" he asks. And did not the Roundheads grind their swords and sing psalms by moonlight before defeating Charles I? Summing up his argument, he turns to speeches and literature. It is his proposition that they are generally written at night, utilizing moonlight as well as midnight oil.[50]

No less a personage than Emerson was his next victim. Brooks pokes fun at his essay, "Representative Men," which describes the several degrees of human greatness. "But the American philosopher," Brooks complains, "did not illustrate his subject by every-day life examples." Outstanding heroes like Napoleon, Socrates, Cromwell, or Washington can not be seen every day. *Punch* had also picked out certain "model men," but Brooks thinks both *Punch* and Emerson have committed the sin of omission. "There should have been the 'Model Post-Office Clerk!'" he exclaims. Here is a man who is seen in every village. He knows everybody and all their business. Not even a bashful lover can drop his letter in the office without being detected by the clerk.[51]

After this contribution, published on June 28, 1851, it was a long time before another appeared. Not until April 10, 1852, did Brooks write another of his "Leaves from the Penobscot." This time his contribution is in the form of two anecdotes. The first deals with a washerwoman who works from house to house doing family laundry. On one occasion the lady of the house gives the hard-working laundress "a cup of warm rum toddy" at the end of the day. Upon tasting it the laundress turns up her nose "in evident disgust." The housewife takes this to mean that she is a "temperance woman," whereupon the washing woman exclaims that she is not—she just does not like "to drink a whole well of hot water to get a thimbleful" of rum. The other anecdote relates the story of "an old-fashioned wealthy codger" who never buys any new clothes. He finally decides to take a trip, however, and purchases a new pair of boots. Going to a hotel he puts his boots in the hall among all the others, and upon arising in the morning he can not find "the old familiar pair." He forgets about purchasing new boots, and the stage is about to depart before he solves his dilemma by selecting a good pair that fitted and giving the porter five dollars to reimburse the owner. "The 'owner' never called: The old gent had bought his own boots!"[52]

The editors of *The Carpet-Bag* added a message at the bottom of these two anecdotes: "Note.—We hope to have more of these pleasant leaves, as they unfold themselves." But the editors were doomed to disappointment—not until November 6, 1852, did Brooks write another article that can be identified. In this issue he began to use the pen name "Jacques" and contributed a piece called "A Waggish 'Dazzle.'" It is a jolly story about a fake professor by the name of "Airpure" who advertises himself as "The Champion of Free Ventilation." Following this, Brooks's sketches appear with greater regularity. Evidently, he had less newspaper writing to do. It is even possible that he severed some of his other writing commitments at this time since his main occupation, beginning in November, 1852, was a paint shop of his own. Probably his contributions to *The Carpet-Bag* were written in his spare moments.

Toward the end of 1852, Brooks began to write more poetry for this humorous weekly than formerly. Several of his verses are very good, such as "The

Slamming of the Blind," which describes how an annoying window shade can interrupt so many things.[53] Another one, "A Bit of Proverbial Philosophy," advises every husband that it is better to have a dirty house than to keep a broom around the premises where an angry wife may grab it and give him a thrashing.[54] To show off his budding talents Brooks next proceeded to compose a piece in Elizabethan English which was entitled "Ye Sawyer."[55] It is not humorous; instead, it describes the tiring work of a poor sawyer who toils all day to support his little boy. In fact, it seems somewhat autobiographical. Brooks probably remembered seeing his own father, a ship carpenter, at work in the yards in fair weather and foul. In brighter spirits Brooks wrote "Apothegms of Wisdom," a set of witty sayings each beginning with a different letter of the alphabet. A typical line: "Kill time with a knitting needle—and bed bugs with a hammer."[56]

One of the writers who worked with Brooks on *The Carpet-Bag* began his duties in the office as a typesetter. In 1851 Charles F. Browne came into the office with his uncle, Dr. Calvin Farrar, who was there to have a pamphlet printed. When the bargain was struck, the publishers agreed to hire young Browne, then about seventeen, to work in the printing rooms in return for the privilege of printing Dr. Farrar's booklet.[57] The young printer was "a tall, red-haired, consumptive-looking" fellow, Brooks recalled in later years, and when he "began to write clever skits couched in rural New English dialect and wonderfully and phonetically misspelled, we were all very greatly amused and besought the young man to do more."[58] His first article, "An Incident," appeared in *The Carpet-Bag* of December 27, 1851.[59] Browne contributed his clever stories under the name of "Chub" or "Lieut. Chubb" (spelled with either one "b" or two), but when *The Carpet-Bag* collapsed went to Ohio. Eventually, he became connected with the Cleveland *Plain Dealer* where on January 20, 1858, he wrote his first "Artemus Ward" letter.[60] From then he was famous, but it was *The Carpet-Bag* which first gave him an opportunity to write. One can well imagine the good entertainment which "Artemus Ward" furnished his fellow workers at the printing office. He possessed one of the important prerequisites for a comedian: he had the facility of "keeping a straight face" while telling his foolishness.[61]

With such an array of good writers *The Carpet-Bag* should have prospered, but it could not keep going. From the beginning it was plagued by financial troubles, and Shillaber admitted that finally "the bill of financial difficulty was reached that could not be surmounted."[62] During its brief two years of life both editors and publishers were changed many times. At the beginning S. W. Wilder and B. P. Shillaber shared the editorial duties, but on September 9, 1851, the publishing partnership of Snow & Wilder was dissolved and a new company was formed on the same day. It was known as Wilder, Pickard & Company and consisted of S. W. Wilder, B. P. Shillaber, and S. T. Pickard. All three men considered themselves not only publishers but also editors. George K. Snow left *The Carpet-Bag*, but he continued to publish the Boston *Pathfinder* and the *Pathfinder Railway Guide*.[63] Having three editors was bothersome enough; however, on March 30, 1852, Silas D. Hancock was admitted to the firm, probably in order to increase the capital. The name of the company remained the same, but now there were four editors.[64] In the midst of their troubles the editors certainly realized that Boston was not patronizing their humor, for with the start of the second volume they confessed that their desire at the beginning of the paper had been to mix humor with "graver matters." "But," explained the editors, "our correspondents—jolly fellows—have had it their own way, and we have become almost unwittingly, but agreeably, the dispensers of their heartiness."[65]

With all their good intentions the exceedingly humorous style of *The Carpet-Bag* remained unchanged, and by June 26, 1852, Wilder and Shillaber were again its editors—as in the beginning. But the very next issue, July 3, 1852, found a change in both the editorial management and the publishing firm. C. G. Halpine joined Shillaber in the editorial chores and the new publishers was Wilder, Halpine & Company. About a month and a half later the firm was again reshuffled and new blood added. Wilder "disposed of his interest" to C. A. Randall because of "ill-health."[66] The new publishers were listed as Randall, Halpine & Company, but the editors remained the same. Halpine was a poor choice for coeditor because he was "a reckless critic" who printed "the old-fashioned slashing" sort of articles which hurt the paper. Such writings poured lead "into the boots of progress"[67] and, needless to say, an alteration had to be made. So, on October 9, 1852, Halpine's name was dropped from the masthead and Shillaber assumed "exclusive control." This change was effected by the dissolution of Randall, Halpine & Company. George K. Snow, one of the original publishers, bought back the stock and attempted to revive the tired weekly. He altered the typography of the paper and introduced the "new minion type—two size[s] smaller" than that with which it had been printed. This smaller type allowed the publisher to print more material in the same amount of space. Without enlarging the paper he combined it with his own Boston *Pathfinder,* which preserved its own masthead and occupied only a small section of *The Carpet-Bag.* This merger multiplied the advertisements many times their former number and gave *The Carpet-Bag* a new lease on life.

Although there were no more shifts in editors or publishers, *The Carpet-Bag* was doomed. In desperation, new ways were sought (toward the last of March, 1853) to prolong its life. First, the publisher announced that it was his "intention to alter the Carpet-Bag to a monthly publication of the most unique, novel and interesting character." The new monthly was to be called *The Pocket Carpet-Bag* and was to be duodecimo in size with a gilt-edged top. Each issue was to be complete in itself and contain about one hundred pages. The price was to be twelve and one-half cents for single copies or $1.50 per year. Plans were so far advanced that the initial number was scheduled for the first of April, and it was announced that "Jacques" had "contributed a charming poem for its pages."[68] The second big alteration was to be in the editorship. "I have been offered . . . the editorial management of the Carpet Bag!" Noah Brooks confided to his Castine friend. "It seems rather funny but the publisher is in earnest and offers quite an inducement. I may accept but cannot be sure. I have one month to decide and in the meantime, keep dark on this subject and don't tell any one of it," he cautioned.[69] "The present editor, Mr. Shillaber," Brooks explained, "is about to [re]join the editorial corps of the 'Morning Post,' and, of course, will have to give up his connections with the Carpet Bag." The publisher was insistent that Brooks accept the job and assured him it would require only four or five days' time each month. The salary was to be $250 per year, and the decision had to be made before the middle of April. Brooks was undecided, but was confident that the new post would not "much affect my painting business as I shall still be able to attend to it without the two pursuits coming in collision." One thing he was certain about: if he accepted the position, he would devote his career more to "literary pursuits" than painting.[70] But he never had to make a decision; *The Carpet-Bag* died with the issue of March 26, 1853, and thus the new monthly edition never made its appearance. There simply "was no room in Boston for an exclusively comic paper."[71]

Besides Boston's lack of interest in such a paper, there was another factor involved in its demise. *The Carpet-Bag* had published a brutal satire upon the 1852 presidential contest between Generals Scott and Pierce.[72] Both political parties felt the sting of its biting humor. One whole year before the election, *The Carpet-Bag* had manufactured a presidential candidate out of whole cloth. On November 1, 1851, it endorsed "Ensign Stebbings" and informed its readers that "to-day we fling to the breeze our banner, inscribed with the name of Ensign Jehiel Stebbings." His motto was "All things to all men." Stebbings was from "Spunkville" and was a military hero of the Alamo as well as the Mexican and Aroostook wars. He had been wounded many times; while defending the Alamo he was stabbed. To make a story better *The Carpet-Bag* waged a mythical fight with various other newspapers. When the "opposition" charged that Stebbings had received his knife wound in the back, the supporters of the Ensign replied: "Where else could the Ensign be wounded in a hand-to-hand fight? No Mexican ever dared to face him. His foe crept stealthily behind him, stabbed him, and retreated."[73] Even after the election Brooks penned an article entitled "Stebbings in the South." It is dated "Tuscaloosa, Ala., Nov. 12th," and informs *The Carpet-Bag* editors that their ticket has been defeated in Alabama. "No doubt you have long before this heard," Brooks wrote under his pen name, "the result through the Magnetic Paragraph, but as that medium is inclined to be rude, particularly when the news is shocking, I thought a more delicate medium of communication would be acceptable." It seems that "Jacques" had fought gallantly for Stebbings, but unfortunately, he was the only supporter of the Ensign who was qualified to vote.[74] Such clever political wit made many enemies in both camps and helped to end *The Carpet-Bag*. And yet, as late as January 15, 1853, the editor was ready to enter Stebbings in the 1856 presidential contest.

The Paint Shop

After Brooks found that artistic painting would not put bread and butter on the table, he drifted into journalism; but there was paint in his blood even though the quill fitted his hand better than the drawing pencil or brush. From the time that Brooks arrived in Boston, painting of one kind or another occupied a large part of his life. While he was studying art he earned at least part of his living by doing ordinary house painting and like tasks. On these jobs he worked with other men, but with whom he started working is not certain. He probably started with William Sargent, with whom he boarded, or with Frederick Thomas Somerby (1814–1871). As early as 1848 Brooks was assisting another painter,[75] and in 1850 he was busily engaged in painting and trimming the steamship *Ocean* as she lay in dock at Chelsea. In addition to these routine painting skills, he learned other associated trades such as glazing.[76]

By 1852—if not before—Brooks was associated with Somerby at No. 62½ Cornhill Street in Boston. When the owners of this building tore it down, the two painters were forced to move to No. 5 Union Street in March of 1852.[77] Somerby and Brooks had many things in common. Somerby was an artist who had also given up trying to earn a living at this profession. He now advertised to paint "signs, banners, military standards" and do ornamental work.[78] Like Brooks, he too was a writer—a very prominent one in his time. He served as correspondent for both the Boston *Post* and the *Spirit of the Times*, but his close literary connection with Brooks was on *The Carpet-Bag* staff. There, he wrote under the name of "Cymon," and he contributed steadily to that comic weekly from its very first number. He was known throughout

Boston for his many pranks and hoaxes. His major work was a book entitled *Hits and Dashes*, a collection of his many newspaper sketches, which was published in 1852 and found a ready market.[79]

Brooks's business in the paint shop consisted largely of ornamenting furniture with pictures of flowers or landscapes. He received the furniture from the manufacturer and worked "by the job" so that he was "not obliged to go and come at any particular hours." By his own admission, the work was profitable although "mechanical" instead of artistic. Naturally he was not satisfied with this ornamental painting, but he fully realized that "it requires much time, practice, and study to make an artist finished enough to make Art ... a vocation and means of liv[e]lihood." While he was partially resigned to the fact that he would never be an artist, he nevertheless continued to paint landscapes and read books and articles about artists and their masterpieces.[80]

Later in 1852, Brooks and Somerby moved their establishment to No. 16 Union Street, just a few doors from their old location. At this time Brooks ran his first newspaper advertisement as an independent painter. To the public he offered his talents as a landscape and ornamental painter of cottage furniture.[81] He did not suffer for lack of business, and as the winter months approached, trade increased.[82]

Although Brooks and Somerby shared the same building, there is nothing to indicate that they were business partners. Both men advertised separately.[83] Perhaps they realized that with their writing duties it would be difficult for one man to keep a shop open for business every day. With this arrangement they could share the onerous task of shop keeping. The idea of two journalists trying to keep a place of business and write at the same time reminds one of the Lincoln and Berry store at New Salem, Illinois. Lincoln probably thought that Berry would look after things while he read, talked or joked, and Berry probably thought that Lincoln would look after business while he performed the duties of constable and attended court in Springfield. Considering their many distractions, it is amazing that Brooks and Somerby remained in business as long as they did. In addition to the many hours which Brooks spent in writing and other activities, there was another serious handicap to his business venture. He had a dislike for work. "Business is quite brisk here," Brooks wrote in the early part of 1853, "and I have quite as much as I can attend to, though I cannot attend to much just now, for the weather is so delightful that [it] is almost impossible to stay indoors." He was daydreaming about Castine and "new pleasant localities." His mind was far from the business at hand. But he concluded that he probably would not have time to visit Castine in 1853 because of his other trips. Many invitations to visit surrounding towns like Newburyport, Amesbury, etc. had been extended to him, and then there was the proposed vacation to New York to see the great fair.[84]

"Jacques" continued to ornament cottage furniture, but he never gave up his artistic hobby. During March of 1853, he painted a panorama which was exhibited at a fair held at Medford, Massachusetts. It was called the "Lunar Pantoscope," and the school of modern art would have loved it. Brooks jestingly described it as a "faithful and accurate delineation of the Moon—scenery and people, &c." Actually, it was a phantasm, and showed "several views of notable places and objects in the Moon; amongst them a shower bath on a large scale for the extinguishing of fires." The scene portrayed a "large house on fire" which was pulled on wheels under the "shower bath" and thereby extinguished. A group of Brooks's friends accompanied him to Medford on an excursion to view the paintings on display.

About a week after this trip he wrote that he was back "at work on furniture, which is not a very desirable or pleasant job, it's so *mechanical*, one pattern used time after time; however, *it pays*." Then, too, the pleasant weather kept his mind on other possible excursions out of town.[85] Regardless of his inclinations, Brooks had to do a certain amount of painting to earn extra money to supplement the income he derived from writing. Always borrowing money from friends,[86] he lived entirely beyond his means. He had to be the gentleman at all times. For example, he kept a servant and a carriage at his "residence in Chelsea,"[87] and frequented the American House on Hanover Street quite often—probably for his noon meals.[88]

During the last part of June in 1853, Brooks and Somerby again moved to a new business location. What prompted this relocation is not known, though it may have been lower rent. "We have found a room for our business at last," Brooks informed [George] Witherle, "[a]t No 27 School St. near the City Hall. Only Somerby and I are going to occupy it." Their new business site was "rather small but very convenient and airy." "The windows," he explained, "overlook the garden . . . in front of the city buildings in School St."[89] Prior to their tenancy the place had been occupied by a sculptor, Thomas A. Carew,[90] who probably selected it originally because of its pleasant view and numerous windows.

Brooks could have made a good living if he had planned better. He spent about the same amount of money regardless of how much he made. If the jobs were fewer, he just borrowed more. Although his brother-in-law owed him some money from the family estate, Brooks never borrowed from him or asked for his share. "Mr. Gay and I have never '*hitched horses together*' at all," he admitted. Benjamin D. Gay, who had married Noah's oldest sister, Phebe, was "averse and opposed" to his "setting up" for himself in business. Noah said that Gay was conservative "in his idea of business," but then admitted that he himself was "addicted in the contrary direction."[91] Evidently Brooks understood his weakness, but did not have the strength of will to combat it.

During the summer of 1853, Brooks was in serious monetary trouble and was borrowing heavily to supplement his earnings. But in spite of this, the fun and trips went on unabated. To celebrate the Fourth of July he planned a trip to Lowell, Massachusetts. At another time that summer, Charlie Wilder, Esther Wilder, Gilla Hubbard, and Brooks went on a fishing excursion. "We went down in omnibuses and private carriages," he related. At Chelsea Beach they chartered a schooner yacht and fished off the shore of Nahant. Unless Wilder paid most of the expenses, such ventures must have seriously depleted Brooks's capital. Fortunately, after he returned from the trip to Lowell he obtained a large interior decorating job. This was a contract to redecorate the Howard Athenaeum, a job which took more than two weeks to finish.[92] The Howard Athenaeum was a prominent theatre, located upon the street after which it was named. Brooks explained that theatres used the names lyceum, museum or athenaeum since Boston people thought "theatre" was "too vicious."[93]

With cash in his pockets once more, he quickly changed his mind and decided to take his usual summer vacation at Castine. His vacation would afford him an opportunity to write and "paint some views from nature," and he informed George Witherle that he wanted to rest and not have so many parties and excitement as usually occurred on his visits there.[94] Not satisfied with one vacation a year, he left Boston again on October 20 with Wilder for an extended tour. They first visited Wilder's old school at Monson, Massachusetts, then traveled on to Springfield to see the "Great Exhibition of Horses." That evening (October 21) they continued on to New Haven where they saw some of their "acquaintances" who were attending college there. The afternoon of the twenty-second found them on their way to New York; here, they spent five carefree days at the Crystal Palace Exhibition and other interesting places. Instead of returning to Boston by rail, they bought passage on a steamer—Brooks always enjoyed the sea. The trip was not without some profit, and upon his return, Brooks used the excursion as a basis for several articles, which he published.[95]

When winter came, the crisp air again turned his attention back to serious scholarly pursuits.[96] Throughout his life he served as secretary in many organizations. His ability to compose rapidly was generally recognized by his comrades, who quickly handed him the pen. The Chelsea "Union Course of Lectures" boasted a fine group of speakers, including Thomas Starr King and George W. Curtis.[97] King was a Unitarian minister and a very popular lecturer who had also contributed to *The Carpet-Bag*.[98] Curtis at this time was the editor of *Putnam's Monthly* and lectured widely.

Previous to his Boston days religion had always been a formality with Brooks. As a boy he generally stayed at home while the family attended church services, but in Chelsea he frequented the Congregational Church of Reverend Isaac P. Langworthy,[99] with Charlie Wilder.[100] Even though he went to church, religion meant little to Brooks. While gazing far across the beautiful mountain peaks in New Hampshire in 1851, he wrote: "If ever I feel more of that 'religious sentimentality,' at one time or another, it is when I gaze on scenes like this."[101] His religion was "theoretical" and intellectual to the point of having no "*practical* belief of any kind." Then, in 1854, Brooks suddenly became frightened with the prospect of eternal damnation and was converted. From that moment forward, he was an ardent, practicing, orthodox Congregationalist.[102]

Financial troubles and itching feet prompted Brooks to leave Boston in the spring of 1854. As early as the previous November he had determined to move on. "It is quite certain," he wrote, "that I shall go West early in the spring and it would not be convenient or pleasant for me to go east [that is to Castine] before I leave here." But to George Witherle he confided the fact that he still had the kindliest feeling toward his home town. Then he made a prophecy and a promise: "If in the Western world to which my feet are tending, I shall ever rise to station of influence or honor, of public or of private trust, I shall, while I give my meed of gratitude to my native place, be made to credit the most which I am and shall have, to Massachusetts and its quickening influences." For it was in Boston that he had learned to write for publication, appreciate art, read good literature, and express himself on canvas with brush and pencil. In spite of his advancements and self-education, however, he blamed himself for not having accomplished more. He complained that his ambition was "kept down by a sluggish will," his "activity of mind" was "balanced by indecision of character," and his "thirst for knowledge" was "neutralized by slovenly habits of thinking and study."[103]

"Jacques" was too hard on himself. He had made great strides toward his future profession, although at the time he was not certain that it would be journalism. If *The Carpet-Bag* had not expired just when he was asked to be its new editor, he certainly would not have left Boston when his paint store failed. But recognition in Boston came slowly because of the number of good writers working there; Brooks probably reasoned that he could do better farther west where the country was newer. So, he closed his shop and left. The new occupants of his business site were Cyrus and Darius Cobb,

FIGURE 2. Earliest known photo of Noah Brooks, perhaps taken in Boston. Author's collection.

portrait painters.[104] Somerby disappeared from the ranks of the Boston painters, and the Cobbs had the entire shop. Evidently they, like the sculptor who had occupied the room before Brooks and Somerby, liked the good lighting and pleasant view.

Years after his unsuccessful business venture at No. 27 School Street, Noah Brooks returned to this familiar scene and did some "mousing in a bookstall" there.[105] Did he still feel the hurt of his earliest failure in business, or did he chuckle to himself as he recalled this unsuccessful venture? Brooks never revealed the answer, but he could have afforded to chuckle, for he had become one of the best known newspaper editors on the East Coast.

CHAPTER III

Five Years in the Midwest

The Paint and Furniture Business

When Noah Brooks left Boston, after his unsuccessful business venture, he moved to the midwestern town of Dixon, Illinois, located in Lee County upon the beautiful Rock River in the northern part of the state. Here the old wagon road to the Galena lead mines had crossed the river and the town of Dixon had sprung up at the ferry. Joseph Ogee, a Canadian half-breed, started a ferrying service there, but in March, 1830, he rented his ferry to a newcomer, John Dixon (1784–1876). After operating the business for nearly two years on this basis, Dixon purchased the ferry from Ogee on January 27, 1832, for the sum of $550. As the location had previously been called Ogee's Ferry, the new name Dixon's Ferry followed quite naturally. Along with the ferry Dixon purchased Ogee's cabin, which was constructed in the style of a blockhouse. Around this nucleus a prosperous frontier town developed.[1]

Commercial opportunities were good in Dixon, and many New England merchants transferred their business there. Among them were several relatives of Noah Brooks. His brother, Joseph Barker Brooks, who had previously been in partnership with S. K. Upham at Boston, transplanted his roots to Dixon about 1844 where he started a general store on Water Street.[2] He sold everything from nails to lumber wagons and saved his earnings.[3] In fact, he "did the largest business of any merchant in this section," the old settlers recalled.[4] As soon as his business was on a firm basis, he married the local school teacher, Miss Ophelia A. Loveland, on January 6, 1847.[5] After establishing a prosperous merchandising business, he sold out his store on March 21, 1854, to Webb, Rodgers & Woodruff,[6] but he did not retire. Instead, he and

John Daley established a large grist mill where they carried on a thriving trade. The local paper proudly announced that they had "three run of stone . . . running constantly night and day." Their firm was known as the Dixon Mills, and the following year—1855—the two partners doubled the size of their building and added four more "run of stone."[7]

With this increasing prosperity J. B. Brooks decided to build a residence which would be the show place of Dixon. By the latter part of April, 1855, the basement was finished and the workmen were ready to start the brick work.[8] Since 1852 Dixon had had a brick kiln,[9] and he took advantage of this local product to construct a beautiful three-story brick home which still stands in magnificent grandeur at 303 East Everett Street. Without waiting for the new plaster to become dry, he moved into his new house and caught pneumonia, which caused his death on December 18, 1855.[10] Some idea of the elegance of this place is realized when one notes the price it brought in 1861. Charles Godfrey purchased it for $8,000, a very large sum of money at that time.[11]

"Barker" Brooks, as he was called, had always been a willing servant of the community. In his native home of Castine he had been a member of the fire engine company, and likewise in Dixon he served the town well. In 1851 he was one of the directors of the Dixon Bridge Company, and in 1854 he was the chairman of the board of supervisors for Lee County. Whenever there was a job to do, he was willing to do his full share.[12]

Noah Brooks's brother-in-law, S. K. Upham, after being in California since 1849, returned east and settled in Dixon also. In April, 1853, he and a man by the name of Peacock opened a lumber yard on Water Street, near the bridge. He too was a successful merchant and continued in this business until his retirement in 1876, at which time his partner was Charles F. Emerson. Upham died on February 13, 1883.[13]

Another brother-in-law, Benjamin D. Gay, moved to Dixon at the same time Noah Brooks did. During the summer of 1854 he came west to try his hand in this prosperous community, but he died suddenly on March 29, 1857, while walking home from church.[14]

So when Noah Brooks moved to Illinois, he was once again among his relatives. Before leaving Boston, he asked Barker to build him a paint shop in Dixon. His brother not only accomplished this, but also lined up some jobs for him before he arrived. Noah reasoned that, with a capital of $700, he could reestablish himself in business. Gay, his brother-in-law, lent him some of that needed cash, and various friends supplied the rest.[15]

When his Chelsea friends discovered that Brooks was leaving, they gave him a farewell party on May 8, 1854, and presented him with a rosewood writing desk completely equipped. The following day he left Boston by railroad and proceeded to Albany, Buffalo, and Cleveland. Here it was necessary to change trains for the trip to Toledo and Chicago. After resting overnight at one of the most expensive hotels in Chicago, the Tremont, he left on the Aurora line for Mendota, which was the end of the line at that time. From there he rode a stagecoach into Dixon, a distance of twenty miles. On May 12 he arrived at his destination, eager and well satisfied with the general appearance of the place. "I like Dixon very much better than I expected to," he confessed. His new paint shop was not quite finished when he arrived nor had his goods from the East made their appearance, but there was work waiting for him. His brother Barker had seen to that. One of his first jobs was a fancy sign for Lem Atherton. There was also a meeting hall to fresco and "lots of other work." Nevertheless, Brooks had learned but little from his Boston experience. Instead of doing the painting himself, he had brought with him a man to do the work, a hard-working fellow by the name of Edward Pasco.[16] Brooks hated the menial labor and desired to be a manager even though his business did not warrant such a delegation of painting chores.

On June 8 he opened his new paint store, on Galena Street, near Front Street and the Post Office. Instead of specializing in ornamental painting—as he had done in Boston—Brooks announced that he would do house, sign, and carriage painting in addition to fancy ornamental work. Besides painting, he offered his services in those skills which he had learned from other painters in Boston: glazing, gilding, graining, and the imitating of marble. And he kept mixed and dry paints, putty, glass, and paint brushes which he sold both retail and wholesale. The Dixon *Telegraph* vouched for his ability as a sign painter and recommended him to the townsfolk.[17] His career in Dixon seemed fairly launched.

On November 1, 1854, less than six months after opening the shop, he formed a partnership with John G. Brooks (1830–1859), who probably contributed whatever capital he had, and business continued at the same location.[18] Although his associate had the same surname, he was not related to Noah.[19] John seems to have been originally from Connecticut, but it was at Chelsea that Noah met him.[20] During Noah's stay in Boston, they had been close friends and were often together.[21] Little is known about John except that he had a great interest in music. In Chelsea he played in the local brass band, and upon moving to Dixon, became secretary of the Dixon Musical Association, the conductor of which was J. T. Little.[22]

As soon as Noah arrived in Dixon, he began coaxing John Brooks to join him. John answered that he would come if Noah thought he could be of any assistance in the paint shop. But John was not a painter; indeed, he had no trade at all.[23] Evidently, their partnership was an arrangement for the sake of companionship instead of business. Noah did not like the actual work, and John did not know the painting business. As a result, they hired other men to do the painting for them. When George L. Howell and Philip Maxwell Alexander opened a new hardware store on Galena Street, the Brookses got the contract to paint the interior of the building, but they did not do the work themselves.[24]

In 1855 the Brookses added paper, twine, and glazed sash to their stock in an effort to increase trade.[25] Since they wished to operate on a larger scale, their small building did not afford enough room. When Barker Brooks began the erection of a brick building in the new Nachusa Block on Galena Street[26] in September of 1854, Noah and John decided to move their concern into this. Accordingly, on May 30, 1855, they announced that they had relocated their business in the new block, just across the street from their old store.[27] Their former site was taken by Andrew J. Brubaker who opened "an extensive grocery and provision establishment" there.[28] With more available space, the partners added a new line of business: furniture. It was purchased in the East and much of it was custom-made to their own specifications. Next, coffins (ready-made or custom-made) and cabinets were added to their growing stock. Such an extensive inventory required much capital, and it had to be borrowed from Gay, Upham, or Barker Brooks. Unfortunately, there was keen competition for the furniture trade in Dixon. On the same street, on the corner of Galena and Water, there was another furniture store operated by George W. Baker.[29] It is doubtful if there was a big enough market for two such stores at this time. Nevertheless, the Brookses continued to buy a large stock of fancy furniture in all kinds of woods. And they offered for sale such expensive items as imported window glass. The editor of the local paper remarked that he had taken "a look through their ware rooms and [was] actually astonished. Chairs of all descriptions, French sofas, Marble topped and rosewood centre tables, Ladie's [sic] toilet Bureaus, hat-racks, 'whatnots' so ons and soforths, etc." "We presume," the editor continued, "that a more elegant stock of furniture cannot be found west of Chicago."[30]

There was no lack of work in the house-painting business, but the Brookses were not doing the jobs themselves. Constantly they advertised for house painters to execute their orders.[31] Instead of pursuing this profitable trade, they sold this branch of the business (including the glazing work) to their foreman, Edward Pasco, on November 1, 1855. By this time, Brubaker had sold out his grocery business, and Pasco moved into the building formerly used by the Brookses. Pasco had been doing well and was getting good prices for his work. He was even executing the fancy sign work which Noah should have been doing. Many of the business signs had been painted by Pasco even before this transaction, a step which marked the beginning of the end.[32]

Just what amount of capital the Brookses had invested in their goods in 1854 is unknown, but, in 1855 their stock was valued at $1,085.[33] With addition of more and more furniture, their capital investment jumped to $4,560 in 1856.[34] In order to remain solvent they had to have cash sales. "We must rigidly adhere to the cash system," the Brookses announced to the public, "and in all cases but one price will be asked and that the cash price."[35] The year 1856 was a bad one for winter sales. At times it was 32° below zero. "The severity of the weather which keeps farmers at home, and stops emigration has tended to make business very dull, so that, without any especial panic, we have just now the hardest time for money every known in this country, scarcely any trade in the place, and nothing selling," Noah complained. Nevertheless, his optimistic nature caused him to add "the prospects for a brisk spring trade, are, however, very good, and if we can hold on until then we shall do well."[36] In an effort to increase business they advertised in both of the local papers regardless of political affiliations. But instead of limiting their purchasing until the merchandise on hand began to move, John Brooks went to New York that year to buy more.[37]

Although his financial position in 1856 was extremely precarious, Noah Brooks decided to get married. This step must have surprised even his close friends, because he had not supported the doctrine of working in double harness and in 1850 had flatly denied any thought of marriage. "As for Wedding cake, it *was* invented by Satan for the destruction o[f] mankind," he said, and further maintained that "it was . . . the veritable 'fruit of that forbidden tree which brought death into the world and all our sin.'"[38] Of course, part of this vituperation was in fun, but his letters give no indication of any serious matrimonial intentions until February, 1856. At this time he suddenly told his old friend, George Witherle, that he expected to return to Boston "about the last of April" to be married. From the content of this letter it would appear that not even Witherle knew much about the coming event.[39]

According to plan, Brooks returned to Boston sometime before May 16. He was suffering from the effects of a severe cold,[40] but regained his health in time for his scheduled marriage to Miss Carolina Augusta Fellows at 3 P.M. on May 29, the ceremony being performed by the Reverend Mr. Leeds in St. Peter's Church of Salem, Massachusetts. Charles Tilden Wilder, Noah's "trusty friend & right hand man," served as groomsman in the simple ceremony. There was no wedding cake or celebration; the newlyweds left immediately for a brief honeymoon in New York. If Brooks kept to the schedule which he had previously announced, he was introducing his bride about Dixon within ten days after their marriage.[41]

Noah had met his wife-to-be in Salem while visiting his sister Marianne,[42] but he never mentioned her name in his letters until December, 1852.[43] And even then he was very cautious when speaking of her; a few months before his marriage he begged Witherle to keep this news a secret.

Caroline was the daughter of Oliver and Sally (Foster) Fellows and was baptized with her sister, Mary Ann, on June 3, 1832, in South Church of old Salem. She was born, however, in 1827—not in 1832. Her baptism, if the record is correct, was postponed for five years; Noah Brooks indicated on her tombstone that her birth occurred in 1827, and relatives confirmed the fact that she was older than Noah. Her father was called "Captain" and at one time was a ship caulker. Likewise, two of her brothers followed the sea and lost their lives in sailing mishaps. With their nautical backgrounds the young couple had many things in common.[44]

It is almost certain that they did not set up housekeeping for themselves in Dixon. "You shall see me under the shade of a big elm tree which grows in front of S. K. Upham's house," he predicted in April of 1856, "where I shall probably board this summer."[45] This arrangement, no doubt, proved too congested for all concerned, for by August of that same year, one of his Dixon friends wrote that "Noah Brooks talks of taking Mrs. [J. B.] Brooks['s] house & boarding her & her family & I don[']t know but am inclined to think that you & I shall have to travel, but I guess we won[']t be troubled to get boarding places in town now as boarding houses are more plent[iful] than boarder & money." It is easy to see why Noah wanted to rent this house. His brother's widow was now alone in her large three-story dwelling which was large enough for two families. One of the widow's boarders further commented that "she had rather keep it herself till [next spring] but he is very anxious to get it."[46] It seems reasonable to assume that he did rent the widow Brooks's home—or one floor of it—for a while. In 1858, however, he noted in his diary that he was boarding at Yeakle's for $2.50 per week.[47] Since his wife was with him at this time, the price probably included board for both of them.

With definite responsibilities for the first time in his life, Noah Brooks needed a steady income. Unfortunately, he found himself bankrupt within a few months after his marriage. On November 29, 1856, he and John were forced to execute an assignment of their stock to S. K. Upham, brother-in-law of Noah, and John V. Eustace, a local attorney and land agent, "for the benefit of creditors."[48] Their last advertisement appeared on December 6, notice of their failure having reached the newspaper office too late to stop this insertion. A week later the assignees announced that they were going to sell the merchandise at cost in order to settle the affair quickly. The surprising statement in this notice was the value of the saleable goods. The inventory disclosed that they were worth $10,000,[49] a fantastic amount of capital to be invested in a furniture store that was located in a pioneer town. But if Upham and Eustace thought that they could dispose of the furniture and other goods quickly, they were doomed to disappointment. It simply did not sell, and after many fruitless months Upham and Eustace gave notice that they were going to auction off the entire stock on September 10, 1857. Among the many items which the auctioneer, A. L. Porter, put on the block were 500 chairs, 1,000 rolls of wall paper, 50 boxes of glass, and countless pieces of furniture.[50] The outcome of the sale is not known, but most of the stock was probably purchased by Cyrus A. Davis, who opened a new furniture store "at the old stand" of Noah and John Brooks in November of 1858.[51] If this assumption is correct, then Upham and Eustace did not get matters settled until two years after the business had failed.

One reason for Noah Brooks's failure was the business recession which struck Dixon in 1856. "I guess these hard times will tell who is doing business on borrowed capital," John Howell prophesied later that year.[52] The Brookses were operating on borrowed money, but as one Dixonite remarked about Noah, "he proved to be a misfit in that line of business."[53] Then too, as in Boston, there were many other activities which occupied his time.

Community Activities

Upon his arrival in Dixon, Brooks commented that there was an "indifference to religion" in the town, "but they are making up somewhat, and have just started a Sunday School, and who do you guess is Superintendent. No less a person than my *venerable self!*" The position was tendered to him upon his first Sunday in Dixon, matters having been all arranged previously.[54] His relatives, evidently, suggested him for this post. Within a few months after the founding of the Sunday School, there was a movement started for the establishment of a church. "An Ecclesiastical Council will be convened at Exchange Hall (Stiles' and Webb's new block)," one of the local papers announced, "on Friday Sept. 29th at 4 o'clock P.M. for the purpose of organizing a Congregational Church in this place." Among the founders were Mr. and Mrs. S. K. Upham and Noah Brooks. Their first services were held at Exchange Hall in October, 1854, with the Rev. S. D. Peet serving as pastor. Two years later, the congregation moved to a brick building formerly occupied by another denomination. By 1856, if not sooner, Noah Brooks was a deacon as was his brother-in-law, S. K. Upham.[55] He was also secretary of the Dixon Bible Society, having been first elected at the annual meeting on December 31, 1854, and reelected the following year. The Society had been active for six or seven years prior to Brooks's arrival in Dixon.[56] From the time of his conversion in Boston to the end of his life, Brooks maintained a deep interest in religious matters.

Everything cultural was also of interest to him. Even in Dixon he kept up his subscription to the *Atlantic Monthly*, though he could ill afford it,[57] and at one time he contemplated writing a history of his home town—Castine, Maine.[58] Musical affairs in Dixon brought forth his singing talent, and when the local citizens gave an "old Continental Concert" in 1858, he appeared in the fun-loving cast of amateurs and sang "Capt. Kidd."[59] Previously, when Asa Hull had established a Musical Academy in Dixon on November 1, 1856, Noah and John quickly endorsed the institution and recommended it to the local inhabitants.[60]

Noah also sketched and painted for the local art contests. At the first annual fair of the Lee County Agricultural Society, held at Dixon on October 18–20, 1854, he exhibited three oil paintings and one pencil sketch, all of which were awarded prizes totaling $7.00. To him, the Lee County Fair offered an opportunity for artistic recognition, and at the conclusion of this successful exposition he was one of the first to pledge his support to the Society for the following year.[61] And for the second annual county fair he entered an oil painting under the name of Noah and John G. Brooks. Since his store partner was not an artist, Noah probably added John's name to bring their painting establishment before the public.[62] At another time he used his talent to benefit the newly established Congregational Church. In the early months of 1855 this organization wished to build a permanent place for its services, and he painted coats of arms upon window curtains for their fund-raising fair.[63]

As at Boston, he also painted landscapes for sale. "It affords us great pleasure," the local editor commented, "to notice a painting, executed by Noah Brooks, Esq., of this city of the old block house [John Dixon's log cabin] and its surroundings as it stood on First and Peoria streets in 1837 on our arrival on Rock River. It is a matter of astonishment to the old settlers who have viewed the picture, how Mr. Brooks could have given it the almost perfectly natural appearance which it presents—himself having never witnessed the original." Brooks was aided in his difficult task by Dr. Oliver Everett (1811–1888) who had come to Dixon in 1836. Everett sketched from memory a picture of the old landmark which Brooks used as a model. Since John Dixon was still living at the time, he probably gave Brooks oral descriptions of his cabin and the ferry site.[64] Brooks also made a pencil sketch of old Fort Dixon as it appeared on the north bank of Rock River during the Black Hawk War.

After the many opportunities for literary activities which Boston had afforded, Brooks found the town of Dixon sadly deficient. To improve the town's cultural opportunities, he and others organized the Dixon Lecture Association to bring Eastern talent into their growing community. With his previous experience in the literary groups at Chelsea, it was natural that Brooks should become a leader in this movement. The fact that the newspaper announcements (signed by the committee) carry his name last, seems to indicate that he also prepared most of their publicity as part of his editorial work on the *Telegraph*. In September of 1854, the Dixon Lecture Association asked for the "hearty cooperation" of the citizens in order to assure their enterprise. Good ticket sales, they announced, would bring the best speakers in the country to this Rock River town. The prime movers of the Association were W. W. Curtis, L. W. Atherton, B. F. Shaw, H. T. Noble, F. R. Dana, and Noah Brooks.[65]

The public response to their plea was extremely gratifying, and sufficient funds were subscribed in advance to permit the engagement of such outstanding figures as Bayard Taylor, Josiah Quincy Jr., Parke Godwin, and William Stark.[66] Quincy led off with the first address in December of that year,[67] and was followed by Godwin, Taylor, and two additional attractions not listed in the first program: Horace Mann and James Russell Lowell. With such fine talent the Association enjoyed great success and quickly chose a group of officers to carry out plans for the coming year. L. W. Atherton became president; F. A. Soule and H. T. Noble, vice-presidents; Noah Brooks, secretary; and C. N. Levanway, treasurer.[68] Again, Brooks's energy and writing ability were recognized, and the quill was given to him.

When the lecture group met in 1855 to choose officers, Brooks was again named secretary.[69] He and his colleagues now did a superior job in obtaining outstanding speakers. News of their lecturers attracted attention in distant places. The Cincinnati *Columbian* commented: "Decidedly the best course of lecturers for the coming winter that we have yet seen noticed, is announced for the spirited little town of Dixon, in Illinois. The programme contains the names of the best speakers and thinkers of the age, and the list is superior to any yet announced, even in our leading metropolitan cities. Honor to Dixon!"[70]

This was no idle boast. The Dixon programs featured Parke Godwin, John G. Saxe, Ralph Waldo Emerson, T. Starr King, and others.[71] Emerson, however, was poorly received. On January 3, 1856, he read an essay entitled "Beauty," the one that he gave most often on his western lecture tours. "Many that heard Mr. Emerson," reported one of the editors, "were pleased, but we must beg leave to differ with those who consider it a 'popular lecture.'—The lecture bore evidence of ripe scholarship, and c[o]ntained many instances of history, but it had little that was original. It was delivered in a most miserable style. It would have been quite interesting to read, some rainy day, [b]ut to pay $50 to hear him read it was 'paying too much for the whistle.'"[72]

It was partly due to Emerson's unpopular lecture that the Dixon Lecture Association failed to gain support for the following season. As the time for lectures approached in 1856, adverse sentiment cropped out in the local press. Prior to this, the Dixon *Telegraph* had ardently supported the Dixon Lecture Association, but with the "tightness of the money market" and the poor quality of the former speakers, it advocated that some of the local men address the community and save the "cool fifty" expended for each lecturer. "It is true," the paper admitted, "that the rare intellectual treats which we received from [T. Starr] King, [E. H.] Chapin, [John] Pierpont, and a few others, amply remunerated our citizens for all the trouble and expense of organizing the association. But our eastern fifty dollar lecturers were not all T. Starr Kings."[73]

With this blast, the Lecture Association withered, but in 1857 there was one Eastern speaker in Dixon—probably without any previous arrangement with the defunct group. This man was Horace Greeley, the editor who was later to become Noah Brooks's employer. He lectured on February 13 at Exchange Hall on the subject of "Europe." It would be interesting to know how Brooks felt about this famous man; the other citizens of Dixon expected him to appear "with either the right or left boot-leg outside of his pantaloons" or "his cravat or dickey" awry. However, to their surprise, Greeley presented a well-groomed appearance, which belied the popular opinion held of him.[74]

Land Speculation

With the hope of making some easy money, Brooks became engaged—on a small scale—in land speculation. On December 15, 1854, he purchased 166.22 acres of internal improvement land in Lee County in $498.66, being three dollars an acre.[75] After holding this property less than a year, he sold it on August 14, 1855, to Peter Bressler for $831.00.[76] This gave Brooks a profit of $332.34. He also bought forty acres in Ogle County on January 15, 1855, for the same price, three dollars an acre.[77] But after five months he sold it to Elias B. Stiles (on June 23) without realizing one cent of profit.[78] The reason for this sale remains a mystery; he probably needed cash as this time for his painting business.

Journalism and Politics

When Noah Brooks moved to Dixon, there was no publication in that Rock River community such as the Boston *Carpet-Bag*. On December 25, 1858, however, there appeared the first issue of a paper called *Life in Dixon Illus-trated*. Its chief contributors were James H. Boyd, Noah Brooks, W. W. Curtis, Jason C. Ayers, and B. F. Shaw.[79] Although the first issue was in December, a notice in one of the local papers would seem to indicate that it was later issued only on the Fourth of July.[80] The Dixon people must have enjoyed Brooks's literary contributions, because years later one of the pioneer citizens of the town recalled a very clever bit of writing which Noah penned after several of the local boys had killed a muskrat. He called the story "Amos Krat," and gave the animal such human characteristics that the "killers" felt remorse for their heedless deed.[81]

But *Life in Dixon* was not his chief literary effort. Newspaper writing was the thing which he did best, but this fact was not self-evident to him. While operating his paint and furniture store, he also held the post of editorial writer on the Dixon *Telegraph*.[82] It was the oldest newspaper in Lee County, having been started on May 1, 1851, and was owned by John V. Eustace at the time of its sale to Benjamin F. Shaw on April 20, 1854. One week later, Shaw assumed the editorship of this weekly organ. The new owner and publisher was "a broad-minded man, sincerely honest in every line he wrote, always a 'machine' politician in the best sense."[83] Brooks's first personal contact with the editor, who was one year younger than he, may have been in November, 1854, when he painted the new sign for the *Telegraph* office. In his editorial column Shaw commended Brooks for his fine work.[84] How much of the editorial work Noah did is not certain. At times he signed his articles "B," but these are generally special communications such as his coverage of an execution at Rock Island.[85] Other contributions, no doubt, were written by Brooks and left unsigned or hidden under different pen names. He well could have written "A Little too Punctual—A Steamboat Sketch" which is signed "The Old 'Un."[86] It deals with events which Brooks could easily have witnessed in New York and has the earmarks of his style, but such articles cannot be positively identified. He must have contributed countless lines of type, for after he had left Dixon he related, rather bitterly, that Shaw would not "have this child to make his thunder for him."[87] With his valuable jour-nalistic experience in Boston, he probably did much of the work for Shaw.

It was largely Brooks's connection with the Dixon *Telegraph* that brought about his acquaintance with Abraham Lincoln. "As one who dabbled a little in politics and a good deal in journalism, it was necessary for me," Brooks recalled, "to follow up some of the more important mass meetings of the Republicans."[88] During the 1856 presidential campaign, John C. Frémont headed the first national Republican ticket, and Brooks—a former Whig like Lincoln—became an ardent supporter of this new party. The Dixon Frémont

Club was organized on July 12, 1856, with his partner, John G. Brooks, serving as a member of the welcoming committee for the forthcoming Dixon ratification meeting.[89] Noah also was a member of the Frémont Club and campaigned enthusiastically for the Republicans; in fact, on September 13, 1856, he was asked "unanimously" to address the local club at one of their meetings.[90] But the important event for the Dixon Republicans was the "Fremont Ratification Meeting," which was held at Dixon on July 17, 1856. It was at this time that Brooks met Lincoln and formed a friendship with him which was quite active "during and after the Fremont campaign."[91] "Five or six times" when Lincoln was in the Dixon area in 1856 Brooks chatted with him about politics and other events.[92]

The local advocates of Frémont made great preparations for the ratification meeting and announced that "the following speakers are expected to be present: Joseph Knox, Judge Kneeland, Francis A. Hoffman[n], Dr. Egan, John Wentworth, Judge Deim, T[h]os. Turner, and several others are invited to be present."[93] There was no mention of Lincoln's having been invited, but nevertheless he appeared and was the principal speaker. Court business took him to Chicago on the evening of the fifteenth,[94] and the local Republican leaders saw a wonderful opportunity to utilize Lincoln's great speaking ability. When one of the Chicago papers learned about his visit, the editor wrote: "While here it is hoped he will consent to address the people upon the great political issues of the day."[95] Nor was this wish in vain; the editor proudly proclaimed two days later that Lincoln had consented to appear and speak at the Dixon and Sterling meetings.[96]

"Although the farmers had commenced harvesting, there were about 1,500 people present," the Dixon *Telegraph* recounted.[97] However, one of the best contemporary reports of this meeting appeared in the Chicago *Journal*:

A very large and enthusiastic meeting of the citizens of Dixon and the surrounding country ratified the nominations of Fremont and Dayton yesterday. The assembly organized about 2 o'clock. J. J. Beardsley [of Rock Island], district elector, led off in an excellent speech. He was followed by Hon. A. Lincoln, State elector, in a speech of great power over two hours in length. It was one of the ablest efforts of that distinguished man—clear, concise and convincing. Mr. L. was frequently interrupted with applause, and on concluding, three cheers from the yeomen went up which made the welkin ring. Mr. [John] Wentworth followed, when the meeting adjourned till evening. On reassembling J. C. Vaughan [of the Chicago *Tribune*], J. F. Farnsworth [of De Kalb County] and Thomas J. Turner [of Freeport] each effectively addressed the large audience, which with undiminished numbers remained until after twelve o'clock that night. The assembly was composed of a large share of Democrats, the leaders of that party heretofore, all now united in support of Fremont and Dayton. The meeting adjourned to meet again to-day at Sterling.[98]

One of Brooks's friends later retold the story of Lincoln's appearance that day at Dixon. "Lincoln spoke in the grove in the court-house square," this unknown acquaintance wrote, and "[Noah Brooks] and I sat together and made a little fun of his excessively homely appearance. He was dressed in an awkwardly fitting linen suit, evidently bought ready-made at a country store, and intended for a man at least five inches less in stature than he was, the vest and trowsers not meeting by at least an inch and a half, and the last-named garment being short at the feet."[99]

Brooks was probably introduced to Lincoln during the recess between the afternoon and evening sessions; if he had met Lincoln before he spoke, his appearance upon the platform would not have been so shocking. But it was Lincoln's logic which made a lasting impression upon Brooks. Four years later he wrote the fullest account of this speech yet discovered, probably from skeleton notes taken for the *Telegraph* and never used. This local paper did not carry the story on July 26, but it was only a brief notice. Brooks, in retelling the event, said that Lincoln was then called the "Henry Clay of Illinois" and continued with this report of Lincoln's Dixon address:

> There was an irresistible force of logic, a clinching power of argument, and a manly disregard of everything like sophistry or claptrap, which could not fail to arrest the attention and favorably impress the most prejudiced mind. A prominent democrat riding by the Court House square, where the speaking was going on, stopped his horse for a moment to hear the man who he had met before at Springfield, and so completely did he become drawn into the train of his argument that he staid silently listening to the end of the speech. Hard headed old Democrats who had withstood the arguments and truths of scores of able men were forced to confess that their reason was led captive while they listened to the plain, straight-forward and sledge-hammer logic of the speaker. When he first rose to the stand, his pleasant, but by no means handsome face, irradiated by a genial smile—almost everyone was disappointed at the personal appearance of Lincoln. Tall, spare, sallow in complexion, square-shouldered, with long arms hanging awkwardly by his side, his small head covered with short dark hair brushed carelessly back from his high square forehead, the new speaker, who had been preceded by long John Wentworth [J. J. Beardsley], of Chicago, was not one who was calculated to make at once a favorable impression upon the audience. But when, after briefly sketching the history of the much agitated question of slavery in the United States and Territories, he began to argue therefrom the reasonableness of what was asked by the North, and the madness and folly of

the demand of the South that all governmental power and legislative action should be subservient to the interests of her own peculiar institutions, his manner and appearance were entirely lost and forgotten in the magic of his eloquence and in the fund of irresist[i]ble argument which he poured forth. His manner, never tedious or harsh, became instinct with life, energy and elective vivacity. Every motion was graceful, every inflection of his voice melodious, and when, dropping for the moment, argument, he good-naturedly appealed to his fellow-republicans to admit certain alleged charges, and then went on to show how, notwithstanding all this, the platform and principles of the party were untouched and uninjured, his consummate shrewdness and long-headed, astute perceptions of the truth never failed to touch the audience with a sudden shock of pleasure and surprise, which brought forth spontaneous bursts of applause from friends and opponents.

The chief characteristic of this, as of all other speeches to which we have ever listened from him, was the simplicity of statement, the honest admission of all truthful objections, and the utter absence of everything like sophistry and cunning advantage of verbal trickery. There was no wire-drawn argument to prove that the speaker was right in his conclusions, and that all others were wrong—but every hearer could not fail to be impressed with the fact that the great principles of right and justice had sank deep into the mind of the speaker, and from these flowed the perspicuous statements which overwhelmed all who heard him.

He was always good-humored, witty and ready with a repartee for all those foolish fellows who will persist in making asses of themselves by interrupting a public speaker. Said he to one "irrepressible" muggins who had been unusually impertinent and persistent: "Look here, my friend, you are only making a fool of yourself by exposing yourself to the ridicule which I have thus far succeeded in bringing upon you every time you have interrupted me. You ought to know that men whose business it is to speak in public, make it a part of their business to have something always ready for just such fellows as you are. You see you stand no show against a man who has met, a hundred times, just such flings as you seem to fancy are original with yourself; so you may as well, to use a popular expression, 'dry up' at once." The individual was obliged to see the force of the remark and at once subsided.[100]

Such was Brooks's first contact with the man whom he was later to know intimately. The following day at 2 P.M. Lincoln spoke for two hours at Sterling, "much to the satisfaction of all who heard him." He was followed on the stand by John Wentworth of the Chicago *Democrat*.[101] As Sterling is only ten miles down the Rock River from Dixon, Brooks probably joined the Dixonites who accompanied Lincoln to this speaking engagement. And when Lincoln spoke on August 16 at Oregon (Ogle County), Illinois, Noah Brooks also attended this Republican rally and became better acquainted with Lincoln. While taking notes for the Dixon *Telegraph*, Brooks met Lincoln and the two "crawled under the pendulous branches of a tree, [where] Lincoln, lying flat on the ground, with his chin in his hands, talked on . . . ."[102] Brooks later gave this account of their discussion:

> We [I] had previously been introduced to LINCOLN [at Dixon], and while wandering about the grove, during the preliminary business of the meeting, we met him, and sat talking with him for an hour or more, on the probable result of the campaign, future of the Republican party, and of the national interests therein involved. He had no hope that Fremont would be elected, and deduced conclusions from premises which after events completely justified— He was disappointed at the nomination of Fremont, and charged it upon the wicked doctrine of availability, which would ruin any party. He believed that the progress of Republican sentiment would be such that in 1860 every free State would go for the Republican nominee, provided he were an exponent of the principles of the party, and not committed to any extreme or radical measures. The candidate for 1860, he said, should be a national, conservative man, unhackneyed by political tergiversations, and untrammeled by party obligations. A man fresh from the people, who should be able to embody in himself the expression of the popular will, and to thoroughly sympathise with the popular sentiment. Against the violent doctrines of some Republicans who were prominent in Illinois politics, he expressed himself in decided terms, saying that such men and the false impressions they made would lose the State to Fremont.[103]

Brooks liked Lincoln and his political thesis, and according to his own statement, their friendship in Illinois continued "through the Lincoln-Douglas canvass, two years later."[104] But it is impossible to ascertain which of the debates he attended. If he could raise the money, he probably attended several of them. He certainly must have joined the Dixon delegation when Lincoln debated with Douglas at Freeport on August 27, 1858. On this occasion there was a special train from Amboy, Dixon, and Polo which paused at Dixon while carrying Lincoln himself to Freeport.[105] The next time that Brooks saw Lincoln after the 1858 debates, the Springfield lawyer was president of the United States.

Farming in Kansas

The next chapter of Brooks's life emanated from his political affiliations and business failure. In the summer of 1856, excitement over the Kansas-Nebraska issue was very evident in Dixon. When the Anti-Nebraska party assembled at Bloomington on May 28, 1856, the representatives from Lee County included

Brooks's employer, B. F. Shaw of the *Telegraph*, and his brother-in-law, S. K. Upham. As an aftermath to this convention, a similar meeting was held at the courthouse in Dixon on June 3. John Dixon presided at this anti-slavery gathering, with Shaw serving as secretary. Over $1,000 was contributed by those attending in an attempt to make Kansas a free state. Upham and John Brooks subscribed generously to the fund.[106] Later, when James Gillpatrick, a Baptist minister formerly of Maine, revealed the use of force at Kansas elections, Brooks was among the native sons of Maine who testified to the minister's trustworthiness and personal character.[107] Such reports and political agitation convinced Brooks that he should move to Kansas and work actively for her admission into the Union as a free state.

When Brooks decided to become a Kansas farmer, his wife went back to Salem, Massachusetts, and lived with her mother.[108] Kansas at this time was no place for a girl raised in the city. To show their appreciation for his services as Sunday School superintendent, the Congregational Church of Dixon presented him with a silver goblet[109] about six and one-half inches high, decorated with oak leaves and acorns. It carries this inscription:

> Noah Brooks.
> Presented by the Dixon Congregational Sabbath School
> May 1857.

Severing his ties with Dixon, he left for Kansas Territory a few minutes before midnight on May 14. He had little money, but he hoped to become a successful farmer in this new region. The first part of his journey was by rail to St. Louis. At this time, however, it was necessary to leave the train on the east bank of the Mississippi and cross the river on a steam ferry boat. It was 5:30 p.m. when he arrived so he went immediately to Barnum's Hotel on Second and Walnut Streets. Although he was in severe financial difficulties, he stayed on—as usual—at "the best-reputed hostelrie of the city." On the sixteenth he visited the museum and was especially interested in its exhibit of prehistoric animal skeletons. After a brief tour of the museum, he left that afternoon by train for Jefferson City, Missouri, which he reached at 8 P.M. At this point, he booked passage on a river steamer, the *New Lucy*, for a pleasant trip up the Missouri River. The fine food on the steamer was the greatest point of interest to Brooks on this journey. On May 19 he arrived at Quindaro, a settlement on the Delaware Indian Reservation, and boarded a stagecoach for Lawrence, Kansas, that same morning. After a hard ride the passengers were at their destination by 6 P.M., Brooks's reward was a good night's sleep, and the following morning he started on his way to Topeka. When he arrived there that evening he was very tired and decided to remain in town on the twenty-second for a rest. The next day he continued on toward Manhattan by stage, a distance of sixty miles, and on the twenty-fifth he jolted into the frontier town. His next problem was to secure transportation to his land claim, which was beyond Fort Riley on the Republican River. After some searching, he succeeded in engaging a wagon and driver for the last leg of his journey. When darkness fell before he reached his destination, Brooks and the driver stopped at the cabin of the Yonkins where they ate "friend antelope, cakes and coffee." He arose early on the morning of the twenty-sixth, crossed the river, and found the small group of friends who were awaiting his arrival.[110]

The "devoted band of 'Free State' enthusiasts," as Brooks later called them, were from Dixon and vicinity.[111] The party consisted of Joseph B. and Benjamin F. Quinby, a man by the name of Payne, and John G. Brooks. The two Quinby brothers and Payne were from Grand Detour, a small town about six miles above Dixon on Rock River. "The rest of the party," Brooks related, "started before I did, and drove the cattle into the Territory." By the time Noah arrived, the four other men had constructed log cabins and were well established on their claims.[112] John and Noah lived with the Quinbys and held all their equipment in partnership, planning to build a cabin of their own later. The neighbors of this little band were John King, Jerry and Will Yonkins.

The locations of their claims was fifteen miles up the Republican River from Fort Riley, in what is now Clay County. "We hold 160 acres each by right of pre-emption," Brooks declared, "and claim an additional 160 which we have to pay for as soon as the land comes into market." Their land lay on a stream, then called Elm Creek, which was "well wooded" and supplied them with both fuel and water.[113] The exact location of Noah Brooks's claim can be found since he drew a map of this area and preserved it in his diary. Then too, the Quinby brothers clung tenaciously to their holdings and entered their claims in the land records on September 3, 1860.[114]

These five men seem to have farmed in common. Corn was the crop which they hoped would prove profitable to them, but it was June 6 before they had the ground in shape to plant. This was much too late for a good harvest, and yet they did not complete their planting until June 22. On this date Noah Brooks stated that they had broken and planted a total of forty-eight acres. However, in later years, he recalled that they had "about eighty acres" under cultivation.[115] Perhaps this first reference was only to his and John's farm. His first figure is more plausible considering the fact that the swearing agricultural practitioners were weeding the fields by hand!

Once their meager crop of corn came up, their principal field work was cultivating it. All the men took their turns either hoeing or cooking; Noah

had great abilities along the latter line and even baked cookies for the hungry
toilers on occasion. However, their main staples were pork, corn meal, and
beans. Even beans were considered a delicacy when baked in the ground.
Variety was added to their table fare when they bought a milk cow on July 7
from a group of travelers trekking to California. The price was $20, but hav-
ing fresh milk to drink was worth every penny of the cost. In the evenings,
after hoeing corn all day, they sometimes played backgammon. In addition
to this entertainment, Noah read the several magazines and newspapers to
which he subscribed. By the light of a lamp he also read such books as Charles
Dickens's *David Copperfield* and wrote illustrated articles which he hoped to
sell to magazines. On September 10, 1857, he noted in his diary: "Have written
a letter to Harper's Magazine tonight to see if I can get the 'job' of writing an
illustrated article for them on Kansas. Sent a sample sketch, and an anecdote
for the 'Drawer.'" Although they did not accept a story from him, *Harper's
New Monthly Magazine* seems to have published his anecdote. Material in
this magazine is unsigned, but in the "Editor's Drawer" for June, 1858, there
is a humorous piece which has all the earmarks of Brooks's pen:

> In the office of the Cincinnati House, Lawrence, in Kansas, a party of Free
> State boys were poking their fun at a Westport stage-driver, who, in turn, was
> boasting loudly of what he and his friends had done, could, and would do.
> On being asked, "Why did you run and leave Fort Swansea on the approach
> of the Kansas Militia?" he was posed for a moment; but putting the best face
> on the matter, replied with the usual border oath. "*We couldn't take it along
> with us!*" Hibernian all but the brogue.

Brooks was in Lawrence while on the way to join his partners, and the
term "Hibernian" was one of his favorite words. It is known that he also corresponded with B. P. Shillaber and many others, but the recreation which gave
him the greatest pleasure was sketching. With pencil or water colors he spent
many happy hours, oblivious to troubles or isolation. The front cover of his
diary even contains a beautiful pencil drawing of the Kansas River at Topeka.

Although Noah stayed with the Quinbys at first, it was necessary for
him and John to make other arrangements when, on July 24, 1857, Mrs. J. B.
Quinby and Mrs. Payne joined their husbands. With prior knowledge of
this, Noah and John moved into a tent and began to build a cabin of their
own on June 18. They started the task by cutting the necessary logs, and the
following month they hauled in the timber. John later tried his hand at making shingles, but the task proved too onerous, and they never completed the
building. Instead, they moved into a cabin formerly occupied by the Yonkins.

One of the reasons that Brooks went to Kansas was to aid in keeping the territory free from slavery. He therefore took an active part in the political events of the day. On July 25, 1857, there was a meeting at neighbor Barry's home "for the purpose of choosing delegates to a convention at Manhattan" which in turn was to name a senator and representative to speak for the district in the Territorial Legislature. "The meeting," Brooks write, "was really a 'squatter' meeting; the chairman Mr. Fullington, was squatted on a barrell [*sic*], and the rest of the people were squatted on the ground and around." After discussing their problems, Fullington, Farnham, John G. and Noah Brooks were chosen by the settlers to represent their district at the Manhattan convention. These men joined the other delegates at Manhattan, where S. D. Houston was chosen senator and Dr. Adames was named representative. Brooks reported that the "great question which now divides the Free State party is whether the Topeka Legislature and Constitution shall be suffered to live or not." On October 5, Brooks and his neighbors proceeded to the polling place:

> Things passed off very quietly, and no hard feelings were excited. The Arkansas folks on Chapman's creek are the principle [*sic*] pro-slavery folks in the precinct and they are not very rabid any way. Montague is the pro-slavery candidate for Rep[resentative] to [the] Leg[islature]. The election was held in a log cabin without floor or chimney and in the most unceremonious manner possible. The judges asking information of each other and the voters as to their duties, &c, and telling the voters the names of their candidates [who] did not happen to be on their ticket.

After he returned to Dixon, Brooks summed up the state affairs in Kansas by saying:

> [Robert J.] Walker has gained some access of popularity in Kansas by his persisting in his opposition to the bastard constitution, but he has never been respected or trusted by the Free State party, or any other. His course has been too vacillating and double dealing to ensure him many friends. But he has missed it in trying [to] *reconcile* two opposing factions instead of conciliating a majority. The two great interests can never be joined and the only true policy was to choose and abide by the strongest. Free State men in Kansas only laugh at the Pro Slavery Constitution. They feel assured that Congress will refuse the gross fraud admittance, and with a working majority in the Territorial Legislature, they have the balance of power. But if by any means, by fraud or violence the Lecompton Abortion should recieve [*sic*] the sanction of Congress, the Free State men are prepared to arm themselves to resist it to the bitter end. They have already suffered too much to lightly relinquish their advantage, as they are prepared to shed their last drop of blood in defence

of what they believe to be their just rights. There is more of the old spirit of '76 in Kansas than matter-of-fact politicians and managing outsiders are aware of, and we may be sure that if Kansas has not is rights by law, she will have [them] by force, or thousands will die in the struggle. The force of the pro-slavery party is merely nominal; if a fair vote of the territory could be taken now, there would be ten to one against slavery. You must recollect that the thousands who flocked into the territory after the 5th of April last [1857], were entirely cut off from the vote in October, and the vote on the Topeka Constitution was very light.[116]

Toward the last of July, Brooks had an experience similar to Abraham Lincoln's in the Black Hawk War. Word spread to the settlers that hostile Cheyenne Indians were coming down upon them from the Smoky Hill River, killing both the friendly Potawatomi and the white pioneers. The wives of the settlers hurriedly left for Manhattan and the Brookses struck their tent and went over to join forces with the Yonkinses. Then Major Armistead of Fort Riley ordered the men to arm themselves and meet at One Spring (about fifteen miles from Brooks's claim). About fifteen men from the area joined this militia group and started off looking for Indians only to learn that the stories were greatly exaggerated; the brave Potawatomi had succeeded in driving off the marauding Indians before the militia had arrived. This experience probably furnished many chuckles when Lincoln and Brooks swapped "war stories" at the White House in later years. It is a matter of record that Lincoln often talked to Noah Brooks about his experiences in the Black Hawk War. And he, in turn, surely countered with his Kansas adventures with the Indians.[117]

As usual, Brooks had money troubles in Kansas. By September 13, 1857, his wife was back in Dixon and needed cash for food and lodging. She tried unsuccessfully to borrow money as did John G. Brooks. Upham finally sent thirty dollars to Noah, but it was stolen from the uncertain mails. Their only salvation was the corn crop. The first frost struck on October 12 and the group started to husk their crop on the nineteenth. Neither of the Brookses was a farmer at heart. Noah would rather hunt buffalo than husk corn, and John found the weather was so unpleasant "that he has to give it up." Finally, by October 28, they had about half of it picked and unloaded three loads into their unfinished cabin which served as a corn crib. "The crop," Brooks related, "was light, prices very low and no market accessible short of Fort Riley."[118] Noah and John decided to spend the winter in St. Louis if Upham would send them enough money, but it was not forthcoming. "We shall try and borrow some of our neighbors," he recorded in his diary.

Unwilling to remain on their land any longer, Noah and John left on November 3. The Yonkinses drove them all the way to the Missouri River where they boarded the steamer *Florence* at Leavenworth. They had no money, but somehow convinced the clerk that they would pay their passage fare when they reached St. Louis. On November 14 St. Louis loomed into sight and the two travelers put up at the Barnum Hotel. Where they got the money to pay their steamer debt is unknown—perhaps they never did pay it. They continued on their way and after a short stop at Bloomington, they arrived in Dixon on the eighteenth.

"I intended to have spent the winter [at St. Louis]," Brooks informed a friend, "but found that business was so dull that I could not see any probability of getting anything to do, so we came up to Dixon, where I shall be able to get enough to do to pay expenses, probably, and shall turn my attention to writing somewhat." He liked Kansas and hoped to return if money could be raised "to carry on our improvements of our claims."[119] He never returned, but on January 17, 1899, he was elected an honorary member of the Kansas State Historical Society upon the nomination of Mr. A. B. Whiting, who had lived near him during his brief stay in Kansas.[120] As a result of his membership, Brooks aided the Society in collecting a fine file of newspapers for reference and research work. They were deeply appreciative of his efforts and thanked him with words of high praise, calling him one of "the world's great men."[121]

When Brooks arrived back in Dixon, he had recourse to painting or newspaper writing. S. K. Upham informed him that the furniture which he was trying to tell on assignment would not bring more than fifty or seventy cents on the dollar. In January of 1858, Brooks admitted that he had "gloomy and despondent fits." Business, he said, was dull and there was nothing for him to do. "I am left absolut[e]ly penniless now, and have to begin again, and in these times it is difficult enough even for those who have means," he lamented. In his mind there was just one remedy: move on to another place.[122] However, with his work on the Dixon *Telegraph* and other odd jobs, he evidently earned enough money to support himself and his wife through the trying months of 1858. Despite these efforts, his wife returned to Salem, Massachusetts, on June 28, 1858.[123] In July, Brooks advised a friend that he expected "to take the editor-ship of the Telegraph for three months at $50.00 per month." Evidently, Shaw planned to be absent on an extended vacation during the torrid summer.[124] But the desire to try new regions still lingered with him.

CHAPTER IV

"The Plains Across"

Goes to California

Brooks's active participation in politics continued past his Kansas experiences and the Lincoln-Douglas debates. February of 1859 found him listed among a group of Dixon citizens who petitioned John Dixon to run for mayor.[1] His editorial writing for the Dixon *Telegraph* kept alive an interest in such matters, but his earnings from this work were insufficient to meet his needs. One minor source of additional income came from his paint brush. For example, on January 17, 1859, he sold an oil painting for ten dollars, and in February of the previous year he had received four dollars for doing interior decorating. Since he no longer had a regular painting business, these jobs were only spasmodic. By February of 1859, his financial status was desperate, and he was forced to sell private possessions—such as his pistol—for cash.[2]

There was one romantic escape for those in similar financial conditions in 1859. During the previous September gold had been discovered in the Pikes Peak country of Colorado.[3] When the news of this gold strike reached Illinois it was much too late in the year for the long trek westward, but before the winter was over the boldest of adventurers were leaving Dixon. On the last day of January, 1859, a small group, "being tired of life in Dixon," struck out for Colorado.[4] By February the exodus had become alarming, and the local newspaper complained that the gold rush had carried off "many of our best citizens, heads of families, leaving a score of disconsolate widows to mourn their loss, and, in many instances, heart-broken creditors, to weep over unpaid bills."[5] However, with the advent of March this same editor, B. F. Shaw, left for Pikes Peak himself.[6] Evidently, the fabulous reports of rich gold deposits, which came across his desk, were more than he could resist. Noah Brooks's good friend, Philip Maxwell Alexander (1819–1898), a local hardware merchant, also considered leaving at one time, but being a successful business man he remained at home.[7] Colorado was not the only gold field which attracted the attention of prospectors, for many went to California that same year.[8]

But it was the Pikes Peak region which attracted Noah Brooks's interest. Since he found it difficult to earn a living in Dixon, he decided to join a group of would-be prospectors headed for the Colorado diggings. An advance party, among whom was Frank Kidder Upham, a nephew of Brooks's, left Dixon on April 15, 1859, and proceeded overland to Council Bluffs, Iowa.[9] Their assignment was probably to sound out the returning miners upon the productiveness of the gold veins and make arrangements, if possible, for the long trip to the Colorado country. Noah Brooks and a group of seven others left Dixon on May 10 to join them.[10] There was no doubt about the purpose of their trip then, although in later years Brooks merely stated that he removed to California.[11] The proof is found among the items which he purchased before leaving: a "gold pan" and "$12.50 worth of 'Quicksilver.'"

At 10:30 A.M. Brooks left family and friends and boarded the train for Quincy, Illinois. After staying there that evening, the group left early the following morning, May 11, on the steamer *Pike* for Hannibal, Missouri. From there they traveled across country by railroad to St. Joseph, which they reached at 10 P.M. that same evening. After eating a hearty meal Noah engaged a room at the Allen Hotel. Upon arising the following morning, the twelfth, he discovered (much to his chagrin) that there was no steamer bound up the Missouri River that day. Along with his companions he decided to wait for a steamer, since the stagecoach fare was eight dollars and the ride was not nearly so comfortable. On the thirteenth he struck a bargain with the clerk of the riverboat *St. Mary* to carry his group of eight to Council Bluffs, Iowa, for fifty-five dollars. However, the *St. Mary* was not due to leave that day. So, with time heavy on his hands, he looked the town over. His opinion of St. Joseph was not very complimentary; he wrote that it was "uneven, bluffy and unfinished." There was one place in town that did fascinate him. During his wanderings, he met the scene painter of the local theatre, which was also owned by Allen. The scene painter, Hawkins, and Brooks immediately became friends, with art as a common denominator of interests. Brooks made some drawings which he gave to Hawkins.

Finally, enough passengers accumulated at the pier, and the *St. Mary* sailed at midnight on the fourteenth. She ran most of the night and on the afternoon of the sixteenth arrived at Nebraska City. Brooks noted that it was "quite a large place, very much scattered." Here he first became aware of the many disgruntled Pikes Peakers who had returned. Not a whit discouraged, he remarked that "quite as many are going on as returning." Those returning were doing so merely "on hearsay," since none of the ones he talked to had been over 125 miles west.

On the morning of the seventeenth the little group of Dixonites arrived at Council Bluffs,[12] about four miles from the river. After getting directions Brooks located their advanced party which was camped out on the plains. Council Bluffs made a better impression on him than St. Joseph had. "Council Bluffs," he wrote, "is quite a large and good-looking place." Upham and the others were just having breakfast, so Noah baked some biscuits—the first time he had done any cooking since his Kansas days. His fellow adventurers were "all in good spirits and not at all discouraged by the doleful stories of returning Pike Peakers." For shelter they used a tent which proved very satisfactory, both at Council Bluffs and on the trail westward.[13]

Once at Council Bluffs John G. Brooks, Noah Brooks, and Frank Upham had to purchase equipment and make arrangements for transportation. They succeeded in locating a man who would take them along, but on May 22 a local resident returned from Pikes Peak with "very unfavorable news" which caused many of the men to return home. Among those who turned around and headed back was McIntyre, the fellow who had promised to take Brooks and his friends with his outfit. While other arrangements were being sought, Noah amused himself with sketchbook and pencil.[14] After much diligent searching, he and his party found two young men from Kewanee, Illinois, who agreed to take them "out to Pike's Peak *or* California." Evidently, the discouraging reports had, by this time, made a deep impression upon Noah, but he was determined to try his hand in a new region, even if he had to cross the continent. With their new friends from Kewanee, Leonard Barnard Ayer and Jacob Norton, the party consisted of five members who remained together during the entire trip. Although they all had their personal gear assembled, there still was the matter of teams. On May 25 they purchased an additional yoke of oxen at Omaha for sixty dollars and camped there, ready to start on their long journey. Two days later they struck their tent at 7:30 A.M. and started on their way. Their outfit consisted of a "light wagon" and three yoke of oxen.[15] During the day Brooks counted thirty wagons returning from the gold fields, but this did not dishearten him or his comrades. That night they camped on the Elkhorn after having traveled a distance of twenty miles. Throughout their journey, this was about the average distance covered in a days' drive. The fact that they drove cattle along with a wagon train slowed their travel. At times the cattle strayed away during the night which resulted in a late start the following morning.

The route of the Dixonites followed the Platte River, and here Brooks got his first good look at Plains Indians when some of the Pawnee came through their camp "begging, and selling moccasins." From one of the Indians he bought a pair for eighteen cents. Their village was located upon the Platte and was said to contain about 3,000 people. At the time, they were at war with the Cheyenne and Sioux.

As the gold seekers pressed westward the tide of migration flowed past them in both directions; about as many prospectors were returning as going. But Brooks and his friends were determined to continue on in spite of the discouraging signs. The one thing which Brooks insisted upon was the observance of Sunday as a day of rest. If possible, the group remained in camp on Sundays. Since about the first of June, these five emigrants had been traveling in the wagon train of "an old Californian" and they "resolved to keep along with them if possible." The old Californian was probably John Wise;[16] anyhow, the recognized captain of the train hailed from Marysville, California.[17] Altogether his party numbered sixteen men, and they were driving 150 head of cattle. Three wagons carried all their possessions. At night they sometimes camped in groups of "fifty or more teams."[18]

The emigrants continued along the route which lay on the north side of the Platte, and on June 8 they camped across the river from Fort Kearney, Nebraska Territory. At this point they were forced to cook with buffalo chips in lieu of firewood. Buffalo ranged over the countryside and furnished a welcomed supply of steaks for the hungry men. For variety Brooks baked beans in the ground—the way in which he cooked them while farming in Kansas. He and the others had plenty to eat, but they found it hard to sleep on account of mosquitoes.

As they got closer to the point where they would have to turn south for the gold fields of Pikes Peak, they lost interest in mining. On June 17 Brooks noted their decision in his journal; they had "resolved to keep along" with the wagon train which was headed for California. At Fort Laramie, on June 30, Brooks and his friends were firmly determined to proceed to California, although "many emigrants were diverted from the California route, to Pikes Peak, at Laramie." "Hundreds were crossing the river every day, at $3 per team for ferriage."[19] Many of these emigrants originally bound for California changed their plans "in consequence of the intelligence brought by Greeley who is now at the fort," Brooks noted in his diary, and he believed "Greeley may have been imposed upon" by people who desired his aid in persuading travelers to search for gold and thus cause towns to spring up in the west.[20]

While camped across the river Platte from Fort Laramie on June 30, these five men decided to visit the military post. John G. Brooks and Frank Upham were determined to swim across the river instead of paying the ferry fee. They gave their clothes to Noah who crossed on the boat. Frank made the crossing successfully, but John apparently was seized by a muscle cramp and drowned. This was a "dark and dreadful day" for Noah. He and John had been boon companions since their paths had crossed in Boston. In vain his friends searched; "Jake" Norton and "Barnard" Ayer rode down the river on horseback in an attempt to locate his body. The following day Noah borrowed a horse and also inspected the banks of the river, but without avail. There was little hope that his body would ever be found since "the bottom of the river is quicksand which soon covers anything which lays on it long." "I sometimes feel," Brooks wrote, "as though I were half demented."[21]

On July 2 the little band moved sadly out of camp and continued on their way. The Fourth of July passed without any celebration, and Norton shot four sage hens for their supper while some of the party prospected for gold. They "got the color," but found no large deposits of the precious metal. After traveling about 700 miles on the Platte, they left its north fork on July 11 and pressed on into the region of the Rocky Mountains. The next day they struck the Sweetwater River, and since they found themselves in antelope country, Norton again came to the party's rescue by shooting two which provided plenty of fresh meat for them. As a hunter, Norton had few peers.

They continued along the Sweetwater and reached South Pass, in the present state of Wyoming, on July 19. When they camped at Pacific Springs that evening they were on the Continental Divide. Their next objective was Salt Lake. The road behind them, along the Sweetwater, had been a very difficult 100 miles. There was no timber for fuel, in addition to which there was little feed for the cattle. Also, many of the water supplies were poisonous. As they pushed farther into the Rocky Mountains, prospects looked brighter. To Brooks's artistic eye the scenery was "very grand—high hills on hills, partly covered with pines, but steep and rocky." And in the mountains were antelope which they shot; the dressed meat they cured with salt for future use. The nearer they drew to Salt Lake City, the more Mormons they met "returning, discouraged and disgusted with the state of things there."[22]

The Green River was their next big obstacle. Fortunately, there was a ferry at the crossing, and the fee was only one dollar. The cattle were swum across on July 22 and the men crossed on the ferryboat. It was near this point that the Mormons had burned "a lot of government wagons a year ago." The large black spots on the ground and the ironwork from the wagons gave mute evidence of the hatred which the Mormons bore the United States Government. Some distance from this place they discovered another tragic scene. The previous winter a large train had been snowed in, and the cattle had frozen to death. On the twenty-fifth he wrote a letter to "Maxwell" Alexander and headed it Fort Bridger although his diary shows that he was eight miles from the settlement.[23] The following day at noon they did reach Bridger and discovered that it was a large fort with a good store. Four companies of troops were stationed there in anticipation of more trouble with the Mormons. Again at Fort Bridger they met "many Mormons" who were returning east. These emigrants informed Brooks that hard times had struck Salt Lake City. However, the flow of pioneers toward California greatly exceeded the returning Mormons. The trail to Salt Lake was like a "thorofare" with as many as 100 wagons camping together at one place. Provisions at Bridger were very high. Bacon and sugar were fifty cents a pound, with tea selling for $1.50 and corn, $4 per bushel. Brooks's party was well supplied with everything but flour. This they postponed buying until they reached Salt Lake City where it was much cheaper.[24]

After crossing Bear River the travelers passed into Echo Cañon early on the afternoon of July 28. The walls of the cañon were very high and "beautifully green with lots of berries." It is located in the Wasatch Mountains, and when Brooks left this cañon, two days later, the impression of its splendor was burned indelibly into his mind. While passing through he had climbed some of the peaks for a better view of the scenery. "In my day," Brooks recalled years later, "I have been in many charming places enriched by the hand of Nature or Art, have enjoyed lotos-eating in great content, and have sat at costly feasts; but above all the pleasures that have ministered to the senses in all my years, I still give chief place to those two or three days of camp-life in Echo Cañon."[25]

Evidently, the wagon train was delayed, because Brooks struck out walking for Salt Lake City on August 1. The following day he reached his destination and found some friends from Dixon. His impression of the city was very favorable; it was "beautifully laid out in squares, with shade trees &c.," he wrote. There was no mail for him at the post office, so he loafed around the town and stayed that night with his friends. On the third, his companions made their appearance and camped there. After a welcomed rest, they struck out again on the fifth, headed north around Salt Lake.

Two nights later they had their first experience with a horse-thief. A stranger came into camp and attempted to lead off one horse while riding another. John Wise, standing guard over the herd, shot him off the horse. In some miraculous way, however, he escaped. A few days later another problem presented itself: Brooks's favorite steer lost a shoe. This was remedied when they reached Brigham, then a little village of 300, where the local blacksmith put a shoe on "Tige." Soon the travelers struck Bear River again and discovered that the fee for crossing on the ferry was three dollars—probably more than they wished to pay when their cash was so limited. So they proceeded ten miles farther up the stream and forded it "after blocking up the wagons." Wise's "big wagon" was utilized as a bridge over which the others were pulled. Without ingenuity, these pioneers would have been lost. From here their trail led to Malad City in what is now Idaho. Their trail from there wound around and headed south again. On August 27 they reached the main Humboldt in Nevada. Along this river the cattle found good feed, but wolves abounded in the region and constant guard had to be maintained to protect the herd. Soon the good grazing ran out as the trail led away from the Humboldt and through Smoke Creek Desert. After several trying days they reached mountainous country on September 14. Honey Lake Valley, in California, was a most pleasing sight four days later. Once more grass was plentiful and the countryside was "comparatively settled."

As the wagon train turned southwest the timber grew thicker, making firewood readily available. A good fuel supply was necessary, but Brooks and his companions did not have recourse to the ordinary camp fire, because two good friends, P. M. Alexander and George L. Howell, had constructed a fine camp stove from sheet iron for the emigrants. It even boasted an oven for bread baking. Alexander and Howell operated a hardware store in Dixon, Illinois, and since 1855 they had had a "tin shop" in conjunction with their store.[26] A competent tinsmith fabricated sturdy stoves in this shop for use on the overland route, and as the Dixonites neared their goal, Brooks commended that their "stove works first rate and will last us to California." It was, he boasted, "the best we have seen on the trail by all odds."[27]

When they reached the country of the giant pines more settlements appeared where such staple articles as potatoes could be purchased. September 21 found them in Susanville, a "collection of half a dozen houses and two stores." Here they were able to buy such needed items as "fresh meat, butter, &c.," but the traveling became more difficult. At times the steep roads in the Sierra Nevada Mountains tested the endurance of the oxen. And finally "Tige" was unable to continue. He was taken out of the yoke, leaving "Turk"[28] to carry on with a new partner. "Tige" followed the train, but grew steadily worse. On the twenty-fourth he died, sending a feeling of sadness through Noah. "Tige" had been a noble beast and an affable pet.

On September 28 Brooks and his party could see the Sacramento Valley far below. As they caught their first glimpse of the great valley "mapped out in the hazy glory" of a September sun, they felt that their weary march was slowly coming to an end.[29] To save the oxen, most of the men had walked the countless miles beside the plodding teams. Their last day's tramp was on October 4; at 4 P.M. the wagons rolled into a place called Farley's Ranch. That night they camped in the yard, and the following morning the four men cleaned up their gear. Their destination had been reached, but they decided to move on to Marysville, fourteen miles from Farley's place. With a lightened wagon they rode into the outskirts of town and camped on the banks of the Yuba River. This was their last camp site. "But here we are in California," Brooks related, "provisions out, team 'pretty much gone in,' wagon boxes rather the worse for wear, the ragged cover flapping in the wind, and the whole array of equipage and men pretty accurately represented by that legless, pipeless, battered and shattered camp-stove, which has been banging and rat[t]ling at the tail end of our wagon in all the rain and sun and dust and dirt and rocky roads from Alexander & Howell's store in Dixon to [Farley's] Ranch in Sacramento Valley—like 'the last run of shad,' as one of the party sentimentally observes."[30] The man who made this statement was either Brooks or Upham since they were the only seafaring ones in the foursome.

Paint and Journalism in Marysville

Upon reaching Marysville, on October 5, Brooks "strolled about town" and looked the place over carefully. It was a large community, the third most important city in California at the time, ranking only behind San Francisco and Sacramento,[31] and was located at the junction of the Feather and Yuba rivers. Because of its topography the climate is very pleasant—never getting very cold.[32] Many of Brooks's Dixon friends pushed on to Sacramento,[33] but Marysville suited Noah, especially after he made a few friends there. On his first Sunday, "instead of loafing like most of the newcomers, he slicked up and went to church." The local minister took an interest in him and helped him to get rooted.[34] It was probably this same preacher whom Brooks described as supplementing his salary with bees, the gift of a neighbor.[35] Honey sold for a dollar per pound.

There were many men in the city, like Brooks, who had started "for Pikes Peak, and turned their faces toward California . . . when the bubble burst."[36] But Brooks learned that if a man wanted to work, he could find something to do. This was an important lesson in his life. Without the helping hand of relatives or friends, Noah labored "in any pursuit which appeared most in demand."[37] "Business at this season of the year," he wrote, "is dullest, most of the mine[r]s being obliged to leave their claims among the mountains, and people generally take a breathing spell; but there is nothing of that universal 'blueness' and pinching, tight times, with which I have been unhappily so familiar in the States."[38] Just what he did during his first months in Marysville is unknown. He probably turned once more to house painting or like work.

"I have been doing quite as well here as I expected to do," he confided to a friend, "though just now business is dull, but will soon revive again as the spring comes on." Optimism was always an important facet of his character. However, he did not earn enough money to support his wife back in Dixon. He asked his old friend, Alexander, to loan some money to Caroline until he could send a "draft" to repay him. His rent in Marysville was $25 per month, and board, $7 a week. Then too, he had arrived there broke, needing new clothes and the necessary tools of his trade—probably paint brushes, etc.[39]

With his back against the wall, Brooks worked hard and industriously. In his spare moments he taught drawing and painting. And by April of 1860, he was firmly established and making money. True to his word, he repaid Alexander and felt that he was getting along "first-rate considering all things." After all, he explained, he had arrived there "an entire stranger without 'ary red' and scarcely a rag to my back."[40] Nevertheless, he certainly could have lived more economically than he did. One hotel in town offered both board and room for $9 per week;[41] he paid $7 per week for board alone.

All of the four comrades who had traveled together on the long trek found employment in Marysville. Frank Upham worked as a painter and earned three dollars a day, but his heart yearned for the sea.[42] Instead of returning to a merchantman, however, he later obtained a commission in the regular Army. "Jake" Norton turned his hand to mining and was "well and hearty."[43] Leonard Barnard Ayer became engaged in the meat and grocery business, although he later turned to journalism.[44]

After doing odd jobs and saving his money, Noah Brooks was able to open a paint shop sometime before the first of March, 1860. On that date the local paper announced that he had a studio at No. 33 D Street. It was in an upstairs room and located opposite Wells, Fargo & Company. Here, he again practiced sign, landscape and ornamental painting, and announced that he would "give instructions in drawing and painting." The local editor added that "his studio is well worth a visit."[45] His business card indicated that he was also skilled in fresco painting.[46] Some time later, Noah advertised that he would also take commissions to paint pictures of residences or ranches. In addition, he was desirous of repairing or gilding picture and looking glass frames at his shop.[47]

Before the opening of his paint shop and studio, he was giving lessons in the fine arts. In January of 1860, he wrote that he had "some scholars, and my work gives good satisfaction." "I am very glad to say," he continued, "that the prospects here for me are very good." The climate suited him very well. Personal comfort was always a great factor in his life. "I like the country very much," he admitted. Even in January there were days when no fire was needed in his room.[48] In addition to these factors, his business seems to have prospered, although he was not without competition. As early as September, 1859, there was another young artist in Marysville by the name of Hollis who showed "much promise" of becoming a good landscape painter, Benjamin P. Avery wrote.[49] There was also a house, sign, and ornamental painter, John N. Rohr, with a shop at No. 103 Third Street.[50] But Brooks did not suffer from lack of trade or skill; his main problem was concentrating on the painting business.

Sometime in May or during the first days of June in 1860, he took his first trip to San Francisco. It was a pleasant journey down the Feather and Sacramento Rivers on a steamboat. When he gazed upon the Pacific, fond memories returned. As for the city, Brooks thought that it was a very lively place and did "an immense amount of business, as everything for California passes through" San Francisco.[51] It was probably on this visit that he made arrangements to write stories for a San Francisco newspaper which began publishing in July of that year. This was the San Francisco *Evening Mirror*, and the editors were J. MacDonough and R. M. Daggett, whose offices were at No. 166 Montgomery Street. Brooks's new position was that of "Traveling Correspondent,"[52] and he wrote under the pen name of "John Riverside."[53]

Every year, if his finances permitted it, Brooks took an extended vacation in the summer. Unless he could remain away from work for at least a month, he did not consider that it was worthwhile. True to form, he left Marysville during the latter part of July, 1860, to rest, paint, and hike in the mountains.[54] With the *Evening Mirror* assignment he was assured of having his expenses paid. While on the road to Marysville in 1859, he had passed through the colorful mining country of the Sierra Nevada Mountains, a region later to become famous through the writings of Bret Harte. Brooks retraced his steps and journeyed into the picturesque regions around Downieville, a little town about seventy miles from Marysville. There he lived with the miners in the barracks of the Sierra Buttes Company.

Since there is no complete file of the *Evening Mirror*, Brooks's first newsletters are lost. The first one available was written from Downieville on September 3, 1860. In it he described the town as a busy place "nestled in between the high hills which shut it in on all sides." Located prominently along the main street were numerous saloons which he called "wooden traps baited with whiskey, which crafty men will set wherever three fellows pass." Not caring for whiskey, Brooks drank in the sparkling brooklets which abounded in the area. From his quarters at the mining company's barracks he hiked into the Sierra Buttes as often as possible. On these trips he took along his sketch-pad to capture the beauty of the mountains on paper. The pursuit of this hobby gave rise to an amusing incident which took place one day as he was leaving town. "From one of these *saloons*—save the mark!—a long-legged man came rushing," Brooks related, "as I passed by with sketch-book under arm." "I say mister," cried the stranger, "how is it—are you a-taking the censis?" "No sir," answered Brooks. "I'm Marshill for this deestrict," boasted the stranger, "and I thought I'd like to g'long with yer, if you was."[55]

Even on rainy days he climbed into the picturesque buttes because the rough miners were not the type of companions whom he liked when bad weather kept them close to him in the bunk house. Through the rain he scaled the rocky heights on one such day and sat looking down into the valley in the direction of Marysville. Thus inspired, he composed a poem on this occasion and included it in his newsletter. After lunch he returned and explored the nooks and crannies of the buttes. Nestled away in a secluded spot he found a deserted cabin; upon entering he discovered that the former occupant had enjoyed reading good books. Among the ones left there was "Abbot's Life of Napoleon, in which latter fascinating romance I forgot the inclemency of the remainder of the day."[56] Reading was one of his favorite pastimes—especially historical studies.

At another time, in August, he visited Gold Lake, northeast of the Sierra Buttes. "I spent a short time very agreeably in sketching and viewing the lake and surrounding country," he told his readers, "and with regret left it on the last day of summer for Downieville, and thence home to the Valley."[57] "John Riverside" took leave of the mining country about September 13 and boarded a stagecoach for the return trip to Marysville. In order to view the beautiful scenery from a vantage point, he sat on top with the driver. On the last day of the return trip only one thing marred the pleasure of the ride. Brooks was anxious to finish the journey, but within sight of Marysville the stagecoach stopped for dinner at Zabriskie's. For some unknown reason, he refused the meal and sat atop the coach looking at the horizon. Perhaps he realized that his vacation would soon be over, and he wished to enjoy one more look down into the valley. It was with a feeling of regret that he wrote: "The journey is done, and tall brick blocks replace the sighing pines, level streets seem to surge beneath feet long accustomed to uneven woods and mountain trails."[58] The vacation was over.

The Marysville *Appeal* commented that "the numerous friends of Noah Brooks, the well known painter of this city, will be glad to learn that he has returned with invigorated health from his mountain journey." Then the editors revealed that Brooks had also written articles for them during his stay in the Sierra Nevadas.[59] His reputation as a writer was growing on the West Coast, and he was paid high tribute by the *Evening Mirror*. "The readers of the MIRROR," the editors announced, "have not failed to remark and admire the intelligent, instructive and amusing articles from our correspondent, 'JOHN RIVERSIDE.' They are notably distinguished from the sleepy trash which is thrust upon unwilling readers by certain close contemporaries. 'RIVERSIDE' is a man of observation, mind and genius, and his articles take hold of public attention."[60]

While away, Brooks had missed hearing his old friend, T. Starr King, give the major address at the annual Marysville Fair.[61] Marysville was interested in cultural things; it was a growing city and prosperity was causing it to expand rapidly. "More than two dozen brick edifices, some of them large and handsome," a newspaper in San Francisco reported, "have been built this summer, and still others are in progress."[62] In this city there was even a women's college which had been in existence since 1856. The Marysville Female Seminary was located on E Street, between Seventh and Eighth Streets, and at the beginning of the fall term in 1860 it announced a new faculty member: Noah Brooks, "Teacher of Drawing." But he was about two weeks late for classes, which had started on August 27. The other members of the faculty were Mrs. E. C. Posten, principal, and Miss Mary E. Jewett, assistant principal. "The course of study pursued," they announced, "comprises, in addition to a thorough English Education, all those lighter, and ornamental branches, that are included in the most finished system of female instruction. Ancient and Modern Languages, Drawing, Painting and Music, each receive a proper degree of attention." Connected with the seminary was a boarding house where the principal lived with the girls to guide their "physical, moral and intellectual improvement."[63] It is not known whether or not Brooks was a member of the teaching staff the following year. The faculty was not listed in 1861, and the local directory only mentioned his newspaper connection. As Lincoln once remarked that his greatest honor had been serving as the captain of a militia company in 1832, Brooks probably considered his professorship at the Marysville Seminary as one of his most important achievements.

After returning from his Downieville vacation, he continued to do landscape and ornamental painting, in addition to teaching, but a little more than a month later he closed his painting establishment. For about ten years he had tried to follow two professions: painting and journalism. However, after October 20, 1860, he never operated another paint shop. On that date, this notice appeared in the Marysville *Appeal*:

Change of Proprietorship.—W. L. Cowan has sold his interest in the Appeal to Noah Brooks, retiring with the esteem and best wishes of the remaining proprietors, after seeing the paper established upon a permanent basis. Mr.

Brooks will hereafter share the editorial control of the paper. He is a facile, original and gracious writer, and has won an excellent reputation lately by his contributions to the Appeal and Mirror, over the signature of "John Riverside"; though he enjoyed a reputation long ago as a writer for the press of New England. With his aid, the Appeal will be henceforth more nearly what its proprietors would like to make it, and what the public requires.

The style of the firm will remain as before.

B. P. Avery & Co.

Brooks had somehow managed to save enough money to buy an interest in this daily paper. Published at No. 61 D Street, as "an independent Republican newspaper," the Appeal had been started on January 23, 1860, by George W. Bloor & Company, who hired H. R. Mighels to edit it. Less than four months later, on May 12, William Bausman became the editor. He continued in this capacity until Bloor sold the paper to B. P. Avery, W. L. Cowan and E. Brown on June 6.[64]

Benjamin Parke Avery owned the major portion of the stock and was the senior editor, but when Brooks bought into the company he became the business agent of the Appeal as well as one of its editors.[65] These two men seem to have done most of the editorial writing. Several things had drawn them together. Both were interested in politics and art. Avery had studied wood engraving in New York, and he later wrote articles for the Overland Monthly on the subject of painting. When these two journalists joined forces, the editor of the National Democrat made a pun on their names which the Appeal copied:

Very like a Whale.—The classic editor of the Democrat appears to be getting in a very bad way of late. We trust that the present disastrous tidings from the other side of the Rocky Ridge has not struck in, and so deranged his "intellex" as to induce the repetition of such a horrible pun as the following, which the editor, very conveniently, fathers upon that mysterious Mrs. Harris of his, "a lady of our acquaintance," who is reputed to have asked—

"If I wished to state that I knew a distinguished public man from the South [Preston S. Brooks, (1819–1857)], now deceased, how could I do so emphatically by repeating the names of two Marysville editors?" We gave it up. Her answer was this: "I would Aver I know a Brooks." (Avery, Noah Brooks!")

The man that perpetrated that deserves to be badly punished by election news.[66]

Politics was a serious business in Marysville since the population was nearly equally divided between the Democratic and Republican camps.[67] If the city was to be carried for Lincoln, Brooks had his work cut out for him. He responded during the first part of October by helping to organize a torchlight parade, a mass meeting, and served on one of the local Republican club committees.[68] In an editorial he also told of his personal knowledge of the Illinois lawyer and concluded by writing:

> ABRAHAM LINCOLN is no vulgar ranter, no declaiming railsplitter, devoid of the graces and dignity of manhood, lugging in the claptrap of honest labor to help on his ambitious schemes, but a manly, earnest, simple-hearted and courteous gentleman. We have been disgusted and mortified at the ignorant and unthinking enthusiasm of some of his supporters who would picture him as an unwashed and uncombed, long-legged, uncouth giant, bragging of his railing feats, and swinging his long arms over his discomfited opponents.
>
> Our own personal recollections of him are far different, and reject the too common popular impression of his personal appearance and manner, as we do the horrid caricatures which some of the common engravings of him are. In the parlor or on the stand, affable, courteous, dignified and manly in his bearing, he will fill the Chair of State with all the qualities which that high and noble position demands of its incumbent, and reflect credit and honor upon the mighty nation which soon will call him to its head.[69]

Whether or not Brooks's editorial had any effect upon the voters of Marysville is, of course, unknown, but shortly after the election an early report of the results—44 out of 47 precincts—showed Lincoln leading by the slender margin of nineteen votes. His closest rival was Breckinridge, who had 640 votes to Lincoln's 659. Breckinridge was leading in the county, however, by a margin of 1610 to 1532.[70]

Before the year ended, the *Appeal* announced that it would soon issue a weekly edition in addition to the daily one. It was enjoying a prosperous growth and boasted that its circulation was larger than any other newspaper north of Sacramento. Noah Brooks at last had found his correct niche.

As in the previous communities where he had lived, he became a prominent citizen and leader in Marysville. He acquired membership in Oriental Lodge No. 43 of the Independent Order of Odd Fellows. When this brotherhood dedicated its new building on April 26, 1861, there was a "gala day" of celebration which included a big parade with three brass bands. On this occasion Brooks read a poem, thirty-two stanzas long, which he had composed for this event. It praised the fertile valley wherein Marysville lay and complimented the Odd Fellows on their achievement.[71] Poetry occupied a large place in the cultural interests of this newspaper editor. He read both literature and verse in his spare moments and composed some very good poems. At the Fourth of July celebration in Marysville in 1861, he again read an original poem commemorating California's loyalty to the Union.[72] This subject was of vital interest to him since he was the corresponding secretary of the local Union Club.[73]

As the thermometer reached 100 degrees in July, Brooks's thoughts strayed from the work on his desk to the cooling heights in the distance. But it was the middle of August before he was able to leave Marysville for his vacation. Since mountain climbing was one of his favorite sports, he planned an ascent of Mount Shasta with Richard Goss Stanwood (1830–1917), a prominent lumber man of Marysville.[74] On August 15 Stanwood left Marysville by stagecoach for Yreka, near the northern boundary of California, to make the necessary arrangements for the difficult climb. Brooks was unable to leave on the fifteenth because Avery was absent, and the *Appeal* had to go to press every morning, Mondays excepted. The following day, however, Noah left by coach on the long, hot, and dusty ride to the first station: Oroville, directly north of Marysville. After fifty-one hours of exhausting travel he reached Yreka on the evening of the eighteenth. Stanwood, who had a room at the Union Hotel, met him, and after Brooks had washed up they visited Mr. and Mrs. William S. Moses.

The gear for the ascent had been collected by Stanwood that afternoon, and on the following morning, the nineteenth, a party of six left by coach for the base of Mount Shasta. After a six-hour ride they reached the house of a Mrs. Clarke in Strawberry Valley, which served as their headquarters. The group consisted of Mark Leonard, W. T. Odell, T. T. Canabiss, William S. Moses, Richard Goss Stanwood, and Brooks. Before retiring, they secured climbing staffs and horses. "It having leaked out that Brooks was an editor," Stanwood recorded, "he and I had the best bed, too good for me, in fact, who can't sleep on feathers."

At six A.M. on August 20 the party arose and completed their preparations which were not finished until ten o'clock. Then they rode about nine miles to their first camp in the mountains. Here, they cooked bacon and made a pot of coffee. After resting they moved out again at six P.M. and made another camp near the snow line where supper was prepared. With the moon shining brightly, the adventurers commenced their climb. The group had grown since leaving Yreka. Three more climbers had joined them at Strawberry Valley, making nine in all. Each wore heavy clothing and carried two blankets which served as a bed roll when they stopped to rest. Everyone carried his share of equipment which included a stick of firewood. Moses was interested in making scientific observations, so he had a barometer and thermometer; Stanwood was responsible for the telescope; and Brooks lugged the coffeepot. At first they avoided the snow by choosing a rocky pathway which ran upward for about three-quarters of a mile. At the end of this, they were forced to put on climbers for the snow fields ahead. At eleven P.M. they were about three miles from camp, and the party was badly scattered. Brooks was about four hundred yards behind the leaders, sleepy and somewhat sick at the stomach. By four A.M., on the twenty-first, the stragglers reached the camp which the advance guard had established. The leaders left Brooks and some of the others sleeping in their blankets and pushed toward the top. After a brief and cold sleep Brooks resumed his climbing and reached the peak about two hours after the sun had risen. There on the summit the men built a fire and made coffee; the first, they wagered, that had ever been made on the top of Mount Shasta.

After leaving their names inscribed there, they commenced the descent about ten o'clock. Brooks and Stanwood lingered behind the group, no doubt observing the beauty of the scenery—both were artists. Seeing their party far below, they finally decided to slide down the slopes in their blankets. This maneuver worked very well; the only difficulty was in keeping their speed under control. This they accomplished by dragging their climbers in the snow, but at times they were forced to jump from their makeshift sleds into the snow to stop their excessive speed. Down in the valley, Mrs. Clarke gave the tired climbers a big dinner after which Moses calculated from his observations, that the summit was about 14,000 feet. The accepted elevation now used is 14,161. After bragging a bit about the conquest, they fell into bed and slept soundly.

On the twenty-second some of the fellows sketched the mountain and then boarded the stagecoach for the return trip. At Yreka Brooks collected stories and information for a projected series of articles about northern California and found some new subscribers for the *Appeal*. At two A.M. on the twenty-fourth they continued on toward Tower House. They were in no hurry, however. Stanwood even went fishing on the twenty-fifth. On the following morning they left for Marysville and arrived there at eleven P.M. Brooks and Stanwood were tired, but they went to sleep relaxed. Physical exercise helped Noah to recuperate from his mental fatigue.

Once back at his desk there was much political spade work to be done because his partner on the *Appeal* was running for the office of State Printer in the September election. The Republicans won the election on the fourth with Avery capturing the prize which he sought. His duties, however, did not begin until January 6, 1862.[75] In the meantime, the *Appeal* absorbed its political rival, the *National Democrat*, and enlarged its format to the size of the latter. The two publishing establishments, B. P. Avery & Company and A. S. Randall & Company, lost their identity in the new firm: Appeal Association.

"The paper will continue under the editorial control of B. P. Avery and Noah Brooks," the editors reported, "retaining its individuality in all respects."[76]

In December Brooks was called upon to participate in the funeral services held at San Francisco for Colonel Edward Dickinson Baker, who had been an intimate friend of Abraham Lincoln. In honor of him, Lincoln named his second son Edward Baker Lincoln. Colonel Baker was killed in action at Ball's Bluff on October 21, 1861, and his body was returned to San Francisco for burial. The memorial address at the graveside was given by Rev. T. Starr King on December 11, and Noah Brooks was denoted as a delegate from Yuba County.[77]

When Avery went to Sacramento and assumed his new post, Brooks was left in complete charge of the Marysville *Appeal*. With added responsibility he was very busy, but little information about him is available in 1862. He was a member of the First Presbyterian Church—there being no Congregational Church in the city—and in March he was appointed to serve on a committee organized to increase the membership of the church. Their minister was the Rev. J. H. Brodt whom the congregation invited at this time to serve them for another year. Prior to this appointment he had been on "temporary supply" for six months.[78]

Until tragedy struck him in May of 1862, Brooks was completely happy in California, but on the twenty-first his wife, Caroline, died in childbirth.[79] It was a double blow because the infant son also succumbed.[80] The funeral took place at the First Presbyterian Church at four P.M. on May 22. "After appropriate services . . . with some feeling remarks by Rev. Mr. Brodt, the funeral cortege moved to the cemetery, where the remains of the deceased were committed to the tomb, beneath the warm ray of a genial sunshine, and left to solitude as the concourse withdrew during the mellow evening twilight."[81]

From this sorrowful experience Noah never fully recovered. He seldom referred to Caroline after her death; her memory was too sacred to be disturbed,[82] but after he established his home in the East, he had her body removed during the early 1880s to the family burial lot at Castine, Maine.[83] Here, he raised a monument over her grave with these words carved upon it: "She hath done what she could."[84] She had joined her husband in Marysville after he had become successful there, probably on March 26, 1861.[85]

Although he must have felt very depressed, Brooks did not divorce himself from community responsibilities. Less than a month after the death of his wife, he was working to get a wagon road built from Downieville to Sierra Valley through the Yuba Gap. On June 19 a meeting was held at Sierra Valley, and he was named to a committee of four to draw up the resolutions of the group. With such a road, commercial trade could easily cross the Sierra

Nevada Mountains. Evidently, he had worked with the committee prior to this meeting, because they drew up the resolutions that evening which stated that "this Committee have surveyed the Yuba Gap route and inspected the entire distance of the same from Downieville to this point, and finding it at this season of the year clear from snow or any other impediments in traveling, this summit being of less altitude than the present traveled routes by about 1,700 feet" they agreed that the wagon road was entirely feasible.[86]

Ever mindful of the Civil War which was raging beyond the Rocky Mountains, Brooks also served on a local committee which raised funds for the relief of sick and wounded Federal soldiers. The money was then forwarded to the United States Sanitary Commission at San Francisco.[87] But this was not enough; he wished to get closer to the scene of action. And since he no longer had family responsibilities, he was free to pursue this desire. It is also possible that Marysville held unpleasant memories which time alone would heal. Whatever the reason, he "sold out his newspaper interest, and accepted the position of Washington correspondent of the *Sacramento Union*."[88] When the *Golden Gate* sailed from San Francisco on November 1, 1862, Noah Brooks was aboard.[89] The ship steamed for Panama with 200 passengers, including Senator Harding from Oregon. At the Isthmus of Panama the passengers were carried by rail across the neck of land to Aspinwall where they boarded the steamer *Ariel* for the last leg of the voyage. On the morning of November 24 she steamed into New York harbor,[90] and suddenly the war was very close to Brooks.

CHAPTER V

"Washington in Lincoln's Time"

ON NOVEMBER 30, 1862, his first Sunday in Washington, Noah Brooks attended Dr. Phineas D. Gurley's New York Avenue Presbyterian Church in order to catch a glimpse of President Lincoln. Being "shown into the gallery" he "could not see the President; but, on coming out . . . had a close view of him."[1] "The building was crowded, as usual," Brooks reported, "with dignitaries of various grades, besides sinners of lesser note and rank. Conspicuous among them all, as the crowd poured out of the aisles, was the tall form of the Father of the Faithful, who is instantly recognized by his likeness to the variety of his published likeness. The President and his wife are both in deep mourning for their son [Willie], who died last Spring, and his Excellency has grievously altered from the happy-faced Springfield lawyer of 1856, whom I then met on the stump in Illinois for Fremont. His hair is grizzled, his gait more stooping, his countenance sallow, and there is a sunken, deathly look about the large, cavernous eyes, which is saddening to those who see there the marks of care and anxiety, such as no President of the United States has ever before known. . . . [A]s he moves down the church aisle, recognizing, with a cheerful nod, his friends on either side, his homely face lighted with a smile, there is an involuntary expression of respect on every face, and men, who would scorn to 'toady' to any President, look with commiserating admiration on that tall, mourning figure which embodies Abraham Lincoln, whom may God bless."[2]

During his thirty-one months in Washington, Brooks was to write some 258 newsletters for the Sacramento (California) *Daily Union*, using the pen name of "Castine." Throughout his life, the place of his birth filled him with inspiration. While he was in Washington he wrote: "Your three homes in one picture gives me a glimpse of Castine and is placed under Lane's painting of Castine which hangs in my parlor. I like to look at them and fancy myself back there again."[3] "Sending correspondence from Washington to a paper in California during the war was attended with many difficulties," Brooks related to a reporter on December 13, 1896. "Telegraph tolls for that distance overland were very high and it was only brief dispatches on the most important events that I sent by wire," said Brooks. "I used carbon duplicate copies," he continued, "and one copy of each letter was sent overland by 'pony' express, and another copy would be placed in a tri-monthly budget and sent by steamer" to Panama, where they were transferred to another ship bound for California. It sometimes happened that the pony express "would suffer such delay by being mudbound or snowbound that the copies sent by steamer would get to Sacramento first."[4] Under the best conditions, the overland service required nearly a month to carry the letters from Washington to California, and at times one whole page of the *Union* would be devoted to Brooks's delayed correspondence.

Although Brooks is listed as an editor of the Sacramento *Union*,[5] a more appropriate title would be war correspondent. This position paid him a salary of about $2,500. The *Union* was perhaps the most powerful newspaper on the Pacific Coast at this time. It had been started in 1850 by William Kurtz, Edward G. Jeffries, and Job Court. Two years later it changed hands, passing into the control of James Anthony, Paul Morrill, and H. W. Larkin.[6] "It was an independent journal and discussed all questions with perfect candor and without fear." The miners, isolated high in the Sierra Nevada Mountains, eagerly awaited its arrival by express. Sometimes only a messenger on snow shoes could reach these camps and the fee was twenty-five cents, yet the miners "called the paper their bible." In the opinion of one writer, this newspaper was the deciding factor which held California in the Union.[7] Through his sparkling and candid Washington correspondence for the *Union*, Brooks gained wide recognition, and these articles, carefully preserved in scrapbooks, served as a basis for his later Lincoln writings.[8] For this reason, his reminiscences are more trustworthy than the general run of such writings. A careful check has revealed very few errors in his *Washington in Lincoln's Time* although it was not written until 1894–1895.

"Castine" thought that Lincoln had perhaps forgotten him, so he did not seek the President's company. To his amazement, Lincoln heard of his presence in Washington and "immediately sent word that he would like to see me, 'for old times' sake'; and nothing could have been more gratifying than the cordiality and bonhomie of his greeting when I called at the White House. 'Do you suppose I ever forget an old acquaintance? I reckon not,' he said, when we met," Brooks recounted. The two friends then fell to talking about

Illinois. Lincoln "related several stories of his early life in that region." Particularly, he remembered his participation in the Black Hawk War, and also how Brooks had been discomfited when he told him at Oregon, Illinois, that Fremont would not win the presidency in 1856.[9]

Following this meeting their friendship grew warmer; at first they met about once a week. By July of 1863, Brooks announced that he frequently saw the President, and before the war was over few days passed that did not find Brooks visiting Lincoln. The President did not easily forget friends whom he had known in Illinois. His companionship with "Castine" quickly "ripened into intimacy near and confiding," though Brooks was quick to admit that his friendship with Lincoln was not like that enjoyed by Edward D. Baker or Joshua F. Speed. "It should be said," Brooks explained, "that Mr. Lincoln did not have intimate friends, unless we except a very few. . . ."[10]

"My husband, was so earnest a friend of yours," wrote Mary Lincoln to Brooks, "that we will always remember you, with the kindest feelings & will always be pleased to hear from you."[11] In another letter to him she remarked that "the great affection & confidence my husband, cherished for you, draws you, very near to us."[12] In explaining why he was able to maintain the favored position of Presidential confidant Brooks said: "If I ever had any hold on the President's good-will, it was because I never asked any favor of him, nor allowed myself to be the bearer of the requests of others." And Brooks did not have an ax of his own to grind.[13] With the tiresome press of office-seekers and the worries of military operations, it was pleasant for Lincoln to sit and converse with a discreet friend. Both participants benefited from this relationship: the President found fun, stories, and relaxation while "Castine" enjoyed the honor of associating with the Lincolns.

"Mr. Lincoln spent most of his evenings in his office," John Hay wrote, "though occasionally he remained in the drawing-room after dinner, conversing with visitors or listening to music. . . ."[14] The President's office was a large upstairs room in the east wing of the White House. To this sanctuary Brooks had a ready access. At first he addressed Lincoln by his title, but soon the President said, "Now call me Lincoln, and I'll promise not to tell of the breach of etiquette—if you won't—and I shall have a resting-spell from 'Mister President.'"[15] This was the way his lawyer friends had addressed him on the circuit. By these private conversations the President gained valuable information. "What are people talking about?" he would ask.[16] Being an inconspicuous newspaper reporter, Brooks was able to give him a reliable aid from this correspondence. Not being familiar with naval terms Lincoln would mark, in the margin of his papers, items to be answered. Then he would ask Brooks about them at their next meeting. "I've got a conundrum for you," Lincoln once remarked. "What's the difference between a ship and a bark?"[17] For the son of a shipbuilder this was an easy question, and yet the confidential answer saved Lincoln much embarrassment. On several occasions Brooks served as an unofficial naval aide to the President.

At times he visited with the Lincoln family in the red drawing room or listened to the piano music of some guest musician who played for them in this "favorite sitting room of Mrs. Lincoln." The furniture in this room, Brooks said, was "very rich—of crimson satin and gold damask, with heavily gilded cornices to the windows." If the President learned, while working, that Brooks was in the parlor, he would send word for him to come to the office or library.[18] Often in the seclusion of the White House office they exchanged humorous remarks or read aloud. "Artemus Ward, Petroleum V. Nasby and Orpheus C. Kerr [Office Seeker], three humorists of the war-time," Brooks related, "were Lincoln's favorites." Many of the Nasby letters he committed to memory. "I once heard him repeat one of these letters," Brooks testified, "while I held the book, without missing one material word or phrase." Comic articles were an escape mechanism for the tired President who was generally working under tremendous pressure. And he had his own idea about American humor. Its main qualities, he told Brooks, were grotesqueness and extravagance. To illustrate this he told the story of the woman who was so tall that when she died they had to lay her out in a ropewalk. But there was a more serious facet to Lincoln's mind; one of his favorite poems was Oliver Wendell Holmes's piece, "The Last Leaf." This he knew by heart and sometimes recited it to Brooks.[19]

Although Brooks liked fun and had a merry twinkle in his eyes, he was always very discreet in his articles. Lincoln could be assured that their private conversations would not be published without his permission. As a result, Brooks was often invited to stay overnight with the Presidential family.[20] At other times—especially if Mrs. Lincoln was out of town—he stopped to eat breakfast with Lincoln. With the First Lady absent the President liked a congenial companion to talk with as he perused his morning newspapers. Sometimes he had specific questions to ask. During these conferences Lincoln paid very little attention to what he ate.[21] But "amid all his labors," explained Brooks, "Lincoln found time to read the newspapers, or, as he sometimes expressed it, 'to 'skirmish' with them."[22] If he missed obtaining a morning paper, the Chief Executive would sometimes go out on the street to look for one. Early one morning "Castine" met him on such an errand and promised to "start one up this way" when he found a newsboy.[23]

Lincoln was in the habit of walking over to the War Department late at night in order to read the latest telegraphic dispatches. On some of these excursions Brooks accompanied him.[24] Lincoln always wanted to know the latest happenings and was in the habit of asking Brooks what the news was. "Mr. President," Brooks once replied, "there is no news." "Very well," said the President, "what are people talking about?"[25] Sometimes while Brooks and Lincoln were talking, the pet of the household, Thomas (Tad) Lincoln, would burst into the library. Although always dashing around "with a certain rush and rude strength which were peculiar to him," Tad "had a warm heart and a tender conscience."[26] Brooks, who always liked children, became a favorite of young Tad and after returning to the Pacific Coast was still remembered affectionately by him.[27] Thomas died in 1871, but Brooks never forgot him. When completing his biography of Abraham Lincoln in 1888, Brooks dedicated it "To the Memory of 'Tad.'"

When Lincoln sought relaxation at the theatre he often took Brooks along as his companion. His "theater-going was usually confined to occasions when Shakspere's plays were enacted," Brooks remarked, "for, although he enjoyed a deep hearty laugh, he was better pleased with the stately dignity, deep philosophy, and exalted poetry of Shakspere than with anything that was to be found in more modern dramatic writings." When Edwin Booth played in "The Merchant of Venice," and when Edwin Forrest starred in "King Lear," Brooks was in the box with Lincoln.[28]

After his reelection President Lincoln attended plays more frequently. On November 15, 1864, he was at Grover's Theatre to witness E. L. Davenport in the role of "Hamlet."[29] This play seems to have been a favorite with him; he had previously seen it enacted at the same theatre on March 25, 1863, at which time the newspapers said, "it is rarely that the President appears in places of public amusement."[30] Disliking public notice of his presence, he once entered by the stage entrance in company with "Castine," who afterwards wrote: "It was Mr. Lincoln's delight to sally forth in the darkness, on foot, and, accompanied by only a friend, to visit some theatre to which notice of his coming had been sent only just before his setting out." Occasionally, Lincoln would attend some lighter play such as John Brougham's "Pocahontas," which he enjoyed with Brooks one evening at the Washington Theatre.[31]

This genial reporter also won the confidence and friendship of Mrs. Lincoln. He understood her peculiar mental quirks and learned to admire her spirit and the loyalty she gave to the Union even though some of her own family fought for the South. And she in turn found him to be a staunch friend. After the war she wrote: "I wish you were not, so far removed from us—*true* friends, in *these* overwhelming days of affliction, I find to be very rare. I find myself clinging more tenderly, to the memory of those, who if *not* so remote, would be more friendly."[32] She had good cause to remember him with warm feeling. While grieving for her dead son, "Willie," who had succumbed February 20, 1862, she was induced by "a seamstress employed in the White House" (probably Elizabeth Keckley) to engage the "spiritual medium" Charles Colchester,[33] who promised communication with the deceased boy at a séance. Though invited, Brooks declined to attend this meeting, but curiosity prompted him to go to another "Colchester sitting" a few days afterward. With the aid of a friend, he exposed the medium during the hocus-pocus proceedings, whereupon Colchester struck him on the head with a drum. Later this mountebank sought a favor from Mrs. Lincoln on the threat of having "some unpleasant things to say to her" if she did not comply, and she turned to Brooks for aid. When Colchester appeared at the White House, Brooks identified himself by showing the unhealed scar on his forehead, then warned: "If you are in Washington to-morrow afternoon at this time, you will be in the old Capitol prison." According to Brooks's account, the "swindler" then sneaked out of the White House, never to annoy Mrs. Lincoln again.[34]

After his arrival in the capital, Brooks took up quarters at 289 G Street, North; board and room cost him about $75 per month.[35] Always living in a luxurious manner, he paid considerably more than another correspondent, Henry Villard, who spent only $42 for board and room.[36] The first newsletter which "Castine" wrote from Washington was dated December 2, 1862. The weather was inclement as the third session of the Thirty-seventh Congress opened, and the air was full of unfounded rumors. Washington was a somber place with some twenty-one temporary hospitals scattered throughout the city.[37] To brighten the day for wounded soldiers, Mrs. Lincoln served as a waitress at one hospital on Christmas Day, while Mrs. Stephen A. Douglas presided at another.[38]

At times, Brooks was able to help the President behind the scenes without attracting attention. One such occasion came soon after the adjournment of Congress in March of 1863. The problem involved the secretary of the treasury, Salmon P. Chase, who was a difficult cabinet member to handle. As Edward Bates, the attorney general, noted in his diary, "Mr. Chase's head is turned by his eagerness in pursuit of the presidency. For a long time back he has been filling all the offices in his own vast patronage, with extreme partizans, and contrives also to fill many vacancies, properly belonging to other departments."[39] Chase made changes in the San Francisco Mint and Custom House without consulting Lincoln and in opposition to the California representatives. Highly miffed, Congressmen Frederick F. Low, Aaron A. Sargent, and Timothy G. Phelps disgustedly left Washington en route back to California without mentioning their dissatisfaction to Lincoln. By some means, nevertheless, the President learned of Chase's action and sought to rectify the situation if possible.

The man he chose as mediator was Brooks. Congressman Low had been a banker in Marysville, California, during the time that Brooks had lived there. "One very snowy night in March, 1863 . . . a messenger came to my lodgings," Brooks related, "saying that the President desired me to come to the White House forthwith, if possible. Upon Brooks's arrival Lincoln explained his dilemma and asked Brooks to send a telegram to the congressmen asking them to return to Washington. They were in New York waiting to board a steamer for the voyage back to the Pacific Coast. "With that careful attention to the smallest details which always characterized Lincoln," Brooks explained, "he enjoined upon me that I should send the despatch and collect the charge therefor from him the next time I came to the White House."[40]

When the message reached New York, Phelps had already sailed, but Low and Sargent were still at the Metropolitan Hotel,[41] and they returned to the capital about March 20.[42] There, Lincoln managed to soothe their feelings, and "the treasury department 'slate' was broken, and . . . Lincoln 'paid the bill' [for the telegram] with the most scrupulous exactness."[43] In place of Chase's appointee, Lincoln gave the position of collector at the port of San Francisco to F. F. Low, who then retraced his journey to New York with Sargent about March 23. The President thus maintained the support of the California delegation, but later, in August of 1863, Secretary Chase removed Low. John Hay, one of Lincoln's private secretaries, pointed out to the Chief Executive, "that this was Chase's game and replied good-humoredly, 'I suppose C.[hase] thinks it is to his advantage. Let him have [his appointee.]'"[44]

To escape from the humdrum of his office and to cheer the wounded soldiers, Lincoln often visited military hospitals in Washington. At times he would shake hands with "over one thousand" of the patients, all of whom "seemed highly delighted as the President grasped them by the hand."[45] Brooks accompanied the President, his wife, and Mrs. Abner Doubleday on one of these visits, probably on March 17, 1863.[46]

Moving ahead of the President's party, in the temporary hospital at the Patent Office, was a lady distributing religious tracts. One of the soldiers picked up a leaflet and began to laugh loudly, whereupon Lincoln said: "My good fellow, that lady doubtless means you well, and it is hardly fair for you to laugh at her gift." "Well, Mr. President . . . how can I help laughing a little? She has given me a tract on the 'Sin of Dancing,' and both of my legs are shot off."[47]

Early in April of 1863 General Joseph Hooker, at Falmouth, Virginia, across the Rappahannock River from Fredericksburg, had the Army of the Potomac poised for a blow against the Confederate forces. Mrs. Lincoln decided that the President should pay a visit to the troops, now "ready to march," and thus instill courage into them.[48] Accordingly, a trip was planned which included the Presidential family and a few close friends. April 4 was Tad's birthday, and it was intended that the army review would be a celebration in honor of him. However, "other business . . . intervened, and it was not until the boy's birthday had actually arrived, and with it a present of a fine pony," that the little group was able to leave Washington.[49]

Such an excursion offered the tired President an opportunity to rest from paper work, and he invited some good friends to accompany him. There was a rumor around Washington that Secretary of State Seward wished to go along and offered "to make a stirring speech to the soldiers," but he was not invited.[50] Instead, Lincoln chose Brooks, Dr. Anson G. Henry, an old Springfield friend of the Lincolns and now Surveyor General of Washington Territory, and Captain Medoram Crawford, the commander of the emigrant escort service to the State of Oregon and Washington Territory.[51] Crawford was from Yamhill County in Oregon and a close friend of Dr. Henry. Just half an hour before the party sailed, Dr. Henry suggested that the President invite Attorney General Edward Bates. This was done and Bates "gladly accepted the invitation."[52]

Unfavorable weather had already postponed the sailing and when the steamer *Carrie Martin* slipped away at sunset from her pier in the Navy Yard, it was "snowing furiously." The weather grew worse, the wind blowing up a gale which forced the ship to anchor for the night in a protected cover off Indian Head on the Potomac River. Outside the storm raged, but within there "was a scene which was peculiarly characteristic of American simplicity in the somewhat dingy but comfortable cabin of the steamer on that stormy night, where the Chief Magistrate of this mighty nation was seated familiarly chatting with his undistinguished party, telling stories, or discussing matters military and political, in just such a free and easy way as might be expected of a President who was out on a trip of relaxation from care and toil."[53] Dr. Henry retired after midnight, but Brooks (accustomed to editing a newspaper at night) remained with Lincoln.

They were alone when suddenly the President became serious and asked Brooks how many of the Union "ironclads" would soon rest on the bottom of Charleston harbor. This was his way of informing his friend that a naval attack would soon be launched against Fort Sumter. In his mind he saw defeat for the Navy on April 7, and his prediction proved only too accurate. The conversation turning to General McClellan, Lincoln said, "I kept McClellan in command after I had expected that he would win victories, simply because I knew that his dismissal would provoke popular indignation and shake the faith of the people in the final success of the war."[54] Such intimate revelations never found their way into "Castine's" news column; Lincoln could trust him implicitly in such matters.

It was probably on this cruise that Lincoln spied a vessel on the Potomac which he identified as a "ship." Brooks explained to him that it was a "three-masted schooner" whereupon the President "laughed at his mistake" and promised that in the future he would remember the difference between the two.[55]

The following morning, April 5, the little steamer arrived at the Acquia Creek landing where a special train was waiting for the President and his party. The snow was still falling when they boarded "the rude freight car, decorated with flags," and proceeded to Falmouth station where they were met by Major General Daniel Butterfield, Hooker's chief of staff, and the Philadelphia Lancers, who acted as an escort.[56] The guests were then driven in four-horse "spring wagons" to army headquarters. "Two large hospital tents had been pitched near that of Gen. Hooker, one of which was occupied by Mr. and Mrs. Lincoln and their youngest son; the other was occupied by Judge Bates and three gentlemen from the Pacific Coast, who were in the Presidential party."[57] Bates, however, spent part of his time with a friend of his son, Captain Charles S. Russell of the Eleventh Infantry.[58]

"General Hooker's headquarters are quite simple and unpretentious as those of any of his men," Brooks observed, "as he abhors houses and prefers tent-life, being unwilling, he says, to live in better quarters than his humblest soldier." These tents aroused the curiosity of Tad, who "had made the acquaintance of nearly every [one] before the first day was done." During his first day in camp Lincoln found the weather so inclement that he could do little besides meet the officers of Hooker's staff. With the coming of better weather on the sixth, there was a review of the entire cavalry corps of the Army of the Potomac. Lincoln rode in a saddle which had been given to Hooker by Main & Winchester, saddlers in San Francisco. "The donors," Brooks predicted, "will perhaps, be gratified to learn that so excellent a horseman as the President was the first man to sit astride their magnificent gift." Riding beside the group was Tad Lincoln, "clinging to the saddle of his pony as tenaciously as the best man among them, his gray cloak flying at the head like the famous plume" of Henry of Navarre. It is quite possible that his mount was the pony which he had received on his birthday. The pony could have been transported on the steamer. While Tad was at the front, he was escorted by a young lad who served as Gen. Daniel E. Sickles's bugler. He had come down to the Army of the Potomac from Burlington, New Jersey, at the start of the war and now rode with the best of the soldiers, sporting a sword belt and sergeant's stripes. After the review he initiated Tad into the science of using the lance; the two rambled "around together like brothers."

To view the enemy's picket lines, Brooks rode to the front lines opposite Fredericksburg on the seventh, and Lincoln passed through the tent hospital of General George G. Meade's corps where he shook hands "with every one, asking a question or two of many of them, and leaving a kind word here or there." More reviews of the infantry and artillery followed on April 8; the parade lasted five and one-half hours. Brooks and Lincoln rode in an ambulance over a corduroy road to review General Reynolds's First Corps on April 9, and Lincoln related his experiences as a woodsman:

> We were driving through an open clearing where the Virginia forest had been felled by the soldiers, when Mr. Lincoln observed, looking at the stumps, "That's a good job of felling; they have got some good axemen in this army, I see." The conversation turning upon his knowledge of rail-splitting, he said, "Now let me tell you about that. I am not a bit anxious about my reputation in that line of business; but if there is any thing in this world that I am a judge of, it is of good felling of timber, but I don't remember having worked by myself at splitting rails for one whole day in my life." Upon surprise being expressed that his national reputation as a rail-splitter should have so slight a foundation, he said, "I recollect that, some time during the canvass for the office I now hold, there was a great mass meeting, where I was present, and with a great flourish several rails were brought into the meeting, and being informed where they came from, I was asked to identify them, which I did, with some qualms of conscience, having helped my father to split rails, as at other jobs. I said if there were any rails which I had split, I shouldn't wonder if those were the rails."

At sunset on April 10, after another review, the President and his guests sailed from Acquia Creek on the *Carrie Martin*, reaching Washington later that same night. They were escorted by Generals Carl Schurz and Daniel Sickles. The party was not so large on the return trip; Mr. Bates and Captain Crawford had previously returned to the capital on the eighth.[59]

After this visit Brooks had a good news story to send to California. It was spiced by some exclusive information given to him by the President himself. "One night, while the President and myself were alone together in Hooker's hut, he looked cautiously about him, but in a half-jocular way, and taking a diminutive scrap of paper out of his pocket, gave it to me. On this scrap were written these figures: '216,718—146,000—169,000.'" He explained that the first figure was the total number of men on the rolls of the Army of the Potomac, the second was the actual number of available men, and the third represented the number that might be expected to be available when the army moved out. Then Lincoln added: "You can send that by letter to California, by and by, if you want. It can't get back here in time to do any harm. But don't you ever let on that I gave you those figures. They'd hang me for giving information to the enemy."[60] This military "secret" was included in "Castine's" letter of April 12 and duly appeared in the Sacramento *Union* of May 8, 1863.

The day following their return Lincoln entertained the little group with a dinner at the White House. Dr. Henry and Brooks were there as were Generals Schurz and Sickles. After these guests had gone, the President asked Brooks to remain with him while he worked in his office. As the two started up the stairs Lincoln turned and remarked: "Did you notice how glum Schurz is? He is dissatisfied. Poor Schurz! He seems never to forget that he is an adopted citizen of the country."[61]

The President was "not only invigorated and refreshed by his short outing, but somewhat cheered and comforted by the general appearance of the army and the indications that the coming battle . . . would result fortunately for the cause of the Union."[62] But a few days later something troubled the President's mind; before daylight on April 19 he and General Henry W. Halleck, the general-in-chief, made a secret visit to the Army of the Potomac. They returned that same night, but Brooks informed his readers that he did not know the purpose of the hasty trip "which agitate[d] the minds of the few who kn[e]w of the sudden visit." He speculated that it might mean a change of plans since the army had been held down by the heavy rains.[63]

Hooker's army crossed the Rappahannock on April 29, but the authorities in Washington did not know what was happening because Hooker had cut the telegraph wires before leaving Acquia Creek.[64] Lincoln was anxious beyond words. He scheduled other engagements to keep his mind occupied. On May 6 Brooks and Dr. Henry were waiting in "one of the family rooms of the White House, as the President had asked us to go to the navy-yard with him to see some experiments in gunnery." Before they could leave, however, the unfavorable report on the battle of Chancellorsville reached Lincoln, at about three P.M. His face turned "ashen in hue," and he handed the dispatch to Brooks saying "Read it—news from the army." It was from General Butterfield and revealed that Hooker had been forced to withdraw to his old positions north of the Rappahannock. "Never, as long as I knew him," Brooks recalled, "did he seem to be so broken, so dispirited, and so ghostlike. Clasping his hands behind his back, he walked up and down the room, saying, 'My God! my God! What will the country say! What will the country say!'" Then Lincoln turned and left the room. A few moments later Brooks saw a carriage draw up to the White House. Into it stepped the President; Halleck was already in the carriage when it arrived. At four P.M. they left for the front on a steamer to learn for themselves the true state of affairs. The President, like the weather, was gloomy and uncomfortable. It had been raining for two days.

An attendant soon came into the room and informed Brooks that the President had gone to the Army of the Potomac and would return on the following day. Lincoln had requested that "Castine" should call to see him at that time. Accordingly, on the evening of May 7 he walked over to the Executive Mansion where Lincoln discussed the crisis with him. The picture, Brooks wrote to his readers, was not as bad as first reported. The battle at Chancellorsville, Lincoln said, had forced a change in the plan of attack, but his feigned optimism was mostly for public consumption. "The President," he wrote, "one of the most impressionable, while one of the most resolutely practical of men—comes back satisfied that we have suffered no defeat or loss of *esprit du* [sic] *corps*, but have made a change in the programme (a forced one, to be sure) which promises just as well as did the opening of the campaign."[65]

Though not immediately relieved of his command, Hooker soon was ordered to retire to Baltimore, where he was to remain until further orders. No orders were forthcoming, and he grew impatient. Going to Washington without permission, he sent his card to Brooks's room and asked for a meeting, doubtless in hope that Brooks as a confidant of the President's could explain the cause of the General's misfortunes. Hooker had seen the confidence which Lincoln had manifested in Brooks during the April visit to the Army of the Potomac. While there, Hooker and Brooks had been alone one evening, when "the General standing with his back to the fire-place, alert, handsome, full of courage and confident, said, laughingly, 'B[rooks], the President says you know about the letter he wrote to me on taking command.'"[66] Brooks admitted that Lincoln had read the letter to him before sending it. Whereupon Hooker drew the famous message from his pocket and re-read it to the reporter, adding: "That is just such a letter as a father might write to his son. It is a beautiful letter, and, although I think he was harder on me than I deserved, I will say that I love the man who wrote it." Hooker was very proud of the letter and also showed it to Dr. Henry during the same visit.[67]

Remembering these things, General Hooker asked Brooks what Lincoln thought of him. "Castine" hesitated to reveal the private conversation, but when pressed again by the General he replied that Lincoln regarded him as a father might a lame son. Upon hearing this, tears came to Hooker's eyes and he left. Brooks met Hooker again in March of 1865 and saw him frequently after the Civil War when they often met in the Brevoort House in New York.[68]

Sometime during June or July in 1863 Brooks registered for the draft. His registration form gives his address at that time as the corner of 4½ Street and Pennsylvania Avenue.[69] Whether he was drafted or not is unknown, but it is certain that he did not serve in the Union forces. If he was selected for service, he purchased a substitute to serve in his place.

About the middle of June, 1863, he managed to obtain permission for a cruise down the Atlantic Coast, probably on a Federal gunboat. By June 17 he was at Beaufort, South Carolina, a beautiful little town "embowered in groves of orange and magnolia trees." The following day he visited Hilton Head, about twelve miles below Beaufort. While here he learned about the capture of the Confederate ram *Atlanta* by the Federal monitor *Weehawken* ten miles south of Hilton Head, near Wassaw Sound.[70] A blockade runner, built in Great Britain, had steamed into Savannah, Georgia, only to find that the exit was blocked by the Union fleet. This was the *Fingal* which had been converted into a ram, armor plated and renamed the *Atlanta*. The ladies of the Confederate States raised the necessary money to refit her, and she was affectionately dubbed "The Ladies' Gunboat." On June 17 she steamed out to give battle to the *Nahant* and *Weehawken*. Captain John Rodgers of the *Weehawken* disabled her with several rounds whereupon she surrendered.[71]

Brooks visited St. Augustine, Florida, on June 20. "The harbor," he reported, "is deserted, save when an occasional Government transport makes the echoes with its shrill steam whistle, or a little fishing shallop comes or goes." After this his party turned about and sailed back north, stopping at Fernandina.[72] Back at Hilton Head by June 25, he was allowed to board the rebel ram *Atlanta* which had been captured during his previous visit. She was anchored in Port Royal harbor near the *Wabash*, Admiral S. F. Dupont's flagship. "On our first visit to the Admiral," he related, Dupont "received our party very graciously." The Admiral had been waiting over a year for the *Atlanta* to appear, and he proudly brought her ensign out and displayed it to his guests. It was the new Confederate flag, and the *Atlanta* had been the first rebel ship to fly it. The ensign, according to Brooks, had a "large white field, with a 'union' of bright red one-half the width and one-third the length of the flag. In the union is a cross of blue from corner to corner, forming what is known as the St. Andrew's cross, in which are thirteen white stars."[73]

Upon his return to Washington, Brooks learned that Lincoln and his family had taken up summer quarters at the Soldiers' Home on June 22, but Brooks had little time for visits with the President at this time. The war quickly burst into flames again when General Robert E. Lee invaded the North only to be defeated at Gettysburg on July 1–3 and forced to retreat south. To witness what many believed would be the final battle of the war, Brooks left about July 10 on the Baltimore and Ohio Railroad for Frederick, Maryland. "The train was chiefly filled with soldiers," he declared, "the fag ends of reinforcements which had gone on before, with sutlers, officers returning to their commands after a short leave of absence, newspaper correspondents going to see the fight, and, dotted in here and there, a few sensation seekers bound on the same errand." On this trip he met some old friends from California: Dr. A. G. Soule, formerly at the Yuba County (California) Hospital, and Anton Roman, the well known bookseller of San Francisco with whom he was later to be closely associated.

Brooks hired a horse at Frederick and rode with his friends toward the front lines. En route they saw the body of a man dangling from the limb of a tree. It was the corpse of a Confederate spy who had been caught and hanged.[74] When "Castine" reached General Meade's headquarters, near Boonsboro on Antietam Creek, he obtained a meeting with him on July 11. "The headquarters," he reported, "are in a magnificent grove of tall oaks, free from undergrowth, and the tents and equipage of camp, disposed picturesquely about, give it the appearance of a pic nic or *fete champtetre*, rather than actual war." General Meade, he noted, was "tall, a little past his prime, but straight and wiry; wears spectacles usually; has a sallow face and large eyes, and his hair is quite gray. He is affable but not genial, and dresses very plainly and puts on no airs."[75]

General Rufus Ingalls gave Brooks a cavalry horse and an orderly for a closer inspection of the lines on July 14. To Brooks, on his tour, it was clearly evident that Lee's army had escaped. Filled with disappointment, he returned to Meade's camp, wrote another newsletter, and went on to Washington.[76] By July 18 he was once again back at the capital writing about other matters. The people of the North were greatly depressed by the knowledge of Lee's safe withdrawal across the Potomac; they knew that the war would continue until Lee could be caught and his forces smashed.

Complaining about the July heat in Washington, Brooks longed for a vacation.[77] About August 8 he left for an extended trip through the New England states. In Boston he met his old friend Charlie Wilder, who was about to leave with some companions for a trip to the White Mountains of New Hampshire, and who coaxed Brooks to join the party. With them Brooks journeyed to Mount Kearsarge,[78] then scaled Mount Washington. Leaving them, he traveled on to Vermont and finally to Maine, resting briefly at Bangor, proceeding to Portland, and at last taking the stagecoach to Castine.[79]

This was home to the weary reporter, but the village had changed since the days of his happy boyhood. Grass now grew in the shipyard where his father had constructed some of the finest ships of the day. "The placid waters of the noble harbor," he complained, "are almost unvexed by any keel, and the advent of the daily stage is an event to be celebrated with respected attention."[80] When the shipbuilding industry moved south to Boston and New York, Castine lost her position as flourishing shipping center.

After resting and visiting with his old friends, Brooks returned to Washington by way of Boston and New York at which places he stopped several days. He arrived at the nation's capital on September 18 after more than a month's absence. It felt fine to be back in Washington, although he admitted that it was "not the most desirable place in the world for a place of residence." He then informed George Witherle that he had "given up all ideas of keeping house here on account of the extreme scarcity of houses." His suite of rooms would have to suffice.[81]

Less than two months later, however, he rented a house in Georgetown, a suburb of Washington. It was a small but pleasant residence at No. 128 Green Street to which he moved about the first of November, 1863.[82] Here he had more space and nicer living conditions, but he was farther from his work. Every day he had to travel into Washington in order to obtain the latest news about Congressional actions and military operations. For this reason, it is possible that he spent more of his nights with President Lincoln since it was more difficult to return home every evening.

The big social event late in 1863 was the marriage of Kate Chase, daughter of Secretary Salmon P. Chase, to Senator William Sprague on the evening of November 12. The Senator and his bride left on their wedding trip the following night, but the event was not quickly forgotten. "The whirl of dust of the bridal cortege" had subsided, Brooks reported, "but not so the gentle flow and ebb of small talk which so grand an event" had created. People commented upon the fact that "the President went in solitary state and a white cravat and things; how Mrs. Lincoln did not go because she is yet in black wear and had an opportune chill betimes . . . how the President stayed two hours and a half 'to take the cuss off' of the meagerness of the Presidential party; how the bride wore a regal 'tiara' of pearls and diamonds. . . ."[83]

Mrs. Lincoln did not like Kate Chase, a social and political rival of hers, who wished to be the center of attraction in Washington society, and who had presidential aspirations for her father. Though "Castine" hinted broadly at the reasons for Mrs. Lincoln's non-attendance, he betrayed no confidence—all Washington knew of the bitter rivalry between the two women.

On Saturday evening, November 14, 1863, Brooks chanced to be sitting with the President at the White House. During the course of the conversation the Chief Executive invited Brooks to accompany him on the following day to Alexander Gardner's photographic studio, located at the corner of Seventh and D streets. He explained that it was impossible for him to go at any other time, and the engagement was one of longstanding. The California correspondent readily agreed and joined Lincoln at his White House office on Sunday, the fifteenth.

As they descended the steps to the door Lincoln suddenly remembered that he had forgotten something. Turning around he walked back to the office, picked up an envelope, and rejoined Brooks. Once they were seated in the carriage Lincoln explained that he had brought along an advanced copy of the address which Edward Everett would deliver at the dedication of Gettysburg Cemetery on November 19. The President thought that perhaps he might have time at the studio to read it between sittings. Following this explanation Brooks inquired if his address was written. Lincoln replied that he had written a rough draft but had not finished polishing it yet. He emphasized the fact that it would be "short, short, short."

While at the photographic gallery, the President placed the envelope on a small table beside him. He intended to read Everett's speech between exposures, but he became so interested in talking that he forgot the envelope.[84] When Gardner completed his work, the two friends returned to the White House only to find an office seeker waiting there. Not even on Sunday could the tired President escape from politics.[85]

After the photographer delivered the prints, Brooks was looking at the photograph which has come to be known as Ostendorf Number 78B when Lincoln remarked, "Now I can understand why that foot should be so enormous. It's a big foot, anyway, and it is near the focus of the instrument. But why is the outline of it so indistinct and blurred? I am confident I did not move it." Brooks studied the picture for a moment and replied that it probably was caused by the throbbing of the arteries in the leg which was crossed over the other. "The President," Brooks continued, "very much interested in the discovery, as he called it, immediately took the position of the figure in the picture, and, narrowly watching his foot, exclaimed, 'That's it! that's it! Now, that's very curious isn't it.'"[86]

Lincoln kindly presented to Brooks one of the five original prints which had so interested him. It is an oval picture, twelve inches wide by sixteen inches high and was borrowed many times by artists and sculptors until finally Brooks had to "sequester it under the strictest rules."[87] After his death this rare item was given to the Maine Historical Society at Portland where it remains today.

On November 17 Washington was "all alive with preparations for the dedication" of Gettysburg Cemetery which was to take place two days later.[88]

"Castine" should have been in the retinue of Marshal Ward Hill Lamon who left a day before President Lincoln's party. Lamon was a particular friend of the President and was United States Marshal for the District of Columbia. For the dedication Lamon was appointed chief marshal of the parade, and Brooks is listed among the chosen members of his party.[89] But for some unknown reason Brooks did not go.[90] Illness probably prevented him from hearing Lincoln's famous address.

Lincoln departed from Washington at noon on Wednesday, November 18, on a special train. The following day Mr. Everett delivered his long flowery address and was followed by the President who pronounced "in a fine, free way, with more grace than is his wont . . . his half dozen words of consecration, and the music wailed and we went home through crowded and cheering streets," John Hay recorded.[91] That evening the President and his friends returned to the capital.

After this speech became an epic, a host of theories sprang up in regard to the composition and delivery of it. Brooks revealed his knowledge of the matter thus: "When he came back from Gettysburg, Lincoln told me that he made several changes in the manuscript of his own address after he got to Gettysburg, and others 'as he went along' while delivering it on the field. But all of these changes did not appear in the fac-simile afterwards produced under Lincoln's own supervision. The explanation of this [is] sufficiently obvious. Lincoln, who did not appear to think very highly of his own speech, could not remember just what changes he did make while he read it on the field."[92]

Having always been interested in politics, Brooks was not long in Washington until he began to seek an appointment which would supplement his earnings. During the summer and fall of 1863 his California friends, among whom was A. A. Sargent, made plans to obtain the position of postmaster in the House of Representatives for him.[93] Brooks joined the forces of Schuyler Colfax, who sought the speakership of the House, and Edward McPherson, a candidate for the clerkship. There were more people seeking the postmastership than any of the other small offices, but Brooks thought his chances were good because of his "geographical position." California, he explained, "has never claimed anything here before." The office carried the salary of $2,500 and would not interfere with his correspondence.[94]

When Congress was organized on December 7, 1863, Congressman William Higby of California nominated him for the position of postmaster, but the incumbent, W. S. King of Minnesota, was also nominated and elected on the following day.[95] Brooks explained his defeat quite simply: "not enough votes." "A combination was formed by the friends of a successful candidate for doorkeeper and the friends of my opponent," he added, "and as they had more votes to trade on than I had, they carried the day." However, Edward McPherson was elected clerk of the House of Representatives and Schuyler Colfax became speaker. They in turn appointed Brooks to one of the minor clerkships. It "pays quite as well, and has neither work or responsibility in it, so I have no reason to complain," he proudly announced.[96]

This third session of Congress was particularly generous to newspaper correspondents serving in Washington. Five other reporters for Republican journals were also appointed to positions in the House and Senate. Whitelaw Reid of the Cincinnati *Gazette* became House Librarian; D. W. Bartlett of the New York *Evening Post*, clerk to Committee on Elections; Ben Perley Poore of the Boston *Journal*, clerk to Committee on Printing Records of Congress; Horace White of the Chicago *Tribune*, clerk to the Committee on Military Affairs of the Senate; and J. B. McCullagh of the Cincinnati *Commercial*, clerk to the Senate Committee on Agriculture.[97]

Brooks's duties seem to have been largely in connection with the publications issued by the House of Representatives. He read proof, corrected it, and prepared material for the press.[98] The position afforded Brooks good facilities for his correspondence, but the salary was not as large as that of doorkeeper. When he informed George Witherle that his clerkship "paid as well" as the position of doorkeeper, he was rationalizing. The clerkship paid $1,200 instead of $2,500.

Although Brooks was appointed to his post in December, 1863, his duties did not begin until May 11, 1864, when the second session of the Thirty-eighth Congress met. From this date until June 30, 1865, when he resigned, Brooks enjoyed the privileges of being close to the political events of the day, having a ready access to the floor of the House, and using a desk conveniently located for the writing of his news stories.[99] Besides this, the additional income enabled him to live in a grand style. And his close relationship with the California congressmen had other little advantages too. T. B. Shannon sometimes franked letters for Brooks.[100] Stimulated by his surroundings he formed in his mind the plot for a "great novel" which he thought he would later write.[101] Of course, he never wrote such a book.

When Schuyler Colfax was chosen Speaker of the House, the newspapermen working in Washington decided to give him a complimentary dinner. Colfax was a journalist himself, being editor of the South Bend (Indiana) *Register*. On Saturday night, December 19, 1863, the dinner was served at Willard's Hotel with many of the leading correspondents present. Among them were L. A. Gobright of the Associated Press; Eliah Kingman of the New York *Sun*; John R. Young, Philadelphia *Press*; W. D. Wallach, Washington (D. C.) *Star*; D. W. Bartlett, New York *Evening Post*; Whitelaw Reid, Cincinnati *Gazette*; Ben Perley Poore, Boston *Journal*; L. A. Whitely and James M. Ashley, New York *Herald*; Frank Henry and J. N. Platts, New York *Times*; Adam S. Hill, New York *Tribune*; George W. Adams, New York *World*; Uriah H. Painter and W. B. Shaw, Philadelphia *Inquirer*; J. B. McCullagh, Cincinnati *Commercial*; Noah Brooks, Sacramento *Union*; J. R. McCartney and G. C. Bower Jr., Washington (D.C.) *Chronicle*.

Other guests were Senator Henry B. Anthony of Rhode Island, editor of the Providence *Journal*; Congressman James Brooks of New York, editor of the New York *Express*; Congressman John D. Baldwin of Massachusetts, editor of the Worcester *Spy*; Edward McPherson, Clerk of the House of Representatives, formerly editor of the Harrisburg (Pennsylvania) *Telegraph*; and J. D. Defrees, Superintendent of Public Printing.

"The entertainment," Brooks reported, "was a choice one—both as to the substantial delicacies of the table and the feast of reason and flow of soul which followed thereafter. Sam Wilkeson of the New York *Times* presided, and his speech was the opening one of the evening, being followed by Speaker Colfax, James Brooks" and Senator Anthony. "The symposium was kept up to a late hour, and everybody considered that they had a good time."[102]

CHAPTER VI

Companion to Lincoln

THE SOCIALITES OF WASHINGTON celebrated New Year's Day of 1864 by attending the White House reception. On this occasion President Lincoln appeared to be in much better health than previously. He had suffered from a light case of smallpox, or varioloid, during the latter part of 1863. On November 26 he had become "quite unwell" and was forced to remain in bed for some time.[1] However, on January 1 Brooks observed that the "President looks better than he has since the varioloid." "I don't mean to insinuate," he explained, "that the disease has added any new charms to his features; but his complexion is clearer, his eyes less lackluster and he has a hue of health to which he has long been a stranger. He stood up manfully against the great crush and bore of the hand-shaking like a blessed old martyr, as he is."

For this social event Mrs. Lincoln "left off her mourning garb"; it was the first time since the death of Willie in February of 1862, that the First Lady had not worn black. Instead of her usual somber apparel, she appeared in "a purple velvet dress, decorated with white satin flutings . . . around the bottom; Valenciennes lace was on the sleeves, and an immense train flowed out behind." In Brooks's opinion she had never looked finer than she did in this new gown.[2]

This reception was only the first of a series of parties which followed. "For some reason not specifically apparent," Brooks wrote, "the semi-weekly levees at the White House are unusually popular this Winter." "The levees," he continued, "are held on Tuesday evenings and Saturday afternoons, the former being 'dress' receptions, and the Saturday afternoon levees being less formal in character. The President has been present at all of these receptions, and he intends to meet the people always when his duties will permit."

At receptions, Brooks informed his readers, "Uncle Abraham stands by the door which opens into the Blue Room, flanked by Marshal [Ward Hill] Lamon and his private secretary [John G. Nicolay], who introduce the new arrivals, each giving his name and that of the lady who accompanies him. The President shakes hands, says, 'How-do,' and the visitor is passed on to where Mrs. Lincoln stands, flanked by another private secretary and B. B. French, the Commissioner of Public Buildings, who introduce the party; then all press on to the next room, where they admire each other's good clothes, criticise Mrs. Lincoln's new gown, gossip a little, flirt a little, yawn, go home, and say 'What a bore!' Such is our Republican Court, and the most bored man in it is Old Abe, who hates white kid gloves and a crowd."[3]

Often Lincoln's thoughts were far from the pushing throng which was striving to shake his hand. Once Brooks passed through the reception line with a friend whom he wished to introduce to the President. "The President," Brooks related, "shook hands with me in a perfunctory way, his eyes fixed on space, and I passed on, knowing that he had never seen me or heard the name of my friend; but after I had reached a point seven or eight persons beyond, the President suddenly seemed to see me, and, continuing the handshaking of strangers while he spoke, shouted out: 'Oh, Brooks! Charley Maltby is in town, and I want you to come and see me tomorrow.'" Maltby was an old friend whom Lincoln had known at New Salem, Illinois; he was then living in California and sought an appointment.[4]

At another time, while passing through a similar line, Brooks played a trick on the bored President. Lincoln shook his hand but showed no sign of recognition. Instead of moving on, Brooks stood his ground until Lincoln perceived that something was wrong. Glancing down he recognized "Castine" and seized his hand again with a warm greeting and said, "Excuse me for not noticing you at first; the fact is, I was thinking of a man down South." Later he informed Brooks that the "man down South" was General W. T. Sherman who was then engaged in his famous "march to the sea."[5]

With the advent of 1864, Brooks's newsletters deal more and more with political matters. He spent more of his time observing the actions of the members of Congress. He was, no doubt, familiarizing himself with the duties of a clerk in the House of Representatives, a position which he would hold beginning May 11, 1864. In the reporters' section of the House, called by Brooks the "gallery of the 'third estate,'" he spent many afternoons.[6]

At the request of many members of Congress, Miss Anna E. Dickinson was invited to Washington in January of 1864 to deliver a lecture. She was a prominent and vociferous supporter of the Radical Republicans although not yet twenty-two years old. Following her arrival in Washington, Speaker

Colfax gave a reception on the fifteenth for this young Quaker girl, and the "number in attendance was very large, arrivals and departures being continuous from half past eight until twelve o'clock."[7]

After her brilliant capture of Washington's society, she addressed an audience estimated at over 2,500 on the evening of January 16 in the Hall of Representatives. Vice President Hannibal Hamlin and Speaker Schuyler Colfax escorted her to the rostrum where Hamlin introduced her as "a new Joan of Arc." Brooks noted that she "was dressed in a black silk dress, with a long train, and lighted up with red velvet furbelows; her figure is graceful and full, of medium h[e]ight, and her face is open, sunny and bright. Her eyes are large and dark; her hair is also dark and cut short, curling slightly, after the Rosa Bonheur style."

Her address was "a series of random sketches loosely strung together" and entitled "Words for the House." She praised the ideals of the Radicals and criticized Lincoln for his amnesty proclamation. In the midst of her tirade, the President and his wife entered the hall whereupon Miss Dickinson suddenly recommended that Lincoln be given a second term. Completely surprised, the audience responded with loud cheers. "She will," Brooks predicted, "flash out her brief and splendid career, and then subside into the destiny of all women and be heard of no more."[8]

But at this time politics was in her blood. Later in the year, on May 9, she gave another address at Grover's Theatre. Only a small audience assembled to hear her this time; evidently, the novelty of a woman orator had worn off. She relentlessly scolded "Lincoln, the Cabinet and [N. P.] Banks—the latter gentleman coming in for the largest share of her abuse." And instead of supporting Lincoln for a second term, she now spoke out strongly for John C. Frémont. In Brooks's opinion, she gave "The Pathfinder" the "same flattery with which she bedaubed President Lincoln" formerly. "Played out," suggested Brooks, would "shortly be the epitaph upon her political gravestone."[9]

His prediction was not far from the truth, although she did become a popular lyceum lecturer following the Civil War, and Brooks became well acquainted with her. In fact they became warm friends and exchanged many playful letters.

Although news gathering occupied much of "Castine's" time, he still found many opportunities to participate in the gay social life of the nation's capital. When groups of Californians met for a party, he was generally invited. Once they gathered in Gautier's Restaurant at 4½ Street and Pennsylvania Avenue on the evening of March 8 to bid farewell to one of their number who was returning to California. "The occasion," Brooks reported, "was a very pleasant one to all present."[10] This restaurant probably reminded him of past celebrations and events; he had previously lived at this intersection before moving to Georgetown.

In June the Republican party had an important decision to make. Would they renominate Abraham Lincoln? To buttress their political platform the party name was changed to Union, and the "National Union Convention" scheduled its meeting at Baltimore, Maryland. Before leaving for the scene of the convention Brooks met with Lincoln on the evening June 5 and "had a long conversation with the President in regard to the probable action of that body." He asked "Castine" to bring back "the odd bits of political gossip" which would float around the city and yet escape the newspapers. When asked whom he favored for the second place on the ticket, Lincoln would not name a candidate. Brooks recalled that he was crafty and "rigidly non-comittal."[11] The Chief Executive also refused to reveal his choice to his private secretary, John G. Nicolay, who wrote from Baltimore requesting instructions in this matter.[12]

On the sixth of June every train that arrived at Baltimore was crowded with people, and long before night "the hotels were filled to their utmost capacity with the vast crowds of delegates and seekers after excitement." The next day the convention opened at the Front Street Theatre at 11 A.M. It was a large building, but it was totally inadequate to accommodate the crowd which assembled to witness this event. Being a privileged reporter, Brooks managed to gain entrance to the Theatre before the meeting convened. "I have said nothing about the nomination for the Presidency," Brooks explained, "for it is a foregone conclusion here that Abraham Lincoln will be the nominee of the Convention."[13]

The outcome was as he had predicted with Andrew Johnson being selected as Lincoln's running mate. One important question which the convention had faced, however, was the President's cabinet. "It is notorious," Brooks revealed, "that [Montgomery] Blair cannot stand with [Salmon P.] Chase, nor [William H.] Seward with either of them, upon the propositions concerning the Monroe doctrine or slavery. A change of the Cabinet *must* be made if Lincoln is re-elected, and I am free to say that if the Convention at Baltimore had not believed that it would be made Lincoln could not have been re-nominated."[14]

Upon his return to Washington, Brooks called at the White House and made a "verbal report to the President, and entertained him with an account of the convention's doings of which he had not previously heard." Imagine Brooks's surprise when Lincoln jokingly teased him for not having notified him of his renomination. In the rush and confusion nobody had thought to send a telegram to Lincoln who was waiting patiently in Washington for the results of the balloting.[15]

At noon on June 17 eighteen young women were killed while they were handling ammunition in the Washington Arsenal. Without warning there was an explosion which instantly detonated the "cartridges upon which they were working." Friends claimed the bodies of three of the victims, but the government buried the others with impressive ceremonies on Sunday, June 19. During the Civil War many girls left home to work in the capital; it is probable that the families of these fifteen unfortunate workers were either too far away or financially unable to have the bodies returned. Then too, most of the dead were difficult to identify since the bodies were "burned to a crisp." So, a "pavilion, lined and covered with white, and decorated with flags, was erected upon the [arsenal] grounds, and the coffins . . . were ranged upon an altar in the midst of the same." Among the mourners were President Lincoln and Secretary Edwin M. Stanton, who walked behind the band in the funeral cortège together with employees of the arsenal, members of various benevolent societies, and other dignitaries."[16]

Lincoln was encouraged by his renomination, but the war was not much closer to a successful conclusion. As Brooks sat talking with Lincoln about the Virginia campaign, the President said: "I wish when you write and speak to people you would do all you can to correct the impression that the war in Virginia will end right off victoriously. To me the most trying thing in all of this war is that people are too sanguine; they expect too much at once. I declare to you, sir, that we are to-day further ahead than I thought one year and a half ago we should be, and yet there are plenty of people who believe that the war is about to be substantially closed. As God is my judge I shall be satisfied if we are over with the fight in Virginia within a year. I hope we shall be 'happily disappointed,' as the saying is, but I am afraid not—I am afraid not."[17]

During the first part of May, General Grant launched his Wilderness Campaign with meager results. Then he pushed on to attack Petersburg which guarded the approach to Richmond. The attacks of June 16, 17, and 18 met with failure and Lincoln became anxious about affairs down on the James River. He therefore decided to examine the situation personally. From John Hay's diary it is evident that Brooks was at the White House talking to Lincoln before the Commander-in-Chief left the capital for Grant's headquarters.[18]

At 5 P.M. on June 20 Lincoln and Tad, accompanied by Gustavus V. Fox (Assistant Secretary of the Navy), slipped away from Washington on the ordnance steamer *Baltimore*.[19] This voyage, Brooks stated, excited "the apprehension of our people, always on the alert for bad omens, it being considered that the President, tired of suspense, has gone down to the front to see for himself what is the real state of the case, and what the prospects are."[20]

The steamer *Baltimore* reached City Point on the morning of the twenty-first.[21] Following a brief survey of the troops, Lincoln and his guests shared the table fare of Grant. "Not the least conspicuous and peaceable personage at the table," announced one reporter on the scene, "was little Tad Lincoln, who came down with his pony and diminutive shoulder straps to see the theatre of war." This correspondent noted that Tad was "a perfect boy gentleman" as he poked about the camp with a playmate by the name of "Perry."[22] From this account it appears that Tad had once more taken his pony along with him on the steamer. And to complete the ensemble he wore his uniform; in a rare playful mood, Secretary Stanton had once issued him a commission whereupon Tad ordered a uniform and all the necessary accouterments.[23] Thereafter, he often appeared in his uniform, which was a great source of pride to the boisterous lad.

After the President had thoroughly examined the situation, he left City Point and returned to Washington where he arrived on the afternoon of the twenty-fourth.[24] John Hay observed that the President was "sunburnt and fagged but still refreshed and cheered."[25] However, Edward Bates thought that he was noticeably "disappointed at the small measure of our success, in that region; but encouraged by Grant's persistent confidence."[26] Brooks was again at the White House when Lincoln returned and discussed the situation with him. Grant, remarked Brooks, "seems to arrive at his conclusions without any intermediate reasoning process—giving his orders with the greatest rapidity & with great detail. Uses the theoretical staff officers very little."[27] Lincoln probably replied with his own observations since he had "visited personally, all positions about Petersburg and Bermuda Hundred."[28] John Hay recorded that the President did relate Grant's opinion of his subordinate generals, describing the ones whom he trusted implicitly.[29]

Since the humid summer heat made Washington most uncomfortable, the Presidential family was in the habit of occupying the Soldiers' Home during the hottest days of the season. This residence was located on a wooded hill just north of the capital in the State of Maryland. To open "the President's summer apartments" in this cool secluded retreat, Mrs. Lincoln and her son Robert returned from New York on July 2, 1864. For protection, the Union Light Guard of Ohio served as an escort while the Lincolns occupied these quarters.[30]

They were scarcely settled in their summer home, however, when a Confederate force under General Jubal A. Early launched a daring attack upon

Washington. As the Soldiers' Home lay on the supposed route of attack, Stanton—on the night of July 10—ordered a carriage and a small guard to bring the Lincolns back to Washington. "The lonely situation of the President's Summer residence," Brooks pointed out, "would have afforded a tempting chance for a daring squad of rebel cavalry to run some risks for the chance of carrying off the President, whom we could ill afford to spare just now." In spite of his precarious position, Lincoln was "very much irritated" by Stanton's order.

On the following afternoon, July 11, the Confederates "made a descent upon the Baltimore and Washington Railroad" and tore up part of the track. That night, as Brooks passed the War Department on his way home from work, he observed "an awkward squad of Quartermasters' clerks drilling in the park." The commander of this group was "an impromptu Captain" who had to rely upon the promptings of "his Orderly Sergeant, a messenger in the War Department," for every command that he gave. Washington was beleaguered and every available soldier and militiaman was pressed into active duty for a defense of the city. Part of the burden fell upon Brigadier General P. F. Bacon, "a worthy grocer, who is the militia commander of the District."

At noon on July 12 the enemy forces returned and severed the telegraph lines and removed more of the railroad track. After this bold feint, however, they withdrew, much to the relief of worried Washington. Eager to see the results of this raid, Brooks and a small group rode out on July 13 and "were lucky enough to catch the last glimpse of the clouds of dust which the skedadddling rebel pickets left behind them as they rode off in the direction of Edwards' Ferry." He found traces of the Confederates within five or six miles of the city where they had ridden in from the north on the Seventh Street road before being stopped by Union troops at Fort Stevens. The attackers also had been within seven miles of Georgetown where Brooks lived, but he remained there as did General Halleck who also occupied a Georgetown Heights residence. While the battle was in progress in the west, Brooks could hear the musketry very distinctly at this house, and on the twelfth "the sound of artillery on the north side of Washington was perceptible anywhere in the city."[31]

During the attack, one of the least frightened was Lincoln, who made two visits to Fort Stevens while it was under fire. And on July 12 a man standing close to the Commander-in-Chief was killed by an enemy bullet. The President was eager to trap the invading force, but it escaped. Filled with disgust he returned to his quarters at the Soldiers' Home on the evening of July 14.[32]

Later in the month, Grant moved his troops into position for a blow upon Petersburg, one of the key defenses. This movement was a failure, and on the evening of July 30 Lincoln received dispatches stating that the Union forces "had failed to make any progress." The President, with Captain Gustavus V.

Fox, "immediately went down to the mouth of the James [River] in a naval transport, where Grant met them" on the thirty-first.

Brooks evidently was with Lincoln when he made the arrangements for this trip because he knew exactly when the President would return. On the morning of August 1 Lincoln returned to Washington, and from him Brooks learned that "on the morning of the 30th a mine . . . was exploded under the enemy's works, blowing up an earthwork which was in fact a battery of four guns in positions, manned by South Carolinians." Despite their advantage of complete surprise, the Union army failed to carry the positions and the attack failed. From the President's account "Castine" stated that "in this unfortunate affair there has been a failure on the part of subordinate Generals and of men."[33]

The summer dragged past without the Union armies being able to defeat the wily Lee and his lieutenants. To ensure Lincoln's reelection in November, a notable victory was needed. By August 23 the President was so discouraged that he wrote out a note stating that "for some days past, it seems exceedingly probable that this Administration will not be re-elected."[34] But to all outward appearances his courage never faltered. On the following evening Noah Brooks went to talk with Lincoln and bid him good-by. Brooks was getting ready to leave for Chicago where the Democratic nominating convention was to be held. In the course of the conversation Lincoln—knowing that Brooks would not return immediately—said: "I wish you would write me, say, two letters, giving me an idea of the tone and temper of the convention, and of the delegates, as you meet them." "Write," he instructed [Brooks], "just what you would talk, but wouldn't print."[35] As they parted, Lincoln encouraged his reporter friend by saying, "Good-by; don't be discouraged; I don't believe that God has forsaken us yet."[36]

On the morning of August 25 Brooks started on his journey toward Chicago, but the first part of the trip was not pleasant. That evening he was "weather-bound at Harrisburg [Pennsylvania] on a train burdened with Copperheads, a gale having blown a train of cars off the track ahead of us, and obstructed in various style the way which we were going." As a result, his train did not reach Pittsburgh in time to make connections. He was forced to "wait six hours and a half in that dirty, black and ill-smelling city for a through train to Chicago."

Without further incident, Brooks reached his destination late on the night of August 27.[37] Two days later the Democratic convention convened with "Castine" carefully observing the happenings, both for his newsletters and the confidential reports to Lincoln. That evening he penned a summary of the events and addressed the envelope to John G. Nicolay, the President's private secretary. This subterfuge was probably to keep interested persons from knowing that Brooks was "spying" on the Democrats.

"Agreeably to the expressed wishes of the President," Brooks began, "I will write you a few lines concerning matters and things here. . . ." At the assembly "peace men and measures and sentiments were applauded to the echo, while patriotic utterances, what few there were, recieved [*sic*] no response from the crowd, though that is more noticeable among the outsiders than the members of the Convention." When several resolutions "of an incendiary character" were made, S. S. ("Sunset") Cox tried to stop such measures by proposing that they be referred to a committee and not read on the floor. "But he was ruled out, and some hisses from the outsiders were given him, one calling out, 'Sit down and shut up, you war democrat.'"

Alexander Long resolved that a committee be appointed to petition President Lincoln for a postponement of the draft "until the people had decided for peace or war at the polls." In keeping with this sentiment, the crowd vigorously applauded "Dixie" whenever the band played this tune, but they never cheered "the patriotic airs." "Inconsistent as all this may appear with the other facts," Brooks continued, "it is nevertheless true that the popular current is all in favor of McClellan and it *appears* to be a foregone conclusion that he will be nominated." Delegates from the Northwestern States were not firm supporters of "Little Mac," but he had powerful backing from the East. August Belmont, "with plenty of money to use, heads the McClellan interest, and Cox, Dean Richmond and others are his able colleagues." "They have music, fireworks, &c, and they r[a]n the outside show of Saturday last August 27, when Amos Kendall presided over a convention of 'Conservatives,' which nominated McClellan." This was an advance publicity stunt acted out on the sidewalk to sway the delegates and the onlookers.

"On the other hand," Brooks pointed out, "[Clement L.] Vallandigham, [Fernando] Wood and [George B.] Pendleton are equally determined, but as they lack union upon any one candidate, they are not able to present a strong front as a peace party." Their choice lay among Thomas H. Seymour of Connecticut, James Guthrie of Kentucky, and former presidents Franklin Pierce and Millard Fillmore. Wood "is most bitter and determined and declares that his faction will not submit to McClellan and a war platform; he and such as he point to McClellan's arrest of the Maryland Legislature and kindred acts and sentiments as evidences of a war spirit, while many do not hesitate to say that if a war man is to be nominated, Lincoln is good enough for them."

From "good authority" Brooks learned that Thomas H. Seymour was ready to "sell out his dubious chances for nomination to McClellan for the assurance of Seward's place in the next cabinet." As to the vice-presidency, "Castine" thought that the convention would choose a border state man, although George H. Pendleton was working hard for this position himself.[38]

McClellan won the nomination easily on August 31 and Pendleton was chosen as his running mate. The Democrats at last had a slate and the Republicans had a vulnerable target which was tangible. The shouting was all over, and it was time for Brooks's annual vacation. Accordingly, he journeyed westward to Dixon, Illinois, where he had lived from 1854 to 1859.

"While I am spending a few days of rest in my old Illinois home," Brooks wrote, "I cannot do better, perhaps, than write up a brief account of what I heard and saw at the Chicago Convention after my last letter . . . ." This was his second report to Lincoln. "The nomination of McClellan was a foregone conclusion, the only possible obstacle thereto being the deep determination of the ultra 'peace' men to carry all the points which they could," he stated by way of recapitulation. Vallandigham succeeded in writing the platform to suit himself, although he was forced to tolerate McClellan for the sake of unity. Several "horse trades" secured the nomination for the General. New York swung over to him following the promise that Pendleton would receive the second place on the ticket. Illinois was secured by earmarking the "Chief Justice-ship for Judge [John D.] Caton of Illinois, in case Justice Taney would not die or resign before March 1865!" Seymour was placated by "a written agreement" which promised him the post of secretary of state.

Brooks concluded his resume by saying that the "nomination has already served to unite" the Republicans, "and I feel more encouraged than when I left Washington." He then informed Lincoln that he would remain in Dixon for a few weeks and would be pleased to receive a letter.[39] And the President did acknowledge Brooks's reports with "a short note in reply to the first letter." Lincoln's answer was given by Brooks to an "autograph hunter," however, and has not been located. This note requested Brooks—if he did go to the Illinois State Fair at Decatur—to look up "an old friend of his whose name he gave me."[40]

After resting at Dixon, Brooks went to Decatur, as he had planned, where he wrote a newsletter on September 15. Decatur, he declared, was "an old, ragged, straggling prairie town, dusty and busy, containing some ten thousand inhabitants, on the crossing of the Illinois Central and the Great Western" railroads. The agricultural products interested him, but the drought had hurt their quality. He yearned to see once again the "luscious peaches and melting figs and grapes of California."[41]

Following this excursion he probably returned to Dixon, but by September 30 he was at Burlington, Iowa, attending another state agricultural fair. To reach this city, he boarded a river steamer at Dubuque, on the Mississippi, and traveled down to Port Byron where low water forced him to leave the steamer and finish his trip by train. "It is nearly ten years since your correspondent visited these parts," Brooks told his California readers, "then this whole region was full of life, energy and excitement . . . ." The depression of 1857, he said, had wiped away much of the "western wealth" and left only an "inflated delusion."[42] From this remark it is evident that he was still bitter about his business failure at Dixon.

"Castine" was back in Chicago on October 12 and describing the sights of the city for the Sacramento *Union* prior to his return trip to Washington".[43] When Brooks reached the capital, he sought out the President on October 18 and had a long talk with him. They no doubt discussed the coming November election. "One man alone," observed Brooks, "I always found hopeful, cheerful and intelligently sanguine of returning light—and in those dark days I had frequent occasion to brace up my own courage and faith with the good words of Abraham Lincoln . . . ." The President expressed great satisfaction with Maryland's new constitution which prohibited slavery. With a touch of homely philosophy, he summed up his feelings on the subject by saying, "I had rather have Maryland upon that issue than have a State twice its size upon the Presidential issue; it cleans up a piece of ground." And he knew whereof he spoke, for in his youth he had helped to clear land for the plow and remembered the wearisome labor involved in grubbing out roots.

In addition to the political victory in Maryland, the Union armies had also achieved notable successes since "Castine" had last been in Washington. Sherman had captured Atlanta, Sheridan had swept the Confederate cavalry from the Shenandoah Valley, while Grant continued to press toward Richmond with a determined effort. To bring Brooks up to date, "a confidential friend" allowed him to read and quote from a "recent letter" written by Grant. Said the General, "We think that the people in Richmond believe that they are no longer safe there; so they are leaving."[44]

With the approach of inclement weather, the Lincolns moved back to the White House on October 28 from their "insufficiently guarded suburban residence" at the Soldiers' Home.[45] Four days later, on the evening of November 1, the Negro population of Washington held a "jubilation in honor of the emancipation of Maryland." After religious services at the Presbyterian church on Fifteenth Street they organized an "impromptu torchlight procession, numbering some few hundreds" and marched to the Executive Mansion. Their loud cheering, accompanied by blaring band music, attracted the attention of the President who came outside. "I have to guess, my friends," he said, "the object of this call, which has taken me quite by surprise this evening." The chief spokesman of the group shouted: "The emancipation of Maryland, sah." After hearing the cause of their celebration, Lincoln replied:

> It is no secret that I have wished, and still do wish, mankind everywhere to be free. (Great cheering and cries of "God bless Abraham Lincoln.") And in the State of Maryland how great an advance has been made in this direction. It is difficult to realize that in that State, where human slavery has existed for ages, ever since a period long before any here were born—by the action of her own citizens—the soil is made forever free. (Loud and long cheering.) I have no feeling of triumph over those who were opposed to this measure and who voted against it, but I do believe that it will result in good to the white race as well as to those who have been made free by this act of emancipation, and I hope that the time will soon come when all will see that the perpetuation of freedom for all in Maryland is best for the interests of all, though some may thereby be made to suffer temporary pecuniary loss. And I hope that you, colored people, who have been emancipated, will use this great boon which has been given you to improve yourselves, both morally and intellectually; and now, good night.

Following this brief message the crowd cheered again and again. Then, "after some boggling about the order of march, the dark torchlighters gathered themselves up, and hurrahing, disappeared in the darkness."[46]

Always loving a good joke, Lincoln is said to have told this story when asked who would be the successful candidate in the election:

> "My opinion as to who will be the next President," said Mr. Lincoln, not many days ago, "is very much the opinion that Pat had about the handsome funeral. You see Pat was standing opposite the State House in Springfield, with a short, black pipe in his mouth and his hands deeply buried in his empty breeches pockets."
>
> "Pat, who's funeral is that passing?" inquired Old Jake Miller, who seemed impressed with a belief that an Irishman must know everything.
>
> "Plaize your honor," replied Pat, removing his pipe for a moment, "it isn't myself can say for sartin; but to the best o' my belief the funeral belongs to the gintleman or lady that's in the coffin!"
>
> "Now, it's very much the same," continued Mr. Lincoln, "about the next Presidency. I can't say for certain who will be the people's choice; but to the best of my belief it will be the successful candidate."[47]

Election day, November 8, was wet and dreary as rain fell profusely from the heavens. The White House, John Hay recorded, was "still and almost deserted" since "everybody in Washington, not at home voting, seems ashamed of it and stays away from the President."[48] But just before the time for the cabinet meeting, Brooks arrived and found Lincoln "entirely alone." The President "took no pains to conceal his anxious interest in the result of the election then going on all over the country." To Brooks he confided his thoughts. "I am just enough of a politician," he said, "to know that there was not much doubt about the result of the Baltimore Convention, but about this thing I am far from being certain; I wish I were certain."[49]

As Lincoln was nervous and anxious to such a degree that he was unable to keep his thoughts on routine office matters, he entreated Brooks to remain with him. During the major part of that afternoon they talked and exchanged jokes. The President related, with evident pride, an "amusing anecdote" which had taken place earlier in the day. It seems that in 1863 a live turkey had been purchased for the Christmas dinner at the Executive Mansion; however, with characteristic tender-heartedness, young "Tad" Lincoln "interceded in behalf of its life, and carried the case up to the Executive Chamber, securing a stay of proceedings until his father could be heard from." The boy's argument rested upon the plea that "the turkey had as good a right to live as any body else." The Chief Executive, with fatherly indulgence, spared the life of the bird whereupon it wandered about the White House grounds at will. The soldiers stationed there to guard the President tamed the turkey, which became another one of the numerous pets kept by "Tad."

Now, nearly a year later, when the Pennsylvania troops queued up within sight of the White House to cast their votes for president, "Tad" rushed up to his father's office to point out that even the soldiers were voting. As Lincoln looked down from his window, he noticed the turkey strutting about among the troops. To hear what he would say, Lincoln playfully asked the boy "if the turkey was voting, too." Without pause for thought, "Tad" replied, "Oh, no; he isn't of age yet!" In the President's opinion, this response of his son's "was a great deal better than many of the so-called Lincoln stories."[50]

After dinner that evening, Lincoln left the White House at 7 o'clock with John Hay and "splashed through the grounds to the side door of the War Department where a soaked" sentinel stood guard. The night was "rainy, steamy and dark,"[51] but excitement filled the air. Soon the telegraphic reports of election returns from the various states would be clicking their way into this office. When important events were pending, it was generally here that Lincoln awaited the results.

Later that evening Noah Brooks returned to the White House only to find that the President was at the War Department. Knowing that the guarded door would be opened to him, he proceeded to the telegraph office and joined Lincoln.[52] The little group waited until nearly nine o'clock "before anything definite came in, and then Baltimore sent up her splendid majority of ten thousand plus." When this news was received, Lincoln "only smiled good naturedly and said that was a fair beginning." Soon after this, Pennsylvania reported that Lincoln was leading there. "'As goes Pennsylvania, so goes the Union, they say,' remarked Father Abraham, and he looked solemn, as though he seemed to see another term of office looming before him," Brooks observed.

After ten P.M. the little group "had a fine supper" which Thomas T. Eckert, the chief telegrapher, had prepared. By midnight it was certain that Lincoln had been reelected, but he and his friends continued to read the reports until "about two o'clock in the morning" at which time a messenger from the White House appeared with the intelligence that a "crowd of Pennsylvanians were serenading his empty chamber." Sensing the disappointment of this group if he did not make an appearance, the President left. "Castine" certainly accompanied him back to the White House, because he reported that Lincoln "made one of the happiest and noblest little speeches of his life" to the waiting Pennsylvanians.[53]

Because of the lateness of the hour, Brooks probably remained with the President at the White House instead of returning home. While still discussing the election, Lincoln said: "Being only mortal, after all, I should have been a little mortified if I had been beaten in this canvass before the people; but the sting would have been more than compensated by the thought that the people had notified me that my official responsibilities were soon to be lifted off my back."

The following day, Lincoln asked Brooks to send the election results to Dr. Anson G. Henry of Washington Territory. As he dictated, the Sacramento *Union*'s reporter wrote down the message for Lincoln's old friend.

Washington, November 9, 1864.

To A. G. Henry, Surveyor-General
Olympia, Washington Territory.

With returns, and States of which we are confident, the re-election of the President is considered certain, while it is not certain that McClellan has carried any State, though the chances are that he has carried New Jersey and Kentucky.

Upon finishing this telegram, "Castine" passed it over for Lincoln's signature, but he declined, saying: "Oh no, you sign it for me. You see, it is written that way; and though I should like to please the old doctor, I don't think it would look well for a message from me to go travelling around the country blowing my own horn. You sign the message and I will send it." So, without further comment, Brooks fixed his name to the telegram. But the matter did not end there; several days later, when the election tally had been nearly completed, it became evident that McClellan had also won Delaware. Remembering that he had mentioned only two states as being carried by his rival, Lincoln caused a supplementary telegram to be telegraphed. "Not because the doctor wouldn't hear of it," he explained, "but because he might think it was odd that I should not correct my first statement and clear it up."[54] Such was the way Lincoln's mind worked. He was meticulously careful about details and always wanted his statements to be correct to the last word.

Another example of "his accuracy and memory" was given by Brooks in connection with the election returns. The President kept his own record of the votes and compiled a table "only four weeks after the election." These figures were "collected hastily, and partially based upon his own estimates," but when the official count was tabulated by the chief clerk of the House of Representatives from the official returns sent in by the states, Lincoln's total was found to be just 129 votes short of the official count.[55] And since Brooks was himself one of the clerks under Edward McPherson, he personally prepared a tabulation of the election returns when they arrived. His first table showed both the civilian and army vote, while the second was concerned with the vote of the soldiers alone. According to the official report, Lincoln received 2,219,924 to McClellan's 1,814,228. The soldiers in the Union forces gave him an even larger majority: 121,152 to 34,922.

With this information neatly arranged in columns, together with a statement about the total number of votes cast both in 1860 and 1864, Brooks carried the statistics to the White House only to discover that the President was not there. Writing a brief letter to Lincoln, he left his report. The President read it and carefully filed the figures with his papers.[56]

Happy throngs rejoiced with the President after his victory at the polls. On the evening of November 10 a procession, "gay with banners and resplendent with lanterns and transparencies," marched up Pennsylvania Avenue to the White House where they crowded into the semicircular drive in front of the mansion. The accompanying bands played stirring music while "the roar of cannon shook the sky, even to the breaking of the President's windows, greatly to the delight of the crowd and Master 'T[a]d' Lincoln, who was flying about from window to window, arranging a small illumination on his own private account." Earlier in the evening Lincoln had prepared a little speech, "being well aware that the importance of the occasion would give it significance, and he was not willing to run the risk of being betrayed by the excitement of the occasion into saying anything which would make him sorry when he saw it in print."[57] After he had read his message from a White House window, he remarked to John Hay, "Not very graceful, but I am growing old enough not to care much for the manner of doing things."[58] As to this remark, Lincoln was probably only being modest. Whenever he finished writing a speech, the words were always re-examined and changed until the whole was a polished essay.

After the election Brooks expressed a desire to visit Grant's headquarters on the James River at City Point, Virginia. Lincoln, seeing the opportunity of obtaining an eyewitness account of military affairs at the front, gladly presented him with a special pass and a letter of introduction. On the raw and chilly afternoon of November 14 "Castine" left Washington at 4 P.M. on the government steamer *Cossack*. He was "lucky enough to get one of the boxes which the Cossack people call staterooms," and when he awoke to survey the situation the following morning, the ship was approaching Fort Monroe, which lay on the Chesapeake Bay north of the entrance to the James. At 4 P.M., after a twenty-four hour trip, the *Cossack* reached her destination, a point near the confluence of the Appomattox and James Rivers.

The man who met Brooks and served as his escort to Grant's camp was General Rufus Ingalls, the same officer who had provided him with a horse and orderly upon his visit to Meade's headquarters on July 14 of the previous year. Ingalls, Brooks boasted, was the "general-in-chief of all Quartermasters, past and to come." The small party from the ship proceeded to "the extreme end of City Point" where Grant's headquarters were located. The commander at this time was living very simply in a tent. (Shortly after this visit, however, log cabins were constructed for winter quarters.) Upon entering, Brooks found a cheerful fire burning "in a rude brick fireplace" close to which sat "the chieftain" puffing on his "world-famed cigar." "The cares of the day were over," Brooks found, "and the General received us hospitably and pleasantly, like an honest, simple gentleman. Seats taken and salutations exchanged, we found ourselves in a small wall tent, the rough floor of which was covered by a venerable carpet; the General's narrow bedstead was also up against one side, and opposite it was a rude pine table covered with maps and papers. . . ."[59]

After spending the sixteenth inspecting the countryside around City Point, a little expedition "equipped with our train of orderlies and guide of yesterday" boarded a small steamer on the seventeenth and set out for Aiken's Landing on the James River. This side was near the point where General B. F. Butler had attempted to dig a canal across Dutch Gap. Butler still commanded the troops at Bermuda Hundred, an area on the James just north of City Point. Two new members were added to the little group for this trip: Brigadier General T. Kilby Smith "who has served well in Sherman's army, and is on a visit of inspection here," and Lieutenant Colonel Frederick T. Dent, the brother-in-law and aide-de-camp of Grant. Brooks reminded his

Pacific Coast readers that Dent had formerly been stationed at Colville and Walla Walla in Washington Territory.[60] His position was not the result of mere nepotic appointment since he was a West Point graduate with experience in the Mexican War.

When the diverting excursion to Grant's army ended, Brooks returned to Washington where he gave a report of his findings to the President.[61] At this time, however, it was not military affairs alone that troubled Lincoln. In October Chief Justice Roger B. Taney had died, leaving a vacancy on the Supreme Court. This resulted in a vicious struggle for possession of the coveted office. Salmon P. Chase had resigned from the cabinet in June and was now "turning every stone" in an attempt to gain the chief justiceship.[62] Without a word to the cabinet, Lincoln sent Chase's name to the Senate for confirmation on December 6 and the appointment was accepted by that body.[63] This move may have been a political expedient because the radical wing of the Republican party received the news with ecstasy. As soon as Congress adjourned that evening "a party of them met in a private room in one of the hotels . . . and in their rejoicing over the result nominated Old Abe for the President for 1868, on the third term. They are all in excellent humor and at peace with all the world."[64]

When Brooks called upon Lincoln one day during the first week of December, probably on the fourth or fifth, he found him writing out with pencil, on a piece of cardboard, a little anecdote concerning an experience which he had had with the endless problem of pardon requests for Confederate prisoners. Upon completing the story, the President handed it to Brooks for his perusal. It read:

THE PRESIDENT'S LAST, SHORTEST, AND BEST SPEECH.

On Thursday [December 1] of last week two ladies from Tennessee came before the President asking the release of their husbands held as prisoners of war at Johnson's Island. They were put off till friday, when they came again; and were again put off to Saturday. At each of the interviews one of the ladies urged that her husband was a religious man. On saturday the President ordered the release of the prisoners, and then said to this lady: "You say your husband is a religious man; tell him when you meet him, that I say I am not much of a judge of religion, but that, in my opinion, that religion that sets men to rebel and fight against their government, because, as they think, that government does not sufficiently help *some* men to eat their bread on the sweat of *other* men's faces, is not the sort of religion upon which people can get to heaven."

Brooks noticed and remarked that some of the days of the week were not capitalized, whereupon the President asked his opinion of the semicolon after "a religious man." "Is that the correct punctuation mark, or should that sentence be set off by itself with a full stop?" questioned Lincoln. In reply, Brooks said that it was perfectly correct. Then the President added, "With educated people, I suppose, punctuation is a matter of rule; with me it is a matter of feeling. But I must say that I have a great respect for the semi-colon; it's a very useful little chap."

Following this discussion, the President explained that he wished his little story to be published in the Washington (D. C.) *Chronicle*. "Don't wait and send it to California in your correspondence," Lincoln admonished "Castine." "I've a childish desire to see it in print right away," he admitted. Brooks agreed to have it published, but asked Lincoln to sign his name at the end of the article in order to authenticate it. This he readily did and Brooks took the manuscript to the office of the *Chronicle*, which published it on December 7, but the editor omitted Lincoln's signature, changed some of the words and punctuation, and added this sentence: "We have given as a caption for this paragraph the President's own opinion of his little speech, which he considered his shortest and best, as well as latest." The *Chronicle*, however, delayed publishing the item; this is evident from the fact that Brooks copied the anecdote into his newsletter sent from Washington on December 5.

Brooks prized greatly the original manuscript and retrieved it from the editor after it was printed. It remained in Brooks's possession until after his death at which time the Maine Historical Society received it.

A comparison with the original shows the deviations which appeared in the *Chronicle* version. It appeared on page two as follows:

THE PRESIDENT'S LAST, SHORTEST, AND BEST SPEECH.

On Thursday of last week two ladies from Tennessee came before the President, asking for the release of their husbands, held as prisoners of war at Johnson's Island. They were put off until Friday, when they came again, and were again put off until Saturday. At each of the interviews one of the ladies urged that her husband was a religious man, and on Saturday, when the President ordered the release of the prisoners, he said to this lady: "You say your husband is a religious man; tell him when you meet him that I say I am not much of a judge of religion, but that, in my opinion, the religion that sets men to rebel and fight against their Government because, as they think, that Government does not sufficiently help *some* men to eat their bread in the sweat of *other* men's faces, is not the sort of religion upon which people can get into heaven." We have given as a caption for this paragraph the President's own opinion of his little speech, which he considered his shortest and best, as well as latest.[65]

As the time for the opening of the last session of the Thirty-eighth Congress approached, Lincoln worked hard on his annual message. "I happened to be with him often," Brooks related, "while he was composing his message to Congress . . . ."[66] With first-hand observations of Lincoln while composing, "Castine" explained that "the whole of the compact and able message just referred to exists, or did exist, upon slips of paste-board or box-board. It is a favorite habit of the President, when writing anything requiring thought, to have a number of these stiff slips of board near at hand, and, seated at ease in his arm chair, he lays the slip on his knee and writes and re-writes in pencil what is afterward copied in his own hand, with new changes and interlineations. Then being 'set up' by the printer with big 'slugs' in the place of 'leads,' spaces of half an inch are left between each line in the proof, when more corrections and interlineations are made, and from this patchwork the document is finally set up and printed. The complete collection of original scraps of the manuscript message would be a valuable prize for an autograph hunter."[67]

While Lincoln was writing this annual message, Sherman was on his long march through Georgia to the sea. One evening as Brooks sat alone with the President, Lincoln withdrew one of the little slips of cardboard from his desk and remarked, "I expect you want to know all about Sherman's raid?" Naturally, Brooks quickly said that he certainly did. "Well, then," Lincoln continued, "I'll read you this paragraph from my message." So saying, he read:

> The most remarkable feature in the military operations of the year is General Sherman's attempted march of three hundred miles directly through the insurgent region. It tends to show a great increase of our relative strength that our General-in-Chief should feel able to confront and hold in check every active force of the enemy, and yet to detach a well-appointed large army to move on such an expedition. The result not yet being known, conjecture in regard to it is not here indulged.

Since it contained no real information about Sherman's movements, Brooks expressed his disappointment. The President removed his glasses and laughed heartily at the reporter's discomfiture. Then he said kindly, "Well, my dear fellow, that's all that Congress will know about it, anyhow."[68]

Congress convened on December 5, but Lincoln did not send his message over to be read until the following day. Evidently it encouraged the people because that evening a group serenaded Lincoln and R. E. Fenton, the governor-elect of New York. Fenton responded with a speech, but the President told the people "that he could never yet get over being embarrassed when he had nothing to say, and proposed three cheers for Sherman, which were given with a will."[69] The President's message to Congress even had a strange effect upon old Thad Stevens of Pennsylvania. He had "never 'believed' in Lincoln" and yet he said, either in jest or in seriousness, that it was "the best message which has been sent to Congress in the past sixty years."[70]

Although pleased with Chase's appointment to the Supreme Court, some of his "over-zealous and indiscreet friends" claimed a few days after his confirmation that "the President was coerced into making the appointment." They scornfully announced that the choice was "forced upon the President by men who control confirmations in the Senate." Having heard many of the private petitions of Chase's followers, Brooks related his knowledge of the matter. "I will venture to say," he divulged, "that the President never desired to appoint any other man than Chase to the Chief Justiceship; he never, I believe, had any other intention." To explain this statement, he said that "it is a peculiar trait of his mind that when doubts and objections arise concerning the expediency of certain contemplated acts, he states to those with whom he comes in contact those doubts and objections, not as his, but with the express purpose of having them refuted, controverted and removed, if possible. A careless or unobservant listener goes away confounded and discouraged, but the crafty statesman Lincoln has enjoyed seeing a false position demolished and his own convictions made him stronger."[71]

CHAPTER VII

"The Close of Lincoln's Career"

SOMETIME AFTER JULY 12, 1864, probably in November, Noah Brooks moved back to Washington from his Georgetown residence.[1] The daily trip to and from his home in this suburban community had become burdensome to the busy reporter. His choice of living quarters was an apartment at No. 260 New York Avenue, a suite of rooms formerly tenanted by Senator Charles Sumner. The landlord's name was David A. Gardner, whom Brooks and his roommate, W. E. McArthur, "facetiously dubbed 'The Ancient.'" The location was most excellent since it was in the immediate neighborhood of the White House where Brooks was spending more and more of his time. It is not true, however, as Brooks later reminisced, that "during the greater part of my stay in Washington I occupied the rooms on New York Avenue." Only during the last year of his residence in the capital did he live at this address.[2]

The apartment, as it was described to Sumner in 1851, was "within a hundred steps of [the] State Department, in a house fronting on New York avenue, looking northward. The House is a *frame*—but very neat and suitable looking. The rooms are not large, being front and back parlor on the first floor with basement story underneath. They are very well furnished. You could have any or all meals served in your room from [a] neighboring restaurant. I regard the situation to be eligible as any in town." The rent in 1851 was $35 per month which included the care of the rooms. "Lights, fires and meals [were] furnished extra on terms to be agreed on," and in the years before the war, the Gardner family, who were termed "nice people," rented no other rooms in their house.[3] With the coming of the Civil War, the rent for this apartment probably doubled.

These rooms held many memories for the landlord, who related to Brooks and McArthur some of the former activities of Senator Sumner. The Gardner children "always knew when Sumner was preparing to make a set speech in the Senate, weeks before it was known to the general public," said the landlord. "In the rear of Sumner's apartment was a gallery from which the interior of the rooms could be viewed. The younger members of the Gardner family, with a curiosity natural to youth, would be attracted by the sound of the Senator's magnificent voice rehearsing his speech, and from the gallery they could look in and see him before a pier-glass, fixed between the front windows, studying the effect of his gestures by the light of lamps placed at each side of the mirror."[4]

With the advent of 1865 the President was again besieged by office seekers. "The saying is just as true of a President as of a King," remarked Brooks, "and even now, I suppose, Father Abraham lies uneasy o' nights, as he thinks of the sluice of office-hunting which may shortly be opened upon him by the cruel thoughtlessness of his friends (?), as they call themselves." It was nearly impossible for Lincoln to show an interest in anybody without being asked for an appointment.

One evening in 1863, when the President was relaxing at the theatre with Brooks, James Henry Hackett's (1800–1871) portrayal of Falstaff so pleased and delighted Lincoln that he "expressed himself in warm terms to the player through the medium of the manager." (The date for this particular performance was probably between the 15th and 18th of December in 1863, when a Washington correspondent reported—on the eighteenth—that Lincoln had attended the theatre "the last four nights" in a row to watch Hackett in the "Merry Wives of Windsor.") "Thereupon," Brooks related, "the actor sent the President a book[5] in which he inscribed some pleasant words by way of dedication to Lincoln, who acknowledged the gift in a kindly little note."[6] Hackett then requested that Lincoln give an opinion, in writing, of his acting ability. The President did this, only to discover later that Hackett had published the letter in the newspapers of London.[7] In 1864 the actor returned to Washington and had it announced in the press that the play, in which he was currently performing, was "at the request of the President." Such a cheap play upon his name disgusted Lincoln, but he attended the performance nonetheless.

These incidents were nearly forgotten by Brooks until the first part of January, 1865, when Lincoln summoned him to the White House "very late at night." As "Castine" was about to enter the Chief Executive's office, he noticed Hackett "waiting alone in the corridor outside the President's door." After Brooks had entered, Lincoln asked him "if anyone was waiting without."

Brooks replied that he had "seen the actor sitting there," and Lincoln "made a gesture of impatience and regret, and said that the little courtesies which had passed between them had resulted in the comedian applying to him for an office." Hackett wanted "nothing less than the mission to the Court of St. James'" at London![8]

To escape from his daily toil and bolster his spiritual courage, Lincoln attended Sunday services at the Hall of the House of Representatives on January 15, 1865. His family accompanied him to hear the chaplain of the House preach a sermon, "a glowing eulogium" on Edward Everett, the prominent scholar and orator who had shared the speaking honors with Lincoln at Gettysburg. While the chaplain spoke, no one present in the Hall knew that "the distinguished orator was then no more in life." It was only after President Lincoln and his family had returned to the White House that Everett's death was announced. "That afternoon, the Secretary of State, by order of the President," made the fact known by a public announcement. "In respect to his memory," salutes were fired on the following day, and the public buildings, including the Capitol and White House, were draped in black bunting.[9]

Although the President had great respect for Everett, he did not rate him as an outstanding scholar. On the evening of Everett's death, Brooks was in the Executive Mansion with the Lincolns. The conversation turned to Everett and Lincoln said, "Now, you are a loyal New Englander,—loyal to New England,—what great work of Everett's do you remember?" Brooks was forced to admit that he could think of none. Then Lincoln asked if he remembered any great speech which Everett had made. Again "Castine" pleaded ignorance, whereupon Lincoln, "looking around the room in his half-comical fashion, as if afraid of being overheard," remarked: "Now, do you know, I think Edward Everett was very much overrated. He hasn't left any enduring monument. But there was one speech in which, addressing a statue of John Adams and a picture of Washington, in Faneuil Hall, Boston, he apostrophized them and said, 'Teach us the love of liberty protected by law!'" "That," said Lincoln, "was very fine, it seems to me. Still, it was only a good idea, introduced by noble language."[10]

Following Lincoln's discussion of Everett, Congressman Samuel Hooper and Professor Louis Agassiz sent in their calling cards. Brooks rose to leave only to have Lincoln exclaim with delight, "Agassiz!" "Don't go, don't go. Sit down, and let us see what we can pick up that's new from this great man." However, both Lincoln and Agassiz seemed to sense that they were strangers in each other's field and acted "like two boys who wanted to ask questions which appeared commonplace." The Chief Executive inquired as to the correct pronunciation of the Professor's name, and Agassiz countered by asking

Lincoln if he had ever lectured. The President replied that he had written the outlines for two lectures on inventions[11] which attempted to prove "that there is nothing new under the sun." "I think," Lincoln stated, "I can show at least, in a fanciful way, that all the modern inventions were known centuries ago." The Professor suggested that Lincoln should complete his paper. In reply, the President said that the manuscript was still among his papers. "When I get out of this place," he promised, "I'll finish it up, perhaps, and get my friend B[rooks] to print it somewhere."[12]

"President Lincoln," Brooks pointed out, "likes to relate any good story concerning any of his Cabinet officers, and if their dignity has been taken down a trifle he relished it all the better." In February he told "Castine," "with great unction," a story about Stanton. The Secretary of War had left Washington during the first part of January for a tour of the Southern areas held by Union armies. The trip was one of both inspection and recuperation. As Stanton traveled up Broad River in South Carolina with General J. G. Foster, they were challenged by a picket on the bank. The soldier wanted to know who was aboard the tug. The reply was given with great dignity: "The Secretary of War and Major General Foster." In answer the picket roared back, "We've got Major Generals enough up here—why don't you bring us up some hardtack?" This blunt reply completely deflated Stanton's dignity, and Foster "conceded that his pickets did not have very large veneration, phrenologically speaking."[13]

At another time Lincoln passed on to Brooks a preposterous tale concerning Secretary Gideon Welles. "The story ran," Brooks wrote, "that a dying sailor in one of the Washington hospitals said he was ready to go if he could see his old grandmother at home before he died; and the attendant at his bedside, being directed to ask Secretary Welles if he would personate that relative, the Secretary replied that he would do it with pleasure—but he was then busy examining a model of Noah's ark with a view of introducing it into the United States navy."

The President loved to tell this particular story, and he related it one autumn evening while Brooks was staying overnight with the Lincolns at the Soldiers' Home. There were other guests present, but Lincoln "standing with his back to the fire and his legs spread apart, recited from memory" the fanciful tale with appropriate gestures. Upon completing the story, he turned to Brooks and cautioned him: "Now don't let the Secretary know that I have been telling these stories on him; for he would be dreadfully mortified if he knew it." Brooks was greatly shocked since the President had trusted him on previous occasions with much greater secrets, but when the other guests had left and Brooks was preparing to retire, Lincoln had explained that he had used him as "a friend over whom to hit" the other guests who might repeat the story since they were "leaky vessel[s]," as Lincoln termed them.[14]

At times, Brooks was able to aid Lincoln by delivering personal messages to political figures on Capitol Hill. Since "Castine" often ate breakfast with the President before reporting for work at the House of Representatives, he could perform such tasks easily. One morning, sometime between February 24 and March 3, 1865, Brooks was at the White House when Lincoln asked "if, on arriving at the Capitol, whither I was going, I would say to Senator Sumner that he (the President) would be glad if the Senator would call to see him later in the day, if entirely convenient." Brooks sought out Sumner and told him of the President's invitation. With a great show of importance, Sumner replied, "Let me see. I have an engagement to take luncheon with the Marquis de Chambrun, and later to dine with the British Minister. Yes, yes, I think I will go; I think I will go. Pray tell the President so." To Brooks's way of thinking, "there was no need for Senator Sumner to tell an unimportant person like myself what his engagements with great people were; and he knew very well that I should not see the President again that day."[15]

On inauguration day, March 4, there was a manifestation of great enthusiasm as "various societies" marched through the mud of the Washington streets in cadence with martial music.[16] Though the citizens of the capital were greatly excited, it was just another working day for Abraham Lincoln. On the previous evening he had been busily engaged in the President's room off the Senate Chamber "signing bills with might and main" while Mrs. Lincoln observed the closing hours of Congress from the diplomatic gallery. When Lincoln returned to the White House, it was late. Yet he arose early the following morning and returned to the Capitol. Some bills still remained to be signed".

When the formal procession moved away from the White House toward the Capitol for the inaugural ceremonies, Lincoln was not present. He was still finishing up last-minute business at the Capitol. However, as Mrs. Lincoln's carriage led the procession, "it was just as well, and the cheering crowd thought that the President was within the vehicle."[17]

Brooks witnessed the inauguration from the vantage point of the reporters' gallery[18] and observed that the impressive ceremonies were ruined by the behavior of Andrew Johnson. "The Vice-President elect," Welles confirmed, "made a rambling and strange harangue, which was listened to with pain and mortification by all his friends."[19] On one of the most important days of his life, Johnson was inebriated. In his newsletter "Castine" reported the drunken condition of the new vice-president, and at a later date this report was used against Brooks by his political enemies. But Brooks's account was true. Those present noticed and commented upon the strange behavior of Johnson. Mr. Johnson, reported one newspaper, made "a speech remarkable only for its incoherence, which brought a blush to the cheek of every Senator and official of the government who was present." "It is charitable to say that his condition was such that he was unfit to make a speech. He evidently did not shun Bourbon county, Kentucky, on his way here."[20]

On the night of the inauguration, a gay reception—the last levee of the season—was held from eight to eleven at the White House. "Such was the crowd," related Welles, "that many were two hours before obtaining entrance after passing through the gates." When the weary President retired that night after the press and excitement and work of two hectic days, it was probably with a sense of mixed feelings. He certainly was glad that the tiring ceremonies were past, but ahead lay what he thought would be another four years of trying leadership. The day had been very fatiguing for him, and the weather had added to the unpleasantness, with rain in the morning and mud in the afternoon. In addition, there probably lingered in his mind the shame of Johnson's conduct. There is little doubt that his huge hand also ached from endless handshaking at the reception. The President was a very tired man.[21]

Yet there was no immediate rest for Lincoln; the National Inauguration Ball took place on Monday, March 6, just two nights after the levee. The proceeds of the affair were to be used for the benefit of service men's families. Elaborate preparations were made for this social event, under the direction of B. B. French, who acted as chairman of the general supervisory committee. To assist him, there was also a select group of "managers," among whom were Noah Brooks and his friend Edward McPherson. Each manager wore a distinctive blue rosette to denote his office. Tickets for the ball sold for $10 each and entitled each gentleman to bring two ladies with him.[22]

The site which was chosen for the gala affair was the Patent Office, a huge government edifice which had served previously as a temporary hospital. Now its huge marble halls were thrown open to the public, "making a complete quadrangle of four lighted and decorated halls, a fine sight."[23] The exquisite floors of this building were large blocks of blue and white marble, and the hall which was reserved for dancing was 280 feet long and 60 feet wide. Another of the huge rooms, where couples could promenade, measured 300 feet long. For the Presidential family, a large *dais* had been erected and furnished with sofas and chairs that were upholstered in blue and gold.

It was "a glorious spectacle, such as has not been seen in Washington for years," one reporter observed. About 10,000 people attended, but the immense building was not "uncomfortably crowded." At 10 P.M. a promenade opened the dancing program and was followed by a quadrille. At the conclusion of the first dance President Lincoln and his family made their appearance at 10:30. The Chief Executive walked into the hall with Speaker Colfax, while Mrs. Lincoln was escorted by Senator Sumner. Robert Lincoln, "a fine-looking young man," was dressed in the uniform of a captain in the Army. The President was attired simply in "a plain black suit and white gloves" and presented a marked contrast to his wife who wore a gown of "rich white silk, heavily flounced and trimmed with elegant white point-lace, and a white lace shawl. Her headdress was of delicate lilac and white flowers and her necklace, fan, and other appointments were in excellent taste."

As the guests of honor entered the grand ballroom, there was a great "clapping of hands and waving of handkerchiefs." The President was noticeably tired, but he tried "to throw off care for the time." However, he had ill success and "looked very old; yet he seemed pleased and gratified, as he was greeted by the people." To him, this was just another social event which sapped his strength and stole his needed rest.[24]

Following the dancing and promenading there was a sumptuous dinner with many courses. But Brooks related that the extravagant repast was "all spoiled by the disgusting greediness of this great American people." When the evening was over, the socialites of the capital were happy, but Lincoln had found little respite from his numerous cares. Even before he left for the ball, Chief Justice Chase "spent an hour with the President" and urged him "to exempt sundry counties in eastern Virginia from the insurrectionary proclamation." According to Welles this would greatly benefit the radicals' "sundry purposes." It was nearly impossible for Lincoln to relax and enjoy himself.[25]

As Lincoln's new term of office began, John G. Nicolay, quite unexpectedly, agreed to resign from his position of private secretary to the President and accepted another appointment. On March 11, he was made Consul to Paris to succeed John Bigelow, who had been elevated to the post of Minister. It "was a pleasurable surprise to the Senate" who immediately confirmed his appointment with a unanimous vote. "He will, it is understood, not proceed to Paris immediately," a Washington paper reported, "but will remain at the Executive Mansion for some time."[26] About two weeks later, it was announced that Lincoln's other secretary, John Hay, would also go to Paris as Secretary of Legation.[27] These appointments probably resulted from pressure which was brought to bear upon Lincoln by his wife and other interested persons. Nicolay and Hay were probably glad to leave the White House also; they were dissatisfied with their official duties there.

Prior to his appointment as consul, Nicolay had informed his future wife that "as the matter now stands I am pretty well resolved not to remain here in my present relation after" the second inauguration, "and I think the chances are also against my remaining in Washington."[28] Charles H. Philbrick, an assistant secretary, observed that "Nicolay is gloomy on account of physical and mental trouble. I think if he and I could make an 'even divide,' he taking a part of my 163 lbs weight, and giving me some of his indifference and industry, that we should each be the better for the bargain. Hay does the *ornamental* . . . and the main labor is divided between three of us who manage to get along tolerably well with it."[29]

As for Hay, he did not get along with Mrs. Lincoln at all. He termed her the devil's daughter or the "Hell-cat." On several occasions he had disagreements with her over financial matters. Once Mrs. Lincoln tried to draw the steward's salary from Hay on the ground that there was no steward in the White House and the unpaid money belonged to her. Hay refused. At another time she tried to obtain money from the secretaries' "stationary fund" only to be thwarted by Hay. After several of these encounters, Hay stated that "the Hell-cat is getting more Hell-cattical day by day." And Hay had done yet another thing which displeased the First Lady. He sometimes dined with Kate Chase or escorted her to the theatre, and Kate was Mrs. Lincoln's social rival for the center of attention in Washington. By March 31, 1865, Hay was "thoroughly sick of certain aspects of life here, which you will understand without my putting them on paper."[30]

Whether Lincoln's secretaries were unhappy or merely unable to cope with Mrs. Lincoln's odd mental patterns is unknown. In the course of a bitter dispute with Nicolay in 1891, A. K. McClure disclosed his knowledge of the matter. Nicolay, declared McClure, "was a good mechanical, routine clerk; he was utterly inefficient as the Secretary of the President; his removal was earnestly pressed upon Lincoln on more than one occasion because of his want of tact and fitness for his trust, and only the proverbial kindness of Lincoln saved him from dismissal."[31]

In December of 1864, Brooks had been undecided as to whether he would remain at the capital or not. He missed the sunny climate of California, but admitted that he might "have to stay in Washington." He thought that if he did return to the Pacific Coast, it would be about March 4.[32] His plans, however, were changed radically on January 1, 1865, when Lincoln asked him "to remain at the Capital as his Private Secretary, in place of Mr. John G. Nicolay." The President's "kindly estimate" of his character and ability "were the means of the offer" of this position to Brooks.[33] "The President," Brooks testified, "was then anxious for me to take the place near him, but demurred at my sacrificing so much for the sake of serving him, and offered me the privilege of continuing my correspondence, which pay as much as the salary of secretary." The private secretary to the President received only $2,500. "Castine" told Lincoln that "the sacrifice, such as it was, was mine, and I had a right to make it, a view of the case in which he finally acquiesced, with the understanding that he would make all of the perquisites of the place, living, &c. liberal as possible." "I would have made myself poor," Brooks continued, "for the sake of serving a man so dear to me, and for the sake of serving the Country by saving him for better and higher duties. . . ."

At first, however, "it appeared doubtful if Nicolay could be induced to go abroad."[34] But there were strong forces at work for Brooks's appointment. Speaker Colfax was consulted on the matter several times and favored the Californian for the position of secretary.[35] And other support was soon forthcoming. Dr. Anson G. Henry sailed from San Francisco aboard the *Constitution* on January 4, 1865.[36] He sought a cabinet position or an appointment in the capital, and he was going to lay his petition before his old friend, President Lincoln. At the Isthmus of Panama, Henry transferred to the *North Star* and arrived at New York on January 27.[37] When he reached Washington, Dr. Henry sought the ear of Mrs. Lincoln. On February 8 he acted as her escort to a joint session of both houses of Congress, and in the course of their conversation, the First Lady assured him that "Mr. Lincoln won't refuse any thing you ask him for *I know*."[38] Dr. Henry wished to be named Commissioner of Indian Affairs, but the office was not vacant.

On the evening of March 12, Henry had "a very pleasant" half hour's interview with the President. "My friend Mr. Noah Brooks was with me," related the Doctor. "I have been working ever since I have been here with Mrs. Lincoln," he continued, "to get Nickolay [sic] out as private secretary and Mr. Brooks in his place." Although Henry suggested that Brooks "was capable of rendering him infinitely more substantial service" than Nicolay, Lincoln made no comment. The President had already sent Nicolay's name to the Senate as Consul to Paris and he had been confirmed. Brooks also knew of the President's action and probably had already accepted the secretaryship, but he said nothing. Dr. Henry did not know of the previous arrangements made between Lincoln and Brooks, but concluded that the President would certainly "make Mr. Brooks his secretary." All Lincoln said was that Nicolay would remain with him for two or three weeks.[39] Hay had also been requested by the President "to stay with him a month or so."[40]

In his correspondence, Brooks did not announce his new appointment. According to Dr. Henry, the matter was to be kept a secret until Nicolay left.[41] "Castine" merely mentioned that "the few changes which have been made in foreign appointments have chiefly been made for the benefit of the 'lame ducks,' though not in that category comes John Bigelow, made Minister to France, who is an able Diplomatist, a gentleman and a newspaper man withal, being formerly editor of the New York *Evening Post*. He is succeeded in the Consulship to Paris by J. G. Nicolay, formerly Private Secretary of the President. The new Consul does not go out until about the first of June."[42]

On March 14 Lincoln was forced to remain in bed although he was not seriously ill. He met the cabinet members in his bedroom when it was necessary to have conferences.[43] "The President's health," Brooks reported, "has been worn down by the constant pressure of office-seekers and legitimate business, so that for a few days he was obliged to deny himself to all comers, and now he rigidly adheres to the rule of closing the doors at three o'clock in the [afternoon] receiving only those whom he prefers during the hours of evening." With rest, Lincoln's health improved steadily, but he confided to "Castine" that one of his great sources of worry was congressmen who had failed to be renominated or reelected. The President complained that such politicians always returned to Washington, "like a lame duck, to be nursed into something else."[44]

To escape from his official duties and pressures, Lincoln and his wife left the capital at noon on March 23, aboard the steamer *River Queen* for a trip to City Point, Virginia. "The truth is that the President's health of late has been poor," one reporter explained, "and he has been overrun by office seekers and others who do not allow him an hour's rest. It was, therefore, considered necessary that he should have at least a brief respite, and accordingly he determined to accept General Grant's invitation to visit City Point . . . ."[45]

Noah Brooks was with the Lincolns on this trip, but it is not certain that he left Washington with them on the *River Queen*. Brooks stated that while he was at the front, Lincoln expressed to him "a determination to stay until the first of next week [April 9]." Brooks may have planned to remain with Lincoln until he returned, but sickness forced "Castine" to go back to Washington about April 1.[46]

The tour of the army was a pleasant relaxation for the Chief Executive. On March 25 he and Grant visited Meade's command and reviewed the Third and Fifth Corps. "As the Chief Magistrate rode down the ranks, plucking off his hat gracefully by the hinder part of the brim," wrote Colonel Theodore Lyman of Meade's staff, "the troops cheered quite loudly."[47] On the following day the President, with a large party of guests from City Point, visited the Adirondack Regiment. "Our tall President with his 'stove-pipe' hat was conspicuous, especially on horseback," noted one of the soldiers.[48]

Surrounded by his good friends, such as Brooks, the President forgot some of his cares. "Down the Potomac, he was almost boyish in his mirth & reminded me, of his original nature, what I had always remembered of him, in our own home—free from care, surrounded by those he loved so well & by *whom*, he was so idolized," recalled Mrs. Lincoln.[49]

While Grant, Sherman, Sheridan, and Lincoln were all in a conference at City Point on March 27, Brooks was visiting Fort Monroe, which the Confederates had never been able to capture. "The fort," Brooks observed, "is of hammered stone, many-angled, and bearing a bastion at each angle; it has one row of guns in casement and one tier *en barbette*, I believe they call it—that is to say, mounted on the ramparts. These grim monsters are about four hundred in number when all of the guns are in place, but at present only about two hundred and fifty are mounted, many of the casements being used for dwellings for the officers, storehouses, etc." Most of the cannon were six inches in caliber, but six of the guns were fifteen inches in diameter and were of the "famous Fort Pitt manufacture." The center of attraction for Brooks, however, was the "Union Gun," which was mounted on the beach in a base of granite, iron, and concrete. A brigadier general on duty at the fort explained to Brooks that the gun could throw a shell weighing 400 pounds a distance of about six miles.[50]

When he returned to Washington, Brooks found that General Franz Sigel was in town, "under examination by the Committee on the Conduct of the War." "Your correspondent," Brooks announced, "has the honor of meeting him at breakfast every morning, and while I would express no opinion as to his generalship, I can testify as to his extraordinary capacity for fried potatoes."[51] Soon after Brooks reached the capital, he was forced back to bed with a recurrence of the same malady which had caused his return from the front.

While Brooks was incapacitated, Edward McPherson, his superior as Clerk of the House of Representatives, urged "Castine" to use his influence to obtain Lincoln's permission for the publication of the Lincoln-Greeley correspondence, which had resulted in bringing about the Niagara peace conference with Confederate representatives in July of 1864.[52] The government printer, John D. Defrees, had printed the letters, but they had not been released for publication. The President had been "unwilling just then" to allow Greeley to publish the collection unless the New York *Tribune's* editor would consent to omit one particular passage which alluded to the ruined condition of the country. Greeley would not agree to the editing of this one letter.[53]

On April 5 Brooks informed McPherson that he would "see what can be done, but I have not very strong hopes of his consenting to the publication of the correspondence, as there were one or two other letters which have not seen the light, and other parties than the President, might not be glad to see them printed."[54] One of Greeley's letters to Lincoln had recently been published in England, and McPherson probably reasoned that the government should now release all of the correspondence. But McPherson's request put Brooks in an uncomfortable position; he never wished to use his personal friendship with Lincoln to forward the petitions of others.

Lincoln's absence from Washington postponed Brooks's disagreeable task temporarily, but after visiting the fallen Confederate capital, the President, Mrs. Lincoln, Senator and Mrs. James Harlan, and Senator Sumner embarked at City Point on the *River Queen* at 11 P.M., April 8, for the return trip to Washington. The little group arrived back at the capital on the night of April 9.[55] The President had profited from his vacation and returned "looking well and feeling well,"[56] and Brooks had no desire to disrupt Lincoln's peace of mind.

To discourage McPherson, Brooks related, in a second letter written on April 12, that he had not had "an opportunity of asking the President for that correspondence, he has been crowded all the while since coming back, but I shall see him this week, and will ask him about it." When Brooks wrote this letter, he had already seen Lincoln several times, and it seems doubtful if he ever intended to mention the matter to the President. Perhaps thinking that McPherson could be placated, Brooks proceeded to relate his own knowledge of the matter. "When I saw it last summer," he said, "it was printed entire and was in Greeley's hands, with full consent to print, but he said that though he was willing to publish it, others might not be, and he was not sure that all the correspondence could be accessible to him. So much for his honesty; so, though he may now say that he is . . . willing,—if so, why don't he print it in the *Tribune*? The President said then that he should leave the whole matter in the hands of Mr. Greeley, and he will probably say so now. I suppose you will print the President's speech" of April 11, Brooks questioned McPherson in an attempt to change the subject.[57]

To celebrate the surrender of Lee, many of the government departments closed on April 10. When a group of Treasury clerks were dismissed, they gathered before the White House and serenaded Lincoln by singing "The Star Spangled Banner." The President was eating breakfast with Brooks at the time, but he quickly left the table to learn the cause of the singing. "Seen from the windows," Brooks wrote, "the surface of the crowd looked like an agitated sea of hats, faces and men's arms." The celebrants had brought six "boat-howitzers" with them to aid in the merry-making, and the assembled crowd "filled the whole area in front of the President's house, where they patiently waited for a speech, guns firing and bands playing meanwhile."

Before Lincoln could reach his usual post, young Tad "made his appearance at the well known window from whence the President always speaks, where he was received by a great shout of applause; encouraged by which he waved a captured rebel flag,[58] whereat he was lugged back by the slack of his trowsers by some discreet domestic, amid the uproarious cheers of the sovereign people below." Shortly after Tad's demonstration, the President appeared and the people broke forth with loud cheering again. Lincoln explained that a more formal celebration was being planned for the following day and declined to make a speech. For, said Lincoln, "I shall have nothing to say then if it is all dribbled out of me now."[59]

Then noticing the band, Lincoln remarked that the Confederacy had always claimed one tune which he greatly admired. That piece was "Dixie," he said. According to Lincoln's legal reasoning, "Dixie" was now the property of the United States because "we fairly captured it" on April 8. To confirm his decision, Lincoln explained that "he had submitted the question to the Attorney General that morning and he had decided that the tune was our lawful property." After having his fun with the crowd, Lincoln requested the band to play "Dixie." "I," said Brooks, "stood behind the President, who turned while the band was playing and said: 'I just feel like marching when that tune is played.'" When the musicians finished playing his request, Lincoln proposed three cheers for Grant and his men, three cheers for the Navy, and then left the window after bidding the people good morning.[60]

"So as to be on hand and see the fun afterward," as Lincoln expressed it, the President invited Noah Brooks to dine at the White House on the evening of April 11.[61] After dinner the Presidential family and their guests "lingered at the dinner-table" talking.[62] Then the little group retired to the drawing room to await the expected serenade. As Lincoln entered the room he laid a manuscript on one of the tables, whereupon Brooks showed signs of obvious surprise. Said the President:

> I know what you are thinking about. You think it mighty queer that an old stump-speaker like myself should not be able to address a crowd like this outside without a written speech. But you must remember I am, in a certain way, talking to the country, and I have to be mighty careful. Now, the last time I made an off-hand speech, in answer to a serenade, I used the phrase, as applied to the rebels, "turned tail and ran." Some very nice Boston folks, I am grieved to hear, were very much outraged by that phrase, which they thought improper. So I resolved to make no more impromptu speeches if I could help it.

Subsequently Lincoln explained that it was Senator Sumner who had expressed the attitude of some Boston friends.[63] Then as the Presidential party prepared to go to the upstairs window, Lincoln remarked that he had included in his speech the story of the egg and the fowl because it caught his fancy. "Don't you think that is a good figure?" Lincoln asked Brooks. The reporter replied that "it might be thought inelegant," especially as people had found fault with his phrase, "turned tail and ran," which he had used on a previous occasion. The President only laughed and resolved nevertheless to keep his illustration.[64]

Although the air was full of mist, a huge crowd gathered to hear the President.[65] At an adjacent window with Mrs. Lincoln was another guest, the Marquis de Chambrun, whom the First Lady had invited with a formal note and a "bunch of flowers."[66] Lincoln began to read his address, which was written on loose sheets of paper, only to discover that the candles had been placed too low for him to see clearly. He reached down and took one of the candles in his hand to illuminate the page, but when he reached the end of the first sheet, he found that this combination was totally unworkable. "He made a comical motion with his left foot and elbow," Brooks related, "which I construed to mean that I should hold his candle for him, which I did." "Castine" remained out of sight behind the draperies of the window while holding the light. As Lincoln read, he "let the loose pages fall to the floor one by one," and Tad quickly scrambled about "picking them up as they fell and impatiently [called] for more as they fluttered from his father's hand." Upon finishing the address, Lincoln turned to Brooks and said, "That was a pretty fair speech, I think, but you threw some light on it."[67] Then the tired President returned to his room and stretched his long body out upon a sofa to rest.[68]

The President and his lady had previously announced their intention of witnessing Miss Laura Keene's performance in the play "Our American Cousin" on Friday evening, April 14, at Ford's Theatre on Tenth Street. Lincoln then secured the promise of General and Mrs. Grant that they would accompany them to the theatre on that evening. However, in the early afternoon of April 14 the General informed the President that he and his wife would be unable to attend because of a planned trip to visit their children at Burlington, New Jersey.

When Lincoln learned that the Grants would not attend the performance, he asked Major Thomas Eckert of the telegraph office if he would accompany him. Secretary Stanton refused to allow the Major to go.[69] Later that afternoon, Brooks "filled an appointment by calling on the President at the White House, and was told by him that he 'had a notion' of sending for me to go to the theater that evening with him and Mrs. Lincoln; but he added that Mrs. Lincoln had already made up a party to take the place of General and Mrs. Grant, who had somewhat unexpectedly left the city . . . ." Mrs. Lincoln invited Major Henry R. Rathbone and Miss Clara Harris.

"The afternoon and evening of April 14, 1865," Brooks recalled, "were cold, raw, and gusty. Dark clouds enveloped the capital, and the air was chilly with occasional showers."[70] But in spite of the gloomy weather, Lincoln "was unusually cheerful that evening, and never was more hopeful and buoyant concerning the condition of the country." Brooks lingered with the President until it was time for the Lincolns to leave for the theatre. In the meantime, Speaker Colfax had joined "Castine" at the White House. Turning to Mr. Colfax, Lincoln said, "You are going with Mrs. Lincoln and myself to the theatre, I hope." Colfax declined the invitation on the grounds that he was leaving the city early the next morning.[71]

Brooks and Colfax then walked out to the driveway with the Lincolns. "His conversation," wrote Brooks of Lincoln, "was full of fun and anecdotes, feeling especially jubilant at the prospect before us. The last words he said as he came out [to] the carriage were: 'Grant thinks we can reduce the cost of the army establishment at least a half million a day, which, with the reduction of expenditures of the Navy, will soon bring our national paper up to par, or nearly so, with gold; at least so they think.'" With a word of farewell, the "President and wife entered and drove off without any guard or escort."[72]

Brooks turned and walked home to his rooms at 462 New York Avenue where he probably composed his newsletter for the day. It was one of the shortest that he ever wrote, covering less than one column in the Sacramento *Union*.[73] But he was not feeling well. "The evening inclement," Brooks explained, "I stayed within doors to nurse a violent cold with which I was afflicted; and my room-mate, McA[rthur] and I whiled away the time chatting and playing cards. About half-past ten our attention was attracted to the frequent galloping of cavalry, or the mounted patrol, past the house . . . . After a while quiet was restored, and we retired to our sleeping-room in the rear part of the house. As I turned down the gas, I said to my room-mate: 'Will, I have guessed the cause of the clatter outside to-night. You know Wade Hampton has disappeared with his cavalry somewhere in the mountains of Virginia. Now, my theory of the racket is that he has raided Washington, and has pounced down upon the President, and has attempted to carry him off.'" "Will" McArthur replied, "What good will that do the rebs unless they carry off Andy Johnson too?"

While Brooks and McArthur slept, Lincoln was slowly dying from the effects of a pistol bullet which John Wilkes Booth had fired into the President's brain. When dawn came on April 15, there was "a heavy rain" falling and "the sky was black."[74] As the daylight crept slowly out of the east, Brooks was suddenly awakened by "a loud and hurried knocking on my chamber door, and the voice of Mr. Gardner, the landlord, crying, 'Wake, wake, Mr. Brooks! I have dreadful news.'" Quickly Brooks sprang out of bed, unlocked the door, and heard Gardner's account of Lincoln's assassination. "I sank back into my bed, cold and shivering with horror, and for a time it seemed as though the end of all things had come," Brooks recalled. For him, his plans were suddenly shattered. Never would he serve as private secretary to the dying Lincoln.

"When we had sufficiently collected ourselves to dress and go out of doors in the bleak and cheerless April morning," Brooks said, "we found in the streets an extraordinary spectacle. They were suddenly crowded with people—men, women, and children thronging the pavements and darkening the thorough-fares. It seemed as if everybody was in tears." Brooks and McArthur learned that the President was still alive but that there was little hope for his recovery. At 7:22 A.M. Lincoln expired. Later, "Castine" and his roommate wandered "aimlessly up F street toward Ford's Theater" where they "met a tragical procession. It was headed by a group of army officers walking bareheaded, and behind them, carried tenderly by a company of soldiers, was the bier of the dead President, covered with the flag of the Union, and accompanied by an escort of soldiers who had been on duty at the house where Lincoln died."[75]

As Brooks surveyed the situation along the Washington streets, he noted gloom everywhere. "Nature seemed to sympathize in the general grief," he wrote, "and tears of rain fell from the moist, and dark sky; while the wind sighed mournfully through the streets, crowded with sad-faced people, and broad folds of black flapped heavily in the wind, over the decorations of yesterday's rejoicings."[76]

On the evening of April 17 the remains of Abraham Lincoln were placed in the casket and removed from the guest room, where they had lain, to the great East Room of the White House. "The room was on the occasion draped in deepest mourning," Brooks recounted, "the chandeliers and lusters covered with crape, the mirrors and paintings hanging with black barege, and the columns and pilasters with black cloth. In the middle of the room was erected a catafalque, upon which the coffin rested. The structure was about fifteen feet high, and had an adorned canopy of black cloth, supported by four pillars, and lined with fluted white silk; from the edges of the canopy heavy curtains of black fine cloth were draped, being looped back at the corners, and adding a gloom to the dear face lying within."

Before 11 A.M., the time when the general public was allowed to view the body, Brooks called at the Executive Mansion on the morning of the eighteenth where he observed that "the scene was most solemn and impressive. Oppressive silence pervaded the mansion, and there, within the room where every sojourner at the National Capital had seen so much of youth, brilliancy, life and pride of life, all of that remained of one of the great ones of the earth lay rigid within the somber shades of his funeral canopy." In May of 1861—in this very room—President Lincoln himself had caused the body of Colonel Elmer E. Ellsworth, his personal friend, to lie in state following his death at the hands of an enraged Confederate citizen. Now, he too would be buried from this room.

After Lincoln's corpse had lain in state for a day, the funeral was held at noon on the nineteenth in the same East Room. Although Brooks was present, he never revealed where he sat. It is probable that he occupied a seat "at the foot of the catafalque . . . in a semi-circle of chairs for the family and friends" of the deceased President. Of the immediate family, only Robert Todd Lincoln was present, "Mrs. Lincoln being unable to leave her room on account of nervous prostration, superadded to a slight fever." General Grant was seated near the head of the casket and "often moved very deeply by the solemn services." The Rev. Dr. Gurley, who had been the President's pastor, preached a solemn sermon which was "impressive and clear, without being specially eloquent or thrilling." There was no music during the services.

Precisely at two o'clock the funeral procession moved away from the White House and marched to the Capitol. "Just before the procession begun to move," Brooks reported, "the Twenty-second Pennsylvania Colored Infantry landed at the wharf from Petersburg; they marched up to a position on the Avenue, and, when the head of the column came up, struck up a dirge and so headed the procession to the Capitol." At the Capitol the casket was removed from the "funeral car and placed within the rotunda . . . which had been darkened and draped in mourning, and a catafalque erected for the reception of the remains." Quietly the throngs of onlookers and officials dispersed, leaving only an honor guard with the body.

On the following day the coffin was again opened and "a great crowd" surged through the rotunda to pay their last respects to their martyred President.[77] "While this solemn pageant was passing," said Brooks, "I was allowed to go alone up the winding stairs that lead to the top of the great dome of the Capitol. Looking down from that lofty point, the sight was weird and memorable. Directly beneath me lay the casket in which the dead President lay at full length, far, far below; and, like black atoms moving over a sheet of gray paper, the slow-moving mourners, seen from a perpendicular above them, crept silently in two dark lines across the pavement of the rotunda, forming an ellipse around the coffin and joining as they advanced toward the eastern portal and disappeared."[78] This was "Castine's" last observation of a man whom he had loved and revered.

When the special funeral train started on its long circuitous journey toward Illinois on April 21, Mrs. Lincoln and her two sons were not aboard. They remained in the White House, President Johnson having use of the second-floor office only. Mrs. Lincoln was so distracted that she was unable to follow her husband's body, but Brooks announced that she would move to Chicago when she was able to travel. Robert later traveled to Springfield for the services there. As "Castine" talked with the widow, he became convinced that she was in dire financial circumstances, and he appealed to the public for aid to Mrs. Lincoln. Unknown to Brooks, she was already mentally unbalanced on the subject of money.[79] Lincoln had left a large estate for his widow and sons.

CHAPTER VIII

Naval Officer and Newspaper Editor

Naval Officer at San Francisco

With the death of Lincoln, Brooks's future became uncertain. The loss of the secretaryship, however, was not as great as his loss of a beloved friend and companion. As Brooks explained it, there was "no man outside of my own family circle [who] was ever so much to me."[1] As a token of Lincoln's esteem for him, Mrs. Lincoln presented "Castine" with one of the favorite canes which the President had carried during his night wanderings. It had been given to Lincoln by a naval officer and was fashioned out of an oaken timber which had been retrieved from a vessel sunk during the battle of Hampton Roads. "The ferule," as Brooks described the cane, "was an iron bolt from the rebel ram *Merrimac*, and another bolt from the *Monitor* furnished the head of the cane."[2]

Soon after Lincoln's death Brooks decided to write a character sketch of him for the *Congregationalist*, a religious magazine. "But the matter grew on my hands," he related, "being interwoven with other traits of his character, until I made up an article of twenty-five pages foolscap, which I now think I shall publish in Harper's Monthly. . . ."[3] His paper was finished by May 10, and nine days later Brooks announced that "my article on Mr. Lincoln will be out in the July number of Harper's Magazine." The July issue had already been made up, but the editor removed "a couple short papers" to make room for Brooks's contribution, which was his first major writing on Lincoln.[4]

With Lincoln dead and the Civil War ended, Washington held little interest for Brooks, who yearned to be back in California. "As early as the 1st of January 1865," Brooks revealed, "our late President . . . told me that it had been decided not to renew the commissions of the Naval Officer and Surveyor of the Port of San Francisco; that, as I was remaining away from California unwillingly, I had better take one or the other of these positions, unless I chose to remain at the Capital as his Private Secretary . . . ."[5] "At first, when it appeared doubtful if Nicolay could be induced to go abroad," Brooks explained, "I accepted from Mr. Lincoln the promise of a lucrative place in San Francisco, and had well-nigh concluded to go there when Nicolay concluded to go abroad."[6] The incumbent naval officer as well as the surveyor had proved unsatisfactory, and in October of 1864 an investigation had been "ordered into the affairs of the San Francisco Custom House."[7] William B. Farwell, the naval officer, made a special trip to Washington in February of 1865 in an attempt to save his "official bacon" but was unsuccessful.[8] As early as April 24, 1865, Senator John Conness of California determined to secure for Brooks the position in San Francisco which Lincoln promised him. "But," said Brooks, "I shall not make any application for myself, and unless Conness can compass the matter, I shall remain where I am, going away only during the hot weather."[9] On May 4 Senator Conness and Representative William Higby (also of California) recommended the appointment of Brooks as naval officer and Thomas B. Shannon, a former congressman, as surveyor of the port.[10] Two days later, President Johnson approved the nominees and sent their names to the Secretary of the Treasury since the offices were under his jurisdiction.[11]

With the support of Senator Conness, Brooks was hopeful of obtaining the appointment and thought that his chances were very good. If successful, he planned to sail for California on June 16.[12] While awaiting a decision, Conness, Higby, and Brooks joined a "little party of Californians, accompanied by a few ladies," and visited Mount Vernon during the first week of May. The War Department placed a steamer at their disposal, and the sightseers sailed to their destination, only to discover that the water was too shallow for them to reach the pier at the Washington estate. With Congressman Higby at the tiller, the other gentlemen rowed the ladies ashore in a small boat. As Brooks viewed the burial vault of George Washington, he was reminded of Lincoln. "Such men as these," he thought, "can never die, though the mortal part may perish." Then the group moved to the mansion where they inspected every nook and cranny before leaving.[13]

When Brooks returned to Washington there was no news from the Treasury Department, and he wondered if he would "secure the place which Mr. Lincoln offered me."[14] But there were news stories to write for the Sacramento *Union*, and Brooks noted the changes which had occurred in the military. "Grant has become a peaceful bureau officer," he observed, "and we can see him any day riding about the streets of Washington with his traditional cigar in his mouth, followed by no Staff, but with only one orderly riding at a respectful distance in the rear. Sheridan, the fiery, matchless Sheridan, short, well made, wiry and terrier-looking, has dismounted at last."[15]

On May 19 Brooks gleefully informed McPherson: "I have secured my California appointment . . . but, unless you object, I would like to have my name remain on the pay-roll [as clerk in the House of Representatives] until July 1st, and will, before leaving send you a formal resignation for that date. I do not enter upon my new office until July 20."[16] To another friend, Brooks explained that his appointment as naval officer was "a sort of legacy from Lincoln."[17] The position was a lucrative one, paying $4,500, and only one other office in the custom house at San Francisco paid a larger salary: the collectorship.[18] News of Brooks's appointment was not officially released to the newspapers until June 10.[19] James W. Simonton, a political enemy of Brooks, sneered at him and wrote: "In point of personal character this appointee has a decided advantage over most of those who owe their success to Senator Conness, if that can be called 'success' which takes a man out of an honorable and influential profession, and makes him the agent and instrument of an unscrupulous politician, who tolerates nothing less than slavish obedience in those who like official crumbs of favor from his table."[20]

Later in May, Brooks paid a visit to the United States Arsenal where the conspirators in Lincoln's murder were being tried in the penitentiary. "The trial," said Brooks, "from being a secret one, has come to be open, only a pass from the President of the Court, procured without difficulty by any loyal person, being required to obtain admission."[21]

There was another place that Brooks wished to visit before returning to California. "It has always been my intention to visit the Gettysburg battlefield," Brooks confessed, "and I shall not be satisfied to go back until I do. . . ."[22] However, his time was strictly limited since he expected to sail on June 16. And yet another event occurred which disrupted his schedule. "Having lately accepted the appointment of member from California on the Examining Board of Visitors for the Naval Academy," Brooks disclosed, "I am afraid that I shall not have time to visit Gettysburg. The examination lasts until the end of the first week in June, and my time for visits will be very short, if I go on the 16th" of June.[23]

The regulations of the Naval Academy state that the "Secretary of the Navy will, when expedient, annually invite a Board of Visitors, such as he may judge well qualified, to attend at the Academy during the June examination, for the purpose of witnessing the examination of the several classes, and of examining into the state of the police, discipline, and general management of the institution; the result of which examination they will report to the Secretary of the Navy."

For Brooks, the appointment to this naval examining board was a great honor. The other distinguished members were: Vice Admiral David D. Farragut, president; Rear Admiral David D. Porter; Captain John L. Worden; C. B. Boynton of Maryland; John C. Green of New York; J. M. Forbes of Massachusetts; Joseph T. Mills of Wisconsin; Horace Maynard of Tennessee; and J. N. A. Griswold of Rhode Island.[24]

The United States Naval Academy at this time was in Newport, Rhode Island, having been transferred there from Annapolis, Maryland, at the beginning of the Civil War. The upper class cadets were housed in a large hotel, "quite unfitted for the purposes for which it is used, but has been made to answer a temporary purpose," reported Brooks. There were 500 midshipmen at the Academy and the lower classmen were living aboard "four or five" ships which were anchored in the harbor. "The frigate Sabine is used as a practice-ship for apprentices," Brooks informed his readers. The frigate Constitution and sloop-of-war Santee were assigned to the midshipmen; the Macedonian, another sloop, was utilized for heavy gunnery practice, while the steamer Marblehead served for engineering studies. For short cruises the cadets sailed on the yacht America. One duty of the Board of Visitors consisted in selecting ten of the best apprentices from whom the Secretary of the Navy would choose several for appointment to the Academy. There were about 200 apprentices (from middle and lower class families) who sought midshipmen appointments, and when Brooks witnessed their examinations on June 8, he was favorably impressed. "The drill and practice in gunnery and seamanship of these boys was very good indeed," he reported.[25]

When the examinations at the Naval Academy were finished, Brooks determined to see the battlefield of Gettysburg, and he postponed his sailing date. On June 14 he explored the terrain and retold the story of the battle—which he termed the "American Waterloo"—for the benefit of his readers. To close his newsletter, Brooks quoted the portion of Lincoln's Gettysburg Address which implores the living to remain dedicated to the completion of the unfinished task of securing freedom.[26]

After Lincoln's assassination, Dr. Anson G. Henry admitted that "the great attraction for remaining" in Washington "has been taken away," yet he still wished to be appointed Commissioner of Indian Affairs.[27] However, Dr. Henry was not so fortunate as Brooks, since Johnson "was willing to carry out the intention of Lincoln, but left it to Secretary [of the Interior James] Harlan." That functionary," complained Brooks, "like the rest of the Washington officials, has no special desire to recognize any claims not rammed home upon him, so the Pacific coast has no representation in the administration here."[28] Henry had previously resigned from his post as Surveyor General of Washington Territory and was without a job. Johnson finally came to his rescue and named him Governor of Washington Territory,[29] but the office carried the meager salary of $1,500.[30] Dr. Henry was not completely disappointed, though, because he had few personal friends in Washington, D.C.[31]

Brooks wrote his last Washington newsletter on June 28, 1865, and together with Dr. Henry proceeded to New York for passage back to the Pacific Coast. They "passed a day or two"[32] in New York before sailing at noon on July 1 aboard the Atlantic Mail Steamship Company's *Ocean Queen*, a vessel of 3,000 tons.[33] Three days out of port and the passengers "assembled under the awning on the Hurricane-deck and organized in regular style" for a Fourth of July celebration. Dr. Henry was chosen president and "made a good little speech, chiefly referring to our late President." After a series of addresses by other passengers, Noah Brooks recited a poem which he had composed especially for the occasion. Singing and fireworks completed the festivities.[34]

The *Ocean Queen* on July 11 steamed into the port of Aspinwall where the passengers disembarked and traveled across the narrow neck of land on the Panama Railroad. At 5 P.M. they reached the Pacific and had "a short run on shore" since their ship did not sail for California until the following morning at 7 A.M. This steamer was owned by the Pacific Mail Steamship Company, and the travelers were "heartily glad to be domiciled, at last, in the splendid saloons" of the *Constitution*, a ship of 4,400 tons. The monotony of the trip was broken on July 17 when the ship stopped six hours at Acapulco to take coal aboard; most of the passengers went ashore to stretch their stiff legs.[35] After a voyage of thirteen days and six hours out of Panama, the *Constitution* docked at San Francisco on July 25. Brooks and Henry immediately engaged rooms at the Occidental Hotel, one of the finest in the city.[36]

The day after the arrival of Brooks and Shannon, one of the morning newspapers announced that the new officials of the Customs House would assume their duties immediately and reported that "the commercial public, after recent events, feel a sense of relief in the change, in the hope that the course of proceedings so destructive to general interests may be altered in new hands, and that in accordance with the spirit of the law, the interests of San Francisco commerce will be recognized as identical with those of the Government. Much is hoped for from the known character of the new appointees." "We presume, however," the editor continued, "that all the charges and difficulties met with during the past two or three years will be better understood when the judicial investigations are concluded."[37]

But Brooks and Shannon did not take possession of their offices on the twenty-sixth. The afternoon papers reported that the new appointees would not claim their offices until August 1. "Applicants for positions," the *Bulletin*, said, "will therefore have to hold on a few days longer. Whether the new officials design carrying out the 'rotation' system by a general removal of their subordinates is not yet known."[38]

"The office which I hold," Brooks related, "is purely administrative, being supervisory and controlling the financial business of the Custom House. The accounts of the Collector pass through the Naval Office, where they are examined, compared and checked each day, so that, with an efficient and honest Naval Officer no fraud by dishonest Collectors or Cashiers is possible."[39] The collector of the port was General John F. Miller,[40] and his records were scrutinized by Brooks in his offices on the third floor of the Custom House.[41]

Since Congress was not in session when Brooks was appointed, the President had issued him a temporary commission on July 26, 1865.[42] Brooks had left his bond and signed oath with the Treasury Department prior to his leaving Washington, and on July 27 Nathan Sargent, Commissioner of Customs, notified Brooks to assume his duties as Naval Officer.[43]

About 10 A.M. on July 28, as Dr. Henry's coach left the Occidental Hotel for the docks, Brooks bade him farewell. Henry was "glad to be so near his own home, and we talked cheerfully of the future," Brooks recalled. As the vehicle was crowded, Brooks did not ride with the Doctor to his ship, the *Brother Jonathan*, which was sailing that day for ports along the Pacific Coast. When they parted with a handshake, neither realized that their close association was finished.[44] At 2 P.M. on July 30 "the steamship Brother Jonathan struck a sunken rock, and sunk in less than an hour, with all on board, except sixteen persons, who escaped in a small boat, the only survivors of the ill-fated ship." Governor Henry and his bitter rival, Victor Smith, were among those drowned.[45]

Brooks moved out of the expensive Occidental Hotel shortly after his arrival in San Francisco and rented quarters in the Cosmopolitan Hotel on the southwest corner of Bush and Sansom Streets.[46] However, in the spring of 1866 he "became sick of hotel life" and with a friend rented "a furnished house" at 915 Sutter Street. Brooks said that it was a "snug little cottage on one of our sightly San Francisco hills" where they had a "man maid-of-all-work, a garden, dog, and all the surroundings of a real home."[47]

While Brooks was in California, he and Mrs. Lincoln continued their friendship by correspondence. At first he believed that she was in dire need. "President Lincoln," Brooks pleaded to his readers, "left his family in anything but easy circumstances, as he had but little more than a modest homestead when he was elected, and the great expenses of the White House have absorbed nearly all of his official salary, which has not been increased with the increased cost of living."[48] With this thought in mind, Brooks solicited money for Mary Lincoln's relief, and one unnamed gentleman sent the widow $400 in gold. Brooks also collected and forwarded $2,000 in gold to her in November in 1865.[49]

The Springfield (Massachusetts) *Republican* was one of the first newspapers to state that President Lincoln had left a large estate and that the funds being raised for Mrs. Lincoln's relief were unnecessary.[50] Nevertheless, Mrs. Lincoln's account of her financial difficulties was believed by the general public. Gradually, however, it became known that Mrs. Lincoln's mind was not rational when money or property was concerned. On December 14, 1865, old Thad Stevens stood up in the House of Representatives and stated that instead of the usual appropriation of $20,000 for White House refurnishing, $30,000 was needed since "the house is now, owing to circumstances which have occurred, almost totally unfurnished."[51] This was a veiled hint that Mrs. Lincoln had removed government property from the Executive Mansion when she left. Later the newspapers seized upon this bit of scandal. "The reports concerning Mrs. Lincoln's conduct at the White House I have noticed with great pain," Brooks declared, "more especially, as I have reason to believe they have foundation in fact. I know that Mrs. L[incoln] is disposed to absorb a good deal, to put a fine point on it; and, before I left Washington, I felt uneasy at indications which I observed. I have, also, always believed that she was disposed to give currency to understated reports concerning Mr. Lincoln's estate, for obvious reasons; and these things have pained me exceedingly when I have remembered how free, generous and child-like in his money matters Mr. Lincoln was, and, more especially, how scrupulously exact and honest he was in all his dealing with public, as well as private property. This matter has added only another regret to the thousands which I have had at the death of my beloved friend . . . ."[52]

But Brooks defended Mrs. Lincoln publicly and did everything which he could for her comfort. When the widow fancied that she needed money, she wrote to Brooks from Chicago on May 11, 1866, enclosing stock certificates which she thought might be sold in California. She had held the stock for some time; in July of 1865 she had contemplated sending the certificates to Brooks but then changed her mind. "I thought it best," she concluded, "not to send, for the present, those claims to Mr. Brooks. Some months later, perhaps, it would be better. Anything, *we do* is seized on. An especial way, of 'being cared for, by the American people.'" The name on the mining stock was "Frances T. Lincoln," which indicates that Mrs. Lincoln did not wish it known that she was a stockholder. One certificate, No. 81, was from the Indian Queen Mining Company of Virginia City, Nevada Territory, and was issued on November 3, 1864, for twenty shares, each valued at $500. Another certificate, No. 67, issued on the same date, was from the Empress Eugenie Gold and Silver Mining Company of Virginia City and represented twenty-five shares of capital stock, each worth $1,000. The third claim was drawn from the First National Petroleum Company, which purported to own land in Tulare County, California. The certificate, No. 178, was originally issued to Caleb Lyon[53] at San Francisco on April 13, 1865, and was for five hundred shares at five dollars each.[54]

"I may as well explain," Brooks said, "that the 'claims' referred to in Mrs. Lincoln's letter were certain shares of 'wildcat' stock, sent to her in her days of prosperity, and which the poor lady thought might be sold for a small sum."[55] Brooks was unable to find a buyer for the stock and dismissed the matter from his mind until late in 1867 when the editor of the *Territorial Enterprise* at Virginia City, Nevada, accused Mrs. Lincoln of unscrupulous practices. Brooks quickly sprang to her defense. "We are not aware," he replied, "that any White House lobbying was ever performed in consideration of these shares having been sent to Mrs. Lincoln, but do know that they have been lying in this city for a year or two . . . ." Without success he had sought for "some financier who could give any accurate information as to what particular portion of the land of sage-brush and wild-cats was the fortunate region where the 'Indian Queen' and 'Empress Eugenie' are located." As a parting shot, Brooks stated that he would turn "over to the lucky bidder at a very liberal discount from its per valuation" the mining claims which the Nevada editor thought were so valuable.[56] Brooks could not sell either the mining stock or the petroleum claims.

Since Brooks's temporary commission as naval officer had been issued by the President while Congress was in recess, Johnson formally nominated him to that position on December 29, 1865. This nomination was read to the Senate on January 29 1866, and was referred to the Committee on Commerce.[57] On February 13, 1866, this committee reported favorably upon Brooks's nomination, and he was confirmed by the Senate on February 15.[58] President Johnson then gave Brooks a permanent commission, dated February 15, 1866, which was to run for the term of four years.[59] On March 1 the Treasury Department notified Brooks that his appointment had been confirmed and requested him to send an official surety bond to Washington.[60] It was not until June 1, 1866, however, that Brooks acknowledged the receipt of his commission as naval officer.[61]

Just five days after his commission was issued, Brooks learned from telegraphic reports that there was talk in Washington of abolishing his office. "I am now comfortably settled," Brooks explained, "and though I had no special anxiety to take the place, as you well remember, I should dislike to be abolished, now that I am fixed." "I often wish that I were in the Reporter's Gallery again," he continued, "and if I am 'abolished' here, may turn up" in Washington again.[62] The office of naval officer was not abolished, but Brooks was removed before the year was out. On August 21, 1866, President Johnson appointed Thomas Gray naval officer,[63] but Brooks did not learn of his removal until August 24. The Radicals in Congress were opposed to Johnson's policies of reconstruction, and he in turn was removing those officials who supported the Radicals. "The President," a Washington correspondent wrote on the day that Brooks was removed, "is getting a very good edge on the official guillotine, and it begins to work better than formerly."[64]

Brooks's political stand for the Radicals seems to have been the cause for his removal. "I am what is known as a 'radical,'" explained Brooks, "in fact, we are all 'radicals' out here, if by that term is meant an adherence to the right, determination that equal and exact justice shall be done to all races, and denial to the rebels and rebellious States all political rights, forfeited by rebellion, until they have complied with conditions precedent. So, being a radical, I have been reported to headquarters, and off goes my head, my successor, a copper-johnson, being due here from Washington in a week or two. That is all right, and I go out of office with the proud consciousness that I might have kept, but was too manly to deny my manhood, and too fearless to hide my convictions of duty for the sake of place. Johnson has done his worst with me, but I have just begun with him; his edict remits me to my pen and to the public press, where I have never spoken with an uncertain sound; so I shall be writing editorials; if I live, long after A. Johnson shall have disappeared from the troubled sea of public life, like an exploded bubble."[65] The local press confirms Brooks's explanation of his removal. The San Francisco *Call* reported that Brooks was "looked upon as an opponent of the national administration,"[66] and the Marysville *Appeal* said that he was known to "sustain congressional policy."[67] Brooks himself had said in February of 1866 that his sympathies were with Congress "which appears to be exercising its legitimate prerogatives."[68]

There was yet another factor involved in Brooks's removal. J. W. Simonton, the editor of the San Francisco *Bulletin*, reported that "for the information of those who have not this personal knowledge to guide their opinion in the case, let me say that Mr. Brooks was not removed for any supposed adhesion to radicalism. Senator [Cornelius] Cole, doubtless, can testify to that, if evidence in the case is wanting . . . . It is no secret, however, that the new Senator [from California] has never approved of Mr. Brooks's appointment, that he has no confidence in his fitness for the position, and that he looked upon his nomination as discreditable to the Government. That he made representations at Washington against the late Naval officer is also well known, and Mr. Brooks's removal is doubtless the result of those representations; so the effort to excite Radical sympathy for the ejected must fail, so long as Mr. Cole is claimed to belong to the Radical camp." And Cole had worked for Brooks's removal. On August 6, 1866, Cole informed his wife that "Noah Brooks will *go out*, for his lying about me. Capt. Gray takes his place."[69]

Although belonging to the same political party, Senators Cole and Conness were opposed to each other.[70] Brooks had always supported Conness and had incurred the hatred of Simonton and Cole in April of 1865 by showing Simonton to be a liar. Simonton had stated that Caleb T. Fay was removed from the position of assessor of the first district of California because of the efforts of Conness, Higby, and Shannon. Brooks, having access to the records, published Simonton's letter to the Secretary of the Treasury which asked for Fay's removal.[71] Simonton and Cole were in the same political machine, and Simonton probably used his influence with the new senator for Brooks's removal. Brooks had no use for Cole either and remarked that his election as senator boded evil. "It is a great pity," wrote Brooks, "for Cole is not a man of any standing, except for honesty." Simonton later turned on Cole and published uncomplimentary articles about him, but Simonton quickly realized his error and begged for reconciliation. Cole, however, never forgave Simonton.[72]

After Brooks's death, yet another reason was given for his removal by Johnson. A correspondent in Los Angeles stated that Brooks's "sarcastic article about the inauguration of Johnson" was the cause of his removal.[73] It is true that Brooks had reported that Johnson was "in a state of manifest intoxication" at the time of his inauguration as vice president,[74] but other reporters told the same story and if this offended Johnson he certainly would not have appointed Brooks. "Castine" later changed his opinion of Johnson's behavior and wrote that "the lapse of March 4th is now understood to have been only a temporary and single departure of his. The disgrace will not be repeated." By way of explanation, Brooks reported that Preston King of New York had taken Andrew Johnson "under his wing immediately after his unfortunate inaugural in March, and has never left him since, day or night."[75] It is entirely possible that Brooks's political enemies called attention to his report of the inauguration, and that the "Castine" letter added fuel to the fire which consumed Brooks. However, it is known that Johnson was removing officials who were not complete supporters of his and replacing them with his own followers. During the recess of Congress in the summer of 1866, Johnson removed 199 men from important offices.[76]

Until Thomas Gray arrived in San Francisco on September 25, 1866, Brooks continued to perform the duties of naval officer. Johnson later submitted Gray's name to the Senate for confirmation on January 3, 1867, but on March 1 that body rejected Gray's nomination together with a long list of appointments which Johnson had made during the recess of the Senate.[77] The following day the President nominated Andrew J. Bryant for the position and he was confirmed the same day.[78] Bryant had previously been superintendent of the United States Mint at San Francisco, having been appointed at the same time as Brooks. On March 9, 1867, Bryant assumed the duties of naval officer, and the long struggles over this office ended.[79]

Returns to Journalism

The ex–naval officer returned to the field of journalism where he became known as a versatile writer and a prominent California editor.[80] "A large daily newspaper, radical Union in politics, with a capital of $150,000" was being organized, said Brooks, "when the news of my removal (Aug. 24) came out." The publishers were having difficulty finding a man to put in the editor's chair, but when Brooks's removal came "like a special providence," they appointed him managing editor.[81] The name of the new Republican organ was the San Francisco *Daily Times*. As early as July 12, 1866, both the *Alta California* and the *Bulletin* of San Francisco announced that a new daily newspaper was being organized; however, it was not until the latter part of October that the name was disclosed.[82] Even before its first issue, the policy of the *Daily Times* was disclosed by a paper which Brooks had formerly edited. "*The Times*," said the Marysville *Appeal*, "will assume and maintain a fearless stand on the side of the Union . . . . The Radical Union men hope to have in the *Times* an organ which will give forth no uncertain sound; doubtless the loyal community will not be disappointed."[83] The publisher of the new San Francisco daily newspaper was the Times Publishing Company, located at 336 Montgomery Street, but Brooks established his office at 521 Clay Street where he employed his nephew, Frank Upham, to aid him with the work.[84]

Before the *Times* was ready to begin publishing, Brooks returned to Marysville, California, to participate in the sixth annual program of the Northern District Fair. At 8 P.M. on September 6, 1866, the president of the association introduced Brooks, who then read an original poem of his to the crowd assembled at the Pavilion on the fair grounds.[85] The title of the composition was "The Transition," and it was later published by the Northern District Agricultural Society.[86] The style of the poem closely resembles Oliver Goldsmith's "The Deserted Village."

After weeks of planning, the *Times* issued its first number on November 5, 1866. It was a morning paper which went to press every day with the exception of Sunday; in addition, there was an evening edition for northern California and also a weekly edition. Under Brooks's supervision was an able staff of reporters and contributors who made the *Times* "a paper of high literary standing."[87] Among the correspondents was Petroleum V. Nasby, and in the editorial rooms were William Bausman and N. S. Treadwell, while O. B. Turrell served as foreman of the typesetters. The nominal editor-in-chief was James McClatchy, but Brooks managed the paper and served as chief editorial writer, with a salary of about fifty dollars a week.[88] One paper declared that his editorials were "dignified and decorous," but was of the opinion that the types were "a little flashy," though the flashiness probably would "wear off in the contemporary friction" to which they would be subjected.[89] The *Times* itself admitted that it would have a difficult time in San Francisco since there were eleven newspapers in the city.[90]

Within three weeks after the first issue of the *Times*, McClatchy disagreed with the owners of the newspaper and returned to the Sacramento *Daily Bee*, leaving Brooks in complete charge of the *Times*.[91] A few days after this, Brooks discovered that one of his typesetters possessed rare literary abilities. The foreman, O. B. Turrell, informed the Editor-in-Chief that "one of the compositors in his department had written several editorial articles, by way of experiment; and they were very good, so the foreman thought." Unfortunately, the printer had not saved his compositions, but the foreman promised that he would bring Brooks one of the articles which the typesetter had written. "A few hours later," Brooks recalled, "a bundle of sheets of Manila paper was laid on my desk by Mr. Turrell . . . who, with a smile, said that the young printer had happened to have ready an article which he was willing to submit to my judgment." "I read the paper," said Brooks, "at first with a preoccupied mind and in haste, and then with attentiveness and wonder. Considering the source from which it came, the article was to me remarkable." Its title was "The Strides of a Giant" and it described the expansion and development of Russia. After a thorough search of the current magazines, Brooks decided that the article was not plagiarized and published it on November 30, 1866, under the title of "The Two Giants," including in the title the United States, with which the author had also dealt.

It was not until Brooks had printed two or three other articles by the same typesetter that he learned the author's identity. His name was Henry George. When Brooks walked into the composing room one day to meet the promising writer, he found him to be "a little man, so short that he had provided himself with a bit of plank of which he stood at a case too tall for him. He was apparently then about twenty-five years old, but in fact was ten years older, as he was born in 1831. His auburn hair was thin, and the youthfulness of his face was disputed by the partial baldness of his head; his blue eyes were lambent with animation and a certain look of mirthfulness." As Brooks grew to know Henry George better, he found the typesetter to be "bright, alert, good-humored, and full of fun; yet his talk showed that he was a thinker, that he thought independently of all writers, and that he had wide, serious, and original views of life." Within a few weeks Brooks promoted George to the editorial staff when a vacancy occurred. "He was given a comfortable salary," Brooks reported, "and from that time forth he set type no more." As the genius of George became evident, the former typesetter advanced to number three man, ranking only behind Brooks and William Bausman. Advancement then came rapidly until the reading public excitedly talked of Henry George, read his famous book *Progress and Poverty*, and discussed his single-tax theory. In later years Brooks often saw Henry George in New York and was proud of the fact that he had started the philosopher and politician on his way to fame.[92]

But not all of Brooks's work on the *Times* was as pleasant as the discovery of Henry George. On the very day that the *Times* published its initial issue, November 5, 1866, one of Brooks's bitter enemies, James W. Simonton, assumed control of the New York Associated Press as general agent, replacing D. H. Craig.[93] The Associated Press held a strict monopoly on the telegraphic news service, and Simonton quickly stopped the news dispatches to the *Times*. Only three large papers in California had ready access to Eastern news: the *Alta California* and the *Bulletin* of San Francisco and the *Union* of Sacramento. Senator Conness had previously fought to break this monopoly in California but failed. In November of 1866 the Western Associated Press challenged the power of the New York Associated Press, and to make good their bid for independence, many of the prominent California editors proceeded to New York where they made a contract with the United States and European Telegraphic News Association. D. H. Craig, the former general agent of the New York Associated Press, became their agent.[94]

Among those editors who fought valiantly for independence was Noah Brooks. On March 4, 1867, he arrived in New York after "a long and boisterous passage" by water from San Francisco and by March 13 he had secured telegraphic service for the *Times*. "We had had a long and bitter controversy with our competitors in the field for the telegraphic dispatches," Brooks explained, "and have finally succeeded in 'laying them out,' my visit here having placed matters in a shape which will be permanent." "We are making a good newspaper, I think," he continued, "and it is a decided success."[95] The tight monopoly of a few large California newspapers—a monopoly which was so tight that members alone could print Eastern news on the day that it was received—was broken by Brooks for the San Francisco *Times*, and his victory allowed other small newspapers to develop and grow.[96]

His business finished, Brooks immediately decided to take a vacation. "Before my return to California," he announced, "I shall go to Chicago, and shall visit Dixon, my friends being ignorant of my arrival here as yet, I suppose." He had already spent one Sunday in Boston, chatting with his old friends, and he intended to spend several more weeks in New York before leaving the Midwest.[97] By April 1 Brooks was back in New York and staying at the Astor House, and within a week after his return from Chicago and Dixon he went to Washington, D.C., where he sought a contract for printing the laws of California.[98] The editor of the *Times* still had influential friends in the capital, but if he secured the contract he failed to mention it to George Witherle after returning from Washington. Brooks paid another visit to Boston and then made plans for sailing on April 11.[99] If he did sail on this date, he was aboard the *Henry Chauncey* when she steamed out of New York harbor bound for Panama, where she connected with the *Golden Age* for the last leg of the voyage to San Francisco.[100]

After gaining such a notable victory for the *Times*, Brooks "fell out with the president of the board of trustees of the paper, Mr. Annis Merrill," during the first part of June, 1867, and resigned, taking with him William Bausman, the assistant editor.[101] "The chairman of this board had personal ambitions," explained Brooks, "which did not harmonize with that political independence with which I conducted the paper."[102] With Brooks's resignation, Henry George became editor of the *Times*, but there were no ill feelings between Brooks and George. "We often talked together [in New York] about the old times in San Francisco," Brooks testified, "and many a hearty laugh we had over our amusing adventures in the editorial conduct of the 'Times.'"[103]

Within a few days after his resignation from the *Times*, Brooks became the managing editor of the San Francisco *Alta California*.[104] He probably assumed his duties on June 16 when the firm of Frederick MacCrellish & Company was formed; prior to this, four men were listed as having editorial control of the paper: Frederick MacCrellish, William A. Woodward, O. M. Clays, and

John McComb. The *Alta California*, a morning newspaper, was published at 529 California Street, and Brooks moved his residence from Sutter Street to 338 Montgomery Street.[105] The real power behind the *Alta California* was MacCrellish, who guided the editorials along the lines of the Republican party. He himself assumed the editorship of the paper in 1882.[106]

The *Alta California* was one of the oldest and most influential newspapers in California, having begun its career under the name of the *Californian* about 1848. On November 18, 1848, it combined with the *Star* and was known as the *Star and Californian*, but on January 4, 1849, the paper changed its name to the *Alta California* and appeared weekly until December when it became tri-weekly. On January 22, 1850, the *Alta California* became a daily and gained strength in 1856 by supporting the vigilance committees.[107]

To assist Brooks with the writing, there were "four or five different persons associated on the editorial staff" of the *Alta California*.[108] Among these journalists were M. G. Upton, Colonel John C. Cremony, William Bausman, and John McComb, the "foreman, local editor, and general factotum of the *Alta*."[109] Francis Bret Harte also contributed "occasional editorial articles" to the *Alta California*,[110] and introduced Brooks to an "eagle-eyed young man of tousled hair and slow speech" who called himself "Mark Twain."[111]

Samuel Langhorne Clemens, better known as Mark Twain, had been a correspondent of the *Alta California* prior to the editorship of Brooks. John McComb was a warm friend of Twain and had engaged him to write letters to the paper. With this contract, Twain sailed from San Francisco on December 15, 1866, bound for New York. He wrote newsletters on the way and continued to correspond after reaching New York. While traveling to St. Louis he noticed an advertisement of a Holy Land excursion to be made on the *Quaker City*. This notice stimulated Twain's traveling interest, and he immediately asked if the *Alta California* would furnish expense money in return for articles. Reservations for the trip had to be made by April 15, 1867, and Twain was without funds. McComb was convinced that the letters would stimulate the sale of the paper, and the ticket money, $1,250, was given to Twain at the New York office of the *Alta California* when he presented an updated note from John Murphy saying that the management had agreed to his proposed trip. The *Quaker City* sailed from New York on June 8, 1867, and returned after a long cruise on November 19, 1867. During this period, Twain wrote fifty-three letters to the *Alta California*.[112]

Mark Twain had agreed to write fifty letters "of a column and a half each, which would be about 2,000 words per letter, and the pay to be twenty dollars per letter."[113] "I am going on this trip for fun only," he confided to a friend. "I have to keep up my San Francisco correspondence, of course," he admitted, "and must write two letters a month for the New York Tribune (they pay best and that is what I work for) till we reach Egypt, and then I have to write of-tener."[114] As Twain's letters reached San Francisco they were edited by Brooks, who later stated that he had also been consulted about sending Twain on the *Quaker City* trip.[115] At that time he was the managing editor of the *Times*, not the *Alta California*, and he added that "it was McComb's influence, more than mine, that gave Clemens the job of writing the Quaker City letters."[116] However, when Mark Twain's first letter, written from the Azores on June 19, 1867, arrived at the office of the *Alta California*, Brooks was by then the editor, and he published it on August 25. This is confirmed by Twain himself who recalled that "Noah Brooks was editor of the *Alta* at that time, a man of sterling character and equipped with a right heart."[117] "It was my business to prepare one of these letters for the Sunday morning paper," Brooks explained, "taking the topmost letter from a goodly pile that was stacked in a pigeonhole of my desk. Clemens was an indefatigable correspondent, and his last letter was slipped in at the bottom of a tall stack." "It would not be quite accurate to say that Mark Twain's letters were the talk of the town," Brooks recalled, "but it was very rarely that readers of the paper did not come into the office on Mondays to confide to the editors their admiration of the writer, and their enjoyment of his weekly contributions. The California newspapers copied these letters, with unanimous approval and disregard of the copy-rights of author and publisher."[118]

After Twain returned to the United States he agreed to write a book for the American Publishing Company of Hartford, intending to use his *Quaker City* letters "to fill it out with." But in March of 1868 he learned that the *Alta California* had secured a copyright to the letters and "meant to publish my letters in book form in San Francisco." Twain immediately sailed for California to inquire into the matter.[119] The proprietors of the *Alta California* had learned "through the medium of the Associated Press," that Twain was preparing to publish his newsletters, and they "were wroth." The owners of the paper "regarded the letters as their private property," Brooks explained, and they immediately made "preparations to get out a cheap paper-covered edition of those contributions."

"Amicable counsels prevailed," Brooks reported, and "the cheap San Francisco edition of the book was abandoned."[120] With much relief, Twain wrote on May 5, 1868, that "the *Alta* has given me permission to use the printed letters. It is all right now."[121] With the aid of these letters, Twain wrote *The Innocents Abroad* in sixty days, and when it appeared in 1869 the preface stated: "In this volume I have used portions of letters which I wrote for the

Daily Alta California, of San Francisco, the proprietors of that journal having waived their rights and given me the necessary permission." But Twain
remained bitter about the incident, and in speaking of Noah Brooks, he
remarked that Brooks had been "quite eloquent in praises of the generosity
of the *Alta* people in giving to me without compensation a book which, as
history had afterward shown, was worth a fortune. After all the fuss, I did
not levy heavily upon the *Alta* letters."[122] It was probably during this mis-
understanding between Twain and the *Alta California* that Brooks, trying
to conciliate the two, experienced Twain's "powers of sarcasm and a relent-
less rancor in his contempt." Brooks later told William Dean Howells that
"he would rather have any one else in the world down on him than Mark
Twain."[123] However, there was no ill feeling between Twain and Brooks, and
in speaking of the book which caused him so much trouble, Brooks remarked
that "there is no parallel in any other language of the long-sustained and
gleaming humor of Mark Twain's 'Innocents Abroad.'"[124] And Twain continued to joke with Brooks while they were both in San Francisco. To gain
publicity for his lecture of July 2, 1868, Twain composed and published the
following letter:

> San Francisco, June 30th [1868].
>
> Mr. Mark Twain—Dear Sir,—Hearing that you are about to sail for New York
> in the P.M.S. Company's steamer of the 6th of July, to publish a book and
> learning with the deepest concern that you propose to read a chapter or two
> of that book in public before you go, we take this method of expressing our
> cordial desire that you will not. We beg and implore you do not. There is a
> limit to human endurance.
>
> We are your personal friends. We have your welfare at heart. We desire to
> see you prosper. And it us upon these accounts, and upon these only, that
> we urge you to desist from the new atrocity you contemplate.
>
> Yours truly,

Among the sixty "signers" Twain forged the name of Noah Brooks and
ended the list with "Various Benevolent Societies, Citizens on Foot and
Horseback, and 1,500 in the Steerage."[125]

The *Alta California* continued to grow and expand with Brooks as its editor. In 1869 it absorbed the San Francisco *Times*, and this move must have
pleasured Brooks, since he had once resigned as editor of this paper because
of difficulty with the owners.[126] An increased salary, no doubt, caused Brooks
to seek better living quarters, and he moved to 926 Jackson Street in 1868 or
1869. Here he remained until he left San Francisco.[127]

Work with Young People and Recreation

In addition to his editorship of the *Alta California*, Brooks conducted a "semi-monthly newspaper for young folks" and wrote articles for eastern journals. However, the name of the juvenile publication which he edited has not been discovered. It was in San Francisco that he developed his interest in writing children's stories, and his nephew, Frank Kidder Upham, testified that Brooks's "favorite field is that of fiction writing for young people."[128] As a member of the First Congregational Church[129] he took an active interest in helping boys and was proposed for membership in the Young Men's Christian Association on September 16, 1867. He became a member on October 21 and the following year (on August 3, 1868) was elected president of the Y.M.C.A. The genial editor was re-elected on August 2, 1869, and served until August 1, 1870. It was during his presidency that a building fund was raised, and Brooks supervised the campaign. The business of the Association was of great interest to him, and he was an active president, regular in his attendance.[130] For recreation and good fellowship, Brooks joined the Pacific Lodge No. 155 of the Independent Order of Odd Fellows in which organization he held the scarlet degree.[131] This was probably the extent of his club activities since the Bohemian Club, where Brooks visited in later years, was not formed until after he had left San Francisco, but the camaraderie there would have been to his liking.[132]

Assistant Editor of *Overland Monthly*

When the *Overland Monthly* was established in 1868, Brooks became more closely associated with Bret Harte, although he had known Harte since about 1862. A mutual friend, Thomas Starr King, had introduced the two young writers, and as King and Brooks entered Harte's little office in San Francisco, King remarked, "Now I want you to meet a young man who will be heard of far and wide some of these days." Harte at this time held the position of clerk in the surveyor general's office, although Brooks in recalling the event confused this position with his later appointment as clerk to the superintendent of the United States Branch Mint in San Francisco.[133] Brooks and Harte immediately became fast friends since they had many common experiences and interests: both were Eastern men who had drifted to California and achieved success in journalism after vainly pursuing various other occupations. Both had traveled through the mining regions of the beautiful but rugged Sierra Nevada, where they studied the resourceful sourdoughs and recorded their observations in delightful stories—Brooks in the San Francisco

Mirror and Harte in the *Overland Monthly*. In art they also had a common bond of friendship.

During the gubernatorial campaign of 1867, Brooks and Harte went to Sacramento where they witnessed the antics of a politician whom Harte later used as a prototype for his fictional character Colonel Culpepper Starbottle. This politician, related Brooks, "wore a tall silk hat and loosely fitting clothes, and he carried on his left arm by its crooked handle a stout walking stick. The Colonel was a dignified and benignant figure; in politics he was everybody's friend." On another occasion Harte and Brooks were walking down Montgomery Street when they were accosted by an old settler who had landed prior to California's admission to the Union. This argonaut addressed Harte in the hopes of receiving an invitation to a nearby saloon for a drink. "Harte entertained the most cordial contempt for this class of ne'er-do-wells whose only claim to social recognition was their early arrival," Brooks revealed. In the midst of the ensuring conversation, William C. Ralston, a prominent banker, passed and greeted Brooks and Harte. "Who was that sharp-faced galoot?" questioned the old pioneer. When informed who Ralston was, the argonaut replied, "Don't know him; I reckon he's one of the new fellers; came in fifty-one, p'raps?" Harte quickly caught "the seedy aristocrat's meaning" and asked with contempt, "Are you one of the d—d fools who were here when the water came up to Montgomery Street?" In earlier years, the bay had reached to the exact spot where Harte and Brooks then stood talking to the old-timer.[134]

In Brooks's company, Harte found encouragement and understanding. As editor of the *Alta California* Brooks received many exchange papers, and from these he clipped for Harte the notices of his work which appeared in the foreign and Eastern papers. Once, while Harte was reading these notices, he remarked: "These fellows see a heap of things in my stories that I never put there." The proximity of their offices made frequent visits possible since Harte's secluded writing den at the Mint was "but a few steps from the leading newspaper establishments." Harte would often open the door to Brooks's office "late in the afternoon, with a peculiar cloud on his face," and Brooks knew that Harte had come to go out to dinner with him. "It's no use, Brooks," Harte would confess. "Everything goes wrong; I cannot write a line. Let's have an early dinner at Martini's." After a pleasant chat with Brooks over a pleasing dinner, Harte would recover his equanimity, return to his desk, and work late into the night.[135] It was difficult to remain gloomy or uninspired with Brooks as a companion, because he was cheerful, full of fun, and optimistic. And, if he had a good story, he would give it to Harte for his use.[136]

During the early part of 1868, Anton Roman, a genial German bookseller in San Francisco, made plans to establish a monthly magazine which would supply the literary needs of the Pacific Coast. "By 1868," Roman recalled, "my book-selling and publishing had brought me a personal acquaintance with most of the contributors to the current literature of the Coast." Roman was convinced that there was abundant material for a publication which would rival the *Atlantic Monthly*, and San Francisco seemed to be the logical place for such a magazine because of its geographical location. The main problem was to obtain a suitable editor for the management of the new magazine, and one of the writers with whom Roman discussed his plans was Noah Brooks, then editor of the *Alta California*. Brooks had known Roman in California before he went to Washington, and during a trip to the front in July of 1863 they had met and together toured the Union army in Maryland.[137] The other writers who helped Roman form his plans were W. C. Bartlett of the San Francisco *Bulletin*, John and Theodore Hittell, John F. Swift, Benjamin P. Avery, Charles Warren Stoddard, George B. Merrill, Samuel Williams, and B. B. Redding. Many conferences were held until all the arrangements were carefully complete. Stoddard recommended that Bret Harte be named editor, but Roman was afraid that Harte, would put too much emphasis upon literary matters for the general reader. To balance the magazine, Roman suggested that Brooks and Bartlett become joint editors with Harte; however, these two newspaper editors pleaded that they did not have enough free time to assume so much responsibility. But after due deliberation, Brooks and Bartlett did agree to accept the position of assistant editors, much to the satisfaction of Roman.

"No name but Harte's was ever proposed for the editorial management of the new periodical," wrote Brooks. But Harte was not convinced that there was enough literary talent on the Pacific Coast to supply material for the magazine. Only after the little group of advisors had agreed to furnish articles for the first six months, did Harte consent to accept the editorship. He further stipulated that his control of the magazine was to be absolute, the articles were to be unsigned and he was to have an assistant to help him. After agreeing on Harte's terms, the publisher's main worry was to get the editor himself to write a story for "at least every other number."[138]

By the latter part of March the necessary arrangements were finished, and the *Overland Monthly* marched "steadily along to its fate, which will be in July—but what I know not," remarked Bret Harte.[139] Roman had secured enough advertisements to insure an income for the first year of $900 per month, and he himself guaranteed a monthly circulation of 3,000 copies. The grizzly bear, emblem of California, was adopted for the cover of the new periodical, but at one of the conferences somebody questioned the attitude of the bear who was pictured growling defiantly. Harte, in reply, picked up his pencil and sketched a railroad track under the bear's feet, explaining as he drew that the grizzly was disputing an onrushing locomotive which symbolized the coming expansion and growth of California. This figure became the vignette of the *Overland Monthly*.[140]

"There were not many writers of fiction in our ranks," Brooks reminisced, "and Harte and I confidently agreed that we would each write a short story for the first number of the new magazine." They had four months in which to prepare the stories, but when the *Overland Monthly* appeared in July of 1868, only Brooks's was there in print. Among the other contributions were Benjamin P. Avery's article on "Art Beginnings on the Pacific," and Mark Twain's sketch called "By Rail through France," which did not impress either the editor or his associates since it lacked the humor of his previous writings.[141] "Harte, with many sighs and groans, confessed that he had been unable to finish the first short story that he had ever undertaken in his life."[142] Editor Harte had "filed and polished his first story so long that it was not ready" for the press in time.[143] He had, however, composed a poem which he entitled "San Francisco from the Sea." Several reasons probably accounted for Harte's failure to complete his short story. In the months before the first number of the *Overland Monthly* went to press, Harte spent most of his time visiting away from San Francisco with Roman and his family.[144] These trips posed several problems for Harte who needed just the right conditions to write. "His writing materials, the light and heat, and even the adjustment of the furniture of the writing room, must be as he desired; otherwise," added Brooks, "he could not go on with his work."[145] It is doubtful if Harte found these ideal conditions while traveling the countryside. And he was not willing to submit a story for public view without polishing it to perfection. "The care for minute details, the painful elaboration of his work, and the frequent rewritings of his sentences, so characteristic of Bret Harte," explained Brooks, "gave to his finished product an exquisite fineness and polish that were all his own." The editor who succeeded him stated that Harte preferred violet ink, wrote in a legible uniform hand on unruled notepaper, was a slow composer and seldom left a page "without some erasures upon it." His sentences were laboriously chiseled, and there was a great waste of paper in the process.[146]

Brooks related an example of Harte's composition by way of explaining his fastidiousness. "Going into my own editorial room, early one forenoon," he wrote, "I found Harte at my desk, writing a little note to make an appointment with me to dine together later in the day. Seeing me, he started up with the remark that my early arrival at the office would obviate the necessity of his finish the note which he was writing, and which he tore up as he spoke." After Harte left the room, Brooks chanced to look into his wastebasket to discover "a litter of paper carrying Harte's familiar handwriting; and turning over the basket with quiet amusement" Brooks found "the rejected manuscript of no less than three summons, which any other man would have disposed of in something like this order: 'Dear Brooks: We will dine together at Louis Dingeon's at 6:30 P.M. to-night.'"[147]

An associate editor with Harte, Brooks soon discovered that his position was "more nominal than actual."[148] The other associate editor, W. C. Bartlett, related that Harte conferred with them, "but in the end followed his own counsel. All he wanted of his friends was good papers, and he would attend to all details."[149] And yet Harte complained to an Eastern publisher that he was unable to write sketches for him because all of the editorial work of the *Overland Monthly* fell entirely upon him.[150] Brooks did share the editorial labor with Harte by reviewing books, but the editor insisted upon writing all the material for the column called "Etc." "Harte and I wrote the notices of new books," Brooks recalled, "he writing by far the greater part; and we used to strive good-naturedly for the privilege of reviewing books that were destined to be 'scalped.' With the confidence of youth, it was easier for us to scalp a poor book than to do full justice to a worthy one." "As a book-scalper," Brooks admitted, "Harte greatly excelled. His satire was fine and keen."[151] There was one occasion when Brooks had to make a major decision in the absence of Harte and Roman, who were in Santa Cruz. It concerned Harte's story "The Luck of Roaring Camp" which he had failed to complete for the first number. When the manuscript reached Bacon & Company's press to be set in type, one of the proof-readers, Sarah B. Cooper, "declined to have any hand in the proof-reading or publication of a story in which one of the characters was a soiled dove, and another of the dramatis personae remarked: 'He rastled with my finger, the d—d little cuss!'" The matter was referred to Brooks who surprised the printer with "a burst of laughter." He, however, advised the printer to wait until Roman returned to San Francisco since Brooks knew that Roman would never consent to his editing of Harte's story. Upon the return of Harte and Roman the story went to press as written and both the "printing-office and vestal proof-reader survived the shock."[152] In speaking of this event in an interview, Harte gave an account which does not agree with either Brooks or Roman. According to Harte, he discussed the matter upon his return with Brooks, "an intimate friend of mine." Brooks, said Harte, "was not personally opposed to the story, but felt that that sort of thing might be injudicious and unfavorably affect immigration. I was without a sympathizer or a defender. Even Mr. Roman felt that it might imperil the prospects of the magazine."[153]

Rarely did Harte discuss his stories while they were in progress. "He never let the air in upon his story or his verses," reported Brooks. Once, however, he came to Brooks with a problem: "How long [would] a half sack of flour and six pounds of side-meat . . . last a given number of persons?" "This was," Harte confided, "the amount of provision he had allowed his outcasts of Poker Flat, and he wanted to know just how long the snow-bound scapegoats could live on that supply." Brooks helped him to figure out the answer, but evidently Harte found the result unsatisfactory for when "The Outcasts of Poker Flat" appeared in the *Overland Monthly* of January, 1869, no exact amounts of food were specified.[154] Brooks took a deep interest in Harte's work and later explained just what it was that made his stories the classics which they have become. "Bret Harte's humor," Brooks wrote by way of analysis, ". . . is nearly allied to the tenderest pathos. Harte, as an express messenger and rider, spent years in unconsciously collecting impressions and skeletons of stories, and when he began to weave these into fiction and verse, a world of readers was astonished and delighted. I may add that Harte was just as much astonished as anybody else. His humor is as distinctively American—racy of the soil . . . as any ever produced on the continent."[155]

Brooks also drew from his actual experiences for the stories which he wrote for the *Overland Monthly*. His tales were also full of local cover which he had gained from frequent trips and hiking expeditions in California. He possessed the knack of putting himself so thoroughly into the plot of the story and writing with so much realism that his accounts were taken by many readers to be true experiences. In all, Brooks contributed fifteen articles to the *Overland Monthly* for which he received an average payment of about thirty-two dollars.[156] His style and subject matter were so similar to Bret Harte's that Samuel Bowles, editor of the Springfield (Mass.) *Republican*, copied one of Brooks's stories and attributed it to Harte since the authors' names were withheld until the last issue of each volume.[157] This story was probably Brooks's first contribution to the *Overland Monthly*, a clever piece called "The Diamond Maker of Sacramento" which Bartlett said was one of the best stories Brooks ever wrote.[158] Brooks himself passed it off as "a trifling sketch founded on the actual experience of a California genius who actually did produce diamond dust by exploding carbonic acid under an enormous pressure."[159] The plot centers around a physician, whom Brooks calls "John Barnard,"[160] and involves his tireless research for an artificial method of producing diamonds. He finally forsakes his medical practice for endless chemical experiments. After many explosions, which sometimes wreck neighboring houses, the persistent doctor produces a diamond "about the size of a large pea." However, he never succeeds in repeating this feat, and as he lies dying, destitute and forsaken, he makes an attempt to reveal the secret to his wife, but after uttering "take of carbonic acid" his jaw falls, and the "cherished secret died with the baffled Diamond Maker of Sacramento."[161]

Brooks wrote nothing for the August issue, but the following month he contributed a clever story called "The Haunted Valley" which has its setting in the Sierra Nevada. An artist, George Wilder,[162] is wandering aimlessly in the pleasant heights sketching, hunting, fishing, and collecting botany specimens when he suddenly discovers one day a "colossal Shape" in a valley hidden behind a waterfall. Thenceforth, Wilder ceases to paint and searches for the mysterious phantom only to lose his life while crossing a bridge of snow in pursuit of the figure. "There was one wild cry," Brooks revealed, "a hand stretched out imploringly toward the wreath of mist that wrose slowly from the further brink, and no sign of life remained save far above where the truth-telling Indian Captain Dave looked down on cataract, rock and foaming stream, and then silently turned away to tell the tale that I have told to you."[163] As in many of Brooks's tales, the central figure, Wilder, has many of the characteristics of Brooks himself because he wove his own experiences into his stories.

Brooks wrote rather commonplace stories for October and November, but his contribution for the December number was outstanding. It is entitled "Lost in the Fog" and is a phantasy somewhat similar to Friedrich Gerstäcker's "Germelshausen" which was written in 1862. To earn his passage, Brooks purports to have shipped as an able seaman on a twenty-ton schooner, the *Lively Polly*, sailing from Bolinas Bay to San Francisco. Without warning, a fog drifts in and envelops the schooner and the captain gets drunk. After drifting aimlessly for two days, they reach a strange port which is flying the Mexican flag and is called San Ildefonso. The inhabitants have had no contact with the outside world for forty years and believe that Mexico still owns California. From bits of information gleaned from the towns people, the crew determine that the little place is south of San Francisco, and as soon as a fair tide comes they sail back there. Brooks relates that he later tried several times to rediscover the lost town, but could never find it.[164] This story proved to be very popular and gained widespread fame when it was reprinted by Charles Scribner's Sons in *Stories by American Authors*.[165] It was such a realistic sketch that it "was absorbed into the current history of the times, so that, years after, somebody writing a biographical sketch of the author, soberly said that he had been cast away in a fog, and had made some remarkable antiquarian discoveries."[166]

The *Overland Monthly* for January 1869 contained a piece by Brooks entitled "Our Brother from California" in which he tells the story as if he were one of the sisters of the principal character, Charlie Storrs.[167] Because jobs were scarce in Boston, Charlie had gone to California in 1849. Twenty years pass and the sisters learn that Charlie is returning. On Christmas Eve they are startled to find two men both looking like their brother Charlie. As it turns out, Charlie Storrs had played a trick on his sisters by bringing back with him Charlie Blake, his good friend who closely resembled him.[168]

The following month Brooks wrote a story which, in part, pokes fun at Darwin's *The Origin of the Species* and is entitled "Mr. Columbus Coriander's Gorilla." The plot is perhaps weaker than his best stories, but the ending is very clever. It involves the study of a gorilla in a menagerie for an article on the origin of man. The "animal," however, turns out to be one of Brooks's friends dressed up in a gorilla skin.[169]

After only eleven months of publication, Roman sold the *Overland Monthly* to John H. Carmany & Company who published it at 409 Washington Street. However, Carmany agreed to issue the magazine under Roman's name for another year.[170] According to Roman, ill health forced him out of the business, and he sold the monthly to Carmany for $7,500 and further agreed not to reenter the magazine field for a period of ten years.[171] Harte retained the editorship and demanded a salary of $200 a month with exclusive control of "its literary and critical conduct."[172] In addition to his salary, Harte was also to receive $100 for each story or poem which he wrote for the *Overland.* As Carmany later complained, he "spent thirty thousand dollars to make Bret Harte famous—that being the amount I lost on the management of the *Overland.*"[173]

Brooks continued to assist Harte with the magazine, and the July issue of 1869 carried one of his most fascinating tales of the Sierra Nevada region. A miner, Obed Murch, is tamping powder into a hole when his rock hammer sends a spark into the explosive. The resulting detonation blows the tamping iron—twenty-two inches long and one-half inch in diameter—completely through his head from chin to crown. Murch does not die and the local doctor performs a successful operation, but since the victim has little money, Dr. Peletiah Otis informs Murch that he will cancel the fee if Murch will agree that give him his skull after death. Murch consents to the terms but moves constantly from one mining community to another only to find that Dr. Otis is following him. Finally Murch dies, the doctor obtains his skull, replaces the iron rod, and ships it to an Eastern college where a night watchman later discovers a headless shape searching through the cabinets for its head. When

FIGURE 3. Noah Brooks in San Francisco, about 1870.
Author's collection.

the phantom finds the gruesome object, he holds it up and says, "Yes, you bet that's me!" The watchman had seen the ghost of "The Man with a Hole in His Head."[174]

But not all of Brooks's stories for the *Overland* were fiction. In December of 1869 he wrote a treatise on China's new position in the civilized world and charged her with using Oriental cunning instead of sincerity.[175] Nearly a year passed before he wrote a story for Harte, and again it was a true experience which he had witnessed in Washington during the Civil War. It deals with the life story of Princess Salm-Salm.[176] And even after Brooks left California he continued to send an occasional story to the *Overland.*

The *Overland* lost its prestige when Harte left San Francisco in 1871. As early as December of 1870 rumors were abroad that Harte was leaving for the East, but the *Alta California* denied these reports and declared that he would remain in San Francisco as editor of the *Overland.*[177] But Harte did leave California to join the staff of the *Atlantic Monthly.* According to Brooks, "Harte hated the materialism and ungracious atmosphere of San Francisco, and he could never be reconciled to the commercialism that pervaded every rank of society."[178] On February 1, 1871, the evening before Harte's departure, a group of his literary friends (including Brooks and Samuel Bowles) gave a farewell dinner to Harte in one of the private rooms of Louis Dingeon's restaurant. "For once," Brooks recalled, "we all 'talked shop' unreservedly, and with numberless personal allusions and illustrations that were interesting—to us at least." When the party finally broke up it was nearly 5 A.M. and the hour was rapidly approaching for Harte to board the Overland Express for his journey east.[179]

Sarah B. Cooper became the editor of the *Overland*, and she lamented the loss of Harte by asking if there could "be no perfect colors and no maturity with a perfect fruiting in authorship, without a touch of frost somewhere east of the Hudson River?"[180] And the magazine was doomed when Brooks also left San Francisco on May 10 that same year. He had been one of the guiding spirits of the *Overland* and "one of the most accomplished journalists that has ever been connected with the California press."[181] Harte and Brooks were the giants of the struggling magazine and without them it soon faded into obscurity.[182]

CHAPTER IX

Night Editor in New York

The New York *Tribune*

Although Brooks had a good position as managing editor of the *Alta California*, he wished to return to the East, where talented young writers were gathering. Accordingly, he wrote to Whitelaw Reid, who ran the New York *Tribune* for Horace Greeley, and inquired about a position. Reid, whom Brooks had known in Washington during the Civil War,[1] replied on January 15, 1871, that there was an editorship vacant, but quickly informed Brooks that the salary was not tempting since only a few of the senior editors received fifty dollars a week. Reid tried to discourage him, but Brooks was determined and on March 21 Reid finally offered him the position. The hours, as Reid explained, were from dinner to 2 A.M. and the work consisted of writing editorial comments upon the latest news. With Brooks's previous experience, Reid gave him the same salary as the older *Tribune* editors: $200 a month. After putting his affairs in order, Brooks left San Francisco by rail on May 10 and traveled back to Dixon, Illinois, where he visited with friends until the week of May 22, at which time he proceeded on to New York.[2] When he arrived, Greeley, the editor-in-chief of the *Tribune*, was visiting in the South,[3] but Reid was there to explain the policies of the paper to Brooks.

Just where Brooks lived during his first year in New York is not known, but within a year or two after his arrival his address was 59 West 9th Street, in the section known as Greenwich Village. By about 1874 he had moved closer to his work and was living at 30 West 23rd Street. His favorite eating place was the Brevoort House, located at 11 Fifth Avenue, where he frequently dined with General Hooker, who resided there.[4] This hotel specialized in French cuisine and was especially patronized by artists and journalists.[5]

The *Tribune* building, located on the corner of Nassau and Spruce Streets, was an old, dilapidated, five-story brick structure which had been built in 1845.[6] Here the editors and writers climbed the "steep stairs" each day to the "shabby room" on the third floor where their desks were located. This editorial room was "a long, narrow apartment, with desks for the principal editors along the sides, with shelves well-loaded with books and manuscripts, a great heap of exchange papers in the midst, and a file of the Tribune on a broad desk, slanting from the wall." Dust was everywhere. Greeley's "little snuggery" was nearby, and from this "ancient chamber" he supervised the paper when he was in town.[7] "There were not desks or chairs enough," related one of the editors, "and sometimes we had to wait in turn for them, standing until they became vacant." Isaac H. Bromley once asked Clarence Cook, the art critic, if he was finished with his desk. Upon hearing that he was, Bromley said, "Then scrape away all the blood and feathers and let me sit down."[8] Not only was there a scarcity of furniture, but the few pieces were in "a state of well-nigh hopeless decrepitude, and scarcely a chair [remained] with a full complement of its original legs, the place of the missing member or two being supplied often with a piece of board nailed to the side."[9] Brooks complained to the foreman about these deplorable conditions and asked for "a comfortable arm-chair." "The hard-worked night editor," he explained, "needs to take a rest at intervals, and there is nothing but an imposing stone or turtle for him to impose his bones upon."[10]

Most of the editors began their labors about 5 P.M., and by 7 "the business of the night" began in earnest. From then on there was a constant scurrying about of writers or typesetters until 2:30 A.M. when most of the editors finished their labors.[11] At 5 the morning edition emerged from the presses and went on sale in the streets. It was said in humor that the uniform of the night editors was "shirt-sleeves and moustache,"[12] and Brooks joined these men whose task it was to compose the many editorials which the *Tribune* published daily. He did not, however, contribute to the weekly edition, which was written by Greeley and one or two of his assistants.[13] Brooks's ability was quickly recognized, and he was given complete charge of "the editorial page during the night." "The position, on the whole," remarked Brooks, "is a pleasant one, though laborious and responsible."[14] Among newspaper men there was a "solemn tradition" that the senior night editor of the *Tribune* "always goes crazy,"[15] but there were several compensations for the responsibility involved: the hours were only from 9 P.M. until 2 A.M. and the salary was $65 a week.[16] If the compositors were happy when Greeley no longer composed so many of the editorials, their joy was short lived since Brooks's backhand scrawl was nearly as illegible as Greeley's pinched script.

Brooks was popular with the other editors, and the younger writers considered it a great privilege to sit and listen to his fascinating stories while they drank their midnight coffee. There were "coffee and cake saloons" all along Park Row where the journalists gathered to drink "coffee in earthenware cups as heavy as bombshells" and much "hot soda biscuits upon which you deposited pats of very yellow butter." During these half-hour rest periods "distinctions of rank were sunk" and everybody relaxed in an atmosphere which smelled of "old leather and old clothes." Now and then Mark Twain and Bret Harte would join Brooks's group, and the laughter would grow "so loud that the dingy, taciturn company at the other tables would look at us suspiciously, wondering how we could be so gay in a world that was so dark and joyless to them."[17]

Harte and Brooks renewed the intimate friendship which they had formerly shared in San Francisco. Before Brooks arrived, Harte learned of his plans and exclaimed with glee to Sam Bowles: "Brooks is coming to New York to live, and then he and I will found the Society of Escaped Californians." In New York Harte and Brooks frequently shared the same coach on their way to the heart of the city, and once, Brooks related, while they were "waiting on Broadway for a stage," Harte asked him for twenty-five cents. "I haven't money enough to pay my stage fare," explained Harte. Brooks quickly handed him a quarter since he knew that Harte was constantly in financial difficulties. "Two or three weeks later," Brooks continued, "when I had forgotten the incident, we stood in the same place waiting for the same stage, and Harte, putting a quarter of a dollar in my hand, said: 'I owe you a quarter and there it is. You hear men say that I never pay my debts, but (this with a chuckle) you can deny the slander.'" Harte incurred many debts in New York and he paid few of them.[18]

During the years that Brooks worked on the "Great Moral Organ," as Whitelaw Reid termed the *Tribune*,[19] it had "the most remarkable group of editorial writers which any American newspaper had seen."[20] Greeley had gradually drawn "to his paper some of the best writers and editors of the country, as well as valuable correspondents from abroad."[21] Even as notable as was the staff of the New York *World*, "it was not as strong or as solid as the staff" of the *Tribune*.[22] Probably the most remarkable feature of the *Tribune* was its founder and editor, Horace Greeley. He was a unique personality and, as Brooks described him, "was notable for his foibles, as well as for his commanding traits of character." "In some directions his judgment was immature, even childish," confided Brooks, "in other directions his sagacity was an inspiration of genius." A typographical error in his editorials "drove him into spasms; then his maledictions on the offending typesetter and proof-reader were something blood-curdling to hear." He also affected contempt for college men and "was accustomed to say, with great emphasis, 'Of all cattle, the most useless in a newspaper office is a college-bred man!'" But, as Brooks noted, "during my term of service on the *Tribune* a majority of the men on the staff were college-bred men."[23] Greeley was a "self-made man" who looked "with a kind of bland toleration upon the arts,"[24] and yet he hired editors who were themselves experts in these fields.

When Brooks joined the *Tribune*, the managing editor, Whitelaw Reid (1837–1912), actually controlled the paper more than Greeley. George Ripley maintained that Reid was "the ablest newspaper manager he ever saw."[25] Reid, a graduate of Miami University in Ohio, had joined the staff in 1868 and was frequently referred to as "Uncle Whitelaw;"[26] however, his bearing belied this appellation. As seen on Broadway, he appeared "dark, tall, straight, and handsome, but haughty in bearing; a man not likely to be mistaken for a trifler, irresolute and vague of purpose, or for a renegade to ambition. There was an air of puissance and of assured authority about him, and a glance revealed a martinet." But at times he exhibited great kindness.[27]

Another of the outstanding writers on the staff was John Hay (1838–1905), a graduate of Brown University. Reid had brought Hay to the paper in 1870, having known him in Washington during the Civil War. At that time, however, Hay disliked Reid because, as a reporter for the Cincinnati *Gazette*, he had been unfair to Lincoln. In fact, Hay tried to get Reid removed from the Western Associated Press in 1863.[28] But these previous differences were quickly forgotten, and of all the writers on the *Tribune*, Reid was closest to Hay.[29] Hay boasted that he wrote what he pleased,[30] and Mark Twain said that Hay was the only editor on staff who was not afraid of Greeley.[31] Everybody in the *Tribune* office was delighted by Hay's "wit and kindness."[32] Frequently, Bret Harte would drop into the office to exchange pleasantries with Hay, who always had a ready pun.[33] Whenever a celebrity died suddenly, Brooks generally wrote the obituary since he composed readily. On one such occasion, as Brooks was returning from the library with an armful of books "in a peculiar jog-trot gait that he adopted when in a hurry," he chanced to pass Hay's desk. Without pausing in his writing or looking up, Hay quipped, "as if merely thinking aloud: 'Books in the running Brooks.'"[34] As a result of his diplomatic service in Europe, Hay was a valuable editorial writer of foreign politics.

Oliver Johnson (1809–1889) owned stock in the *Tribune* and edited the weekly edition. In addition to his *Tribune* work, he edited *The Christian*

Union.[35] The literary editor was George Ripley (1802–1880) who had organized the Brook Farm movement. Ripley had been on the staff since 1849,
succeeding Margaret Fuller, and was a graduate of Harvard. In American
literature he was an expert. Every morning he came to his desk "fresh and
smiling; he chatted pleasantly with his assistants for a little while; but as soon
as he began work he worked in earnest, not with headlong haste but with a
steadiness that engrossed his whole mind for the time being." After Greeley's
death, Ripley was elected president of the Tribune Association and received
$75 a week.[36] John R.G. Hassard (1836–1888) served as music critic and later
wrote literary reviews.[37] He received his schooling at St. John's College in
Fordham, New York. Charles Taber Congdon (1821–1891) attended Brown
University three years before joining the *Tribune* in 1857 and was one of the
leading editorial writers on the paper. Another of the talented editors was
Isaac H. Bromley (1833–1898) who joined the *Tribune* "early in 1873." He was
a Yale graduate and wrote in many fields. His contemporaries remembered
him as never smiling while telling the "most amusing things, never laughed
at his own jokes, being in that respect like Mark Twain." Bromley left the
Tribune in 1883 to become the editor-in-chief of the New York *Commercial
Advertiser*, at which time one journal stated that "Mr. Bromley is an experienced and able journalist, and the public have reason to expect much of a
paper over which he presides."[38] Joseph Bucklin Bishop (1847–1928) started
as a reporter for Greeley in 1870 after graduating from Brown, but he quickly
advanced to the editorial staff.

In 1865 William Winter (1836–1917) became the dramatic editor after
graduating from Harvard.[39] In addition to his editorial work, Winter wrote
several biographies and books about the stage. The distinguished poet, Edmund Clarence Stedman (1833–1908), contributed poems and also occasional
editorials about the stock market where he earned his living as a member of
the Stock Exchange. Stedman, a Yale man, also wrote a series of travel letters
for the *Tribune* in 1872 entitled "Old Colony Letters."[40] In addition to these
well known men, there were other writers who were entitled editors of the
Tribune. These were: W. C. Wyckoff, Z. L. White, J. S. Pike, W. M. O'Dwyer,
C. S. Hunt, J. L. Hance, P. T. Quinn, William H. Trafton, E. E. Sterns, H. J.
Ramsdell, A. B. Crandell, D. Nicholson, H. H. St. Clair, and Clarkson Taber.

The *Tribune* also employed seven women as occasional editors or correspondents. Mrs. Ellen Louise Chandler Moulton (1835–1908) lived in Boston
and from 1870 until 1876 wrote a column entitled "Boston Literary Notes."
At her home, 28 Rutland Square, she held weekly receptions for writers,
artists and musicians. Her salon was the nucleus for culture in Boston for
half a century.[41] Kate Field (1838–1896) served as European dramatic corre-

spondent for the *Tribune* during her frequent travels in England and wrote a column called "Dramatic Straws."[42] She was better known as an actress, but her correspondence was also greatly prized by Greeley. One of the first women ever to write editorials for a metropolitan newspaper was Mrs. Lucia Isabella Gilbert Calhoun Runkle (1844–1923) who joined Greeley's staff in 1865. At first she wrote about "codery and fashions, and society doings, strictly feminine twaddle," but later she composed leading editorials on the slaughter houses of Paris and New York. From these Greeley launched his attack upon the deplorable conditions in the New York meat plants.[43] Mrs. Runkle also contributed to *Harper's Magazine* and served as associate editor with Charles Dudley Warner on the thirty-volume set of *Library of the World's Best Literature* which was published in New York from 1896 to 1898. In 1869 she married Cornelius A. Runkle, who was the legal counsel for the New York *Tribune* and had his office at 320 Broadway where he associated with the lively coterie of *Tribune* editors.[44] The Runkles lived at Berkeley Heights, New Jersey, and frequently Brooks was their guest on holidays and over weekends.[45] Brooks was Mr. Runkle's "most intimate friend," and when his daughter was born, she was named Bertha Brooks Runkle in honor of the *Tribune*'s night editor who became her godfather. She also called him Uncle Brooks although his friends often referred to him as "Brooksy."[46] Upon the death of Mr. Runkle, the widow sold the Berkeley Heights home in 1889 and moved into an apartment at 175 West 58th Street in New York where Brooks continued to visit both mother and daughter.[47] He was very proud of Bertha who became a celebrated writer at the age of twenty when she sold "The Helmet of Navarre," a romance of "sword-and-plume," to *The Century Magazine* in 1900.[48] She had studied her brother's assignments during his four years at Harvard and thus obtained a fine education.[49] The other women editors on the *Tribune* were Mrs. Rebecca Harding Davis (1831–1910), Mrs. G. H. S. Hull, Miss Nellie Hutchinson, and Mrs. Laura Lyman.[50]

The genial foreman of the *Tribune* office from 1844 until 1877 was Thomas Newberry Rooker (1815–1898) who started setting type for Greeley on April 10, 1841, when the first issue of the *Tribune* was printed. In 1868 he became the secretary of the Tribune Association, in which capacity he signed the pay checks of the entire staff and managed other business matters.[51]

Although the editors of the *Tribune* worked at a rapid pace, they found time to relax at a social functions, and in celebration of Horace Greeley's sixty-first birthday, this gay group of writers gathered at the home of Dr. Alvin J. Johnson at 323 West 57th Street on February 3, 1872. In addition to the staff, Mark Twain, Bret Harte, F. B. Carpenter, and Anna E. Dickinson were among those present.[52] It was probably at this party that Brooks renewed his acquaintance with Miss Dickinson, whom he had known in Washington during the Civil War. They evidently became quite fond of each other because they began corresponding, and Anna inquired of Mrs. Runkle about him. "He is so quiet and self-contained," replied Mrs. Runkle, "that you must know him well to understand him. But he is as pure and delicate as a woman, as generous as you are, and deeply and sweetly religious in the true sense . . . . He has a very great admiration for you . . . . He says that you are a revelation to him: a creature of new parts."[53] Brooks kept up a steady flow of letters to Anna, but she did not often attend the frequent parties at Mrs. Runkle's.[54] Instead she sometimes went to Long Branch, New Jersey, with John Hay and Whitelaw Reid, but since Brooks had to edit the *Tribune* while they were absent, he missed seeing her. Brooks complained that he was "cooped up in the office of the Great Moral Organ, doing work for three," while Anna, Hay and Reid were having a good time at Long Branch. "I am a sort of male Cindarella—a scrub," joked Brooks, "in the world's back kitchen."[55] And when Anna did visit the *Tribune* in November of 1872, Brooks was not there. He was greatly disappointed and asked her if she were "coming this way any more, ever."[56] Since Anna continued to lecture and travel around the country, they kept up a kittenish correspondence throughout the early 1870's, but nothing serious ever came of their friendship; Anna never married nor did Brooks remarry, although he frequently escorted Miss Jessie Bross who was the daughter of William Bross, at one time lieutenant governor of Illinois. Miss Bross, however, married Henry D. Lloyd of the Chicago *Tribune* on December 25, 1873.[57] It would seem that Brooks was determined to win recognition as a writer and did not wish to have family responsibilities.

As the hot summer of 1872 progressed, Brooks's thoughts strayed from his editorials to a vacation in his "ancestral Maine." "If I were not a salamander," complained Brooks, "I should not be alive to hint of the horrors of our night office, our slave-pen." On many occasions the temperature in the Tribune Building, even at night, was 99°. Sam Bowles of Springfield, Massachusetts, urged him to stop there for a few days, and during the last week of August Brooks left his desk for a two weeks' vacation at Castine. In the midst of his rest, a telegram from Whitelaw Reid sent him out to campaign in Maine for Horace Greeley, who was running for the nation's highest office. In opposition to Grant the Liberal Republicans had met in convention at Cincinnati and nominated Greeley in May. The Democrats, seeing a chance to split the power of the Republicans, also nominated Greeley in July at their convention in Baltimore. Brooks left his "dear old native place" and plunged into Greeley's campaign, which also took him to New Hampshire where he visited his old friend Charlie Wilder. Although this political activity curtailed his relaxation, Reid extended Brooks's vacation from fourteen to twenty-three days.[58]

Greeley was beaten by Grant at the polls on November 5, and the defeat hastened the editor's death which came on November 29. The editorial staff of the *Tribune* held a meeting on Sunday, December 1, and formed a committee to draft "suitable resolutions" and make the necessary arrangements for the funeral. Charles T. Congdon was chosen chairman on the motion of J. R. G. Hassard, and Noah Brooks was named secretary.[59]

With the death of Greeley, the stock of the *Tribune* was sold in 1873, most of it to Reid who increased the number of shares to 200. No other stockholder held more than twenty shares, which in 1883 were valued at $10,000 each.[60] After this change of ownership, Brooks wrote in January of 1873 that the Great Moral Organ "flourishes, Reid being regal in his splendors." "We get on admirably," he continued, "and make a capital paper *I* think. It would seem that so much talent and enterprise must pay. It will—I believe, though it is too soon to be sure of it now. We are to have a new building next summer and appearances generally are flattering and encouraging. Reid as Editor and Manager; the rest of the force is as before, mine being the laboring car."[61]

On the last day of July in 1873, Brooks announced that "the town is fearfully hot, dull and wearisome." He longed "for a taste of the briny," which in this case was the Isles of Shoals, and invited Anna to accompany him there. Mrs. Moulton, he assured Anna, had promised to go with them, but Anna was called to Pittsburgh and could not go. Brooks had recently written a flattering review of Mrs. Celia Thaxter's book, *Among the Isles of Shoals*,[62] and he wished to see this famous summer resort. The Isles of Shoals are about eight miles off the New Hampshire coast, and the Oceanic House, where Brooks stayed on Star Island, had just opened on July 8. Mrs. Thaxter's home, on Appledore Island, was "a center for the literati of the hotel."[63] Brooks left New York about August 23 and stopped for a day at Boston before continuing on to Star Island, which he found "just lovely." "It is a lotos-eating life one lands there," he related. At the Oceanic House the guests relaxed in their old clothes and received all the comforts and services of a metropolitan hotel. The only disappointment for Brooks was his visit to Mrs. Thaxter's. She acted like a "lioness" who looked his call as an impertinence and gave the impression of being a "superior genius."[64]

Brooks returned to his labors greatly refreshed, but as the snows came he complained that the *Tribune* "is unusually exacting this winter, and I go nowhere." He missed the gay parties at Mrs. Bullard's and Mrs. Runkle's, but in January of 1874 he found time to visit Hartford, Connecticut, where he spent a pleasant weekend with Charles Dudley Warner and his wife.[65] During the spring, however, Brooks became more dissatisfied with Reid. When Reid became the editor-in-chief, he offered his old position of managing editor to Edmund Clarence Stedman, who refused the offer because of ill health.[66] This may have rankled Brooks, who was in line for the promotion. His relationship with Reid did not improve, and some few days before the middle of June, 1874, Brooks quit the *Tribune*. Reid, he said, had become "so internally top-loftical that there is no living with him." "For a long time," explained Brooks, "I have borne this abuse and insolence, until I found that he mistook my patience and magnanimity for mean-spiritedness. He sought to impose on me in all sorts of brutal and ungentlemanly ways; so I concluded that I might as well leave peaceably." He gave Reid a week's notice and concluded that the editor-in-chief had the worst of it since he "lost a faithful and hardworking assistant by his foolishness, and hurt himself more than me."

The New York *Times* and Associated Activities

Brooks took a two-weeks' vacation, during which time he spent five days with the Warners in Hartford. Upon his return to New York, he immediately obtained a position as night editorial writer on the New York *Times*.[67] This post was similar to the one he had held on the *Tribune* except that the hours were shorter: he worked only three hours. This, Brooks said, was "such a respite that I continually fancy that I am loafing and must go to work by and by. My new place fits admirably; I write no politics and have a very easy time of it."[68] Later, however, he did write political editorials and also reviewed books.[69] Although Brooks served on the *Times* for ten years, little is known about his work there. The *Times*, located at 41 Park Row, was Republican in politics, but was conservative and did not campaign for radical social changes as did the *Tribune* under Greeley. The editors of the *Times* were competent writers, but the staff was not nearly as outstanding as that of the *Tribune*. The managing editor of the *Times* from 1872 until 1889 was John C. Reid; the editor-in-chief when Brooks joined the staff was Louis J. Jennings, but in 1876 John Foord succeeded Jennings and served until 1883.[70] The founder of the *Times*, Henry J. Raymond, had once worked for Greeley on the *Tribune*, but on September 18, 1851, Raymond printed the first issue of the *Times* in a basement at 113 Nassau Street.[71] There was great editorial strife between the *Times* and *Tribune*, and the latter once stated that the livelihood of the *Times* was merely publishing lies about the *Tribune*.[72] To gain circulation, the *Times* in 1883 slashed its price from four cents to two, and the *Tribune* was forced to lower its price from four to three cents.[73] Gradually the *Times* fought its way to the position of eminence which it holds today.

Brooks continued to live at 30 West 23rd Street until about 1876 when he moved to 180 Fifth Avenue. Then about a year later he rented a suite of rooms in the Lotos Club at 147 Fifth Avenue. He could ill afford such accommodations and at times was forced to borrow money to pay his bills[74] since he had saved little money while on the *Tribune* and probably lost most of his savings by speculating in the stock market on Pacific Mail. When this stock suddenly dropped in 1872, Brooks lamented, "I am ruined in the fall."[75] In 1882 he moved to The Cumberland at Fifth Avenue and 22nd Street in order to have accommodations for two relatives who moved in with him. It was "an apartment house for bachelors," and Brooks's rooms were on the ninth floor where the view of the city was superb. "From my window," he commented, "I can see the East River, Long Island, and glimpses of the Sound." The building was fireproof and had an elevator which ran all night—a great convenience for a night editor. The relatives moved to Newburyport, Massachusetts, in May of 1882, but Brooks probably remained at The Cumberland until he left New York in 1884, although he spent much of his time in the Lotos Club and received his mail there.[76] His calling card gave the Lotos Club as his address and bore his personal monogram, which consisted of the letter "N" intertwined with a honeybee, thus giving his initials: N. B.[77]

Shortly after Brooks assumed his new post on the *Times*, he gave Sam Bowles a dinner party at the Lotos Club on July 10, 1874; the other guests were Mr. and Mrs. Alfred Wilkinson, Mary Mapes Dodge, and Louisa May Alcott.[78] Bowles, who was visiting in New York, again dined with Brooks at the Lotos Club two days later.[79] Their friendship was of long standing, and they enjoyed each other's company until July 25 when Bowles sailed on the *Batavia* for a two-month tour of Europe with a Springfield friend, Chester William Chapin, who was president of the Boston & Albany Railroad.[80] At times, Brooks's social engagements kept him so busy at night that he was forced to do much of his editorial writing during the day.[81] He was greatly interested in both the opera and theatre. A stellar performance always sent him scurrying to the box office for tickets. When the great actress Charlotte Cushman gave her farewell performance at Booth's Theatre in New York on November 7, 1874, Brooks invited Anna Dickinson to accompany him, but she did not return to New York as expected, and Brooks was forced to go with a group of friends.[82] Likewise, when Kate Field, one of his personal friends of the *Tribune* days, made her debut a week later as Peg Woffington in the play "Masks and Face," Brooks joined the crowd of "men and women of the first rank in literature, art, and society" who thronged to Booth's Theatre and crowded the galleries as well as the main floor to see her brilliant performance.[83] Brooks had many friends among the actors and actresses of the stage, and he was a welcome guest at their parties and clubs. When a farewell breakfast was given to Edwin Booth on June 15, 1880, at Delmonico's prior to his departure for Europe, Brooks was among the invited guests who included

Lester Wallack, Lawrence Barrett, Joseph Jefferson, P. T. Barnum, and many others.[84] As an artist and a patron of the fine arts, Brooks also gave freely of his time for the promotion of painting. When the Society of Decorative Art sponsored a series of six lectures on art at Association Hall, running from October 29 to December 3, 1878, Brooks served on the lecture committee to procure speakers. This group was attempting to raise funds and stimulate interest in their loan exhibition of about 100 paintings which were displayed in the picture gallery of the National Academy Building. The opening lecture by Charles Dudley Warner on Egyptian art was well attended.[85]

During the summer of 1875, the streetcar companies of New York City introduced "a little musical instrument known as the bell-punch" in order to insure the full payment of fares. This little gadget was worn around the neck of the conductor who punched each ticket with it and thus registered the fares as they were paid.[86] "In the dusk of a summer evening," soon after the introduction of the bell-punch, Isaac H. Bromley of the *Tribune* and Brooks, then with the *Times*, were riding to work on car No. 101 of the Fourth Avenue line when Bromley noticed a new sign in the car which read:

> The conductor, when he recieves [sic] a fare, will immediately punch in the presence of the passenger,
>> A blue trip slip for an 8 cent fare,
>> A buff trip slip for a 6 cent fare,
>> A pink trip slip for a 3 cent fare.

Brooks was dozing, but Bromley's "attention was riveted to the notice." He read it again and again until suddenly he shouted, "It's poetry, by George! Brooks, it's poetry." Brooks, who was startled by the sudden outburst in the quiet car which carried no other passengers, sat up and hastily asked, "What's poetry? What are you talking about?" In reply, Bromley read the notice, leaving out the word "immediately." After mumbling the words over "in a sleepy way," Brooks remarked, "That's so." He tried to doze off again, but the words kept his attention focused on the sign. Both Bromley and Brooks kept repeating the little jingle until they reached Printing House Square. The following night they again boarded the same car; after a while Brooks became inspired and "burst forth with the additional line" which completed the poem: "All in the presence of the passenjare." Music was finally composed for the poetry, and the little song was introduced by Bromley in the editorial rooms of the *Tribune* where W. C. Wyckoff, the scientific editor, and Moses P. Handy made a few changes and added a chorus which began "Punch, boys, punch; punch with care." The night editors frequently sang the little ditty to pass away the weary hours, but "it was not intended to give the poem to the public."[87] On the night of September 27, 1875, however, one of the editors of the *Semi-Weekly Tribune* wrote down the words in shorthand as they were sung, and the following day he published the poem for all to read.

HORSE-CAR POETRY

The conductor when he receives a fare,
Must punch in the presence of the passenjare,
    A blue trip slip for an 8 cent fare,
    A buff trip slip for a 6 cent fare,
    A pink trip slip for a 3 cent fare,
All in the presence of the passenjare.

Chorus.
Punch, boys, punch; punch with care.
    A blue trip slip for an 8 cent fare,
    A buff trip slip for a 6 cent fare,
    A pink trip slip for a 3 cent fare,
Punch in the presence of the passenjare.[88]

Although the poem appeared on page 6 with no word of explanation, it was immediately picked up and copied by other newspapers from coast to coast; the verses took the country by storm. To protect their brain child, the originators published the words and music which they copyrighted under the title "Song of the Horse-Car Conductor,"[89] but the authors remained anonymous. Mark Twain read the little piece in a newspaper and was fascinated by it. By January 10, 1876, he had completed an amusing article about the "Horse-Car Poetry"[90] which he published in the *Atlantic Monthly* of February under the title "A Literary Nightmare." "I came across these jingling rhymes in a newspaper, a little while ago, and read them a couple of times," explained Twain. "They took instant and entire possession of me," he added. He then proceeded to tell how the poem kept running through his mind until he was unable to write or talk intelligently without repeating the harassing lines.[91] Twain's article drew more attention to the already famous poem, and in later years this jingle was credited to him in spite of Bromley's story about its origin which appeared in *Scribner's Monthly* for April, 1876.[92] Brooks frequently related to friends or fellow club members how Bromley and he had discovered the sign in the horse-car which led to the famous poem.[93] The upshot of the satirical verses was the rapid abandonment by the streetcar companies of the bell-punch system which was so obnoxious to conductors, drivers, "car-starters," and passengers.[94]

By the end of 1875 the Remingtons at Ilion, New York, were manufacturing in quantity a new device which was termed the "Typewriter."[95] It was a clever machine and greatly facilitated the preparation of manuscripts, but few of the noted authors, with the exception of Mark Twain, who purchased a machine in 1874, learned to operate the typewriter. Even in the late 1890's there was only a small number of journalists who used the machine in their work.[96] Brooks, however, was composing his personal letters on a typewriter as early as April of 1879.[97] He evidently purchased his own machine which he kept at his quarters in the Lotos Club.[98] It was not until ten years later, however, that Brooks received nation-wide recognition for his skill with the typewriter. In March of 1889, while Brooks was in Washington attending the inauguration of Benjamin Harrison, a reporter from the New York *World*, Edward S. Van Zile, fell to talking with Brooks and learned that he composed on a typewriter. This interview was published in the *World* of March 7, 1889:

> Noah Brooks and William D. Howells are among the few well-known writers who have learned to manipulate the typewriting machine. Mr. Brooks, who has been used to dictating his literary productions to a stenographer, now sits down to his typewriter and plays on the keys as he composes. He finds this process saves a good deal of time.

Many other papers copied this story and Brooks finally exclaimed that he was tired of reading about it in the press.[99] Brooks, whose handwriting was almost illegible, began to use the typewriter as a matter of convenience, but Howells adopted the machine because "an injury to his wrist made it difficult for him to write with a pen," and for this reason he sometimes felt it necessary "to offer a timid apology for the presence of the writing machine" in his study.[100]

On July 7, 1880, before Brooks left New York City for his summer vacation, he was called upon to attend the funeral of George Ripley, his former colleague on the *Tribune* staff. Prominent members of the literary world served as pallbearers, including Edmund Clarence Stedman, Whitelaw Reid, and Professors Vincenzo Botta and Edward L. Youmans.[101] A few weeks after this, Brooks journeyed north for a pleasant rest at Bar Harbor, Maine, after which he returned to his labors on August 29, but the *Times* editors always managed to find time for fun and frolic, and they took Mr. and Mrs. Laurence Hutton on an all-day water excursion to Sea Cliff and Glen Island on September 7. On such occasions, the editors invited prominent writers, such as William Winter, to join them on their outings.[102]

The Critic Established

American scholars had long felt the need for a magazine which reviewed literature, fine arts, music, and drama, and this need was fulfilled by the appearance of *The Critic* in New York on January 15, 1881. Among the prominent writers who helped to organize this magazine was Brooks, who also contributed heavily to it, but his articles are unsigned.[103] Charles E. Merrill purchased the major portion of the stock in the Critic Publishing Company, and the new magazine was edited by Jeanette L.[104] and Joseph B. Gilder, a sister and brother of the noted editor of the *Century Magazine*, Richard Watson Gilder, who thought that their establishing of the magazine was "a wild thing to do," but admitted that they had "lots of encouragement."[105] The editors of *The Critic* were described as "two strong, unassuming people, full of humane feeling and art feeling, upright in both."[106]

In the beginning, *The Critic* was issued every two weeks, contained fourteen pages, and sold for ten cents, but on January 13, 1883, it became a weekly, "the first purely critical weekly" to secure a permanent footing in New York.[107] With an increasing circulation, *The Critic* absorbed a competitor on January 5, 1884, and became *The Critic and Good Literature*; however, it reverted to its original title on January 3, 1885, and in 1893 J. L. and J.B Gilder purchased the controlling interest in the Critic Publishing Company from Merrill and published the magazine themselves.[108] But as competition grew, *The Critic* was forced to become a monthly magazine in August of 1898. From its frequent moves of one location to another, it would seem that publishing costs were causing the owners to seek lower rents in an effort to survive, and in 1901 the magazine collapsed. By this time there were too many literary journals for them all to flourish, but *The Critic* had been a pioneer in its field and had stimulated an interest in American culture. At the suggestion of one of its readers, *The Critic* had conducted a poll in 1884 to determine which American authors corresponded to the "Forty Immortals" of the French Academy. Although Brooks did not win a place among the first forty, he received many votes and was listed among America's favorite writers.[109]

A Tour of the West

When the Northern Pacific Railroad completed its transcontinental line in 1883, Brooks was invited by Henry Villard to go on the special excursion which was planned by way of celebration. Villard, who became president of the Northern Pacific in 1881, had probably known Brooks in Washington since he too had served as a correspondent during the Civil War.[110] The first spike of the Northern Pacific road had been driven at Kalama, Washington, on May 18, 1871,[111] and twelve years later, in the month of May, plans were being formulated for a spectacular tour of the new line. By May 3 Brooks had received his invitation for the "grand excursion to San Francisco and Oregon." The trip, Brooks was informed, would last five or six weeks, and he had some doubt if the *Times* would allow him to remain away from his desk for that length of time. "But I shall go if I can," Brooks concluded, although it meant that he would have to forego his annual summer vacation in Castine.[112] The editor-in-chief of the *Times* consented, however, and Brooks informed Villard on July 19 that he accepted "with pleasure the invitation to join the opening excursion over the road, to start from New York during the latter part of August."[113]

The German guests, whom Villard had invited from Europe, left New York aboard the first section of the excursion train on August 28.[114] The following day a second section of the train pulled out of Grand Central Station, carrying writers, reporters, and other dignitaries. With this group was Noah Brooks, who was acting as the official representative of the New York *Times*.[115] On August 31 "the American portion of Villard's guests" reached Chicago where they were feted in high style at special banquets and taken on tours of the Board of Trade, the Pullman factories, and the stockyards before leaving Chicago on September 1. The following day a third section, comprising the "Chicago and Northwestern division of the Villard party," was made up and left Chicago bound for St. Paul.[116]

At 9:35 A.M. on September 3 the correspondents' train arrived at St. Paul where the reporters were taken on a tour of the city. Ten carriages were required to accommodate the gentlemen of the press when they left St. Paul at 12:30 A.M. for Minneapolis where the citizens eagerly awaited the distinguished members of Villard's party: President Chester A. Arthur, Generals U. S. Grant and Philip H. Sheridan, and Secretary of War Robert Todd Lincoln.[117] That evening the city council of St. Paul tendered a banquet to Villard's guests at Hotel Lafayette on Lake Minnetonka for which occasion the journalists "selected Noah Brooks . . . to respond to the toast, 'The Press.'"[118] However, when this toast was offered, Carl Schurz jumped up and responded instead.[119] Schurz, as editor of the New York *Evening Post* which was subsidized by Villard, had enough influence to ignore the democratic choice of the journalists and speak himself.

When the excursion train left the Twin Cities, another section was added, making four altogether. The German guests were in the first, the English in the second, the press in the third, and the Americans in the fourth. Each section was composed of ten cars which included two diners where the best food and wines were served to the more than 300 passengers who were aboard the four sections. The luxurious service was such that the cost to the Northern Pacific amounted to $500 per guest.[120]

At Fargo, Dakota Territory, General Grant spoke briefly on September 4, and the following day the excursionists reached Bismarck where Villard laid the cornerstone of the new capitol building and climaxed the event by introducing Sitting Bull to the assembled crowd.[121] On September 6 the trains crossed the Missouri River and stopped to give the travelers a short horseback ride to the "Bad Lands."[122] At this stop, Edward P. Mitchell, later the editor-in-chief of the New York *Sun*, walked several miles out into the prairie with Brooks and General H. V. Boynton to observe the quiet countryside.[123] Two days later, on the eighth, the last spike was driven in the new line at a point near Garrison, Montana.[124] With the formal dedication over, the trains continued west to Portland, Oregon, where the tired passengers arrived during the night of September 11.[125] Brooks had witnessed the great opening of the Pacific Northwest to Eastern trade, and on September 17 a freight train, loaded with canned corn, steamed out of Portland, Maine, bound for Portland, Oregon—the first through freight shipment to run over the new road.[126] It is not certain when Brooks returned from the West, but Villard was back in New York on September 26;[127] it is possible that Brooks visited San Francisco, as he had earlier planned, before returning to his night labors on the *Times*.

A Joke on Mark Twain

Some days prior to April 1, 1884, the author George W. Cable conceived a plan for playing an April-fool joke on Mark Twain. While visiting with the Twains, Cable had discovered Mark's aversion to autograph seekers, and determined to play a prank on him. Cable printed the following circular and sent it to 150 of Twain's literary friends:

Private and Confidential

My Dear Mr. _____

It has been agreed among some friends of Mr. S. L. Clemens that all his friends, as far as they will, write to him on receipt of this circular (mailing on such dates as to allow all the letters to reach him simultaneously on the First of April), asking for his autograph.

The consent to co-operate has already been obtained from a number of sufficient to make it certain that the matter will take the character intended for it, and this circular is now mailed to 150 persons for the literary and journalistic guild, in Boston, Hartford, Springfield, New York, Brooklyn, Washington and other cities, each of whom—with yourself—is requested to invite others, ladies or gentlemen, to take part.

It is suggested that no stamps or card or envelope be inclosed with the request; that no stranger to Mr. Clemens and no minor take part.

Yours truly,
Geo. W. Cable.[128]

On Tuesday, April 1, Twain's mail was "swollen to abnormal proportions, and the Hartford postmen were obliged to call in assistance in delivering" the many requests for his autograph.[129] About 200 writers, actors, and notables participated in this joke on Twain and when questioned about "the deluge of applications," he merely remarked that the gesture was but "the outburst of affection of a generous public." Many of the autograph seekers were extremely witty and complimented Twain on books or articles not written by him, such as "The Bread Winners" and "Little Breeches," while others purposely misspelled his name.[130] Among Twain's many personal friends who besieged him for autographs was Brooks, who wrote the following letter:

The Lotos Club
147 Fifth Avenue
March 31, 1884

My dear Mark:

I don't like to trouble an old friend, especially one who is so considerate of the feelings of others as you are, but if you will send me ten or twelve (10 or 12), of your autographs, you will save me a world of bother. I am constantly harassed by applications for the autographs of distinguished people, and I hate to be obliged to deny the applicants. If you will send me the number herein specified, I can satisfy a moderate demand.

Yours faithfully,
Noah Brooks.

Brooks addressed the envelope "Sam'l L. Clemens, Esp Hartford, Conn." and it was duly received at Hartford where the postmaster stamped its arrival as April 1.[131] Evidently, Brooks kept his letter in a serious vein in order to fool Mark Twain more completely, since a comic letter would have indicated immediately that a great hoax was being enacted.

The American Copyright League

American authors had long expressed a great dissatisfaction with the copyright laws since their works were being pirated by foreign publishers without payments or royalties. Foreign writers also had their works published in this country without compensation. The solution was an international copyright law, and the American Copyright League was organized by Edward Eggleston, Richard Watson Gilder, and George Parsons Lathrop in 1883 "to urge a reform of American copyright law" and abolish "all discriminations between the American and the foreign author." The movement was organized in New York, but there were corresponding members located in other cities. The executive committee, which was established during the first month of 1884, consisted of John Bigelow, Hjalmar Hjorth Boyesen, Noah Brooks, Robert Collyer, Howard Crosby, Edward Eggleston, Sydney Howard Gay, Richard Watson Gilder, Parke Godwin, George Walton Green, Laurence Hutton, Brander Matthews, H. C. Potter, Allan Thorndike Rice, Edmund Clarence Stedman, Richard Henry Stoddard, Bayard Tuckerman, Charles Dudley Warner, and E. L. Youmans. George Parsons Lathrop served as secretary for the 150 members who established their headquarters at 80 Washington Square.[132]

To raise the necessary funds for their operating expenses, the American Copyright League sponsored a series of authors' readings in the spring of 1885. The first performance was given on April 28 at the Madison Square Theatre where every seat in the house was sold. At 3:30 P.M. George William Curtis, who acted as chairman opened the program by speaking briefly "of the property-right of the author in the work of his hand and brain, and said that the question in what way best to secure the rights of authors—which was the object of the American Copyright League—was a matter for further consideration." After these remarks, Julian Hawthorne read and many other authors followed, including William Dean Howells, who gave a few selections from one of his current novels. It was 6 P.M. before the program was finished.[133] The following afternoon the Madison Square Theatre was again filled to capacity for the second day's performance. Henry C. Potter presided and introduced the many writers as they appeared to read. When Mark Twain was introduced to the throng, near the end of the program, he appeared in evening dress and "began by saying, in his nasal drawl, that he knew it would be night before they got to him," so he wore a dress suit. After having his fun with the appreciative audience, Twain read a humorous sketch entitled "A Trying Situation" which "kept his hearers in continual merriment, that at times bubbled over into uproarious laughter." Before the last author had performed, it was 6:40, but the audience had enjoyed every minute of this rare entertainment.[134]

The series of readings was a great success, and swelled the treasury of the American Copyright League,[135] but it was not until 1891 that the hard work of the League resulted in the International Copyright Law which was put into operation by presidential proclamation. To celebrate their success, the League gave a dinner at Sherry's in New York on April 13, 1891. "It was a double celebration," wrote one reporter, "first, in honor of the passage of the new Copyright Law, and second, in honor of the eighth anniversary of the Copyright League." The tables were arranged in the shape of a horseshoe as a symbol of the League's good luck. Edmund Clarence Stedman presided and introduced the long list of distinguished speakers who included Senator O. H.

Platt, Henry Cabot Lodge, William McAdoo, and many others. Brooks, who was also present, made a few brief remarks before the program ended,[136] but he complained the next day that "the official speeches . . . were too long, and we were too late in getting to work."[137] However, the authors had achieved their goal and had well earned a long evening of dining and boasting.

Short Stories and Children's Literature

In addition to his laborious newspaper writing, Brooks composed many magazine articles during his thirteen years in New York—1871 to 1884. For *Scribner's Monthly*, which began in November of 1870 and then changed its name in November of 1881 to *The Century Magazine*, Brooks contributed fifteen articles besides numerous editorials and book reviews which were not signed.[138] His first story for *Scribner's Monthly* was entitled "The Cruise of the *Balboa*: A Story of the Pacific Seas" and appeared in the March number of 1872. From "one grain of fact," Brooks wove a fascinating web of fiction concerning the sea—a subject which he knew so well. Although he possessed a fertile imagination, Brooks rarely formed a story from whole cloth. Rather, he used some facts and changed the names of the participants and rearranged the events in such a manner as to be wholly confusing. To test the merit of "The Cruise of the *Balboa*," he first told it to a group of friends who were gathered one evening at the Runkles'.[139] His audience liked the story very much, and Brooks sold it to *Scribner's Monthly*. Brooks puts himself into the narrative in the character of a Mr. Waller, who owns a coffee plantation at Baranchy, Peru. On June 1, 1867, Waller is at the port of Callao where he purchases a shipment of Chinese coolies for the plantation. To transport them back home, Waller charters the *Balboa*, but while at sea the slaves mutiny, kill the captain and crew, and take over the ship, intending to sail back to China. Waller and his Chinese foreman survive the onslaught by locking themselves securely in one section of the ship where there is a large supply of food, but the coolies know nothing about navigation and sail in circles for months until Waller and his foreman are finally rescued by a group of whalers who take them off the ship through a porthole. Waller finds himself in the Aleutian Islands on June 20, 1868. The coolies, however, continue to sail the weather-torn *Balboa* until August 27 when she drifts into the Bay of Hakodad in Japan. Forty-six coolies are still alive, but they had stripped every vestige of identification from the ship, and in bewilderment the port authorities allow them to leave. Waller manages to obtain passage back to Callao where he learns of the phantom ship's appearance in Japan and knows that it is the *Balboa*.[140]

Brooks told the story with so much realism and knowledge of seamanship that many sailors who read it were deceived. "More than one seafarer
wrote to the amused author for additional particulars, and one writer actually contributed to the archives of the Navy Department a report of certain
'additional facts, which as an officer of the navy, had come under his observation.'"[141] This officer, who was stationed at Philadelphia, claimed to have
been on the *Iroquois* when the *Balboa* was picked up: "So there is one of the
elect deceived," chortled Brooks.[142] "The Cruise of the *Balboa*" is perhaps the
best piece of fiction which Brooks ever wrote; it combines adventure with
suspense in a highly skilled manner.

The Orient fascinated Brooks, and he wrote three articles about Japan for
Scribner's Monthly, the first of which gives a brief history of the country and
concludes that "the awakening of a great people, like that of Japan, is one
of the marvels of the time."[143] The second describes the artistically painted
Japanese fans which formerly sold so readily in the United States at ten cents,
each of which was a work of art.[144] In another article he presents an interesting
study of Japanese art with many illustrations, probably from his own collection. "Japanese art," Brooks pointed out, "may be said to preserve a perennial
freshness and youth; but no department of it has made the slightest advance
in centuries."[145]

Some of Brooks's stories are based on actual incidents which he had observed in his boyhood at Castine. He changed the names, couched the tales
in the quaint dialect of the New Englanders, and flavored them with salt air.
"The Waif of Nautilus Island"[146] relates the rescue of an unknown child from
the wreck of an East Indiaman which sinks on a reef off Nautilus Island. The
little waif is raised to womanhood by her rescuers, Miah and Thankful Morey,
only to die when the ice that she is walking upon along shore breaks upon
and carries her back "to the sea whence she came."[147] In "The Apparition of
Jo Murch" Brooks describes a lad who runs off to sea at seventeen and years
later turns up in New York, where he relates his many tall tales of adventure
to Brooks.[148] In this story there are many true incidents camouflaged and
skillfully "woven into the web of fiction." The sailor whom Brooks used as
the model for Jo Murch was a chap by the name of Jim Connor. "He actually
did turn up here and go through some of the pranks alluded to in my story,"
revealed Brooks to a friend in Castine.[149] "The Phantom Sailor" describes a
seaman who comes to "Fairport" (the name Brooks always used for Castine)
and purports to be first, Lafayette Hubbard, then Bill Drinkwater, and later
Obed Morey—all three of whom had previously been lost at sea. The parents
of the lost boys are all completely fooled by the impostor, and each family
treats him as their son. Some local boys, however, discover the fraud and

the phantom sailor disappears. Eleven years later, Brooks is sent by his editor to interview an eyewitness to a lighthouse disaster. The witness, Daniel More, turns out to be the man who tried to fool the Castine people. Brooks recognizes him by his tattoos, whereupon More admits that he was the man who had impersonated the three seamen as a lark, having sailed at one time or another with all three.[150]

In June of 1873, Brooks wrote a biographical sketch of Bret Harte and, against his better judgment, signed for it.[151] "You know it is a difficult thing to handle," explained Brooks, "considering how Harte's personal feelings have been bruited about. But I think I managed it skillfully."[152] When the study of Abraham Lincoln's life became popular in the late 1870's, Brooks contributed three papers on Lincoln, each relating personal experience with the martyred president.[153] These articles are interesting and also highly valuable as source material since Brooks enjoyed a position of confidence with Lincoln for several years. In 1882, Brooks also wrote a historical sketch of Castine, Maine, for *The Century Magazine*,[154] and the following year he shortened this article, "added a few lines to it, polished it here and there," and published it in the *Magazine of American History* as a biographical sketch of the Baron de St. Castin for whom the town was named.[155] The result, Brooks related, was "an article which reads very well for a historical magazine."[156] Although Brooks had a deep love for history, he disliked the footnotes and intense research which characterize scholarly journals.

In 1873 Scribner & Company of New York inaugurated a new monthly juvenile magazine called *St. Nicholas*, and they selected Mary Mapes Dodge to edit it with Frank R. Stockton as assistant editor.[157] Mrs. Dodge quickly gathered around her the most outstanding juvenile story writers in America, and soon *St. Nicholas* won the reputation of being the best children's publication in the English language.[158] By 1875 *St. Nicholas* had absorbed five other children's magazines which greatly increased its popularity and subscription list.[159] It was in the pages of *St. Nicholas* that Brooks established his reputation as a writer of children's articles and books. *The Book Buyer* and *The Literary World* considered Brooks's juvenile stories as American classics which every boy and girl should read.[160] Years afterward, men recalled Brooks's fascinating stories which they had read as boys.[161]

Brooks was a contributor to the first number of *St. Nicholas*, which appeared in November of 1873, and during his residence in New York he wrote a total of thirteen stories for this magazine, several of which ran serially and were then published as books. This first story is entitled "By the Sea" and is autobiographical, telling of his boyhood in "Fairport" where he had gathered mussels, dug clams, built rafts, and climbed over the "rude wooden wharves that skirted the ancient town." It was here that he heard countless yarns from the many sailors who came into port.[162] From his experiences as a youth in Castine, Brooks also relates the adventures of some lads who steal a boat, row out to a large rock in the harbor where the rotten craft breaks up a reef, and are marooned over night. Brooks's companions were adventurous lads, and "the boy who, at the mature age of twelve, could not row crosshanded, bait a cod-line, or steer a boat, was not of much account."[163] Another of his stories is based upon the historic British landing at Castine in 1777 with a liberal touch of fiction for the plot. Oliver Perkins, a lad of sixteen, grabs his gun and rushes to repel the redcoats, and a century later one of the local farmers plows up a small skull at the scene of the battle. Lying beside it is "a tom-cod sinker;" Oliver Perkins had carried his fishing tackle with him into battle and had never returned.[164]

Two of Brooks's articles for *St. Nicolas* are true stories which he published under the name of "John Riverside," the pen name which he had used in California while writing for the San Francisco *Evening Mirror*. In the first of these, "An Adventure with a Critic," Brooks casts himself as "Ned McGilp," an artist but "not a great painter," who is sketching in the mountains of California when he suddenly discovers that a large black bear is behind him, watching. In terror McGilp runs, but the bear merely knocks the easel over, licks the paint from the canvas, and strews the paints about before leaving. McGilp repaints the picture with himself seated before the easel and the bear looking over his shoulder. "The figure of the black bear in the painting excited so much curiosity and comment when it was exhibited," said Brooks, that it "sold for a high price." And with the article, Brooks printed a picture of his painting.[165] The second of his true stories is entitled "The Dotterels' Luck" and relates a happening which Brooks had observed on his way to California in 1859. The Dotterels discover gold in the craw of a duck and by tracing the ducks back to their feeding ground they find a rich gold strike.[166]

The best known story which Brooks wrote for *St. Nicholas* ran serially from November, 1875 to October, 1876, and is entitled "The Boy Emigrants," a novel that is based upon the journal which he kept on his journey from Illinois to California in 1859. Brooks puts himself in the story as "Montague Perkins Morse," a former resident of Boston who had "been in the dry-goods trade," but got tired of selling goods over the counter." The rest of the characters are modeled after the men who accompanied Brooks on the trip: "Barker Barnard Stevens" is Leonard Barnard Ayer, "Arthur Stevens" is Jacob Norton, "Tom Fender" is Frank Upham, and "Hiram Fender" is J. G. Brooks. The story follows Brooks's diary closely and relies but slightly upon imagination. There is only one major deviation; "Hiram Fender" completes the journey to California, but in 1859 J. G. Brooks was drowned while swimming across the Platte River. The tale made an instant hit with the young readers of *St. Nicholas*; they plagued the editor with so many questions about Brooks that Mrs. Dodge published a sketch of his life, complete with a picture.[167] "The Boy Emigrants" received more compliments from the children than any other story in *St. Nicholas*. Some thought it was "the best story ever published."[168]

When the last installment of "The Boy Emigrants" was printed, the editor announced that it was to be published in book form; "Mr. Brooks knows a boy's heart through and through, and his fine story, with its wealth of strong narrative, exciting scenes and incidents, and true lessons of self-reliance, ought to be read by every boy in the land."[169] In January of 1877 *The Boy Emigrants*, published by Scribner, Armstrong & Company, made its appearance in the bookstores and was praised in glowing terms by many reviewers. "The writer possess a singularly happy talent for description, his language is picturesque and impressive, and his lively narrative will be sure to win the sympathy and applause of every boyish reader," said the New York *Tribune*.[170] Another reviewer praised Brooks for writing a truthful, manly novel instead of an "improbable adventure" story which so many authors fabricate for children. "One of the best of the new school of writers for juveniles," said this reviewer, "is Noah Brooks, the journalist."[171] A new edition was issued in 1887 and when the 1891 printing appeared, one literary magazine named it as the "book of the month" for children.[172] New editions were printed again in 1903 and 1914, and it is still in print. The continued sale of *The Boy Emigrants* gave Brooks a modest royalty payment every year after its publication.[173]

"I have begun on my Castine story, and have finished two chapters," reported Brooks on August 31, 1879. "It will be called 'The Fairport Nine,' the name of the town being thinly disguised under the title which I have used before now for Castine," he continued, "I shall introduce Castine scenery and incidents, and a mixture of Castine names," confided Brooks, "but not to make any of the characters recognizable."[174] The first chapter of this serial, however, did not appear in *St. Nicholas* until May of 1880. The story revolves about the adventures of the boys with whom Brooks played during his boyhood. They have a baseball team called the Fairport Nine whose rivals are known as the White Bears, a group of rough youngsters who spend more time with the whaling fleet than in school. After losing the first championship game to the White Bears, the Fairport Nine beat their rivals in the second match. In this tale Brooks is "Billy Hetherington," who plays either center field or right field. During the time that the White Bears are at sea, the Fairport Nine organize a military company in which Billy Hetherington is the standard bearer. Brooks later admitted that "the boys in 'The Fairport

Nine' were real boys, and I was one of them." He was, in fact, the standard bearer of the military company of twelve boys, who in 1840 were called the Hancock Cadets, and the flag which Brooks had carried was found in 1895 at Castine and returned to him. It had fifteen stars on a field of white and was trimmed with red material from a dismantled ship's cabin curtains.[175]

Upon the completion of "The Fairport Nine" in the October issue of 1880, it was announced that the story would be issued as a bound volume,[176] and before the end of the year it was published by the press of Charles Scribner's Sons with illustrations drawn by A. C. Redwood. One reviewer remarked that the book displayed "good English and good hearty fun." "Without other proof it could be easy to deduce from the book itself that its author was once a boy, and recollects particularly well how it feels to be one."[177] *The Fairport Nine* was a successful book and was reissued in 1889. After observing how well American boys liked baseball stories, Brooks wrote another one based upon the same subject: *Our Base Ball Club and How It Won the Championship*. E. P. Dutton & Company published this volume in 1884. It tells of the baseball team of "Catalpa," Illinois, on the "Stone River." Dixon, Illinois, on the Rock River is actually the scene of Brooks's tale, and Albert G. Spalding (1850–1915), who was president of the Chicago Baseball Club and a manufacturer of baseball equipment, wrote an introduction for Brooks. Spalding was born at Byron, Illinois, which is not far from Dixon.

Brooks also wrote several historical sketches for *St. Nicholas*, the first of which was "The Children's Crusade," a study of the youths who journeyed to the Holy Land in a futile attempt to free it from the infidels in 1212.[178] In a short study of George III of England, Brooks outlined the king's life and showed that he was not the monster which American tradition made him.[179] When President James A. Garfield was assassinated, Brooks lamented the nation's loss and wrote a brief biography of the martyred president, with special emphasis upon his youth.[180] Turning to the sea once more, Brooks related for *St. Nicholas* the story of Captain David Porter's valiant naval engagement in 1814 with the British ships *Phoebe* and *Cherub*. Although Porter was defeated, Brooks stressed the brave determination of the American captain and from this drew a moral for his youthful readers.[181] From his close observations of "Tad" Lincoln during the Civil War, Brooks, who had learned to know and love this merry sprite, wrote an article which revealed the mischievous antics of Lincoln's spoiled son.[182]

While in New York, Brooks also contributed an occasional story to the *Overland Monthly* of San Francisco. He rewrote the historical sketch of Japan which he had published in *Scribner's Monthly* of April, 1872, and it appeared in the *Overland* as "A Chapter of Condensed History."[183] Since Brooks had left

San Francisco in 1871, the *Overland* had changed hands several times, and by 1883 it had fallen into disrepute because of the dishonesty of the editor. Warren Cheney had plagiarized a sketch of Bret Harte written by Edmund Clarence Stedman, and a contributor, Annie Montague, had signed her name to a poem written by James Russell Lowell. "The magazine is a standing libel on the literary people of the Coast," said one reporter, "and unless it gets a change of heart and pays for contributions, the sooner it dies the better for the credit of the State."[184] But Brooks, out of loyalty to the magazine which he had helped to found, continued to support it. In 1883 he wrote one of his best stories for the *Overland*, entitled "Saville: A Symposium and a Tragedy." It is a psychological tale involving five friends who are in the habit of eating together at their club. Brooks takes a place in this group as "Perkins," a "night leader-writer on one of the great dailies." One of the men, Saville, suddenly dies and when the remaining four gather at the club for their first meal since Saville's death, they fall into a discussion of the hereafter. Perkins states that, as an orthodox Congregationalist, he is sure that Saville is in heaven, but some of his friends—being agnostics—argue that no living man knows where Saville has gone. The dinner ending, Perkins leaves the club and boards the elevated train for his newspaper office. While en route, the brakeman is killed, and Perkins, who knows the young chap, whispers in the ear of the dying man, "Good by, and remember me to Saville." Later that night, after his labors are finished, Perkins returns to his apartment where he relaxes in his favorite chair. Suddenly he sees the figure of Saville coming out of the gloom and hears him say, "Well, Perk, I got your message; and how are all the malefactors?" This was the term Saville had always used when speaking of the little group who dined together. The following morning Perkins awakens with a start to find that he is still sitting in the chair, the victim of a vivid dream.[185]

For another magazine, *The Californian*, Brooks composed a story which had an unusual origin. Being afflicted with insomnia, Brooks was advised to use bromides to induce sleep. The use of this drug caused him to dream about a plot which he recalled upon awakening.[186] After inventing a connecting link, he published the story as "The Honor of a Family."[187]

Considering Brooks's daily newspaper labors, his output of fiction and historical writings was most prolific. And it was during these fruitful years in New York that he established his reputation as a popular writer for both young and old. Although he had won recognition in California, his reputation was, for the most part, local, but with his relocation in New York, he received nation-wide praise as a versatile and talented author.

CHAPTER X

A Club Man in New York

WHEN BROOKS WENT TO New York in 1871, the city had about 100 clubs with a total membership of 50,000.[1] The Nineteenth Century was a sociable era; nearly every professional or business man belonged to one or more clubs. When the day's work was finished, members went to their clubrooms to rest, relax, smoke, and meet their friends. Such a man was Brooks. "He is thoroughly a club man," said one reporter, "he enjoys a good dinner and a good story, and can himself give one and tell the other." Brooks is described as being "a very comfortable and pleasant looking person . . . amiable and genial, full of anecdote, reminiscence and narrative." He was "everybody's friend, apparently," remarked one observer, "and has a kind word and helping hand for every needy or unfortunate person." Since Brooks never remarried—relishing his freedom too greatly, as he expressed it—clubs took the place of family life for him,[2] and "socially he was most happily equipped: in friendship he was fastidious, sincere, devoted."[3]

The Lotos Club

The first organization Brooks joined was the Lotos Club, founded by six young journalists on March 15, 1870, and incorporated on the twenty-ninth of the following month.[4] Brooks became a member in 1873 and remained active in the Lotos until his resignation sometime between 1887 and 1890. The club took its name from a poem by Alfred Lord Tennyson entitled "The Lotos-Eaters,"[5] a term which signifies a pleasure seeker.[6] The Lotos Club was formed as a "meeting ground for the younger men" of art, literature, music, drama, journalism, and other professions,[7] in "protest against the conservative methods and autocratic ways of certain members" of The Century Association.[8] Knowing that artists, musicians, and actors could ill afford the initiation fee of $200, the founders put an article in the constitution which allowed an artist to contribute a painting valued at $200 and authorized the directors to remit any part of the fee for a professional actor or musician.

The first quarters of the Lotos Club were located at No. 2 Irving Place, where the members were somewhat cramped in their small parlors. Nevertheless, they found room to give special dinners and receptions to the outstanding men of letters and art who were visiting in New York.[9] Very early in its existence, the Lotos Club initiated a weekly Saturday night meeting at which time the members gathered for a dinner and a program of music and recitation.[10] "A charming literary coterie that frequently gathered around" one of the dinner tables comprised Henry Watterson, George Alfred Townsend, D. G. Croly, Stephen Fiske, Noah Brooks, Isaac H. Bromley, and E. W. Vanderhoef. Their "conversation or discussion was most brilliant and ever interesting," reported one member, "for all named are charming conversationalists, quick at repartee, refulgent with reminiscence, as graphic and forcible in speech as with their pens." These authors, once started, could relate interesting happenings by the hour, "if their engagements permit them to remain" at the club all evening.[11]

Another feature of Lotos Saturday Nights was an art exhibit. In the spring of 1872 the club began to collect works of art and built an annex to the house which served as an art gallery.[12] Brooks, who himself owned a valuable collection of paintings,[13] aided the Lotos Club in obtaining "a notable collection of specimens of the best wood engraving of modern times."[14] The Saturday art exhibits, which once numbered fifty-five canvases, were left up through Monday when the club held its regular Ladies' Day program.[15] During the winter months, the Lotos Club gave special musical and literary programs on Monday afternoon for women guests. After the formal program, the ladies were invited to inspect the paintings currently being shown in the gallery. One such exhibition was devoted to French painting with examples from "the different epochs in the art history of that country."[16]

When Brooks joined the Lotos Club in 1873, Whitelaw Reid was president, having been elected that year to heal the rent which had developed between two factions in the club.[17] Reid united the divided elements, but the club still faced a financial problem. To raise funds, the Lotos members decided to publish a limited-edition volume which would contain original contributions written by the many talented members. John Brougham and John Elderkin were selected to edit the book, and Wilkie Collins, Whitelaw Reid, Mark Twain, John Hay, P. V. Nasby [David Ross Locke], and many others composed choice pieces for it. Brooks wrote of his experiences [in] "In Echo Cañon" while en route to California in 1859.[18] It is full of local color and describes the beautiful scenery of the Wasatch Mountains. One of the members, William F. Gill, was a publisher, and he not only contributed a story but also printed the volume at his press on Washington Street in Boston. *Lotos Leaves: Original Stories, Essays, and Poems* was scheduled for publication in November of 1874,[19] but it was not until the following year that the collector's item was finally issued.

After serving three terms as president, Reid declined to run for office in 1876. When the annual election was held on March 18, John Brougham, who had been first vice president, was chosen president, but sharp opposition developed over the remainder of the slate as proposed by the nominating committee. Without Reid, the members again divided into two factions. Isaac H. Bromley and Noah Brooks "came within a few votes of being chosen respectively First and Second Vice-President." However, the committee's choices, F. A. Schwab and George H. Story, were finally voted into the contested offices.[20] Reid's term expired on April 1, and on the eighteenth a complimentary dinner was given to him at which time "a choice collection of pictures was exhibited in the dining-room and gallery."[21] But before the year was out, a special election was held. In November Brooks was chosen second vice president, replacing George H. Story; the other officers remained as before. In honor of his election, a complimentary dinner was given to Brooks at the club house on November 25.[22] Brooks helped to unite the club again, and when the annual election was held a few months later, on March 17, 1877, "the regular ticket was elected without opposition." John Brougham was reelected president, Brooks moved up to become first vice president, and Charles I. Pardee replaced Brooks as second vice president.[23] Brooks served as first vice president from 1877 to 1882, and in the absence of the president frequently presided over many of the dinners given to notables. He handled these assignments very well; George Edgar Montgomery said that Brooks was the "presiding genius" of the club.[24] At other times, he was called upon to placate annoyed members and keep the Lotos Club running smoothly. When Mark Twain went to Europe in April of 1878, he wanted to resign, but Brooks dissuaded him by promising to put him on half dues during his absence. While in Paris, however, Twain again decided to resign, and Brooks wrote him a friendly letter which tactfully reiterated that he was still on half dues and owed the club only $41.25.[25] Twain kept his membership.

On May 1, 1877, the increased prosperity of the Lotos Club was manifested when it moved from No. 2 Irving Place to the Bradish Johnson mansion at 147 Fifth Avenue, near Twenty-first Street.[26] Seventy new members had swelled the membership to 350, the limit at that time being set at 400. Their new quarters were "on an ample and luxurious scale" with "[many] of the original rich furnishings intact." A Saturday night housewarming was held on May 19 with the usual Ladies' Day reception taking place on the following Monday. Brooks was a member of the art committee which was placed in charge of the new exhibition of paintings hung in one of the parlors.

On the first floor of the new club house were the parlors and dining room; the library, private dining rooms and card room were located on the second floor; and the smoking and billiard rooms were in the basement.[27] On the third floor were "elegant quarters" for a few bachelor members of the club. Soon after the Lotos moved to this location at 147 Fifth Avenue, Brooks rented a suite of rooms in the club as did Colonel Thomas Knox, who also was a juvenile story writer.[28] Here in the quiet and comfort of his apartment, Brooks did much of his writing. He also ate breakfast at the club where the cook, on cold winter mornings, pampered the resident breakfasters by warming their plates at the fireplace. Brooks loved good food and occasionally would send to Maine for "a fresh Penobscot salmon" which the Lotos Club cook would prepare for him.[29] The club had a cat by the name of Richard, and in the mornings this mascot loafed in Brooks's bedroom or sitting room until Brooks would take the cat to breakfast, which for the night editor was always at a late hour. The brownish-yellow cat always sought out Brooks's rooms whenever the Lotos Club entertained ladies because he disliked women. Brooks and Richard were fast friends, but in the summer of 1883 the cat had to be destroyed. He had fallen into a bucket of mortar, while the club house was being repaired, and was severely burned.[30]

Whenever a dignitary visited New York, he was sure to be invited to a Lotos Club dinner. Besides its close ties to art and literature, the Lotos also had "strong affiliations with the stage" and was "always foremost in giving banquets and receptions to representatives of the English theatre."[31] The renowned composing team of William S. Gilbert and Arthur S. Sullivan were feted at the club on November 8, 1879, and Brooks—always on hand for such events—enjoyed meeting and conversing with them.[32] The actor John Gilbert was also the guest of the club on November 30, 1878, when ninety members welcomed him to their hearth. "After the speech making was over and the company had thinned out a little," the guest joined John Brougham and Lester Wallack in singing and telling stories until "a late hour."[33] On April 14, 1883, Oliver Wendell Holmes appeared at the club as an honored guest and received a great ovation from the members.[34] Even the quiet General Grant was persuaded to make a speech at the reception on November 20, 1880.[35] Mark Twain enjoyed the atmosphere of the Lotos and was sitting in the parlors on the afternoon of August 5, 1885, when the funeral procession of General Grant passed. Twain also took room and board at the Lotos upon occasion.[36]

The Lotos Club celebrated its tenth birthday on March 27, 1880, by giving a banquet and inviting the presidents of eleven other clubs. Reid retold the history of the Lotos, and later "a large silver tankard, with two handles, embossed at the base with double-eagle gold pieces, and bearing on its side the design of a Lotos flower, was set before Noah Brooks, at his place opposite the president." Brooks presented the cup to the club by saying:

> I am charged with the pleasant duty of delivering into your custody the loving cup which has been prepared by the members of the club for its use. Its inscription fitly sets forth and commemorates the foundation of the club. We have left, as you see, after the $20 gold pieces—the double eagles—spaces for the mementos of future decennials, and when eight of them are furnished, eighty years will close their course. Edward the Good was stabbed in the back while drinking from a tankard, but it is to be hoped that no member will be stabbed in the back while drinking from this loving cup. And as it passes from lip to lip, and hand to hand, it seems to me that you and I and all of us will unite in the words of our poet, Mr. William Winter.

Brooks then read Winter's poem, "A Lotos Flower,"[37] and handed the cup to Reid, who called upon Dr. A. E. Macdonald, the secretary, to respond in behalf of the entire club.[38]

John Brougham, who had been president of the Lotos Club from 1876 to 1878, died at his home at 60 East Ninth Street on June 7, 1880. He was a noted actor and playwright and one of the oldest members of the club. Brooks immediately called a special meeting of the Lotos to make suitable arrangements for the funeral; Thomas W. Knox, who also lived in the club, served as secretary.[39] Brougham, an intimate friend of Brooks,[40] had been ill since he had returned from a tour on November 7, 1877, and Brooks often presided in his stead at club functions.[41] The funeral was held on June 9 at the Church of the Transfiguration on East Twenty-ninth Street, commonly called "The Little Church around the Corner." It was the favorite church of New York actors and received its nickname from Joseph Jefferson. When his good friend George Holland died in 1870, Jefferson was asked to make funeral arrangements at one of the prominent churches in the city, but the minister told Jefferson that his church would not bury an actor. The man of God, however, added that "there was a little church around the corner" that would give Holland a simple funeral service. "Then if this be so," exclaimed the angry Jefferson, "God bless 'the little church around the corner.'"[42] The name stuck and was revered by the stage people.[43] A large delegation of Lotos members attended Brougham's funeral, and Brooks served as one of the eight pallbearers.[44]

Brooks had loved "Uncle" John Brougham, as he called him, and since the actor had died in debt, Brooks quietly redeemed one of his notes at Tiffany's.[45] And when William Winter edited a biography of the famed actor, Brooks was asked to tell of Brougham's connection with the Lotos Club. It was "a labor of love," as Brooks expressed it, but he cheerfully agreed to furnish a chapter for Winter's book.[46] In September[47] Brooks wrote the chapter "Brougham in His Club Life"[48] which the editor of *The Critic* termed "gentle and genial."[49]

When Brougham retired from office in 1878, Whitelaw Reid again became president of the Lotos Club and retained the office for the next ten years. During this time, the heir-apparent—Brooks—remained as first vice president and resigned about 1887. However, on March 22, 1890, when the Lotos Club celebrated its twentieth anniversary, Brooks returned from Newark, New Jersey, to attend the dinner meeting. The speaker of the evening was Robert G. Ingersoll, but the other members responded with speeches as various toasts were proposed. Brooks spoke for "The Press."[50] Sometime after this, the club moved to "a handsome brownstone building" at Fifth Avenue and Forty-sixth Street.[51] In 1909 the Lotos moved again, this time to 110 West Fifty-seventh, and today the famous club is found at 5 East Sixty-sixth where they continue to sponsor the arts and provide luxurious accommodations in their beautiful club house which was constructed in the French Renaissance style of architecture in 1900 at the expense of a daughter of William H. Vanderbilt.[52]

The Century Association

In 1880 Brooks was elected to membership in the oldest and most distinguished club in New York: The Century Association, more commonly known as The Century Club. No "mere accidents of birth and fortune" could win a man admission to The Century; the standards of this club were based on "brains, culture, and achievement." "Rising young men in letters, art, and the professions, who will grow up with the institution and reflect lustre on its annals" were the ones sought out for membership.[53]

The Century was founded on January 13, 1847, and the membership was originally limited to 100, as the name indicates. When Brooks joined the Association, its quarters were at No. 109 East Fifteenth Street and the president was Daniel Huntington, who had been elected to office in 1879. Henry Codman Potter was elected to the presidency in 1895, and was still in office at Brooks's death in 1903. Brooks never held an important office in The Century, but it was one of the clubs in which he retained membership until his death. One does not lightly renounce his membership in this exclusive club. In 1899, however, he changed his membership from resident to non-resident because of his frequent travels while in retirement.[54]

While Brooks was a member, it was reported that The Century was "one of the very few clubs that are always full and always have from 150 to 200 applicants for admission." Forty new members were all that could be elected in any one year. The initiation fee was $100 and the yearly dues were about $40. The regular dinner meetings were held on the first Saturday night of each month, and at these affairs there was "genuine intellectual companionship" with no speeches or formalities. In the club house, which had been built especially for The Century, there was usually an exhibition of paintings in the halls. The library and reading rooms were always open, and here the members dropped in to read or chat in the evening.[55]

At the regular monthly meetings, or at "any event of more than ordinary interest," Noah Brooks was sure to be present with such friends as Edmund Clarence Stedman, Richard Henry Stoddard, E. L. Youmans, Horace White, Lawrence Barrett, Edwin Booth, and many others.[56] Raphael Pumpelly, a traveler, mining expert, and author who frequently visited the club, said that these men were "the brains of the metropolis" and among them his education was greatly broadened.[57] Another visitor to the club termed its members "the cleverest men of a nation whose chief characteristic is cleverness."[58] George Augustus Sala remarked that at The Century he had met "literature, art, and science in combination with stewed oysters and hot 'whiskey skins.'"[59] Brooks found a ready place among his fellow Centurions and quickly won recognition as "a good story teller."[60] And Henry Holt recalled the club members singing the "Song of the Horse-Car Conductor," which Brooks had helped to write, while Quincy "Mike" Ward did a jig in time to the music.[61]

In 1891 the Century Association moved to No. 7 West Forty-third Street, its present home. As Brooks's prestige in the club increased, he was able to obtain membership for friends of his, such as Charles de Kay, whom he proposed for election in 1896. Augustus St. Gaudens and Edmund Clarence Stedman, close friends of Brooks, seconded de Kay's nomination, and he was accepted into The Century.[62] Brooks took a great interest in The Century's library, which contained 14,551 volumes at the time of his death, and frequently contributed books to it.[63] Other members also gave generously to the library.[64]

When Brooks died, his fellow Centurions paid him a noble tribute. "He was a valuable newspaper man," wrote the club historian, "widely informed, facile, often brilliant, with a trustworthy *flair* for that which interests the public," and displayed a genial humor toward his friends whom he judged solely upon their individual merits. Brooks had brought honor to this club.[65]

The Authors Club

When Brooks arrived in New York, there was no author's club, although such an organization had previously existed for short periods of time. In April of 1837 an authors' club had been started with Washington Irving serving as president; Fitz-Greene Halleck was vice president, and James Fenimore Cooper was one of its members.[66] But this club died out, and another, called the Broadway Literary Club, was organized during the Civil War.[67] It too was of short duration, but in 1882 Charles de Kay decided that New York needed an authors' club where literary men could assemble in good fellowship and talk shop. Other writers agreed with him and promised to help organize a club.[68] On the evening of October 21, 1882, Noah Brooks, Edward Eggleston, Laurence Hutton, Charles de Kay, Brander Matthews, and Edmund Clarence Stedman met at the home of Richard Watson Gilder, No. 103 East Fifteenth Street, just a few steps from The Century Association. Gilder, a brother-in-law of de Kay, lived in a large picturesque residence which had formerly been a stable. These seven men organized the Authors Club and agreed to invite twenty-five other authors to membership. The following week the founders and charter members met at the home of Stedman and appointed a committee to draft a constitution. The work was largely done by Edward Eggleston, and on November 13 the group assembled at Laurence Hutton's home and adopted the constitution.[69]

Immediately the organization was beset with discord since at least two of the members aspired to be first president. To avoid hard feelings, it was finally decided that there would be no president—only an executive council of nine to be elected each year. The council was to choose its own chairman for each meeting. One fourth of the members were to be out-of-town authors, and no woman writer was eligible since the men wished to smoke and feared that women might object to their pipes and punch. The entrance fee was established at $15; annual dues were $10. Since the club had no permanent quarters, the members agreed to hold their fortnightly meetings at their own homes.[70] When it came to selecting the official spelling of the club's name, the members decided that it should be written "Authors Club," without an apostrophe. "No, gentle compositor," cautioned one of the members, "do not put an apostrophe in that title; for the apostrophe is the sign of possession, and the sensation of possession is so rare among authors that they do not use its symbol in the name of their Club."[71] Once this spelling was termed a

O. B. Bunce.   G. C. Eggleston.   Laurence Hutton.   Noah Brooks.   G. P. Lathrop.   R. U. Johnson.
AT THE AUTHORS' CLUB, NEW YORK.—[See page 831.]

FIGURE 4. Noah Brooks at the Authors Club, New York. From *Harper's New Monthly Magazine* 73 (October 1886), 812.

blunder,[72] but de Kay sprang quickly to the defense and nothing more was ever heard of the matter.[73]

The first regular meeting of the Authors Club took place at Laurence Hutton's on November 28, 1882, and Henry M. Baird, Noah Brooks, Edward Eggleston, Edwin L. Godkin, Laurence Hutton, Charles de Kay, Charlton T. Lewis, Edmund Clarence Stedman, and Richard Grant White were chosen as the executive council members for the first year. Brooks served on this governing body again in 1883, 1886, 1887, and 1891. In 1892 the term of office was extended to three years, and Brooks was again chosen to the council, but in 1895 he refused to take a seat because he was in retirement and found it difficult to be present at meetings. During his terms on the council, Brooks was frequently chosen chairman and presided at many of the meetings.[74]

There were thirty-six members at the meeting of November 28, and the temporary limit was fixed at fifty. In addition to the seven founders and the members of the executive council, they were: H. M. Alden, W. L. Alden, John Bigelow, Vincenzo Botta, H. H. Boyesen, John Burroughs, S. S. Conant, George William Curtis, Henry Drisler, George C. Eggleston, Sydney Howard

Gay, Parke Godwin, John Habberton, J. R. G. Hassard, Bronson Howard, Clarence King, Jonas M. Libbey, Hamilton W. Mabie, W. S. Mayo, George Edgar Montgomery, Frederick Law Olmstead, Raphael Pumpelly, Allen Thorndike Rice, Richard Henry Stoddard, and E. L. Youmans. With the support of these men, the club continued to grow and expand until London, England, took notice of the New York club and organized an author's club in 1892.[75]

The constitution of the Authors Club stated that "no person shall be eligible to membership who is not the author of a published book proper to literature, or who has not a recognized position in other kinds of distinctively literary work." This qualification for membership was made broad enough to admit editors who had not written a book, and occasionally the bars were let down even further. William Carey was admitted to the club in 1887 on the basis of his sonnet to Beethoven,[76] and two years later one writer stated that the club had some members who, "though charming fellows, cannot be said to have a recognized position in distinctively literary work."[77] But the Authors Club was meant to be "an informal, brotherly organization of literary men." It excluded "from its rules and its practices everything that might impose restraint upon social liberty" because it was easier to welcome an interested person to membership than reject him.[78] And the club was noted for its freedom from quarrels and strife.[79] Its aims "are more social than literary, its design being to bring the older men in letters into more intimate relation and fellowship with the younger."[80] The Authors Club, however, did have one goal which it pursued with firm determination: an international copyright law. When this law was finally placed on the statute books, one writer reported that "there is no doubt that the passage of the copyright law was due to the formation of the Authors' Club, and this is, doubtless, only the first of a long series of important measures in behalf of literary workers that it will start and encourage."[81]

Since the Authors Club had little money and wished to keep expenses to a minimum, its meetings "for the first year or two" were held "here and there, sometimes at the houses of different members and sometimes at restaurants."[82] At first the fortnightly meetings were held on Wednesday evening and were graced with punch, cigars, and pipes, but later the meetings were held on Thursday night. The club met only during the fall, winter, and spring months.[83] During February and March of each year, the club also held four afternoon receptions for the wives and daughters of the members; prominent women authors were also invited to these receptions.[84] The first guest to be entertained by the Authors Club was Matthew Arnold, who was given an informal reception to the Hotel Dam on February 28, 1884. Although the reception was scheduled for 8:30 P.M., few of the authors arrived until 9. At that time Charlton T. Lewis, the chairman for the evening, introduced Arnold, who spoke very briefly. James Herbert Morse noted in his diary that Arnold's face and head were "large but not out of proportion to the rest of him." In honor of the event, Macmillan & Company presented to the Authors Club a nine-volume set of Arnold's works which became the nucleus of the club's library. At 11 Arnold left the party, but Brooks and many of the seventy-five writers present chatted until midnight.[85]

By the early months of 1884 the Authors Club was holding its meetings at the rooms of the Tile Club, organized by a small group of talented young painters, at 58½ West Tenth Street. To reach the Tile Club, one had to proceed "through a long, narrow, low-arched alley way leading between whitewashed walls, then through a slender backyard." The rooms were furnished simply with two large tables and a number of chairs, but the walls were "prettily hung with pictures and other ornaments" which belonged to the Tile Club. The authors "arrived in goodly numbers about ten o'clock, and dropped off at twelve or later." They chatted of their work while they drank punch, brandy, or whisky and smoked either clay pipes or cigars—all of which were furnished by their club.[86]

Although the Tile Club members were hospitable, the Authors Club longed for its own rooms, and on May 29, 1884, they held their first meeting at their own quarters, located at 19 West Twenty-fourth Street. For $600 a year, the authors leased from the Fencing Club three rooms on the second floor where "the flow of literary conversation is occasionally interrupted by the sound of clashing arms, upborne from the floor beneath—the *salle d'armes* of the Fencing Club." Frank Lathrop and Clarence Cook decorated and furnished the rooms with a few pictures and some rugs. The library, as yet, consisted only of Matthew Arnold's works, but "the elegant piece of furniture," observed Morse, "is a long table of cherry wood on which our little supply of viands was set out." Simple cane-seated chairs completed the furniture.[87] By 1886 the club rooms were adorned with a few engravings and half a dozen oil paintings, "loans only, for the Club is not a rich man's Paradise." There was also "a bronze bas-relief of Bayard Taylor" and some casts of Greek sculpture. "For comfort," Morse added, "we still keep the cane-seat arm-chairs, along with two or three corner benches." "Pipes," he said, "strew the mantel piece, and a punch bowl in a corner speaks of the Thursday night convivialities." A large bookcase now held the works of the 150 members, and there were magazines and newspapers in the reading room.[88] In 1889 the library, rapidly growing, boasted several hundred volumes.

On every second Thursday, at about 10 P.M., from thirty to fifty authors gathered in the club rooms for a brief business session that was usually interrupted some thirty minutes later by the loud tones of an Oriental bronze gong which summoned the authors to a "good supper" prepared by a caterer and spiced with an "abundance of bottled beer and good punch." Each member was entitled to bring one guest. With dinner over, the members gathered in small groups to smoke and talk.[89] A typical coterie which usually gathered around one of the smoking tables consisted of O. B. Bunce, George C. Eggleston, Laurence Hutton, Noah Brooks, George Parsons Lathrop, and Robert Underwood Johnson. Brooks, with a twinkle in his eyes and smoking his favorite cigar, would relate countless tales to his companions while they puffed on their long-stemmed clay pipes and listened with interest to this fascinating conversationalist.[90] At council meetings, after the business discussion had ended, Brooks would also reminisce about Bret Harte or others until the little group finally adjourned to the Assassin's Den for a glass of beer before going home.[91]

Whenever a foreign writer of repute visited New York, he generally was invited to a reception at the Authors Club.[92] J. M. W. van der Poorten Schwartz, who lived at Chateau de Zuylestein near Leersum, Holland, was given honorary membership.[93] The only woman to receive such an honor was Harriet Beecher Stowe.[94] At times the club gave receptions to publishers,[95] but generally they honored the contemporary idol of the literary field, often one of their own number. On April 22, 1886, William Dean Howells was given a reception which proved to be "by far the most interesting event in literary circles this winter." The Fencing Club allowed the authors to use their large first-floor room where the table was set for more than a hundred. E. P. Roe arrived early, bringing with him a large box full of trailing arbutus which he and Hamilton Gibson distributed as boutonnieres to the members as they arrived. When Professor Boyesen appeared, he immediately "lighted a pipe of majestic proportions" which prompted the other authors to do likewise. When George Cary Eggleston, the chairman, arrived with Howells, they were greeted with much applause. Then all fell to talking and smoking until "the few chinks between the authors had been duly filled with blue smoke" at which time the gong sounded to announce the beginning of the meeting. A few speeches, each limited to two minutes, were made and then dinner was served. Mark Twain arrived late, but Morse gave him his chair which was opposite Howells. "When the eating was done," Morse wrote, "we had speeches from the late comers, Mark Twain speaking twice in fact," once for the publishers—when J. Henry Harper declined to respond to Eggleston's toast—and once for himself. It was a memorable event and brought together "a truly representative assemblage of American literarians."[96]

On February 18, 1887, the Authors Club was incorporated under the laws of New York State, with the certificate being signed by the nine trustees:

Noah Brooks, George C. Eggleston, W. Hamilton Gibson, Ripley Hitchcock, Bronson Howard, Thomas W. Knox, James Herbert Morse, Edward Munroe Smith, and Alfred Butler Storey.[97] After incorporation, the club continued to expand and in January of 1890 it was decided to raise the membership limit from 150 to 300.[98] Then in April Andrew Carnegie, a member of the club, offered the executive council $10,000 "for the encouragement of literature." The council accepted the generous gift, but decided to invest the money and spend only the interest.[99] For one reason or another, the Authors Club found it necessary to move in 1892, and they selected temporary quarters at 158 West Twenty-third Street where they held their first meeting in December.[100] Many of the members desired to purchase a permanent club house, but some of the older men believed that "the popularity which the Club has enjoyed thus far has been due largely to the modest way in which it has been conducted."[101] The will of the younger men prevailed, however, and the club decided to raise the necessary funds for permanent quarters.

Rossiter Johnson, John D. Champlin, and George O. Eggleston suggested that the club publish a limited edition book,[102] such as the one written by the Lotos Club in 1875. By April of 1892, plans for such a volume were completed, and Rossiter Johnson announced that the book would contain "stories, essays, poems, and sketches written specifically for it by members of the Club." Only 251 copies—of which one was for the club's library—were to be published, and the price for this unique book was set at $100.[103] Slowly the manuscripts were assembled, sent to the De Vinne Press toward the end of 1892,[104] and finally appeared late in 1893 under the title of *The First Book of the Authors Club: Liber Scriptorum*. Over 100 authors contributed to it and each autographed all 251 copies. The paper, bearing the watermark of the Authors Club, was made in Holland, and the volumes were bound in leather, "tastefully stamped and tooled . . . with artistic luxuriousness."[105] The sale of *Liber Scriptorum* brought the club a profit of over $20,000 which was used to buy "leather-covered morris chairs, soft rugs, handsome bookcases, and other luxuries" since the club had learned in the meantime that Andrew Carnegie contemplated giving them permanent quarters and they would not need to build a house.[106]

For *Liber Scriptorum* Brooks wrote an autobiographical sketch about the books which he had read as a boy when there were few books written especially for children. Although Brooks himself was one of the writers who remedied this situation, he does not mention his own writings. He merely says that he is glad to have "lived long enough to see so vast a volume of valuable literature provided for our boys and girls."[107]

To celebrate its tenth birthday, the Authors Club held a banquet at the St. Denis Hotel on February 28, 1893. Brooks returned to New York for the gala occasion and sat at the main table with the other founders of the club. "The dinner," said Morse, "was unusually brilliant, more good speakers than we could use." After the brief addresses, everybody scurried about collecting autographs on the colorful menu which had been printed especially for the event. One writer observed that since the Authors Club had passed its first ten years, "there remains no doubt of its establishment as a permanent institution."[108]

The cornerstone of the Carnegie Music Hall, at Seventh Avenue and Fifty-sixth Street, was laid on May 30, 1890, and Carnegie built club rooms in this grand structure. When they were completed, Carnegie offered them free to the Authors Club. In February of 1894, a committee, consisting of Harry Marquand, John Champlin, and James Herbert Morse, was appointed to consider Carnegie's generous offer. At first the committee objected to accepting the quarters gratis, but after much discussion they agreed to accept the proposition.[109] In the meantime, the Authors Club held its meetings at the hall of the Architectural League while preparations were being made for the move into their new quarters[110] where at last they had room for the library and mementos of the club. In grateful appreciation of Carnegie's generosity, the original manuscript of *Liber Scriptorum* was given to him.[111] Even for some time prior to their move into the Music Hall, however, the Authors Club had been "in a most flourishing condition,"[112] and the library had grown to "several thousand volumes."[113] In 1896 a prize of $100 was offered for the best bookplate design; George Wharton Edwards's drawing won and was immediately copyrighted by the club.[114] Alexander Black, the literary editor and art critic of the Brooklyn *Times*, served as "honorary librarian" of the club's growing collection.[115] Occasionally, the library was used by scholars for research, but the rest of the quarters were generally vacant except for the evenings of the fortnightly dinner meetings.[116]

At times the club gave dinners in its club rooms for some noted author, such as Stephen Crane who was feted by Ripley Hitchcock on March 7, 1896.[117] But for the larger celebrations, when 150 or more writers and guests would assemble, the dinner meetings were held at hotels. Richard Henry Stoddard was given such a banquet at the Hotel Savoy on March 25, 1897.[118] Stoddard's social interests were centered at the Century and Authors clubs, and before his death he gave the major portion of his private library to the Authors Club. After his death, the remainder of his books were presented to The Century Association.[119] Not all the meetings of the club were social, however; whenever a good literary cause needed support, the authors were sure to note the matter and give it attention. When Emile Zola, the French novelist, sprang to the defense of Alfred Dreyfus, who was falsely accused of treason by French military authorities, the Authors Club scheduled a meeting for March 10, 1898, to take action "in the cause of human liberty and constitutional justice."[120]

Whenever Brooks was in the vicinity of New York, he worked actively with the Authors Club. In 1898 he was assigned to the committee in charge of amending the constitution,[121] and he maintained his membership in the club until his death. In 1919 the Authors Club received $250,000 from the estate of Carnegie, and this large sum, when added to the $50,000 already in the club's treasury, made the Authors one of the richest organizations in New York.[122] But as New Yorkers gradually lost their taste for clubs, the Authors Club too declined; at the time of this writing, the club has no permanent quarters and only an occasional meeting is held.

The New England Society

In addition to the Lotos, Century, and Authors clubs, Brooks also became a member of two other organizations while he lived in New York. On February 14, 1872, he was elected a member of the New York Chapter of the New England Society, and on July 13, 1883, he was chosen a corresponding member of the Maine Historical Society.[123] He took little part in the activities of the latter, but he participated quite actively in the New England Society, an organization which was founded on May 6, 1805, and whose object is to promote and study the history of New England. To be a member, one must be a native or descendant of a person born in the New England States. Brooks maintained his membership in the New York Chapter until the year of his death.[124] Whenever he was called up to serve on committees or make arrangements for meetings of the New England Society, he cheerfully responded. In 1882 he was named to the dinner committee for the annual meeting which was to be held on December 22, in commemoration of the Pilgrims' landing, and since Brooklyn had just organized a chapter, Brooks was asked to secure prominent speakers before they could be contacted by Brooklyn. Accordingly, he wrote to Mark Twain in April:

> Lotos Club,
> 147 Fifth Avenue.
> April 27th, 1882.

My dear Mark:

You will shortly receive from Judge Horace Russell a letter asking you to speak at the next New England dinner of the New York Society. We are early in the field, this year, as the Brooklyn chaps have organized a society of their own, and we want to corrall [*sic*] the best talent in the country before they get

around. I am on the dinner committee, this year, and have taken the burden
of lassoing several speakers. Judge Russell volunteered to write to you, and
I agreed, in order to make things solid, to write an informal letter to let you
know that one of the Fifty-niners[125] who knows your real strength in eating
and drinking is after you, too. You will have from this until December to get
good and ready in, and so I hope you will say to Russell, when he writes you,
that you are just dying to go it.

Faithfully yours,
Noah Brooks

S.L. Clemens, Esq.
Hartford, Conn.[126]

Because of his long friendship with Brooks, Mark Twain agreed to speak
at the New York meeting of the New England Society. When the seventy-
seventh annual dinner was held at Delmonico's, Brooks was among the 230
members and guests who assembled for the celebration. Among the prominent speakers were Joseph H. Choate, Chauncey M. Depew, General U. S.
Grant, and many others. Grant made a few brief remarks and then reported
to the audience that "Mr. Twain says he will say what I was going to say." A
"great burst of laughter" ensued since Grant was to have spoken about the
United States and Twain was scheduled to reply to the toast "Woman, God
bless her!" Undaunted, Twain rose very deliberately, took his cigar from
his mouth, and "dropped his eye-lids on his mischievously twinkling eyes."
Grant quickly turned his chair toward the speaker to see how Twain would
proceed to bridge the gap which he had created. "With a funny nasal drawl
and in a most deliberate manner," Twain extricated himself by explaining
that he esteemed "it a very great honor . . . to be deputed by General Grant
to speak in honor of this great country." Twain then gave the speech which
he had prepared on women.

The New York Chapter had "a notable and brilliant" meeting, but the new
Brooklyn Chapter, which held their first meeting on the same night, did not
have one notable speaker at their table. Brooks and his associates had stolen
the march on them by securing the available celebrities months ahead of the
December 22 banquet.[127]

CHAPTER XI

The Fruitful Years

The Newark *Daily Advertiser*

In 1884 Brooks resigned as editorial writer on the staff of the New York *Times* to become the editor-in-chief of the Newark (N.J.) *Daily Advertiser*. "I take the post because it pays a large salary, larger than I have here," explained Brooks. His new position had several other good features: the *Daily Advertiser* was issued in the evenings, which meant that there would be no night work for Brooks, and the editor's labors were light, requiring only four hours of work "in the middle of the day."

The *Daily Advertiser* was Republican in politics and owned by Thomas Talmadge Kinney (1821–1900), who had inherited the paper in 1880 from his father, William Burnet Kinney. The first number of the *Daily Advertiser*, edited by Amzi Armstrong, had been published by George Bush & Company on March 1, 1832, but the following year this Whig organ was purchased by William Burnet Kinney who served as editor until President Taylor appointed him minister to Sardinia in 1851. At this time, his son Thomas became managing editor and served until Dr. Sanford B. Hunt was appointed editor-in-chief. Hunt held this position until his death on April 27, 1884,[1] and his ability and hard work had made the *Daily Advertiser* "the most influential newspaper in the State" of New Jersey.[2] Upon Hunt's death, Thomas Kinney selected Brooks to carry on this reputation. "The *Advertiser* is to be congratulated upon having secured so able a successor to the late Dr. Sanford B. Hunt," one writer noted.[3]

Brooks planned to assume the editorship on June 2 and explained to his old friend Witherle that the owner was "a rich man" who wanted a reliable editor in charge while he traveled in Europe.[4] The circulation of the *Daily Advertiser* was about 6,800, but there was no Sunday issue. Brooks was given complete charge of the editorial policy and enjoyed "an entirely independent position."[5] Little is known of his work on the *Daily Advertiser*, but he did "snatch enough time from office duties to write an occasional short story" about New England life for a syndicated series which appeared in many other papers.[6] For his own paper, Brooks also reviewed books[7] and by 1886 his reputation caused manufacturers to seek his endorsement for their products. For the Waterman Fountain Pen Company he wrote this testimonial: "A year's assiduous work with the pen, testing it in *various ways*, has proved to me that your 'Ideal' is the only perfect instrument of the kind."[8]

Upon moving to Newark, Brooks rented rooms at 534 Broad Street, but in 1885 he moved to The Aldine at 2 Lombardy Street, an apartment building on the northeast corner of Broad and Lombardy. It was the first apartment house to be built in Newark and was also the first to have an elevator. At the time of this writing this site is occupied by the modern office building of the New Jersey Bell Telephone Company. Because his apartment suited him and was close to the *Daily Advertiser*, which was located at 788 Broad Street, Brooks remained in The Aldine until he left Newark.

Clubs and Other Activities

Since New York was just thirty minutes by rail from Newark,[9] Brooks returned there "every two or three days" to meet his old friends at the Authors, Century, and Lotos clubs. He was "thoroughly a club man,"[10] and in 1893 his name was added to the exclusive New York *Social Register*.[11] But Brooks also took an active part in the clubs of Newark. His creed was "life *is* worth living,"[12] and in Newark he helped to organize the Wednesday Club, a group which met at one of the local restaurants to have dinner and discuss literature. It was "a man's organization and everything about it is informal and restful," declared Brooks. He invited his old friend Edmund Clarence Stedman to attend one of their meetings to be held March 21, 1894; Stedman accepted the invitation and joined in the discussion of American fiction.[13] Brooks was also a member of the Fortnightly Club, "a select organization of about a dozen men of literary inclinations,"[14] the Essex County Country Club, whose object was to encourage sports, and the Essex Club, a social organization.[15]

In Newark, Brooks became a member of the South Park Presbyterian Church where Dr. James P. Wilson was the pastor. It was said of Brooks by friends "that there was no detail of the church work that was so insignificant that he would not give his attention to it." Dr. Wilson and Brooks became "warm friends," and when Wilson died, Brooks helped to erect a memorial tablet in the church to honor the departed minister. At the unveiling of this plaque, Brooks also gave the address which was termed "one of his most inspired compositions." "It made a profound impression upon all who heard it," friends recalled.[16]

A considerable portion of Brooks's income was spent in helping orphans or sons of poor families to obtain college educations. While in Newark, Brooks "always had a boy or two in tow," Mrs. Bertha Bash declared.[17] He also retained his ardent interest in politics and spoke at various political gatherings in Newark. Once, while he was speaking in the north of end of the city, the audience noticed that Brooks "kept away from the front of the stage and was apparently disconcerted, for several times he made a move as if to step forward and then would look down, halt, and move back." In decorating the hall, the committee had draped the American flag in such a manner that it lay on the front of the platform. Finally, Brooks stopped speaking and in a whisper asked one of the officials to remove the flag. As the flag was removed, the audience "broke out into a storm of applause," and Brooks explained that he "feared that he might inadvertently step on it." His patriotism was genuine, and he taught the audience a lesson that they would long remember.[18]

To enable Newark to hear prominent lecturers, Brooks sometimes pleaded with his New York friends to come and speak. In 1891 he asked Edmund Clarence Stedman to "read us a lecture," assuring him that the audience would number about 1,000.[19]

Brooks quickly made many new friends in Newark, and among them was E. Q. Keasbey, a prominent lawyer who delighted in hearing Brooks's many stories. "As a raconteur," said Keasbey, "he was unsurpassed."[20] Another of his companions was Monsignor George Hobart Doane, of St. Patrick's Church, who remarked that Brooks "was the most delightful and companionable man I ever knew."[21]

As a rule, Brooks spent his summer vacations at Castine, but in 1891 he rested at Fabyan House in New Hampshire.[22] He had just recovered from a siege of carbuncles which had troubled him since the early part of January. At times he had been obliged "to stand at the dinner table or take my meals off the mantel-piece." Finally, he was forced to spend two weeks in bed before recovering. "It was the first times in years that I have been confined to the house," Brooks complained.[23] In general, his health was good and he was able to write numerous articles, books, and stories in addition to daily editorial chores.

Literary Work

By 1884 Brooks was recognized as one of the most outstanding writers ever to come from Maine.[24] The following year he was invited to the banquet given by Charles Scribner's Sons on March 21 to honor their most outstanding authors,[25] and in 1886 Boston paid tribute to Brooks for his writings.[26] He had "a decided knack at short stories,"[27] and many of them were used as lead articles in *St. Nicholas* where he continued to publish children's stories during his residence in Newark. Soon after going to Newark, Brooks wrote "The Biography of Richard," a sketch of the Lotos Club cat whom he had known and played with during his residence at the club,[28] but it was nearly two and a half years before Brooks interrupted his other writings to contribute another story to *St. Nicholas*, an autobiographical piece entitled "A Lesson in Patriotism" which tells of his boyhood participation in a military play group at Castine.[29] "Ran Away to Home" appeared next in *St. Nicholas* and is another of Brooks's Castine tales. A young lad is sent on a visit to his aunt, who lives eighteen miles from Castine, but homesickness seizes him and he runs home.[30]

When *St. Nicholas* decided to have "an all-around-the-world year" in 1889, Brooks sketched the life of the explorer Henry M. Stanley under the title of "The White Pasha." It received much advanced publicity since Stanley was a popular and romantic figure.[31] As most boys love dogs, Brooks next composed a story featuring the heroic deeds of some famous dogs. This study, "Among Dogs of High Degree," also describes the various breeds.[32]

In the November, 1890 issue of *St. Nicholas*, the first chapter of a new serial by Brooks appeared. It was "The Boy Settlers," based upon the journal which Brooks kept while in Kansas during 1857 and written in the same vein as *The Boy Emigrants*.[33] In this adventure story, however, Brooks disguised the actual participants to such a degree that it is impossible to identify them, although the narrative does follow the activities of the little group of Illinois men who had attempted to establish farms in Kansas. In September of 1891 Charles Scribner's Sons published the story as a book which was dedicated to John Greenleaf Whittier "whose patriotic songs were the inspiration" of the original "boy" settlers in 1857. At the same time, Brooks's earlier book, *The Boy Emigrants*, was reissued as a companion volume with a matching binding.[34]

The Boy Settlers received glowing reviews in the literary magazines; *The Dial* reported that "the style is brisk and to the point, and the narrative is full of the adventure and exciting incidents of a settler's life in the new, rough country. Such books are excellent reading for boys."[35] *The Book Buyer* promptly named it a "book of the month,"[36] and its steady sale prompted the publishers to reprint it in 1906 and 1924.

Occasionally Brooks contributed articles to other magazines besides *St. Nicholas*. For adult readers he wrote a psychological tale called "The Hereditary Barn" which was published in the *Overland Monthly* of October, 1886. The plot revolves around the history of "a big barn, black with age, but substantial, and more suggestive of wealth and comfort than even the old farmhouse itself." This old barn is on the old Joslin farm which Brooks avers is in the vicinity of "Fairport." In 1807 Elkanah Joslin hangs himself because the Embargo Act has ruined his trade and he will not resort to smuggling—he is "an uncompromising church-member." His son Jotham also hangs himself "from the very identical beam" just ten years later because tuberculosis has ruined his health. With this second suicide, the neighbors declare that the barn is surely haunted, and in 1825 Amzi, another son of Elkanah, commits suicide in the same manner after having become a drunkard. After many years these three tragedies are nearly forgotten, but in the 1880's Charlie Joslin is rejected by his sweetheart and suddenly disappears. On the night of his disappearance, lightning strikes the barn and it burns to the ground. Some days later, two men are poking around in the ashes when suddenly they discover a fragment of human bone. They wonder if it is possible that Charlie had also hanged himself before the fire started, but quickly decide that the answer will never be revealed, throw the bone back into the basement, and push the stone foundations into the pit. "And under this tumult of masonry now lay forever hidden whatever of mystery remained of the hereditary barn," Brooks declared.[37]

For *The Critic* Brooks sometimes contributed a letter or reminiscence,[38] and for *The Forum* he wrote a lengthy article expressing his views on journalism.[39] In 1889 *The Book Buyer* obtained his services as a reviewer of the many new books available for the Christmas shoppers. His lengthy survey was published in December under the heading "Books of the Christmas Season."[40] Three months later, he wrote an anonymous sketch of Bret Harte for *The Book Buyer*,[41] and in December of 1890 he again reviewed the "Books of the Christmas Season."[42] In 1892 he reported on his speciality: "Holiday Books for Young People,"[43] but the following year he returned to his usual review of general books.[44] All of these review sections are long and undoubtedly were very profitable to him.

By the summer of 1886 Brooks was working on a new project: a biography of Lincoln for young people.[45] This was Brooks's first major attempt at historical writing and he was unused to the methods of scholarly research, but his personal knowledge of Lincoln made up in part for his lack of training. It was a tremendous task and left him with little time for rest,[46] but the biography was finished in 1888 and G. P. Putnam's Sons published it at both New York and London under the title *Abraham Lincoln: A Biography for Young People*. It was the fourth volume of Putnam's Boys' and Girls' Library of American Biography and received very favorable reviews although some critics pointed out that it was eulogistic. Most reviewers, nevertheless, concluded that Brooks's popularity with the young people would make it a very successful book.[47]

Except for the period from 1862 to 1865, the material for the Lincoln biography was taken from the secondary works of Isaac N. Arnold, J. G. Holland, Ward Hill Lamon, John G. Nicolay, and John Hay, whom Brooks acknowledged in the preface. There are errors in the study, but it is a very readable book—much too good to have been labeled as a book for juveniles. Robert Todd Lincoln, who was very critical of most biographies of his father, complimented Brooks by saying: "The work you have prepared presents the events . . . with a compactness and interest which could not be surpassed."[48]

In 1892 Putnam's Sons reissued *Abraham Lincoln*, but in 1894 they changed the title to *Abraham Lincoln and the Downfall of American Slavery* and added it to their Heroes of the Nations series. Once removed from the category of children's books, it had a wide sale among adult readers and was reissued in 1896, 1898, 1899, 1904, and 1908. In 1901 it was also republished as *Abraham Lincoln: His Youth and Early Manhood with a Brief Account of His Later Life* in the Knickerbocker Literature Series, and Fred De Fau & Company of New York printed it without date as a volume in their Famous Epoch-Makers Series, using the title *Abraham Lincoln*. Deluxe centennial editions were also printed in 1909 by both Putnam's Sons and the National Tribune of Washington, D.C., under the title *Abraham Lincoln: The Nation's Leader in the Great Struggle through Which Was Maintained the Existence of the United States*.

D. Lothrop Company announced during the early months of 1888 that Brooks had been engaged to write a history of California for their Stories of the States article, but for some reason—perhaps lack of time—Brooks never wrote this volume.[49] In 1893, however, Brooks wrote another book for Scribner's Men of Achievement set. It was called *Statesmen* and sketched the lives of Henry Clay, Daniel P. Chase, Abraham Lincoln, Charles Sumner, Samuel J. Tilden, James G. Blaine, James A. Garfield, and Grover Cleveland. Although *Statesmen* never had a large sale, it was reissued in 1904.

Brooks served as editor of the *Daily Advertiser* for nine years, but when the Kinney family sold the paper in July of 1893, he decided to retire,[50] tendering his resignation to take effect on August 1. The tired journalist wished to devote the rest of his life to "purely literary work,"[51] and although not yet sixty-three, he said in the words of Emerson that "it is time to be old, to take in sail." "He felt the need of rest from the exigent demands of daily newspaper work," observed one of the new editors, "and he was glad to quit."[52] To replace Brooks, the new owners hired Frederick Evans Jr. and W. D. Farwell.[53]

Brooks remained at his apartment in Newark to write; he also saw his *Statesmen* book through the press,[54] and then took a trip to Chicago during the last two weeks of September, probably to attend the World's Columbian Exposition.[55] However, his livelihood now depended largely upon his talented pen and his small savings, so he quickly became engaged in free-lance work. For the Christmas issue of *The Book Buyer* in 1893, Brooks evaluated the many "miscellaneous books" on the market,[56] and in later years he continued to review holiday books for this magazine, his speciality being children's literature,[57] although in 1902 he wrote a second sketch of Bret Harte.[58] During his first few months of retirement, Brooks also wrote for *Harper's Weekly*; in December of 1893 it published his historical article on "The San Francisco Vigilantes," and in March of 1894 his sketch of "Governor Werts of New Jersey."[59]

But Brooks's greatest desire—now that he had the necessary time—was to write a book relating his experiences with Lincoln during the Civil War. By the first part of February, 1894, he was working on his memoirs which he hoped to publish serially. This task, said Brooks, was his "life-work, and when it is completed I shall feel that I shall never do anything more important to me or to the literature of the time."[60]

The Century Magazine, which had published the monumental biography of Lincoln by Nicolay and Hay,[61] quickly accepted Brooks's proposed book without seeing the manuscript. The president of the Century Company offered him thirty dollars per thousand words, which he accepted.[62] Although Brooks did not have any chapters ready for publication, he needed money and asked for an advancement of $1,000.[63] The Century Company offered $500,[64] but Brooks refused this amount and the publishers then sent him a check for $750 which was, as they explained, "midway between the two sums named."[65]

With the security of a lucrative contract and a cash advancement, Brooks decided to leave Newark and return to Castine. On April 24, 1894, Newark friends gave him "an informal farewell dinner" and Brooks moved back to his birthplace,[66] which had always brought back to his mind many happy memories. As early as 1866 he had declared that he wished to end his days "in the cool quiet of dear old Castine."[67] For $1,200 Brooks purchased the house (then occupied by Dr. E. E. Philbrook) where "his father's family had lived

FIGURE 5. Noah Brooks in his library at Castine, Maine, 1890s. Author's collection

for many years." It was one of the four famous Jarvis houses built by Hezekiah
Lufkin at an early date, and Brooks promptly named the old homestead "The
Ark" since for many years he had been affectionately called "Uncle Noah."
Later, he built a library on to the south side of this beautiful frame dwelling
and there gathered his many books and mementos around him.[68] He made
arrangements to take his meals with William H. Hooper and in the evenings,
when the family was together, Brooks would tell Hooper how his writing was
progressing or relate incidents from his bounteous storehouse of memories.[69]
When not at "The Ark," Brooks could generally be found visiting with Phoebe
Holmes on Court Street.[70]

Upon his return to Castine, Brooks immediately took an active interest in
the welfare of the village. Frequently he addressed groups of school children
or advised the boys how to become successful citizens.[71] The Castine Library
also benefited greatly from the many books which he donated, a practice
which he had begun many years prior to his retirement,[72] and in March of
1895 he was chosen chairman of the library committee and helped to compile
and publish a catalogue of the library's holdings.[73] When his three-year term
expired in 1898, he was reappointed for another term.[74]

Soon after returning to Castine, Brooks published a collection of his short
stories which had previously appeared in magazines. He chose seven, founded
largely upon incidents observed in his youth, for inclusion in *Tales of the*

Maine Coast.[75] It was his first volume of fiction for adult readers and was published by Charles Scribner's Sons sometime between the second and eleventh of June, 1894.[76] The reviewers welcomed this little book with much praise. Said one critic, it presents "excellently the picturesqueness of the coast and the queer, shrewd characteristics of its people, with their odd memories for important events linked to small personal happenings."[77] And when *The Literary World* selected its list of the best works in the field of fiction for 1894, *Tales of the Maine Coast* was included.[78] The price was one dollar, of which Brooks received ten cents, but the book never had a large sale.

Most of Brooks's time during the early months of 1894, however, was devoted to his series of Lincoln articles for *The Century Magazine*. From his "Castine" newsletters to the Sacramento *Daily Union*, preserved in numerous scrapbooks,[79] Brooks gleaned the necessary facts to bolster his memories of Lincoln and the Civil War. He composed six lengthy articles, the first of which appeared in November of 1894 and the last in May of 1895,[80] for which he received $2,250; he also signed a contract on May 14 with the Century Company for their publication in book form, but he received no further payment except a graduated royalty ranging from ten per cent, for the first 1,000 copies, to fifteen per cent for all copies in excess of 2,000.[81]

When *Washington in Lincoln's Time* appeared (toward the end of 1895), the reading public did not get just a reprinting of the original six articles because Brooks had expanded some of them, altered punctuation, paragraphing, and chapter divisions, and added three new chapters. In the midst of the original articles he inserted a nineteen-page chapter on "The Death of Slavery" and completed the book by adding "Life in the White House" and "The Last Grand Review." These last two chapters total forty-eight pages and contain much valuable information not found in other source material. Therefore, the book is much more valuable for Lincoln scholars than the original six articles in *The Century Magazine*.

The critics warmly praised *Washington in Lincoln's Time* as a great contribution to American history and a treat for the general reader. Brooks, commented one reviewer, "has done many things well, but has written nothing more interesting."[82] The scholarly but infant *American Historical Review* proclaimed that it was "one of the best books of its class,"[83] and the first edition was quickly exhausted. The book was reprinted in 1896 and enjoyed a modest sale for several years. *The Literary Digest* chose two episodes from the original articles for condensation, a great honor for Brooks since this magazine gathered its material from a large number of the best periodicals.[84]

Although Brooks had decided to make "The Ark" his "regular Summer residence,"[85] he left Castine when fall arrived. He disliked cold weather, and perhaps he had also discovered that the library facilities at Castine were not adequate for his writing needs. As late as October 20, 1894, Brooks was still in Castine,[86] but by November he was living in New York City at No. 10 East Twenty-eighth Street,[87] a "narrow stone" apartment house. This building— long since torn down—was then occupied by such famous writers as Richard Harding Davis, Stephen Fiske, and Stephen Bonsal.[88] Brooks maintained a suite of rooms at this address until 1901, although he generally lived there only during the winter months.[89]

When he was not writing in his rooms, Brooks was frequently seen at the various clubs, the Gilsey House at 1202 Broadway, or the offices of the Century Company where he met his old friends and talked shop.[90] And since Brooks knew so many of the prominent literary figures of the day, he was frequently invited to their celebrations. Before Dr. Arthur Conan Doyle returned to England, after visiting the United States in the fall of 1894, he was given a farewell dinner on December 7 in the Aldine Club at Fifth Avenue and Fifteenth Street. Although Brooks was not a member, he was invited and made a speech to the assembled group.[91]

At the same time that Brooks was writing his Lincoln articles at Castine he was also working on a series of articles which trace the history of political parties in America. These three papers were probably finished when Brooks returned to New York in November of 1894 since the initial article appeared in *Scribner's Magazine* the following January while Brooks was traveling abroad.[92] They are written in a popular vein and exhibit little or no research into original source materials. After their appearance serially, they were col-lected without change, a fourth chapter of twenty-seven pages entitled "The Party Platforms of Sixty Years" added, and Charles Scribner's Sons issued the book in 1895 as *Short Studies in Party Politics*.[93] Since it was published in April, the additional chapter was also prepared some time before Brooks left for Europe.[94]

After finishing *Short Studies in Party Politics*, Brooks made plans in January of 1895 for a Mediterranean cruise. Before sailing, he probably received pay-ment from *Scribner's Magazine*, but the amount is unknown. To help pay his expenses he agreed to write a series of travel letters for the New York *Times*, and after years of dreaming about such a trip, Brooks purchased his steam-ship ticket. Back in 1851 he had admitted to George Witherle that "perhaps it would be more of a duty for us to travel in our own land first, but to me it would not be so much of a pleasure as would a foreign tour, and seriously if I had $1000. in my possession I would leave for Europe within a month." "And soberly and sincerely," Brooks continued, "it will ever be one of the first objects of my ambition to do so."[95] As editor of the *Alta California* in

San Francisco, Brooks had published the travel letters of Mark Twain, and later, other friends of Brooks also visited Europe. Their experiences probably increased Brooks's desire to travel abroad.[96]

On January 29, 1895, Brooks sailed from New York abroad the Hamburg-American steamer *Fürst Bismarck* "with a life-long friend, the trip being in reality the fulfillment of an agreement made when they were lads." In addition to the scheduled ports of call, Brooks announced that he wished to visit "Paris and the north of Europe."[97] When the *Fürst Bismark* reached Funchal, on the island of Madeira, Brooks wrote his first newsletter to the New York *Times* on February 6, describing Madeira and the Azores as "islanded points off the western coast of Europe that appear to have preserved the Old World part, the archaic spirit, as it were, more completely than any part of the Continent has maintained it."[98] Five days later he wrote a second letter telling of his experiences at Gibraltar and the French port of Algiers, a city which Brooks found to be exactly as described in a geography book that he had studied in his youth. "Here," wrote Brooks, "are the white buildings rising in regular tiers from the sweeping curve of the shore; and here, high above the modern French city, are the irregular, but equally white houses and mosques of the Moors."[99]

The steamer docked at Genoa on February 13 and Brooks discovered regretfully that Europe was having a phenomenally cold winter. After exploring Genoa he took a train to Nice, France, and then proceeded to Monte Carlo where he saw Arthur Sullivan, whom he had met at the Lotos Club in 1879. This famous composer, Brooks observed, "played at the roulette table with all the bounce of an American 'plunger.'"[100] After returning to the ship, Brooks sailed to Valletta on the island of Malta where he penned another letter on February 19, but the island did not live up to the descriptions which he had read in Homer.[101]

Alexandria, Egypt, was the next stop on the tour and there Brooks boarded a train for Cairo where he met President Charles W. Eliot of Harvard College who was staying at the Hotel du Nil.[102] From Cairo Brooks drove out to see the pyramids and the Sphinx. "One morning," reported Brooks, "too early for the tourist avalanche and the Bedouin swarm, I succeeded in evading the crowds and had a good time inspecting the Third Pyramid, built by Menkaura, around the base of which are strewn many of the granite blocks that once incrusted its surface."[103]

From Alexandria the *Fürst Bismarck* sailed eastward to Jerusalem where Brooks wrote again on March 4.[104] After visiting the many places connected with Jesus Christ, the tourist sailed for Greece. Athens, complained Brooks, was rather disappointing, but "a nearer view of Athens, revealing as it does, the gem of its crown—the Acropolis—sets right all misconceptions."[105] When he reached Constantinople (now called Istanbul), Brooks discovered that near-by Robert College was an American institution, being incorporated in the State of New York with its funds invested in the United States.[106] In a second letter, written on March 13, he related that he had seen the sultan and his huge palace.[107]

When the tour reached Naples on the return voyage through the Mediterranean, Brooks left the *Fürst Bismarck* and traveled north through Europe, visiting London and Paris.[108] He also went to Rome and Milan where he greatly enjoyed the paintings of Leonardo da Vinci. By April 12 Brooks was back in Naples and summed up his travels by saying that "after the pyramids, Memphis, and Jerusalem, even old Rome seems modern and Naples painfully new." London and Paris, he thought, were cities where "the gloss has not yet worn off."[109] Sometime after returning to Naples, Brooks sailed for home and probably returned to Castine as he had planned.[110]

With the memories of the trip vividly in his mind, Brooks wrote a little guide book for tourists who planned to take a Mediterranean cruise,[111] and in December of 1895 Scribner's published it together with numerous woodcuts, a map, and a list of United States consuls.[112] Its sale at $1.25 was not large, but Brooks received nearly nineteen cents royalty on each volume. The reviewers were divided in their opinions of *The Mediterranean Trip*; some thought that the introductory information concerning ocean travel was "a waste of ink and paper," while others pronounced the guide as the best handbook they had seen.[113]

After his return from Europe, Brooks also wrote a story for *Scribner's Magazine* entitled "The Rector's Hat" which is unlike any of his tales. The Rev. Justinian Littlefield is accidentally assaulted and an innocent man sent to prison for the crime. But the judge, after giving the sentence, accidentally discovers that his own son committed the brutal assault and tells the dying minister of his findings. However, the two agree never to speak of the matter again, and the innocent victim remains in prison. In Brooks's other writings fair play and justice always triumph.[114]

About one month after his *Short Studies in Party Politics* appeared, Brooks also published a little volume of 169 pages entitled *How the Republic Is Governed*,[115] the manuscript of which had probably been written during the summer of 1894. It too was published by Scribner's and contains the Declaration of Independence, the Constitution, and seventeen brief chapters dealing with the operation of the various governmental divisions. Like *Short Studies in Party Politics*, it is a popular handbook and received favorable reviews from the critics. *How the Republic Is Governed* is "so indispensable a monitor that it is a wonder it was not written a dozen years ago," declared one reviewer.[116] But during its first year, only 1060 copies were sold, netting Brooks $79.50 in royalties.

Brooks's income from royalties during his retirement was not large, but he received a sizeable payment for every special article which he wrote for various publications. And in addition to his writing, Brooks had yet another source of funds: "a substantial bequest" was left to him by the will of a friend "who held him in high esteem."[117] This benefactor cannot be identified, but it was not the wealthy Charles Tilden Wilder, whom Brooks once said would take care of him, for Wilder's will does not mention Brooks.[118]

With the exceptions of *The Mediterranean Trip* and the revisions for *Washington in Lincoln's Time*, the four books[119] which Brooks published in 1895 were written in the years 1893 and 1894, but on July 9, 1895, Charles Scribner's Sons gave him another commission which put his pen back to work again. He was asked to revise *A Popular History of the United States*, a four-volume set written by William Cullen Bryant and Sydney Howard Gay and covering the years from colonization through the Civil War. It had been published by Scribner, Armstrong & Company to commemorate the centennial of our independence, the first volume appearing in 1876 and the fourth in 1881.

The publisher informed Brooks that a decision had been made "a year or two" previously to revise the set because the Civil War material was too condensed and an additional volume was needed to bring the series up to date. "The field to be covered in the addition is one with which you are so thoroughly familiar that the matter could not we think be formidable to you," editor Burlingame explained to Brooks. The set was to be kept "popular in style" and as the work would be a revision, the publisher offered an outright payment to Brooks.[120]

After pondering the offer, Brooks accepted the commission on July 13 and immediately commenced work while in Castine. The publishers had suggested that Brooks rewrite the end of volume four beginning with the year 1862, but this plan was altered. He began with the election of Lincoln[121] and rewrote the remainder of the volume, a total of 148 pages. Whereas these original chapters had covered the entire Civil War, Brooks's revision carries the story only to the point in 1862 where Hooker replaces Burnside as general-in-chief. Over half of volume five, a huge book of 674 pages, is devoted to the remaining war years with the period 1865–1893 being condensed into 329 pages which include a chapter on "American Art and Literature," a subject which Brooks knew so very well.

This overemphasis of the Civil War was exactly what the publishers wanted; the popularity of war studies at this time was very great, and Brooks had collected much material on the war for his *Washington in Lincoln's Time*. This part of the manuscript was probably written within the period of a few weeks since some of the chapters were in the hands of the editor by the first part of November, just four months after the author had started the project. When Burlingame read the first chapters, he informed Brooks on November 19 that he was greatly delighted, even surprised "in spite of my expectations, at the way the matter has been expanded, brought to scale & vivified."[122]

Brooks time off from his belletristic efforts during the first weeks of 1896 and traveled down to see his niece, Madge Upham Wright, at Cambridge, Massachusetts. Mrs. Wright remarked that he acted as chatty as ever but appeared "somewhat bigger of belly than when I saw him last in 1890." "He seems to enjoy his retreat in Castine," she continued, "and talks more of clams and doughnuts than of the ghosts which must haunt the place."

Until March 2, 1896, Brooks worked at Castine, but after that date he was at his New York apartment where he remained until May 10.[123] His pen fairly flew and the final chapter reached Scribner's in time for publication that year. The title of the new five-volume edition was changed to *Scribner's Popular History of the United States*, and Brooks's name was added to those of William Cullen Bryant and Sydney Howard Gay on all the title pages. Since it was a revised edition, the history was not reviewed again in the periodicals, but the Civil War chapters are enlightening, accurate, and show the intimate knowledge which Brooks possessed of Lincoln and the war itself. The remainder of the history is much condensed and does not have the same appeal as the Civil War material.

While working on *Scribner's Popular History of the United States*, Brooks somehow found time to write articles too. He published a brief story in the February, 1896 number of *St. Nicholas*,[124] and the June issue of this magazine carried the first of his historical articles on "The Story of Marco Polo." This series ran until April of 1897[125] and was largely written from the scholarly translation of Marco Polo by Colonel Henry Yule[126] although Brooks wove in running comments and other historical explanations. The story proved to be so popular that the Century Company, publishers of *St. Nicholas*, decided in 1898 to reprint the articles in book form. Toward the end of the year it appeared and was eagerly read by adults as well as children. The reviewers said it was "highly entertaining and instructive, and not by any means confined to young readers."[127] *The Story of Marco Polo* had a steady sale and was reissued in 1899 and 1920, but after this serial Brooks wrote only one more article for *St. Nicholas*. This tale, published after his death, relates a true experience which Brooks had had with a stray dog while traveling to California in 1859.[128]

Castine had a centennial celebration in 1896 and Brooks was appointed to several committees which had charge of the erection of tablets at historical places, the literary exercises, and the naval and marine display.[129] When he was not writing, these activities occupied much of his time during the summer of 1896. About the first of December he returned to New York where he announced that he would spend the winter in California because he wished to "escape the bad weather which usually comes to this part of the country somewhere between January and April." While in California Brooks planned to write a novel for adults, his first attempt in the field, and revealed that he had in mind the plots for several, one of which called for the co-operation of Henry Watterson.[130]

By December 14 Brooks was in Los Angeles where a reporter for the Los Angeles *Times* interviewed him. "He is writing another book," proclaimed the reporter, "and has chosen his nephew's home as a place where he may work undisturbed."[131] This nephew was Major Frank Kidder Upham who had accompanied Brooks on the trek to California in 1859. Upham had been commissioned a second lieutenant in the Cavalry on November 1, 1864, and, after having made the Army his career, had been retired on February 4, 1892. Soon after this, Upham was named treasurer of the National Home for Disabled Soldiers, located eighteen miles from Los Angeles and covering about 120 acres. The government furnished him with a comfortable little house known as The Rose Cottage because white climbing roses "practically covered the front porch."

Since the cottage was not large and there were three Upham children (John, Ethel, and Edith) living at home, Brooks soon rented a bungalow in Santa Monica where he had ideal writing conditions. Santa Monica was about four miles from Upham's home and Brooks often commuted with the Upham girls who were then going to school in Santa Monica. The climate and the fresh fruit suited Brooks and he became determined to spend his winters in California where he could write and enjoy family life with the Uphams.[132]

When not writing, Brooks traveled around California and thoroughly enjoyed himself. "According to the calendar," Brooks remarked on January 22, 1897, "this is midwinter, or thereabouts; but in this favored clime, with the thermometer at 70° in the shade, with rose-laden vines looking in at one's open windows and a rankly verdurous plain spread all around the town, how can anybody realize the midwinter fact?" If he desired to climb in the snow, Mount Lowe was just forty miles by rail from Santa Monica.[133]

In April Brooks returned to San Francisco—his first visit there in sixteen years, he told the reporters. While looking about the city, he dropped in the

Bohemian Club on the ninth, chatted with George Bromley "about old times in California," and told anecdotes to the other members about Bret Harte, Mark Twain, Isaac Bromley, Sam Williams, Ben Avery, and Sam Bowles. "He is an entertaining talker on many lines," said a local reporter, "and profoundly interesting when speaking of Lincoln." Brooks, who informed his friends that he would remain in San Francisco for two or three weeks, joined Governor James Herbert Budd's party on April 10 and climbed Mount Tamalpais where they spent the night in order to observe the rising sun from the summit on the following morning.[134]

With the coming of summer, Brooks returned to Castine. Since he planned to spend some of his winters in California instead of New York, Miss Sarah Brooks Gay,[135] his niece, began keeping house for him during the months that he lived at "The Ark."[136] He seems to have done little writing during the summer of 1897—the novel which he had contemplated was never published—and in the fall he returned to his New York apartment to write a biography of General Henry Knox who had served George Washington as an artillery expert during the Revolution and later became the first secretary of war. When Brooks related his plans to G. P. Putman's Sons, they agreed to publish a life of Knox but asked that it be completed in time for inclusion in their "Heroes of American History" series which was to be published in 1898.[137]

Once back in New York, Brooks began several writing projects and did not return to California during the winter of 1897–1898. He wrote several feature stories for the New York *Times*[138] and began the tedious task of tracing Knox's life from manuscript sources, as no previous biography had been published. Evidently Brooks complained to the publishers about the research, for on February 12 they wrote giving him encouragement.[139] The largest collection of Knox's papers was, at that time, in the possession of The New-England Historic Genealogical Society at Boston, and Brooks rapidly read through the fifty-five "massive folio volumes" of manuscripts, probably during the winter of 1897–1898.[140]

Brooks welcomed diversions from his literary work and when his old friend Edmund Clarence Stedman, who had moved to Lawrence Park at Bronxville, New York, asked him to speak at the Gramatan Club, the invitation was cheerfully accepted. He stayed with Stedman in his beautiful colonial house called "Casa Laura" and addressed the literary group during the first part of March, 1898. While Stedman and Brooks were walking home after the meeting, Stedman confided: "Noah, I am beginning to realize my age—the young girls let me kiss them." Brooks, who was three years older than Stedman, exclaimed, "Is that all, my boy? When you are as old as I am, you will find the evidence more painful. Bless your soul, *they* kiss *me*!"[141] By this time, Brooks's hair was white and he wore burnsides and a mustache instead of a full beard. His eyesight had failed—probably as a result of his work as a night editor under poor light—and he was forced to reply upon thick-lensed glasses but the merry twinkle still lingered in his eyes.

Occasionally other projects also interrupted his work on Knox. For the thirtieth anniversary of the *Overland Monthly*, the editor decided to publish a special edition in July and he implored Brooks to tell of his experiences as assistant editor under Bret Harte. Brooks complied with the request and wrote a fascinating account of the "Early Days of 'The Overland.'"[142]

After Brooks had returned to Castine in the summer of 1898, the Century Company inquired if he had any articles on Mark Twain which they might publish. "No," replied Brooks, "I have not been writing anything about Mark Twain to be printed in the *Century*." But he informed the editor that he would enjoy writing a few pages entitled "What I Know about Mark Twain's Personal Character," adding in jest that if he did write such an article, *The Century Magazine* would not print it and "Mark would sue me for libel." "But," Brooks offered, "if you really want [an article], I will write 'a very brief notice,' as we used to say in the *Tribune* office, which will cover the Three Old Californians."[143] About ten days later, on August 26, the sketch was finished and mailed to the editor,[144] but in the midst of its writing, Brooks playfully informed Richard Watson Gilder that "if Mark Twain doesn't think it covers him sufficiently, he can add some, himself."[145] The article relates some of Brooks's experiences with Mark Twain in San Francisco, but the statement concerning Twain's trip westward in 1859 is in error.[146]

While in Castine, Brooks also rewrote his popular book *The Fairport Nine*—published in 1880—making it a "somewhat larger volume" which Charles Scribner's Sons published late in 1898 under the title *The Boys of Fairport*. As with the earlier book, the center of attention is the baseball team of "Fairport," and one reviewer remarked that "it is a hearty, healthy story of healthy, hearty boyhood."[147] It proved to be very popular with the children and by 1900 Brooks's royalties on this volume amounted to $235.10, proving again that his real talent lay in the field of children's literature.[148] Scribner's reprinted it in 1919.

Sometime after October 4, Brooks left Castine to spend the winter of 1898–1899 in California with the Uphams.[149] He returned to The Rose Cottage to work on his biography of Knox, but he also wrote a sketch of Henry George for *The Century Magazine*. To refresh his memory, he asked Henry George Jr. for certain pertinent facts about his father,[150] and after incorporating this material the article appeared in February of 1899.[151] Brooks completed his trilogy by writing a sketch of Bret Harte which was published in July;[152] and because Brooks had had a close association with George, Harte, and Twain, these articles are interesting and intimate.

The publishers informed Brooks, while he was in California, that they wished to have the completed manuscript of Henry Knox by November 1,[153] and he returned to New York sometime before April 7.[154] Brooks worked at his apartment until June[155] and then returned to "The Ark" where he completed all but the last three chapters by the middle of July.[156] The editor read the completed chapters and found only one fault with the manuscript: he did not like the short title of "Henry Knox." Instead, he wanted a long title which would give "the best possible emphasis, in these days of crowded book markets, for the announcement of any new book calling for public attention."[157]

After completing the last three chapters, Brooks wrote the preface at Castine in October of 1899, saying that his reason for writing the biography was that "the family of the author was allied to that part of Knox" and tales of Knox's greatness "formed a part of the author's earliest recollections."[158] Actually, the tie was very slight; Senator John Holmes (1773–1843) had married Sally Brooks, sister of Noah's father, in 1800 and when she died in 1835, Holmes then married Caroline Knox Swan, the youngest daughter of Henry Knox. Except for friendship, there was no actual connection between the Knoxes and the Brookses.[159]

When G. P. Putnam's Sons issued the Knox biography in 1900, it was called *Henry Knox: A Soldier of the Revolution* and also bore a long subtitle telling of his many exploits. It was a volume in the "American Men of Energy" series and in general received favorable reviews from the literary magazines, one calling it "a well-made biography," but Oswald Garrison Villard, in reviewing it for the *American Historical Review*, said that it was "stamped with the earmark 'popular'" and was not a scientific or exhausting study.[160]

Brooks's years of retirement—like his editorial years—were busy ones. In June of 1899 the Lothrop Publishing Company of Boston asked him to write a juvenile book for their 1900 list of publications,[161] and in September Dana Estes & Company of Boston also implored him to write them a book.[162] But both of these generous offers were refused by Brooks, who was serving as a contributor and reviser for *The National Cyclopaedia of American Biography*[163] and also aiding Charles Eugene Hamlin in writing the biography of his grandfather, Hannibal Hamlin.[164] Publishers now sought out Brooks since his many writings had won him fame; in 1899 Brooks's name appeared in the first issue of *Who's Who in America* and remained in this directory until his death.

There is no record of Brooks having been in California during the winter of 1899–1900; he probably was at his apartment in New York until summer. While at "The Ark" in June of 1900, he was appointed president of the "Home

Week Association" for Castine, a statewide celebration that was observed by many communities from the sixth to the twelfth of August.[165] Brooks was also elected to membership in The New-England Historic Genealogical Society in 1900, perhaps in recognition for his writing of the Knox biography.[166]

During the summer of 1900, Brooks began writing "The Plains Across," a historical article which is drawn from his diaries kept in 1859. Brooks explained to the editor of *The Century Magazine* that since "it relates personal experiences, not hearsay, it will have a certain value as a contribution to American history." From these same diaries he had earlier obtained the plot and inspiration for his successful story *The Boy Emigrants*. By the last of November he had "nearly finished" the article,[167] but he then stopped to write another book and "The Plains Across" was not completed until a year later.

Brooks remained at Castine until about December in 1900 before leaving for New York; he did not go to his apartment at 10 East Twenty-eighth Street but took up residence in the Gilsey House at the corner of Broadway and Twenty-ninth Street.[168] Here he finished writing a popular history of the Lewis and Clark expedition, using as a basis for his work the four-volume set of Dr. Elliott Coues,[169] and Scribner's published it in October of 1901 as *First across the Continent*. Cyrus Townsend Brady said that Brooks's edition was a "valuable contribution to literature on the subject of one of the most splendid exploits in our pioneer records."[170] Dozens of newspapers praised the book because it would be read by countless young people who would not read a lengthy and scholarly book on the subject. Only *The Conservative* of Nebraska City expressed disappointment, saying that the reviewer had hoped to see a scholarly edition of the two explorers' journals instead of another popular history.[171]

While in New York during January of 1901, Brooks had deviated from his work on Lewis and Clark to write a lengthy sketch of Horace Greeley whom he had worked for as night editor of the New York *Tribune*.[172] It is a charming and informative picture of the eccentric editor and drew a wide audience when it appeared later that year in *The Youth's Companion*.[173] Although written for children, the literary world also enjoyed Brooks's apt characterization of Greeley. And probably before leaving New York, Brooks also composed a long story for *The Century Magazine* entitled "Mrs. Thankful's Charge," an amusing tale about a preacher's wife who replaces her invalid husband in the pulpit at "Fairport" and wins the congregation away from him only to lose her "charge" because of pregnancy.[174]

In the summer of 1901 Brooks returned to Castine and wrote another book for boys called *Lem, a New England Village Boy*. It was also published by Scribner's and seems to be somewhat autobiographical, depicting "a jolly little chap, just as human as all well-organized boys ought to be, in mischief, and consequently in trouble, very often."[175] Upon Brooks's plea for money, the publisher advanced him $750 before *Lem* was published later that same year. Fortunately, it was a successful book and within three months 3,452 copies were sold, bringing Brooks $480.30 in royalties.[176]

When *Lem* was finished, Brooks turned his attention once again to "The Plains Across," quickly finished the historical article in November of 1901, and sent it to *The Century Magazine*.[177] The editor accepted the long-awaited manuscript and told Brooks to name his own price.[178] After some thought, Brooks said $150 and "The Plains Across" was published the following April.[179]

Probably against his wishes, Brooks remained in Castine during the winter of 1901–1902 and his writing halted. Perhaps his bronchitis and lack of funds kept him from going to California. In February of 1902 the Knickerbocker Publishing Company asked him to serve on the advisory council for the publication of the *American National Biography*.[180] He accepted the offer and was asked to submit a list of prominent people from Maine to be included in the series. Forty-one names, including his own, were compiled by Brooks and sent to the publishing company in April.[181] His literary work then ceased until the death of Bret Harte on May 2 after which Brooks wrote three articles relating anecdotes of Harte,[182] one of which was the feature sketch for the Bret Harte Memorial Number of the *Overland Monthly*.

In July, when Brooks was at Castine, D. Appleton & Company asked him to write a popular biography of Sir William Pepperrell (1696–1759) who was born in Kittery, Maine (then a part of Massachusetts), became a well known soldier and jurist, and was created a baronet in 1746—the only New Englander to be so honored by Great Britain. Brooks accepted the task, but he did not live to write the book.[183] Then in August the same publishing firm asked his opinion of Reuben Gold Thwaites's *Father Marquette* which they had published the previous month as a volume in the Appleton Life Histories. "Although an excellent piece of work, as everything Mr. Thwaites does is excellent," the editor complained, "the book does not exactly meet the requirements of the series. It is slightly over the heads of circulating library people."[184] Brooks's opinion of the book is unknown, but he probably agreed with the publishers since his own writing was aimed at the general public.

Although the chill climate aggravated his respiratory trouble, Brook remained at "The Ark" during the fall of 1902. Doctors insisted that his illness was chronic bronchitis and not tuberculosis, although the symptoms were much alike. A constant racking cough kept him in a state of exhaustion,[185] but he continued to write because he needed extra money for the luxuries which he had grown used to having. In the middle of October he wrote an article on Lincoln for the New York *Times*,[186] and in December he asked Scribner's if they would publish a book either on privateering or the Navy. They advised him that these fields were overworked and suggested that he write a book from Zebulon Pike's memoirs.[187]

Finally the cold weather forced Brooks to return to the Gilsey House in New York, but he could find no relief for his cough and Mrs. T. T. Kinney, the wife of the former publisher of the Newark *Daily Advertiser*, insisted that he go to California "for his health."[188] The Kinney family arranged to take Brooks to California in a private railway car because "he was quite ill at the time," recalled William B. Kinney, "and had a most distressing cough." Brooks feared it was approaching consumption, said Kinney, "but the physicians declared that it was not."[189]

In late winter or early spring Brooks went to California[190] with the intention of staying with the Uphams who were then living in Los Angeles. Frank had died in 1899 and his widow, Sarah, had moved into "a moderately small house" and was physically unable to care for Brooks. She therefore engaged a room for him at a nearby boarding house, but his chronic cough frightened the landlady who insisted that he leave. Brooks became huffed and moved to a hotel where he remained until an old friend, J. H. Morse of San Francisco, purchased a house for him at 331 North Marengo Avenue in Pasadena. It was a pleasant little cottage, "set among a bower of roses and a maze of palm trees,"[191] and a Negro servant, hired by Morse, managed the house. Robert Eason, president of the Union Savings Bank in Pasadena, was assigned the task of looking after Brooks's personal and financial affairs.

At first, while Brooks was still able to write, he composed two articles that were published after his death,[192] but when he became more feeble, most of his time was spent in driving about the countryside. By July he could no longer hold a pen and Edith Upham went to his home twice a week to write letters for him. On July 16 Brooks dictated a letter to Monsignor Doane, informing him that his health was very poor and that "his stay in the high and dry climate of Pasadena" had not benefitted him as much as expected.[193] However, Brooks maintained his courage and occasionally invited the Upham girls to have lunch with him at his cottage,[194] but his severe coughing had weakened his whole body. The end of his struggles came at 11:30 P.M. on August 15, and the attending physician, George Deacon, confirmed the cause of death as "chronic bronchitis."[195] Brooks would have been seventy-three on October 24.

Since Brooks had been confined to the house for three months prior to his death, some of the local papers concluded that he must have been a recluse, and as he had not mixed socially with his neighbors, Pasadena did not know of Brooks's literary fame until his papers were opened at the Union Savings

Bank on August 17. Then, the local press compiled a long obituary which was carried in newspapers throughout the United States. Ives & Warren Company embalmed the body, but there was no funeral service at Pasadena, the casket being shipped by Wells-Fargo Express to Castine.[196] Because of his reputation as a writer and because of the lavish way in which he lived, it was assumed by most papers that Brooks had left a large estate. He died penniless, however, leaving the Upham children only the copyrights to his books, which later brought them a few hundred dollars.[197] But it could be said of Brooks as it was of Bret Harte, who left an estate of only $1,800, that if he died poor, it was "only because he lived rich."[198]

On the morning of August 26 the steamer *Silver Star* brought the body of Brooks into the little port of Castine[199] where his executors, William H. Hooper and Charles C. Upham, took charge of the arrangements.[200] That same afternoon funeral services were held in the little village church where the Rev. George M. Adams, the historian of The New-England Historic Genealogical Society, paid a final tribute to Brooks. Adams, a personal friend of Brooks, had been born and raised in Castine, although at the time his home was in Auburndale, Massachusetts. Many of Brooks's intimate friends, such as William Dean Howells, could not attend the funeral, but their letters were read by the minister during the service.

Burial was made in the Castine cemetery, where Brooks's wife had been reburied at an earlier date, and according to his wishes, the word "rest" was inscribed on his tombstone.[201] His life had been long and fruitful; his friends were legion and his contributions to juvenile literature are still remembered although his best known works today are those concerning Lincoln.[202]

Notes

Chapter I. From Maine's "Aristocracy of the Sea"

1. *The Book Buyer*, III, 271 (Aug., 1886).

2. John Conness to Gen. Charles Hamlin, n.p., Feb. 21, 1896, in Charles Eugene Hamlin, *The Life of Hannibal Hamlin* (Cambridge, 1899), 485.

3. James A. Reed, "The Later Life and Religious Sentiments of Abraham Lincoln," *Scribner's Monthly*, VI, 339–340 (July, 1873).

4. William H. Herndon, "Lincoln's Religion," *Illinois State Register* (Springfield), Dec. 13, 1873, supplement.

5. Brooks to Isaac P. Langworthy, Washington, May 10, 1865, pub. as *The Character and Religion of President Lincoln* (Champlain, N.Y., 1919), 9.

6. N.Y. *Herald*, Mar. 13, 1865.

7. Anson G. Henry to his wife, Washington, D.C., Mar. 13, 1865, Henry Papers, Ill. State Hist. Lib.

8. N.Y. *Tribune*, June 26, 1865.

9. "M. L. R." in Chicago *Post and Mail*, July 13, 1875. Broadwell had been involved in settling the estate of Abraham Lincoln.

10. Original photograph in collection of the author.

11. Brooks, *Abraham Lincoln and the Downfall of American Slavery* (N.Y., 1899), v–vi.

12. Robert J. Cole, ed., *Lincoln by Friend and Foe* (N.Y., 1922), 8–9.

13. "Castine" [Noah Brooks], Washington, Apr. 16, 1865, in Sacramento (Cal.) *Daily Union*, May 17, 1865.

14. *The Writer*, VIII, 175 (Dec., 1895).

15. *Reports, Constitution, By-Laws and List of Members of The Century Association for the Year 1903* (N.Y., 1904), 34.

16. Autograph document signed by Brooks, n.d., The New-York Hist. Soc.

17. Edith Upham Boyers to author, Los Angeles, Cal., Aug. 14, Sept. 14, 1951. Mrs. Boyers is Brooks's great-niece and knew him quite well from his California visits. During the last year of his life at Pasadena when sickness hindered his writing, she often served as his secretary.

18. Rufus Rockwell Wilson, ed., *Intimate Memories of Lincoln* (Elmira, N.Y., 1954), 197.

19. George Moulton Adams, "Noah Brooks," *The New-England Historical and Genealogical Register*, LVIII, c (1904).

20. C. H. C. Wright to author, Paris, Me., July 11, 1951. Prof. Wright is a great-nephew of Brooks and knew him.

21. John S. Upham Sr. to author, Los Angeles, Cal., Aug. 4, 1951. Col. Upham, another great-nephew of Brooks, knew him both in California and in Maine. He visited his great-uncle before classes started at West Point.

22. Edith Upham Boyers to author, Los Angeles, Cal., Aug. 4, 1951.

23. Picture of Brooks and his friends in the Authors Club, *Harper's Magazine*, LXXIII, (Nov., 1886).

24. Adams, "Noah Brooks," *The New-Eng. Hist. and Geneal. Reg.*, LVIII, c (1904).

25. C. H. C Wright to author, Paris, Me., July 11, 1951; Edith Upham Boyers to author, Los Angeles, Cal., Aug. 14, 1951.

26. Caroline Ticknor, *Glimpses of Authors* (Boston, 1922), 57–58.

27. Brooks to E. C. Stedman, Newark, N.J., Mar. 3, 1893, Stedman Papers, Columbia Univ. Lib.

28. Laura Stedman, "Confessions of an Album," *The Bookman*, XXXVII, 267–268 (May, 1913). These pages were taken from Stedman's *Mental Photograph Album* and edited by his granddaughter.

29. Brooks became acquainted with this work, John Stevens Cabot Abbott's *The History of Napoleon Bonaparte*, during a hike in the Sierra Buttes near Downieville, Cal., in 1860. While resting in a deserted cabin he found this book and was fascinated with it. "John Riverside" [Noah Brooks], Downieville, Calif., Sept., 1860, in San Francisco *Evening Mirror*, Sept. 10, 1860.

30. His wife, Carolina Augusta Fellows Brooks, who had died in Marysville, Cal., May 21, 1862.

31. Martin Farquhar Tupper (1810–1889), an English poet whose most famous work, *Proverbial Philosophy*, was issued in 1838. Brooks probably met Tupper at the Lotos Club when he was honored there on Oct. 30, 1876. John Elderkin, *A Brief History of the Lotos Club* (N.Y., 1895), 41.

32. Brooks probably wrote "*Dum vivimus, vivamus*" which means "While we live, let us live."

33. The full name of the ship was the *Blessing of the Bay*, and she was launched from Winthrop's farm at Medford. See John A. Goodwin, *The Pilgrim Republic* (Boston, 1888), 586.

34. William Brooke had been a member of Rev. John Lothrop's congregation at Edgerton, England, and when Lothrop left his parish in 1634, William followed the next year. See *ibid.*, 439–440.

35. John Camden Hotten, ed., *The Original Lists of Persons of Quality…Who Went from Great Britain to the American Plantations 1600–1700* (N.Y. 1931), 93.

36. *Records of the Colony of New Plymouth* (Boston, 1855–1861), I, 118. Gilbert, like William, quickly became a leading citizen in the Plymouth Colony. The records indicate that he married Elizabeth Winslow, who was the daughter of Edward Winslow, governor of Plymouth for three terms. Samuel Deane, *History of Scituate, Massachusetts* (Boston, 1831), 224.

37. *Records of the Colony of New Plymouth*, VIII, 196.

38. *Ibid.*, II, 71.

39. *Ibid.*, II, 102.

40. *Ibid.*, II, 139.

41. *Ibid.*, VIII, 180.

42. *Ibid.*, VIII, 199.

43. *Ibid.*, IV, 148.

44. He took the Oath of Fidelity again in 1673 and became an "allowed and approved inhabitant" which entitled him to a certain share of the "common land." Deane, *History of Scituate, Massachusetts*, 223–224, 155.

45. *The New-Eng. Hist. and Geneal. Reg.*, LVIII, xcix.

46. *Records of the Colony of New Plymouth*, IV, 139. When witnessing a transaction, he made his mark instead of signing his name.

47. *Vital Records of Scituate Massachusetts to the Year 1850*, I, 50.

48. *Ibid.*, II, 43.

49. *The New-Eng. Hist. and Geneal. Reg.*, LVIII, xcix.

50. Deane, *History of Scituate, Massachusetts*, 28.

51. George Augustus Wheeler, *History of Castine, Penobscot, and Brooksville, Maine* (Bangor, 1875), 207.

52. *Ibid.*, 179.

53. F. K. Upham, *Genealogy and Family History of the Uphams* (Newark, N.J., 1887), 23; Brooks to George Witherle, Chelsea, Mass., Mar. 3, 1850, Noah Brooks Papers owned by Francis Whiting Hatch, Boston (hereafter cited as Hatch Coll.).

54. George Moulton Adams, *Castine Sixty Years Ago* (Boston, 1900), 10 n.

55. Upham, *Genealogy and Family History of the Uphams*, 23.

56. Barker Brooks to John Holmes, Camden, N.J., Jan. 20, 1814, Holmes Papers, N.Y. Pub. Lib.

57. "Castine," Castine, Me., Sept. 6, 1864, in Sacramento *Daily Union*, Oct. 5, 1863.

58. Castine town records, "Record Book," I, 36. His tombstone at Castine is in error, listing his birth as Oct. 25. He himself always gave Oct. 24 as his birthday, confirming the town records. Brooks's Kansas Diary (1857), Hatch Coll.

59. Castine town records, "Record Book," I, 36.

60. C. H. C. Wright to author, Paris, Me., July 11, 1951.

61. *Municipal Register of the City of Boston for 1851* (Boston, 1851), 127.

62. *The New-Eng. Hist. and Geneal. Reg.*, XXV, 104 (Jan., 1871).

63. Brooks to George Witherle, Newark, N.J., Mar. 9, 1891, Hatch Coll.

64. Brooks, "The Books of an Old Boy," *Liber Scriptorum* (N.Y., 1893), 67.

65. Castine town records, "Record Book," I, 112.

66. Upham, *Genealogy and Family History of the Uphams*, 23–24.

67. Castine town records, "Record Book," I, 112.

68. Upham, *Genealogy and Family History of the Uphams*, 23.

69. Uncle Noah Brooks to Phebe Brooks, Boston, Mar. 23, 1838, Noah Brooks Papers owned by Charles Conrad Wright, Cambridge, Mass. (hereafter cited as Wright Coll.).

70. Castine town records, "Record Book," I, 129.

71. Anon., "The Author of 'The Boy Emigrants,'" *St. Nicholas*, III, 524 (June 1876).

72. Brooks, "A Lesson in Patriotism," *St. Nicholas*, XIV, 340–341 (Mar., 1887).

73. *The National Cyclopaedia of American Biography* (N.Y., 1897), VII, 57. Since Brooks was one of the staff members of this publication, this sketch should be considered as autobiographical.

74. Brooks, "The Books of an Old Boy," *Liber Scriptorum*, 70.

75. Wheeler, *History of Castine, Penobscot, and Brooksville, Maine*, 143–146.

76. *The Critic*, XXI, 124–125 (Sept. 3, 1892).

77. Brooks, "The Books of an Old Boy," *Liber Scriptorum*, 66–72: Brooks to ed. of Dixon (Ill.) *Telegraph*, Marysville, Cal., Nov., 1859, in *Telegraph* of Dec. 22, 1859.

78. Brooks to George Witherle, Chelsea, Sept. 13, 1848; Jan. 19, [1850], Hatch Coll.

79. Brooks to George Witherle, Chelsea, July 14, [1850], Hatch Coll.

Chapter II. Paint and Printer's Ink

1. *The National Cyclopaedia of American Biography*, VII, 57. See note 73 in Chapt. I.

2. The first letter extant written after he left Castine was to George Witherle, dated Chelsea, Feb. 11, 1848, Hatch Coll.

3. He was born in Castine, Me., on Mar. 11, 1811.

4. Upham, *Genealogy and Family History of the Uphams*, 18.

5. *The Boston Almanac*, 1850, p. 106.

6. Brooks to George Witherle, Chelsea, Sept. 16, 1848, Hatch Coll. He gives his location as across the street from the Sandford house, which was on the corner of Shurtleff and Central Avenue.

7. Brooks to George Witherle, Chelsea, Dec., 20, [1850], Hatch Coll.

8. Brooks to George Witherle, Lynn, Mass., Dec. 17, 1848; Brooks to George Witherle, Chelsea, Aug. 13, 1850, Hatch Coll.

9. *Boston Directory*, 1852, p. 272; 1853, p. 296; 1854, p. 323; *The Carpet-Bag*, Oct. 16, 1852. Charles Tilden Wilder was born at Attleboro, Mass., on Sept. 1, 1831, but his parents moved to Chelsea soon after he was born. When his father entered the Union Army in 1863, Charles T. and his brother Herbert A. carried on the business. Their large paper mills were at Olcott, Vt., and Ashland, N.H., where they produced large quantities of paper, mostly for newspaper printing. Charles T. spent most of his time at Olcott supervising the manufacture of the paper. In 1857 Charles T. married Mary E. Ware. *The Dartmouth*, XIX, 10 (1897). Charles B. Wilder, whom Brooks termed "a well-to-do citizen of Boston," was commissioned a Captain in the Quartermaster Corps by Stanton on Feb. 19, 1863, and served as superintendent of the freed Negroes

at Fortress Monroe until 1865 when he was assigned to the War Dept. He was mustered out of service on March 30, 1866. During the Civil War, Brooks saw him frequently in Washington. "Castine," Washington, Mar. 2, 1865, in Sacramento *Union*, Apr. 10, 1865.

10. Statement of C. H. C. Wright, Apr. 5, 1952.

11. Monson Academy, located at Monson, Mass., is a prep school and was founded in 1804. Wilder's activities there cannot be traced because a fire, in Feb. of 1953, destroyed all the school's records.

12. Brooks to George Witherle, Chelsea, Jan. 19, 1850; John G. Brooks to Noah Brooks, Chelsea, May 24, 1854, Hatch Coll.

13. Brooks to George Witherle, Chelsea, Sept., 13, 16, 1848, Hatch Coll.

14. Brooks to George Witherle, Chelsea, Mar. 3, 1850, Hatch Coll.

15. Brooks to George Witherle, Chelsea, Jan. 27, [1850], Hatch Coll.

16. Brooks to George Witherle, Chelsea, Sept. 13, 1848, Hatch Coll.

17. Brooks to George Witherle, Chelsea, Mar. 3, 1850, Hatch Coll.

18. Brooks to George Witherle, Chelsea, Sept. 13, 1848, Hatch Coll.

19. Brooks to George Witherle, Chelsea, Aug. 13, 1850; Jan. 12, 1851; Boston, May 10, 1852; Chelsea, Sept. 12, 1852, Hatch Coll.

20. Brooks to George Witherle, Boston, Nov. 23, 1848; Chelsea, Mar. 3, 1850, Hatch Coll.

21. Brooks to George Witherle, Chelsea, Sept. 12, 1852, Hatch Coll.

22. Brooks's Journal of the White Mountain Trip, Hatch Coll.

23. Brooks to George Witherle, Chelsea, Aug. 31, 1851, Hatch Coll.

24. *The National Cyclopaedia of American Biography*, VII, 75.

25. Edmund Clarence Stedman and Ellen Mackay Hutchinson, eds., *A Library of American Literature from the Earliest Settlement to the Present Time* (N.H., 1890), XI, 482; Adams, "Noah Brooks," *The New-Eng. Hist. and Geneal. Reg.*, LVIII, xcix.

26. Brooks, "A Lesson in Patriotism," *St. Nicholas*, XIV, 340 (Mar., 1887).

27. Brooks to George Whiterle, Chelsea, Sept. 12, 1852, Hatch Coll.

28. Brooks to George Witherle, Chelsea, Aug. 31, 1851, Hatch Coll.

29. Brooks to George Witherle, Boston, June 25, [1852], Hatch Coll.

30. Brooks to George Witherle, Boston, [1853], Hatch Coll. Since few of these weekly publications remain, it is impossible to identify much of Brooks's work. However, some of his early letters written to a boyhood chum are signed "Pierre." This would seem to indicate that he may have used this as a pen name for his first newspaper writings. "Pierre" [Noah Brooks] to George Witherle, Chelsea, Nov. 25, 1848, Hatch Coll.

31. Brooks, "Horace Greeley," *The Youths' Companion*, LXXV, 400 (Aug. 15, 1901).

32. B. P. Shillaber, "Experiences during Many Years," *The New Eng. Mag.*, IX, 94, 153–154 (Sept.–Oct., 1893).

33. John Townsend Trowbridge, *My Own Story: With Recollections of Noted Persons* (Boston, 1903), 179.

34. Caroline Ticknor, *Glimpses of Authors* (Boston, 1922), 192.

35. Trowbridge, *My Own Story*, 180; George W. Bungay, *Off-Hand Talkings; or, Crayon Sketches of the Noticeable Men of Our Age* (N.Y., 1854), 376.

36. Trowbridge, *My Own Story*, 182; *The Carpet-Bag*, July 3, 1852.

37. *The Carpet-Bag*, May 1, 1852; Franklin J. Meine, ed., *Tall Tales of the Southwest* (N.Y., 1946), xxxi, 445.

38. Cyril Clemens examined this file of newspapers and reported his findings in *The New Eng. Quar.*, XIV, 527 (Sept., 1941); Edgar M. Branch, *The Literary Apprenticeship of Mark Twain* (Urbana, Ill., 1950), 6.

39. Marysville (Cal.) *Appeal*, Dec. 19, 1860; Brooks, "American Humorous Literature," MS. in the Wright Coll.

40. Brooks to George Witherle, Boston, Mar. 21, [1853], Hatch Coll.

41. These articles were not continued long. They are found in *The Carpet-Bag*, Apr. 19, 26, May 24, 31, June 21, 28, 1851, and Apr. 10, 1852.

42. *Ibid.*, May 24, 1851.

43. Brooks quotes things from these authors in *The Carpet-Bag*, Apr. 19, May 24, 31, June 21, 28, 1851, Dec. 11, 1852; Brooks to George Witherle, Chelsea, Jan. 27, [1850], Hatch Coll.

44. *The Carpet-Bag*, Apr. 19, 1851.

45. *Ibid.*, Apr. 26, 1851.

46. Brooks to George Witherle, Chelsea, Jan. 12, [1851], Hatch Coll.

47. Brooks to George Witherle, Chelsea, Sept. 12, 1852, Hatch Coll.

48. *The Carpet-Bag*, May 24, 1851.

49. *Ibid.*, May 31, 1851.

50. *Ibid.*, June 21, 1851.

51. *Ibid.*, June 28, 1851.

52. *Ibid.*, Apr. 10, 1852.

53. *Ibid.*, Nov. 27, 1852.

54. *Ibid.*, Dec. 11, 1852.

55. *Ibid.*, Dec. 18, 1852.

56. *Ibid.*, Mar. 12, 1853.

57. Trowbridge, *My Own Story*, 181.

58. Brooks, "American Humorous Literature," MS. in Wright Coll.

59. This is a new discovery. Don C. Seitz's book, *Artemus Ward: A Biography and Bibliography* (N.Y., 1919), identifies "The Surrender of Cornwallis," published in *The Carpet-Bag* on April 17, 1852, as Charles F. Browne's first contribution. See Seitz, pp. 12–16, 319.

60. Seitz, *Artemus Ward*, 23.

61. William Winter, *Other Days* (N.Y., 1908), 198.

62. Shillaber, "Experiences during Many Years," *The New Eng. Mag.*, Ix, 155 (Oct., 1893).

63. *The Carpet-Bag*, Sept. 20, 1851.

64. *Ibid.*, Apr. 17, 1852.

65. *Ibid.*, Apr. 3, 1852.

66. *Ibid.*, Aug. 14, 1852.

67. Trowbridge, *My Own Story*, 185; Shillaber, "Experiences during Many Years," *The New Eng. Mag.*, IX, 157 (Oct., 1893).

68. *The Carpet-Bag*, Mar. 26, 1853.

69. Brooks to George Witherle, Boston, Mar. 21, [1853], Hatch Coll.

70. Brooks to George Witherle, Chelsea, Mar. 29, 1853, Hatch Coll.

71. Shillaber, "Experiences during Many Years," *The New Eng. Mag.*, IX, 157 (Oct., 1893).

72. *Ibid.*, 156.

73. *The Carpet-Bag*, Apr. 24, 1852.

74. *Ibid.*, Dec. 4, 1852.

75. Brooks to George Witherle, Lynn, Mass., Dec. 17, 1848, Hatch Coll.

76. Brooks to George Witherle, Chelsea, Mar., 3, 1850, Hatch Coll.

77. Brooks to George Witherle, Chelsea, Apr. 11, 1852, Hatch Coll; *The Carpet-Bag*, Mar. 27, 1852.

78. *The Carpet-Bag*, Mar. 27, 1852.

79. *Appleton's Cyclopaedia of American Biography* (N.Y., 1900), V, 605; *The Carpet-Bag*, Mar. 29, 1851; Shillaber, "Experiences during Many Years," *The New Eng. Mag.*, VIII, 722 (Aug., 1893); "Cymon," *Hits and Dashes; or, a Medley of Sketches and Scraps, Touching People and Things* (Boston, 1852).

80. Brooks to George Witherle, Chelsea, Apr. 11, 1852, Hatch Coll.

81. *The Carpet-Bag*, Nov. 27, 1852.

82. Brooks to George Witherle, Chelsea, Sept. 12, 1852, Hatch Coll.

83. *The Boston Almanac*, 1853, p. 108.

84. Brooks to George Witherle, Boston, Mar. 21, [1853], Hatch Coll.

85. *Ibid.*, Brooks to George Witherle, Boston, Mar. 29, 1853, Hatch Coll.

86. Brooks to George Witherle, Boston, [1853]; Chelsea, June 26, 1853, Hatch Coll.

87. Brooks to George Witherle, Boston, [1853], Hatch Coll.

88. Brooks to George Witherle, Chelsea, Mar. 29, 1853, Hatch Coll.

89. Brooks to George Witherle, Chelsea, June 29, 1853, Hatch Coll.

90. *The Boston Almanac*, 1853, p. 118.

91. Brooks to George Witherle, Boston, [1853], Hatch Coll.

92. Brooks to George Witherle, Chelsea, June 26, July 10, 1853, Hatch Coll.

93. Winter, *Other Days*, 26; *The Boston Almanac*, 1853, p. 143; Brooks to George Witherle, Chelsea, Nov. 25, 1848, Hatch Coll.

94. Brooks to George Witherle, Chelsea, July 10, 1853, Hatch Coll.

95. Brooks to George Witherle, Chelsea, Nov. 13, 1853, Hatch Coll. Brooks did not identify the paper in which these articles were published.

96. Printed ticket in Hatch Coll.

97. Brooks to George Witherle, Chelsea, Nov. 13, 1853, Hatch Coll.

98. *The Carpet-Bag*, Jan 22, 1853. This was a short sketch predicting what Socrates would do if he were in New York.

99. Brooks to George Witherle, Chelsea, Jan. 29, [1850], Hatch Coll.

100. Brooks's Kansas Diary, Aug. 22, 1857, Hatch Coll.

101. Brooks's Journal of the White Mountain Trip, Hatch Coll.

102. Brooks to George Witherle, Boston, Feb. 15, 1854, Hatch Coll.

103. Brooks to George Witherle, Chelsea, Nov. 13, 1853, Hatch Coll.

104. *The Boston Almanac*, 1855, p. 108.

105. Brooks to the eds. of *The Critic*, Newark, N.J., Aug. 20, 1892, pub. in *The Critic*, XXI, 124 (Sept. 3, 1892).

Chapter III. Five Years in the Midwest

1. Photograph of original bill of sale in Nachusa Hotel in Dixon; Dixon (Ill.) *Telegraph*, Apr. 28, 1859.

2. Dixon *Telegraph*, Dec. 22, 1855.

3. *Ibid.*, May 7, 28, 1851.

4. *History of Lee County* (Chicago, 1881), 237. This statement is confirmed by a check of the land and tax records in the Lee Co. Courthouse.

5. Mrs. J. B. Brooks was born in Bainbridge, N.Y., on Mar. 9, 1826, and went to Dixon in 1841. She died on Apr. 27, 1878. Dixon *Telegraph*, May 2, 1878.

6. *Ibid.*, Mar. 23, 1854.

7. *Ibid.*, Sept. 21, 1854, June 20, 1855.

8. G. L. Howell, to P. M. Alexander, Dixon, Apr. 22, 1855, Beatrice Lanphier Coll., Dixon, Ill.

9. Dixon *Telegraph*, Jan. 31, 1857.

10. *Ibid.*, Dec. 22, 1855.

11. He purchased it on Mar. 18, 1861, from Mrs. Ophelia Brooks; the description of the property is lots 3, 4, 5, and 6 in Block 32 of the original town of North Dixon. Deed Record Book X, 309, Lee Co. Courthouse, Dixon. The Dixon *Telegraph* was in error in its reports of Jan. 17, 24, 1857. Charles Godfrey also bought the Brooks and Daley Mill for $20,000, half of which went to the young widow. Her husband had been as good a business man as Noah was a poor one. In addition to the $18,000 which Ophelia Brooks received from the sale of the property, she was paid $5,000 by the Manhattan Life Insurance Co. of New York who had insured her husband's life. Dixon *Telegraph*, Mar. 8, 1856, Feb. 14, 1857.

12. George A. Wheeler, *History of Castine: The Battle Line of Four Nations* (Bangor, 1875), 88; Dixon *Telegraph*, May 14, 1851, Jan. 21, Feb. 16, May 25, 1854.

13. Dixon *Telegraph*, Apr. 30, 1853, Feb. 15, 1883; *The New-Eng. Hist. and Geneal. Reg.*, XXXVII, 336 (1883). His wife, Marianne, died on Dec. 30, 1870. Dixon *Telegraph*, Jan. 12, 1871.

14. Dixon *Telegraph*, Apr. 4, 1857.

15. Brooks to George Witherle, Boston, Feb. 15, Apr. 28, 1854, Hatch Coll.

16. Brooks to George Witherle, Dixon, May 19, 1854, Hatch Coll; Dixon *Telegraph*, May 17, 1856.

17. Dixon *Telegraph*, June 8, 14, 22, 1854.

18. *Ibid.*, Nov. 2, 1854.

19. Brooks to F. G. Adams, Los Angeles, Mar. 2, 1899, Kansas State Hist. Soc.

20. Brooks to George Witherle, Washington, D.C., Sept. 20, 1863, Hatch Coll.

21. Brooks to George Witherle, Chelsea, July 14, [1850], Hatch Coll.

22. Brooks to George Witherle, Chelsea, July 10, 1853, Hatch Coll; Dixon *Telegraph*, Mar. 15, 1856.

23. John G. Brooks to Noah Brooks, Chelsea, May 24, 1854, Hatch Coll. This is the only letter of John G. Brooks which has been found.

24. G. L. Howell to P. M. Alexander, Dixon, Apr. 22, 1855, Lanphier Coll.; Dixon *Telegraph*, July 25, 1855.

25. Dixon *Telegraph*, May 16, 1855.

26. *Ibid.*, Sept. 21, 1854.

27. *Ibid.*, May 30, 1855, Supplement.

28. *Ibid.*, May 10, 1855.

29. *Ibid.*, Aug. 1, 1855.

30. Printed invoice form of N. and J. G. Brooks, Ill. State Hist. Lib.; Dixon *Telegraph*, July 18, 1855.

31. Dixon *Telegraph*, June 6, Aug. 1, 1855.

32. *Ibid.*, Nov. 7, 1855, May 17, 1856.

33. Collector's Book 1854–1855, Lee Co. Courthouse, Dixon.

34. Collector's Book 1856–1858, Lee Co. Courthouse, Dixon.

35. Dixon *Transcript*, Apr. 2, 1856.

36. Brooks to George Witherle, Dixon, Feb. 14, 1856, Hatch Coll.

37. P. M. Alexander to John Wilson Howell, Dixon, Aug. 11, 1856; John Wilson Howell to P. M. Alexander, Pompey, N.Y., Aug. 20, 1856, Lanphier Coll.

38. Brooks to George Witherle, Chelsea, Mar. 3, 1850, Hatch Coll.

39. Brooks to George Witherle, Dixon, Feb. 14, 1856, Hatch Coll.

40. Brooks to George Witherle, Boston, May 16, 1856, Hatch Coll. Brooks dictated this letter to Charles T. Wilder.

41. Brooks to George Witherle, Dixon, April 16, 1856; Boston, May 27, 1856, Hatch Coll; Dixon *Telegraph*, May 31, 1856; original marriage record is in the office of the city clerk, Salem, Mass.

42. Brooks to George Witherle, Chelsea, July 14, Nov. 19, [1850], June 26, 1853, Hatch Coll.

43. Brooks to George Witherle, Dec. 21, 1852, Hatch Coll.

44. *Vital Records of Salem Massachusetts to the End of the Year 1849*, I, 292, V, 239; C. H. C Wright to author, Paris, Me., July 11, 1951; T. Frank Waters, "Candlewood an Ancient Neighborhood in Ipswich with Genealogies of John Brown, Williams Fellows and Robert Kinsman," *Publications of the Ipswich Hist. Soc.*, XVI, 71–88.

45. Brooks to George Witherle, Dixon, Apr. 16, 1856, Hatch Coll.

46. P. M. Alexander to John Wilson Howell, Dixon, Aug. 10, 1856, Lanphier Coll.

47. Brooks's diary, Hatch Coll.

48. Dixon *Telegraph*, Dec. 6, 1856.

49. *Ibid.*, Dec. 13, 1856.

50. *Ibid.*, Aug. 27, 1857.

51. *Ibid.*, Nov. 4, 1858; a small amount of the stock was sold to John Wilson Howell on Jan. 30, 1857, receipt in Lanphier Coll.

52. John Wilson Howell to P. M. Alexander, Pompey, N.Y., Aug. 20, 1856, Lanphier Coll.

53. E. N. Howell to Frank E. Stevens, Dixon, Oct. 20, 1925, Lanphier Coll.

54. Brooks to George Witherle, Dixon, May 19, 1854, Hatch Coll.

55. Dixon *Telegraph*, Sept. 28, Oct. 12, 1854; *History of Dixon and Lee County* (Dixon, 1880), 13; John Wilson Howell to P. M. Alexander, Pompey, N.Y., Aug. 20, 1856, Lanphier Coll.; Frank E. Stevens, *History of Lee County Illinois* (Chicago, 1914), I, 348.

56. Dixon *Telegraph*, Jan. 13, 1855, Jan. 12, 1856.

57. Brooks's diary, Hatch Coll.

58. Brooks to George Witherle, Dixon, Jan. 21, 1858, Hatch Coll.

59. *Ibid.*

60. Dixon *Telegraph*, Nov. 15, 1856.

61. *Ibid.*, Oct. 26, 1854.

62. *Ibid.*, Oct. 17, 1855.

63. *Ibid.*, Mar. 17, 1855.

64. *Ibid.*, Apr. 28, 1859; Seraphina Gardner Smith, ed., *Recollections of the Pioneers of Lee County* (Dixon, 1893), 282–293; Frank E. Stevens, "The Dixon Abraham Lincoln-Jefferson Davis Tradition," *Lincoln Group Papers*, 1 ser., ed. by Douglas C. McMurtrie (Chicago, 1936), 127. One of Brooks's oil paintings of John Dixon's log cabin is reproduced in Frank E. Stevens, *The Black Hawk War* (Chicago, 1903), facing p. 129. Another of his original paintings of Dixon's cabin, slightly different, is in the Dixon Public Library, a gift of Frank E. Stevens.

65. Dixon *Telegraph*, Sept. 7, 1854.

66. *Ibid.*, Nov. 23, 1854.

67. *Ibid.*, Dec. 23, 1854.

68. *Ibid.*, Dec. 14, 1854.

69. *Ibid.*, Sept. 26, 1855.

70. Reprinted in *ibid.*, Nov. 21, 1855.

71. *Ibid.*, Nov. 14, 1855.

72. *Ibid.*, Jan. 5, 1856.

73. *Ibid.*, Dec. 13, 1856.

74. *Ibid.*, Feb. 14, 1857.

75. Certificate of Purchase No. 2656, Ill. State Lib. (Archives Division). The description of this land is Range 7 E 4, Township 21 N, SW fractional ¼ of Section 7 and was recorded on Dec. 20, 1854. This is also found in *Executive Record*, p. 375.

76. Deed Book P, 343, Whiteside Co. Courthouse, Morrison, Ill. This land, formerly in Lee Co., is now in Whiteside Co.

77. Certificate of Purchase No. 4687, Ill. State Lib. (Archives Division). The description of this land is Range 8 E 4, Township 23 N, SE ¼ of SW ¼ of Section 34 and was recorded on Feb. 8, 1855. This is also found in *Executive Record*, p. 394.

78. Deed Book V, 456, Ogle Co. Courthouse, Oregon, Ill. This transaction was recorded on Dec. 16, 1857.

79. Franklin W. Scott. *Newspapers and Periodicals of Illinois 1814–1879* (Springfield, 1910), 162.

80. Dixon *Telegraph*, July 14, 1859.

81. Grace E. Johnson, "Mrs. E. B. Baker and Others," *Recollections of the Pioneers of Lee County*, ed., Seraphina Gardner Smith, 319.

82. San Francisco (Cal.) *Chronicle*, Aug. 18, 1903.

83. Smith D. Atkins, "Some Illinois Editors I Have Known," *Transactions Ill. State Hist. Soc., 1910*, 40.

84. Dixon *Telegraph*, Nov. 23, 1854; Shaw made it clear in the issue of Oct. 12, 1854, that nothing would appear in the editorial column which was not written by himself.

85. *Ibid.*, July 25, 1855; this signature of "B" was identified as being Noah Brooks's in the issue of Jan. 26, 1860.

86. *Ibid.*, Aug. 1, 1855.

87. Brooks to P. M. Alexander, Marysville, Cal., June 5, 1860, Ill. State Hist. Lib.

88. Brooks, "Personal Reminiscences of Lincoln," *Scribner's Monthly*, XV, 561–562 (Feb., 1878).

89. Dixon *Telegraph*, July 19, 1856.

90. *Ibid.*, Sept. 20, 1856.

91. Brooks to Frank R. Dixon, Castine, Me., Feb. 21, 1896, Judge George C. Dixon Coll., Dixon, Ill.

92. Brooks, "Personal Reminiscences of Lincoln," *Scribner's Monthly*, XV, 562 (Feb., 1878). Lincoln was in the Dixon area at least six times; Dixon, July 17; Sterling, July 18; Galena, July 23; Polo, Aug. 15; Oregon, Aug. 16; and Polo again, Aug. 17. Paul M. Angle, *Lincoln 1854–1861* (Springfield, 1933), 133–138.

93. Dixon *Telegraph*, July 12, 1856. It was probably Dr. William B. Egan of Chicago.

94. Lincoln to J. W. Grimes, Springfield, Ill., July 12, 1856, R. P. Basler, M. D. Pratt, and L. A. Dunlap, eds., *The Collected Works of Abraham Lincoln* (New Brunswick, N. J., 1953), II, 348.

95. Chicago *Democratic Press*, July 15, 1856.

96. *Ibid.*, July 17, 1856.

97. July 26, 1856.

98. Reprinted in *Northwestern Gazette* (Galena, Ill.), July 29, 1856. This account is not mentioned in *The Collected Works of Abraham Lincoln*, VIII, 450. For another good account see Sterling (Ill.) *Republican*, July 19, 1856.

99. Brooks, "Lincoln," *Scribner's Monthly*, XV, 884 (Apr. 1878).

100. [Brooks], "Some Reminiscences of Abraham Lincoln," Marysville (Cal.) *Appeal*, Nov. 4, 1860. It was Beardsley who preceded Lincoln; Wentworth spoke after Lincoln.

101. Sterling (Ill.) *Republican*, July 26, 1856.

102. Brooks, "Personal Reminiscences of Lincoln," *Scribner's Monthly*, XV, 561–562 (Feb., 1878).

103. [Brooks], "Some Reminiscences of Abraham Lincoln," Marysville *Appeal*, Nov., 4, 1860. Since there were three editors on this paper, Brooks used "we" instead of "I."

104. Brooks, *Abraham Lincoln and the Downfall of American Slavery* v.

105. Chicago *Press & Tribune*, Aug. 30, 1858.

106. Dixon *Telegraph*, June 7, 1856.

107. *Ibid.*, Sept. 13, 1856.

108. Brooks to George Witherle, near Fort Riley, Kansas Territory, July 9, 1857, Hatch Coll.

109. This cup is now owned by Prof. C. H. C. Wright, Cambridge, Mass.

110. Brooks's Kansas Diary (1857), Hatch Coll. It cost him $54.15 to make the trip from Dixon to Kansas. Unless noted, the information for his stay in Kansas Territory is from this diary.

111. Anon., "Noah Brooks," *The Book Buyer*, III, 271 (Aug., 1886). Brooks undoubtedly supplied the information for this sketch.

112. Brooks to F. G. Adams, Los Angeles, Mar. 2, 1899, Kansas State Hist. Soc.

113. Brooks to George Witherle, near Ft. Riley, Kansas Territory, July 9, 1857, Hatch Coll.

114. Joseph B. Quinby held SE ¼ Section 17, Township 10, Range 4; Benjamin Frank Quinby held SW ¼ Section 17, Township 10, Range 4. Deed Book G, 92, 93, Clay Co. Courthouse, Clay Center, Kansas. These brothers continued to farm their land and did not return to Illinois when the Brookses did. A check of the Illinois State Census for 1860 does not list them. Ill. State Lib. (Archives Division).

115. Brooks to F. G. Adams, Los Angeles, Mar. 2, 1899, Kansas State Hist. Soc.

116. Brooks to George Witherle, Dixon, Dec. 8, 1857, Hatch Coll.

117. Brooks to Frank R. Dixon, Castine, Me., Feb. 21, 1896, Judge George C. Dixon Coll.

118. Brooks to F. G. Adams, Los Angeles, Mar. 2, 1899, Kansas State Hist. Soc.

119. Brooks to George Witherle, Dixon, Dec. 8, 1857, Hatch Coll.

120. F. G. Adams to Noah Brooks, Topeka, Kansas, Jan. 24, 1899, Kansas State Hist. Soc.; *Transactions Kansas State Hist. Soc.*, VI, 24 (1897–1900). It was in reply to this letter that Brooks told some of his experiences in Kansas.

121. *Transactions Kansas State Hist. Soc.*, VII, 567 (1901–1902).

122. Brooks to George Witherle, Dixon, Jan. 21, 1858, Hatch Coll.

123. Lottie Little Todd to his sister, Salem, Mass., Dec. 21, 1858, author's coll.; Emmie Little's Diary (entry of June 28, 1858), Lanphier Coll.

124. Brooks to Geo. L. Howell, Dixon, July 12, 1858, Ill. State Hist. Lib.

Chapter IV. *"The Plains Across"*

1. Dixon *Telegraph*, Feb. 24, 1859.

2. Brooks's diary, Hatch Coll.

3. For a treatment of the gold rush and its effect upon Illinois, see Wayne C. Temple, "The Pikes Peak Gold Rush," *Jour. Ill. State Hist. Soc.*, XLIV, 147–159 (Summer, 1951).

4. Dixon *Telegraph*, Feb. 3, 1859.

5. *Ibid.*, Feb. 10, 1859.

6. *Ibid.*, Mar. 3, 1859. Shaw returned to Dixon, however, in June. See *ibid.*, June 23, 1859.

7. John Wilson Howell to P. M. Alexander, Pompey, N.Y., June 19, 1859, Lanphier Coll.

8. John Wilson Howell to P. M. Alexander, Pompey, N.Y., Aug. 7, 1859, Lanphier Coll.

9. Upham, *The Descendants of John Upham of Massachusetts* (Albany, 1892), 377.

10. Unless otherwise stated in the footnotes, the source for Brooks's trip to California is his diaries (May 10–Oct. 5, 1859) in the Hatch Coll.

11. Brooks to F. G. Adams, Los Angeles, Mar. 2, 1899, Kansas State. Hist. Soc.

12. This trip from Dixon to Council Bluffs cost Brooks $16.40, which included a few incidental purchases.

13. Brooks, "The Coming and Going of Pete," *St. Nicholas*, XXXI, 538 (May, 1904). This statement is borne out by his diary entry of June 5 and the sketches which he made of their camps. See note 14.

14. Brooks made these sketches on May 20 and 21, 1859, and sent them to George L. Howell (of Dixon) on May 22. They are reproduced in Temple, "The Pikes Peak Gold Rush," *Jour. Ill. State Hist. Soc.*, XLIV, 149. The original drawings are in the Ill. State Hist. Lib.

15. Brooks to ed. of Dixon *Telegraph*, Marysville, Cal., Nov., 1859, in Dixon *Telegraph*, Dec. 22, 1859.

16. Brooks's diary entry of Aug. 20, 1859.

17. Brooks to P. M. Alexander, Fort Bridger, Utah Territory, July 25, 1859, copy in Lanphier Coll., original was destroyed by fire.

18. Brooks to ed. of Dixon *Telegraph*, Rocky Mountains, South Pass, July 19, 1859, in Dixon *Telegraph*, Aug. 18, 1859.

19. *Ibid.*

20. *Ibid.*

21. Brooks to P. M. Alexander, Fort Bridger, Utah Territory, July 25, 1859, copy in Lanphier Coll.

22. Brooks to ed. of Dixon *Telegraph*, South Pass, July 19, 1859, in Dixon *Telegraph*, Aug. 18, 1859.

23. Brooks to P. M. Alexander, "Fort Bridger, Utah Territory," July 25, 1859, copy in Lanphier Coll. His financial condition is illustrated by the fact that he enclosed a letter to his wife; he probably sent it "collect" to Alexander. The letter did not reach Dixon until August 31. George Howell to P. M. Alexander, Dixon, Sept. 1, 1859, Lanphier Coll.

24. Brooks to P. M. Alexander, Fort Bridger, Utah Territory, July 25, 1859, copy in Lanphier Coll.

25. Brooks, "In Echo Cañon," *Lotos Leaves* (Boston, 1875), 206.

26. Dixon *Telegraph*, Aug. 15, 1855.

27. Brooks to P. M. Alexander, Fort Bridger, Utah Territory, July 25, 1859, copy in Lanphier Coll. Brooks never forgot this stove. He mentioned it in his story, *The Boy Emigrants*, written in 1876.

28. Brooks to ed. of Dixon *Telegraph*, Marysville, Cal., Nov., 1859, in Dixon *Telegraph*, Dec. 22, 1859.

29. Brooks to ed. Dixon *Telegraph*, Marysville, Cal., Dec. 18, 1859, in Dixon *Telegraph*, Jan. 26, 1860.

30. *Ibid.*

31. J. A. Graves, *My Seventy in California, 1857–1927* (Los Angeles, 1927), 7.

32. Caroline M. Olney, "Mountains and Valleys of Yuba County," *Overland Monthly*, XL, 567–588 (Dec., 1902).

33. George H. Hare to his parents, Sacramento, Cal., Oct. 5, 1859, in Dixon *Telegraph*, Nov. 17, 1859.

34. C. H. C. Wright to author, Paris, Me., July 11, 1951.

35. Brooks to ed. Dixon *Telegraph*, Marysville, Cal., Dec. 18, 1859, in Dixon *Telegraph*, Jan. 26, 1860.

36. Brooks to ed. Dixon *Telegraph*, Marysville, Cal., Nov., 1859, in Dixon *Telegraph*, Dec. 22, 1859.

37. Anon., "The Author of 'The Boy Emigrants,'" *St. Nicholas*, III, 524 (June, 1876).

38. Brooks to ed. Dixon *Telegraph*, Marysville, Cal. Dec. 18, 1859, in Dixon *Telegraph*, Jan. 26, 1860.

39. Brooks to P. M. Alexander, Marysville, Cal., Feb. 22, 1860, Ill. State Hist. Lib.

40. Brooks to P. M. Alexander, Marysville, Cal., Apr. 3, 1860, Ill. State Hist. Lib.

41. Marysville *Appeal*, Nov. 4, 1860.

42. Brooks to P. M. Alexander, Marysville, Cal., June 5, 1860, Ill. State Hist. Lib.

43. Brooks to P. M. Alexander, Marysville, Cal., Apr. 3, 1860, Ill. State Hist. Lib.

44. Marysville *Appeal*, Nov. 4, 1860. When Noah Brooks left Marysville in 1862, Ayer became an editor and the business manager of the *Appeal*—the position which Brooks had held. Henry G. Langley, ed., *The Pacific Coast Business Directory for 1867*, 165. In 1865 he was also appointed register of the General Land Office of Marysville, a job which paid $500 per year plus one cent per commission. "Castine," Washington, May 17, 1865, in Sacramento *Union*, June 14, 1865; *United States Official Register*, 1865, p. 126.

45. Marysville *Appeal*, Mar. 1, 1860.

46. Personal business card, Hatch Coll.

47. Marysville *Appeal*, Oct. 16, 1860.

48. Brooks to George Witherle, Marysville, Cal., Jan. 18, 1860, Hatch Coll.

49. North San Juan (Cal.) *Hydraulic Press*, Sept. 3, 1859.

50. Marysville *Appeal*, Nov. 4, 1860.

51. Brooks to P. M. Alexander, Marysville, Cal., June 5, 1860, Ill. State Hist. Lib.

52. San Francisco *Evening Mirror*, Sept. 14, 1860.

53. Marysville *Appeal*, Oct. 20, 1860.

54. San Francisco *Evening Mirror*, Sept. 11, 1860.

55. *Ibid.*, Sept. 6, 1860.

56. *Ibid.*, Sept. 10 1860. John Stevens Cabot Abbott (1805–1877), *History of Napoleon*.

57. San Francisco *Evening Mirror*, Sept. 14, 1860.

58. *Ibid.*, Sept. 19, 1860.

59. Marysville *Appeal*, Sept. 15, 1860.

60. San Francisco *Evening Mirror*, Sept. 14, 1860.

61. *Ibid.*, Sept. 7, 1860.

62. *Ibid.*, Sept. 27, 1860.

63. Marysville *Appeal*, Nov. 4, 1860.

64. *Brown's Marysville Directory, 1861*, 22.

65. *Ibid.*, 31; Marysville *Appeal*, Oct. 26, 1860.

66. Marysville *Appeal*, Oct. 24, 1860.

67. C. C. Goodwin, *As I Remember Them* (Salt Lake City, 1913), 111.

68. Marysville *Appeal*, Oct. 6, 10, 1860.

69. *Ibid.*, Nov. 4, 1860.

70. *Ibid.*, Nov. 8, 1860.

71. *Ibid.*, Apr. 27, 1861; Carl I. Wheat, ed., "'California's Bantam Cock'—The Journals of Charles E. DeLong, 1854–1863," *Cal. Hist. Soc. Quar.*, X, 280 (Sept., 1931), entry of Apr. 26, 1851.

72. Marysville *Appeal*, July 6, 1861.

73. *Ibid.*, May 29, 1861.

74. The account of this climb is taken from "An Ascent of Mount Shasta in 1861: (From the Journal of Richard G. Stanwood)," *Cal. Hist. Soc. Quar.*, VI, 69–76 (Mar., 1927).

75. Ernest R. May, "Benjamin Parke Avery," *Cal. Hist. Soc. Quar.*, XXX, 125–149 (June, 1951).

76. Marysville *Appeal*, Oct. 27, 1861.

77. *Ibid.*, Dec. 5, 1861; San Francisco *Evening Mirror*, Dec. 10, 1861.

78. Marysville *Appeal*, Mar. 4, 1862.

79. *Ibid.*, May 22, 1862; C. H. C. Wright to author, Paris, Me., July 11, 1951.

80. Anon., "Noah Brooks," *The Book Buyer*, III, 271 (Aug., 1886); Frederick Evans, "Noah Brooks," *The Lamp*, XXVII, 129 (Sept., 1903).

81. *California Express* (Marysville), May 23, 1862.

82. Newark (N.J.) *Evening News*, Aug. 18, 1903.

83. Information courtesy of Prof. C. H. C. Wright, Paris, Me.

84. Information courtesy of Mr. Noah Brooks Hooper, Castine, Me.

85. San Francisco *Evening Bulletin*, Mar. 26, 1861. There is also a "Mrs. Brooks" listed as having arrived at San Francisco on May 13, 1860. However, at this early date, Brooks was not financially able to support his wife, and for this reason the later date had been chosen as the most likely one.

86. Marysville *Appeal*, June 22, 1862.

87. *Ibid.*, Sept. 28, 1862.

88. Anon., "The Author of 'The Boy Emigrants,'" *St. Nicholas*, III, 525 (June, 1876).

89. N.Y. *Herald*, Nov. 2, 4, 1862.

90. *Ibid.*, Nov. 25, 1862; N.Y. *Tribune*, Nov. 25, 1862.

Chapter V. *"Washington in Lincoln's Time"*

1. Brooks, "Personal Reminiscences of Lincoln," *Scribner's Monthly*, XV, 562–563 (Feb., 1878).

2. "Castine," Washington, Dec. 4, 1862, in Sacramento (Cal.) *Union*, Dec. 30, 1862.

3. Brooks to George Witherle, Washington, Dec. 23, 1863, Hatch Coll.

4. Los Angeles *Times*, Dec. 14, 1896.

5. Ella Sterling Cummins, *The Story of the Files: A Review of Californian Writers and Literature* (San Francisco, 1893), 77.

6. *Ibid.*, 79; Brooks to Isaac P. Langworthy, Washington, May 10, 1865, pub. as *The Character and Religion of President Lincoln* (Champlain, N.Y., 1919), 9.

7. C. C. Goodwin, *As I Remember Them* (Salt Lake City, 1913), 80–81.

8. Brooks to E. E. Hale, San Francisco, Nov. 29, 1865, copy enclosed in letter to Edward McPherson, Feb. 20, 1866, McPherson Papers, Lib. of Congress; Brooks, *Washington in Lincoln's Time* (N.Y., 1895), 1.

9. Brooks, "Personal Reminiscences of Lincoln," *Scribner's Monthly*, XV, 562–563 (Feb., 1878); *Washington in Lincoln's Time*, 2.

10. Brooks, "Personal Reminiscences of Lincoln," *Scribner's Monthly*, XV, 563 (Feb., 1878); "Castine," Washington, July 30, 1863, in Sacramento *Union*, Aug. 24, 1863; Washington, Apr. 16, 1865, in Sacramento *Union*, May 17, 1865; *Washington in Lincoln's Time*, 2; *Abraham Lincoln and the Downfall of American Slavery*, vi.

11. Mary Lincoln to Brooks, Chicago, Dec. 16, 1865, Hatch Coll.

12. Mary Lincoln to Brooks, Chicago, May 11, 1866, Hatch Coll.

13. Brooks, "Personal Reminiscences of Lincoln," *Scribner's Monthly*, XV, 675, 563 (Feb.–Mar., 1878).

14. John Hay, "Life in the White House in the Time of Lincoln," *The Century Magazine*, XLI, 35 (Nov., 1890).

15. Brooks, "Personal Recollections of Abraham Lincoln," *Harper's New Monthly Magazine*, XXXI, 222 (July, 1865).

16. Brooks, "Personal Reminiscences of Lincoln," *Scribner's Monthly*, XV, 677 (Mar., 1878).

17. *Ibid.*, XV, 676.

18. Brooks, "Personal Recollections of Abraham Lincoln," *Harper's New Monthly Magazine*, XXXI, 222–22, 230 (July, 1865); "Lincoln's Imagination," *Scribner's Monthly*, XVIII, 584 (Aug., 1879); "Castine," Washington, Nov. 7, 1863, in Sacramento *Union*, Dec. 4, 1863.

19. Brooks, "American Humorous Literature," MS. in the Wright Coll.

20. Brooks, "Personal Reminiscences of Lincoln," *Scribner's Monthly*, XV, 564 (Feb., 1878).

21. *Ibid.*, XV, 679 (Mar., 1878); *Washington in Lincoln's Time*, 277.

22. Brooks, "Lincoln's Imagination," *Scribner's Monthly*, XVIII, 585 (Aug., 1879).

23. Brooks, "Personal Recollections of Abraham Lincoln," *Harper's New Monthly Magazine*, XXXI, 224 (July, 1865).

24. Brooks, "Personal Reminiscences of Lincoln," *Scribner's Monthly*, XV, 674 (Mar., 1878).

25. Brooks, *Statesmen* (N.Y., 1893), 170.

26. Brooks, "A Boy in the White House," *St. Nicholas*, X, 61 (Nov., 1882).

27. Mary Lincoln to Brooks, Chicago, May 11, 1866, Hatch Coll.

28. Brooks, *Washington in Lincoln's Time*, 70–71.

29. Dated Washington, Nov. 16, 1864, in N.Y. *Herald*, Nov. 17, 1864; Washington *National Intelligencer*, Nov. 15, 1864.

30. Dated Washington, Mar. 25, 1863, in N.Y. *Herald*, Mar. 26, 1863.

31. Brooks, *Washington in Lincoln's Time*, 70, 72, 71.

32. Mary Lincoln to Brooks, Chicago, May 11, 1866, Hatch Coll.

33. Under the advertisements labeled "Astrology" the following notice appears in the N.Y. *Herald* of Apr. 18, 1863: "Colchester, the celebrated medium, having returned from Europe, can be consulted on any affairs of life, past, present or future, at his rooms, No. 1 Waverly place, corner of Broadway. Letters answered by mail."

34. Brooks, *Washington in Lincoln's Time*, 64–66. On Dec. 31, 1862, Mrs. Lincoln went to Georgetown with Isaac Newton to consult a Mrs. Cranston Laury (also spelled Laurie) who "made wonderful revelations to her about her little son Willy." T. C. Pease and J. G. Randall, eds., *The Diary of Orville Hickman Browning* (Springfield, 1925), I, 608 (entry of Jan. 1, 1863).

35. "Castine," Washington, Dec. 2, 1862, in Sacramento *Union*, Dec. 27, 1862.

36. *Memoirs of Henry Villard: Journalist and Financier 1835–1900* (Boston, 1904), I, 154.

37. "Castine," Washington, Dec. 2, 1862, in Sacramento *Union*, Dec. 27, 1862; Washington, Dec. 19, 1862, in Sacramento *Union*, Jan. 19, 1863.

38. "Castine," Washington, Dec. 26, 1862, in Sacramento *Union*, Jan. 19, 1863.

39. Howard K. Beale, ed., *The Diary of Edward Bates 1859–1866* (Washington, 1933), 310.

40. Brooks, "Personal Reminiscences of Lincoln," *Scribner's Monthly*, XV, 568–569 (Feb., 1878); "Lincoln, Chase, and Grant," *The Century Magazine*, XLIX, 610 (Feb., 1895).

41. N.Y. *Herald*, Mar. 20, 1863; N.Y. *Tribune*, Mar. 19, 1863.

42. "Castine," Washington, Mar. 21, 1863, in Sacramento *Union*, Apr. 17, 1863.

43. Brooks, "Personal Reminiscences of Lincoln," *Scribner's Monthly*, XV, 569 (Feb., 1878).

44. Tyler Dennett, ed., *Lincoln and the Civil War in the Diaries and Letters of John Hay* (N.Y., 1939), 80 (entry for Aug. 13, 1863).

45. Dated Washington, May 25, 1863, in N.Y. *Herald*, May 26, 1863. The date of this particular visit to three of the "principal hospitals" in Washington was May 24.

46. N.Y. *Herald*, Mar. 20, 1863.

47. Brooks, *Washington in Lincoln's Time*, 7.

48. "Castine," Washington, Apr. 12, 1863, in Sacramento *Union*, May 8, 1863.

49. Brooks, "A Boy in the White House," *St. Nicholas*, X, 62 (Nov., 1882).

50. Adam Gurowski, *Diary from November 18, 1862, to October 18, 1863* (N.Y., 1864), II, 192.

51. On April 28, 1864, Lincoln nominated Crawford to be collector of internal revenue for the district of Oregon. He was confirmed on May 7. *Jour. of the Executive Proceedings of the Senate*, 37th Cong., 3rd sess., XIII, 508, 525. Prior to this he was Asst. Quartermaster of the Army. For the account of his emigrant train activities, see "Journal of the Expedition Organized for the Protection of Emigrants to Oregon, &c, under the command of Medorem [*sic*] Crawford," Senate Doc. No. 17, 37th Cong., 3rd sess.

52. Anson G. Henry to his wife, Washington, Apr. 12, 1863, Henry Papers, Ill. State Hist. Lib.

53. "Castine," Washington, Apr. 12, 1863, in Sacramento *Union*, May 8, 1863; Beale, ed., *The Diary of Edward Bates 1859–1866*, 287.

54. Brooks, *Washington in Lincoln's Time*, 46, 16.

55. Brooks, *Abraham Lincoln and the Downfall of American Slavery*, 426.

56. "Castine," Washington, Apr. 12, 1863, in Sacramento *Union*, May 8, 1863.

57. Washington (D.C.) *National Intelligencer*, Apr. 9, 1863.

58. Beale, ed., *The Diary of Edward Bates 1859–1866*, 288. His son, Coalter Bates, was a member of this regiment, but he was not present at this time.

59. "Castine," Washington, Apr. 12, 1863, in Sacramento *Union*, May 8, 1863; Anson G. Henry to his wife, Washington, Apr. 12, 1863, Henry Papers, Ill. State Hist. Lib; Brooks, *Washington in Lincoln's Time*, 50–51; Brooks, "Personal Recollections of Abraham Lincoln," *Harper's New Monthly Magazine*, XXI, 227 (July, 1865); Washington *National Intelligencer*, Apr. 14, 1863. For a study of Lincoln as a rail-splitter, see Wayne C. Temple, "Lincoln's Fence Rails," *Jour. Ill. State Hist. Soc.*, XLVII, 20–34 (Spring, 1953).

60. Brooks, "Personal Reminiscences of Lincoln," *Scribner's Monthly*, XV, 673 (Mar., 1878).

61. *Ibid.*, 674.

62. Brooks, *Washington in Lincoln's Time*, 56.

63. "Castine," Washington, Apr. 20, 1863, in Sacramento *Union*, May 18, 1863.

64. "Castine," Washington, May 2, 1863, in Sacramento *Union*, May 27, 1863.

65. Brooks, "Personal Reminiscences of Lincoln," *Scribner's Monthly*, XV, 674 (Mar., 1878); *Washington in Lincoln's Time*, 57–58; "Castine," Washington, May 8, 1863, in Sacramento *Union*, June 5, 1863; John T. Morse, Jr., ed., *Diary of Gideon Welles* (Boston, 1911) I, 294.

66. Brooks, "Personal Reminiscences of Lincoln," *Scribner's Monthly*, XV, 567 (Feb., 1878); Lincoln to Hooker, Washington, Jan. 26, 1863, *The Collected Works of Abraham Lincoln*, VI, 78–79.

67. Anson G. Henry to his wife, Washington, Apr. 12, 1863, Henry Papers, Ill. State Hist. Lib.

68. Brooks, *Washington in Lincoln's Time*, 59–60, 52–53; "Castine," Washington, Mar. 22, 1865, in Sacramento *Union*, Apr. 19, 1865.

69. Draft Records, Group No. 110, National Archives.

70. "Castine," Beaufort, S. C., June 17, 1863, and Hilton Head, S. C., June 18, 1863, in Sacramento *Union*, July 16, 1863.

71. William Cullen Bryant, Sydney Howard Gay, and Noah Brooks, *Scribner's Popular History of the United States* (N.Y., 1897), V, 153–154. Although carrying the names of Bryant and Gay, Brooks wrote this entire volume of the revised edition.

72. "Castine," St. Augustine, Fla., June 20, 1863, in Sacramento *Union*, July 21, 1863.

73. "Castine," Hilton Head, S.C., June 25, 1863, in Sacramento *Union*, July 23, 1863.

74. N.Y. *Herald*, June 23, 1863; Brooks, *Washington in Lincoln's Time*, 84. The spy's name was William Richardson, about fifty years of age. He was hanged on July 6 for

having secret maps and military information on his person while posing as a sutler. Dated Frederick, Md., July 6, 1863, in N.Y. *Times*, July 7, 1863.

75. "Castine," Near Boonsboro, Md., July 12, 1863, in Sacramento *Union*, Aug. 10, 1863.

76. "Castine," Boonsboro, Md., July 14, 1863, in Sacramento *Union*, Aug. 10, 1863.

77. "Castine," Washington, July 28, 1863, in Sacramento *Union*, Aug. 19, 1863.

78. Brooks to George Witherle, North Conway, N.H., Aug. 16, 1863, Hatch Coll.

79. Brooks to George Witherle, Bangor, Me., Aug. 20, 1863, Hatch Coll.

80. "Castine," Castine, Me., Sept. 6, 1863, in Sacramento *Union*, Oct. 5, 1863.

81. Brooks to George Witherle, Washington, Sept. 20, 1863, Hatch Coll.

82. Brooks to George Witherle, Washington, Nov. 14, 1863, Hatch Coll.

83. "Castine," Washington, Nov. 14, 1863, in Sacramento *Union*, Dec. 12, 1863.

84. This envelope is clearly visible in Meserve Nos. 57 and 58. Frederick Hill Meserve and Carl Sandburg, *The Photographs of Abraham Lincoln* (N.Y., 1944). Four different portraits were taken at this time.

85. Brooks, "Personal Reminiscences of Lincoln," *Scribner's Monthly*, 565 (Feb., 1878); *Washington in Lincoln's Time*, 285–287; Brooks to R. W. Gilder, Newark, N.J., Feb. 3, 1894, Century Coll., N.Y. Pub. Lib.

86. Brooks, "Personal Reminiscences of Lincoln," *Scribner's Monthly*, XV, 565 (Feb., 1878).

87. Brooks, "Lincoln Reminiscences," *The Magazine of History*, IX, 107–108 (Feb., 1909). This article was published after his death. He wrote that Robert Todd Lincoln owned one of the five prints and Dr. Anson C. Henry had one but it was lost in a ship disaster. He did not know where the other two were.

88. "Castine," Washington, Nov. 17, 1863, in Sacramento *Union*, Dec. 16, 1863.

89. Ward Hill Lamon Papers, LN 2439, Henry E. Huntington Lib.

90. Brooks to Edward McPherson, Washington, Apr. 24, 1865, McPherson Papers, Lib. of Congress.

91. Dated Gettysburg, Pa., Nov. 19, 1863, in N.Y. *Herald*, Nov. 20, 1863; Dennett, ed., *Lincoln and the Civil War in the Diaries and Letters of John Hay*, 121–122.

92. Brooks to R. G. Gilder, Newark, N.J., Feb. 3, 1894, Century Coll., N.Y. Pub. Lib.

93. Brooks to George Witherle, Washington, Sept. 20, 1863, Hatch Coll.; A. A. Sargent to Cornelius Cole, Nevada City, Cal., Oct. 18, 1863, Cole Papers, U.C.L.A Lib.

94. Brooks to George Witherle, Washington, Nov. 14, 1863, Hatch Coll.

95. N.Y. *Herald*, Dec. 8, 9, 1863.

96. Brooks to George Witherle, Washington, Dec. 23, 1863, Hatch Coll.

97. Detroit (Michigan) *Free Press*, Dec. 22, 1863.

98. Various letters of Brooks to Edward McPherson, McPherson Papers, Lib. of Congress.

99. *House of Rep. Misc. Docs.*, No. 7, p. 2, 38th Cong., 2 sess.; *House of Rep. Misc. Docs.*, No. 19, p. 2, 39th Cong., 1 sess.

100. Envelopes for Brooks's letters to George Witherle, dated Dec. 23, 1863, and June 15, 1864, Hatch Coll.

101. Brooks to George Witherle, Washington, Dec. 23, 1863, Hatch Coll.

102. "Castine," Washington, Dec. 21, 186[3], in Sacramento *Union*, Jan. 27, 1864.

Chapter VI. Companion to Lincoln

1. Dennett, ed., *Lincoln and the Civil War in the Diaries and Letters of John Hay*, 128.

2. "Castine," Washington, Jan. 1, 1864, in Sacramento *Union*, Feb. 4, 1864. The year before Mrs. John A. Kasson had written that Mrs. Lincoln would receive "calls on New Year's in black velvet, trimmed with thread lace." "An Iowa Woman in Washington, D.C., 1861–1865," *Iowa Jour. Hist.*, LII, 73 (Jan., 1954).

3. "Castine," Washington, Jan. 27, 1864, in Sacramento *Union*, Feb. 27, 1864.

4. Brooks, "Glimpses of Lincoln in War Time," *The Century Magazine*, XLIX, 463–464 (Jan., 1895).

5. Brooks, "Personal Recollections of Lincoln in War Time," *Harper's New Monthly Magazine*, XXXI, 227 (July, 1895).

6. "Castine," Washington, Mar. 18, 1864, in Sacramento *Union*, Apr. 20, 1864.

7. Washington (D.C.) *National Republican*, Jan. 16, 1864.

8. "Castine," Washington, Jan. 18, 1864, in Sacramento *Union*, Feb. 22, 1864; James Harvey Young, "Anna Elizabeth Dickinson and the Civil War: For and Against Lincoln," *Miss. Valley Hist. Rev.*, XXXI, 59–80 (June, 1944).

9. "Castine," Washington, May 10, 1864, in Sacramento *Union*, June 6, 1864.

10. "Castine," Washington, Mar. 9, 1864, in Sacramento *Union*, Apr. 9, 1864.

11. Brooks, "Two War-Time Conventions," *The Century Magazine*, XLIX, 723 (Mar., 1895).

12. Dennett, ed., *Lincoln and the Civil War in the Diaries and Letters of John Hay*, 186.

13. "Castine," Baltimore, Md., June 7, 1864, in Sacramento *Union*, July 1, 1864.

14. "Castine," Washington, June 10, 1864, in Sacramento *Union*, July 4, 1864.

15. Brooks, "Two War-Time Conventions," *The Century Magazine*, XLIX, 723, 726 (Mar., 1895).

16. "Castine," Washington, June 14, 1864, in Sacramento *Union*, July 12, 1864; N.Y. *Tribune*, June 18, 1864.

17. "Castine," Washington, June 14, 1864, Sacramento *Union*, July 9, 1864.

18. Dennett, ed., *Lincoln and the Civil War in the Diaries and Letters of John Hay*, 195. Hay's dates are wrong for this trip.

19. Morse, ed., *Diary of Gideon Welles*, II, 55; Washington (D.C.) *National Intelligencer*, June 23, 1864.

20. "Castine," Washington, June 22, 1864, in Sacramento *Union*, July 18, 1864.

21. *The War of the Rebellion: Official Records*, ser. I, vol. XL, July 18, 1864.

22. Accounts dated Point of Rocks, Va., June 22, 23, 1863, in N.Y. *Herald*, June 25, 1864. The playmate was probably Perry Kelly—a "boy of about Tad's age, whose father was a tinner on Pennsylvania Avenue between Seventeenth and Eighteenth Streets." William H. Crook, "Lincoln as I Knew Him," *Harper's Magazine*, CXIV, 114 (Dec. 1906).

23. Brooks, *Washington in Lincoln's Time*, 284.

24. Washington (D.C.) *National Intelligencer,* June 25, 1864.

25. Dennett, ed., *Lincoln and the Civil War in the Diaries and Letters of John Hay,* 195.

26. Beale, ed., *The Diary of Edward Bates 1859–1866,* 378.

27. Dennett, ed., *Lincoln and the Civil War in the Diaries and Letters of John Hay,* 196.

28. Beale, ed., *The Diary of Edward Bates, 1859–1866,* 378.

29. Dennett, ed., *Lincoln and the Civil War in the Diaries and Letters of John Hay,* 196.

30. Report dated Washington, July 2, 1864, in N.Y. *Herald,* July 3, 1864.

31. "Castine," Washington, July 12, 1864, in Sacramento *Union,* Aug. 10, 1864; Washington, July 14, 1864, in Sacramento *Union,* Aug. 8, 1864; *Washington in Lincoln's Time,* 175; Brooks to George Witherle, Washington, July 12, 1864, Hatch Coll.

32. Dennett, ed., *Lincoln and the Civil War in the Diaries and Letters of John Hay,* 208–210.

33. "Castine," Washington, Aug. 1, 1864, in Sacramento *Union,* Aug. 29, 1864.

34. Signed memorandum, Washington, Aug. 23, 1864, in *The Collected Works of Abraham Lincoln,* VII, 514.

35. Brooks, "Personal Reminiscences of Lincoln," *Scribner's Monthly,* XV, 679 (Mar., 1878).

36. "Castine," Washington, Oct. 19, 1864, in Sacramento *Union,* Nov. 25, 1864.

37. "Castine," Chicago, Aug. 29, 1864, in Sacramento *Union,* Oct. 11, 1864.

38. Brooks to John G. Nicolay, Chicago, Aug. 29, 1864, in Robert Todd Lincoln Collection of the Papers of Abraham Lincoln, Nos. 35638–39, Lib. of Congress (hereafter cited as R. T. L. Coll.).

39. Brooks to John G. Nicolay, Dixon, Ill., Sept. 2, 1864, R. T. L. Coll., Nos. 35828–30.

40. Brooks, "Lincoln Reminiscences," *The Magazine of History,* IX, 107–108 (Feb., 1909).

41. "Castine," Decatur, Ill., Sept. 15, 1864, in Sacramento *Union,* Oct. 24, 1864.

42. "Castine," Burlington, Ia., Sept. 30, 1864, in Sacramento *Union,* Nov. 1, 864.

43. "Castine," Chicago, Oct. 12, 1864, in Sacramento *Union,* Nov. 6, 1864.

44. "Castine," Washington, Oct. 19, 1864, in Sacremento *Union,* Nov. 25, 1864.

45. Report dated Washington, Oct. 28, 1864, in N.Y. *Herald,* Oct. 29, 1864.

46. "Castine," Washington, Nov. 2, 1864, in Sacramento *Union,* Dec. 2, 1864. This speech is not printed in *The Collected Works of Abraham Lincoln.* Maryland's constitution was put into effect on Nov. 1. Washington *Morning Chronicle,* Nov. 1, 2, 1864.

47. Report dated Washington, Feb. 20, 1864, in N.Y. *Herald,* Feb. 21, 1864.

48. Dennett, ed., *Lincoln and the Civil War in the Diaries and Letters of John Hay,* 232–233.

49. "Castine," Washington, Nov. 11, 1864, in Sacramento *Union,* Dec. 10, 1864.

50. "Castine," Washington, May 17, 1865, in Sacramento *Union,* June 14, 1865.

51. Dennett, ed., *Lincoln and the Civil War in the Diaries and Letters of John Hay,* 233.

52. Brooks, "Lincoln's Reelection," *The Century Magazine*, XLIX, 865 (Apr., 1895).

53. "Castine," Washington, Nov. 11, 1864, in Sacramento *Union*, Dec. 10, 1864; Morse, ed., *Diary of Gideon Welles*, II, 178.

54. Brooks, *Abraham Lincoln and the Downfall of American Slavery*, 404–405.

55. Brooks, "Personal Recollections of Abraham Lincoln," *Harper's New Monthly Magazine*, XXXI, 228–229 (July, 1865).

56. Undated letter together with two tables of election statistics all in Brooks's hand, in R.T.L. Coll., Nos. 38882–85.

57. "Castine," Washington, Nov. 11, 1864, in Sacramento *Union*, Dec. 10, 1864.

58. Dennett, ed., *Lincoln and the Civil War in the Diaries and Letters of John Hay*, 239.

59. Brooks, *Washington in Lincoln's Time*, 147; "Castine," City Point, Va., Nov. 16, 1864, in Sacramento *Union*, Dec. 23, 1864; Brooks's diary, Hatch Coll.

60. "Castine," Bermuda Hundred, Va., No.v 18, 1864, in Sacramento *Union*, Dec. 23, 1864.

61. Brooks, "Personal Reminiscences of Lincoln," *Scribner's Monthly*, XV, 678–679 (Mar., 1878).

62. Beale, ed., *The Diary of Edward Bates 1859–1866*, 428.

63. Morse, ed., *Diary of Gideon Welles*, II, 192.

64. Report dated Washington, Dec. 6, 1864, in N.Y. *Herald*, Dec. 10, 1864.

65. Original document is in the Maine Hist. Soc; a facsimile is published in Brooks, "Personal Reminiscences of Lincoln," *Scribner's Monthly*, XV, 568 (Feb., 1878) and the history of its composition is found on p. 566. Brooks included this item in his newsletter dated Washington, Dec. 5, 1864, and it duly appeared in the Sacramento *Union*, on Jan. 7, 1865. The Washington (D.C.) *Daily Morning Chronicle* published it on Wed., Dec. 7, 1864. It is published in *The Collected Works of Abraham Lincoln*, VIII, 155, but the date assigned to it is Dec. 6. It was definitely written before this time, probably on Dec. 4 or 5. John G. Nicolay and John Hay in their *Complete Works of Abraham Lincoln* (N.Y., 1905), X, 279–280 give the date as Dec. 3, but this was a Saturday and in the same week as Dec. 1. Lincoln wrote "On thursday of last week." Lincoln's own statement rules out Dec. 3.

66. Brooks, "Personal Reminiscences of Lincoln," *Scribner's Monthly*, XV, 566 (Feb., 1878).

67. "Castine," Washington, Dec. 7, 1864, in Sacramento *Union*, Jan. 11, 1865.

68. Brooks, "Personal Reminiscences of Lincoln," *Scribner's Monthly*, XV, 565–566 (Feb., 1878). The paragraph about Sherman is quoted from *The Collected Works of Abraham Lincoln*, VIII, 148.

69. "Castine," Washington, Dec. 7, 1864, in Sacramento *Union*, Jan. 11, 1865.

70. Brooks to George Witherle, Washington, Dec. 10, 1864, Hatch Coll.

71. "Castine," Washington, Dec. 9, 1864, in Sacramento *Union*, Jan. 11, 1865.

Chapter VII. *"The Close of Lincoln's Career"*

1. On July 12, 1864, when Brooks wrote to George Witherle, he was still living in Georgetown. Later, in the front of a little journal, he wrote: "Noah Brooks. No 460 N.Y. Ave Washington, D.C." and the first entry is Nov. 15, 1864. Hatch Coll.

2. Brooks, *Washington in Lincoln's Time*, 25; *Boyd's Washington and Georgetown Directory*, 1858, p. 122; rejoinder of Brooks in *The Century Magazine*, XLIX, 793 (Mar., 1895).

3. Charles Eames to Charles Sumner, Washington, Sept. 28, 1851, Sumner Papers, Box 17, No. 27, Harvard Lib.; Edward L. Pierce, ed., *Memoirs and Letters of Charles Sumner* (London, 1893), III, 259.

4. Brooks, *Washington in Lincoln's Time*, 25.

5. James Henry Hackett, *Notes and Comments upon Certain Plays and Actors of Shakespeare, with Criticisms and Correspondence* (N.Y., 1863).

6. Lincoln to James H. Hackett, Washington, Aug. 17, 1863, in *The Collected Works of Abraham Lincoln*, VI, 392–393.

7. Lincoln to James H. Hackett, Washington, Nov. 2, 1863, in *ibid.*, VI, 558–559.

8. Brooks, *Washington in Lincoln's Time*, 287–288; "Castine," Washington, Jan. 10, 1865, in Sacramento *Union*, Feb. 22, 1865.

9. "Castine," Washington, Jan. 21, 1865, in Sacramento *Union*, Feb. 20, 1865.

10. Brooks, *Washington in Lincoln's Time*, 304–305.

11. See Wayne C. Temple, "Lincoln the Lecturer" in the *Lincoln Herald*, CII, No. 3, 94–110 (Fall, 1999) and *ibid.*, [CII], No. 4, 146–163 (Winter, 1999).

12. Brooks, *Washington in Lincoln's Time*, 305–306.

13. "Castine," Washington, Feb. 22, 1865, in Sacramento *Union*, Mar. 22, 1865.

14. Brooks, *Washington in Lincoln's Time*, 33–34.

15. Brooks, *Men of Achievement: Statesmen* (N.Y., 1893), 226–227; Marquis Adolpe de Chambrun, *Impressions of Lincoln and the Civil War* (N.Y., 1952), 19.

16. Beale, ed., *The Diary of Edward Bates 1859–1866*, 455.

17. "Castine," Washington, Mar. 12, 1865, in Sacramento *Union*, Apr. 10, 1865; Morse, ed., *Diary of Gideon Welles*, II, 251.

18. Brooks, "Lincoln's Reelection," *The Century Magazine*, XLIX, 871 (Apr., 1895).

19. Morse, ed., *Diary of Gideon Welles*, II, 252.

20. N.Y. *Herald*, Mar. 5, 6, 1865.

21. "Castine," Washington, Mar. 2, 1865, in Sacramento *Union*, Apr. 10, 1865; Morse, ed., *Diary of Gideon Welles*, II, 252.

22. Washington, *National Intelligencer*, Mar. 3, 1865.

23. "Castine," Washington, Mar. 12, 1865, in Sacramento *Union*, Apr. 10, 1865.

24. Washington *National Intelligencer*, Mar. 7, 1865; N.Y. *Times*, Mar. 7, 8, 1865.

25. Morse, ed., *Diary of Gideon Welles*, II, 253–254.

26. N.Y. *Tribune*, Mar. 13, 1865; N.Y. *Herald*, Mar. 13, 1865; Washington *National Intelligencer*, Mar. 14, 1865.

27. N.Y. *Tribune*, Mar. 27, 1865.

28. Helen Nicolay, *Lincoln's Secretary: A Biography of John G. Nicolay*, (N.Y., 1949), 223.

29. Charles H. Philbrick to O. M. Hatch, Washington, Dec. 30, 1864, Ill. State Hist. Lib.

30. Dennett, ed., *Lincoln and the Civil War in the Diaries and Letters of John Hay*, 40, 41, 52, 105, 247.

31. A. K. McClure, "Lincoln and Hamlin," Philadelphia *Times*, July 9, 1891.

32. Brooks to George Witherle, Washington, Dec. 10, 1865, Hatch Coll.

33. "Castine," San Francisco, July 31, 1865, in Sacramento *Union*, Aug. 2, 1865.

34. Brooks to Rev. Isaac P. Langworthy, Washington, May 10, 1865, pub. as *The Character and Religion of President Lincoln*, 9–10; *Official Register*, 1863, p. 14.

35. "Castine," San Francisco, July 31, 1865, in Sacramento *Union*, Aug. 2, 1865.

36. A. G. Henry to his wife, San Francisco, Jan. 2, 1865, Henry Papers, Ill. State Hist. Lib.

37. N.Y. *Times*, Jan. 28, 1865.

38. A. G. Henry to his wife, Washington, Feb. 8, 1865, Henry Papers, Ill. State Hist. Lib.

39. A. G. Henry to his wife, Washington, Mar. 13, 1865, Henry Papers, Ill. State Hist. Lib.

40. Dennett, ed., *Lincoln and the Civil War in the Diaries and Letters of John Hay*, 247–248.

41. A. G. Henry to his wife, Washington, Mar. 13, 1865, Henry Papers, Ill. State Hist. Lib.

42. "Castine," Washington, Mar. 22, 1865, in Sacramento *Union*, Apr. 19, 1865. Nicolay formally resigned his position as private secretary to Pres. Johnson on Apr. 20, 1865. Andrew Johnson Papers, Lib. of Congress. Nicolay, his bride, and Hay sailed on the *City of London* for Liverpool on June 24, 1865. N.Y. *Tribune*, June 26, 1865.

43. Morse, ed., *Diary of Gideon Welles*, II, 257.

44. "Castine," Washington, Mar. 22, 1865, in Sacramento *Union*, Apr. 19, 1865.

45. Report dated Washington, Mar. 23, 1865, in N.Y. *Herald*, Mar. 24, 1865.

46. Brooks to Edward McPherson, Washington, Apr. 5, 1865, McPherson Papers, Lib. of Congress; "Castine," Washington, Apr. 1, 1865, in Sacramento *Union*, May 8, 1865.

47. George R. Agassiz, ed., *Meade's Headquarters 1863–1865: Letters of Colonel Theodore Lyman from the Wilderness to Appomattox* (Boston, 1922), 324–325.

48. John L. Cunningham, *Three Years with the Adirondack Regiment* (Norwood, Mass., 1920), 166.

49. Mary Lincoln to Francis B. Carpenter, Chicago, Nov. 15, [1865], in Carl Sandburg and Paul M. Angle, *Mary Lincoln: Wife and Widow* (N.Y., 1932), 242.

50. "Castine," Fortress Monroe, Mar. 27, 1865, in Sacramento *Union*, May 1, 1865.

51. "Castine," Washington, Apr. 1, 1865, in Sacramento *Union*, May 8, 1865.

52. Brooks to Edward McPherson, Washington, Apr. 5, 1865, in McPherson Papers, Lib. of Congress.

53. Defree's printing is in the R. T. L. Coll., Nos. 34277–80; Morse, ed., *Diary of Gideon Welles*, II, 99, 271–272. The passage which Lincoln objected to was this: "And thereupon I venture to remind you that our bleeding, bankrupt, almost dying country also longs for peace—shudders at the prospect of fresh conscriptions, of further wholesale devastations, and of new rivers of human blood." Greeley to Lincoln, N.Y., July 7, 1864, R. T. L Coll., Nos. 34316–18.

54. Brooks to Edward McPherson, Washington, Apr. 5, 1865, McPherson Papers, Lib. of Congress. From this letter it is known that McPherson made his request to Brooks on April 1.

55. Washington *National Intelligencer*, Apr. 10, 1865.

56. Morse, ed., *Diary of Gideon Welles*, II, 278.

57. Brooks to Edward McPherson, Washington, Apr. 12, 1865, McPherson Papers, Lib. of Congress.

58. This was the flag which Col. Elmer E. Ellsworth had pulled down at Alexandria, Virginia, only to be shot by the enraged proprietor of the hotel. The flag was presented to Mrs. Lincoln who kept it in a bureau drawer. Tad time and again sneaked it out for such display. Julia Taft Bayne, *Tad Lincoln's Father* (Boston, 1931), 39–40.

59. "Castine," Washington, Apr. 12, 1865, in Sacramento *Union*, May 8, 1865.

60. Brooks to E. E. Hale, San Francisco, Nov. 29, 1865, copy enclosed with letter to Edward McPherson, San Francisco, Feb. 20, 1866, McPherson Papers, Lib. of Congress. Brooks quoted Lincoln's words from his journal, which has not been found.

61. Brooks, "Personal Reminiscences of Lincoln," *Scribner's Monthly*, XV, 567 (Feb., 1878).

62. Brooks, "A Boy in the White House," *St. Nicholas*, X, 63 (Nov., 1882).

63. Brooks, *Abraham Lincoln and the Downfall of American Slavery*, 452.

64. Brooks, "Lincoln," *Scribner's Monthly*, XV, 885 (Apr., 1878); *The Collected Works of Abraham Lincoln*, VIII, 404.

65. "Castine," Washington, Apr. 12, 1865, in Sacramento *Union*, May 8, 1865.

66. Chambrun, *Impressions of Lincoln and the Civil War*, 92.

67. Brooks, *Abraham Lincoln and the Downfall of American Slavery*, 453–454; "Personal Reminiscences of Lincoln," *Scribner's Monthly*, XV, 567 (Feb., 1878).

68. Chambrun, *Impressions of Lincoln and the Civil War*, 93.

69. David Homer Bates, *Lincoln in the Telegraph Office* (N.Y., 1907), 367.

70. Brooks, *Washington in Lincoln's Time*, 257.

71. Report from Washington, Apr. 16, 1865, in *Illinois State Journal* (Springfield), Apr. 17, 1865.

72. "Castine," Washington, Apr. 16, 1865, in Sacramento *Union*, May 17, 1865.

73. "Castine," Washington, Apr. 14, 1865, in Sacramento *Union*, May 16, 1865.

74. David Donald, ed., *Inside Lincoln's Cabinet: The Civil War Diaries of Salmon P. Chase* (N.Y., 1954), 267.

75. Brooks, *Washington in Lincoln's Time*, 258–260.

76. "Castine," Washington, Apr. 16, 1865, in Sacramento *Union*, May 17, 1865.

77. "Castine," Washington, Apr. 20, 1865, in Sacramento *Union*, May 19, 1865.

78. Brooks, *Washington in Lincoln's Time*, 266.

79. "Castine," Washington, Apr. 20, 1865, in Sacramento *Union*, May 19, 1865.

Chapter VIII. Naval Officer and Newspaper Editor

1. Brooks to Rev. Isaac P. Langworthy, Washington, May 10, 1865, pub. as *The Character and Religion of President Lincoln*, 7.

2. Brooks, *Washington in Lincoln's Time*, 38.

3. Brooks, *The Character and Religion of President Lincoln*, 9.

4. Brooks to Edward McPherson, Washington, May 19, 1865, McPherson Papers, Lib. of Congress. Brooks's article was published as "Personal Recollections of Abraham Lincoln," *Harper's New Monthly Magazine*, XXXI, 222–230 (July, 1865).

5. "Castine," San Francisco, July 31, 1865, in Sacramento *Union*, Aug. 2, 1865.

6. Brooks, *The Character and Religion of President Lincoln*, 9.

7. N.Y. *Herald*, Oct. 23, 1864.

8. "Castine," Washington, Feb. 22, 1865, in Sacramento *Union*, Mar. 22, 1865.

9. Brooks to Edward McPherson, Washington, Apr. 24, 1865, McPherson Papers, Lib. of Congress.

10. John Conness and William Higby to Andrew Johnson, Washington, May 4, 1865, Treas. Dept. Records, National Archives.

11. Andrew Johnson to Hugh McCulloch, Washington, May 6, 1865, Treas. Dept. Records, National Archives.

12. Brooks to Edward McPherson, Washington, May 5, 1865, McPherson Papers, Lib. of Congress.

13. "Castine," Washington, May 8, 1865, in Sacramento *Union*, June 2, 1865.

14. Brooks, *The Character and Religion of President Lincoln*, 11.

15. "Castine," Washington, May 12, 1865, in Sacramento *Union*, June 8, 1865.

16. Brooks to Edward McPherson, Washington, May 19, 1865, McPherson Papers, Lib. of Congress.

17. Brooks to George Witherle, San Francisco, Sept. 20, 1866, Hatch Coll.

18. *Official Register*, 1865, pp. 119, 117.

19. Report from Washington, June 10, 1865, in N.Y. *Herald*, June 11, 1865.

20. J. W. S., N.Y., June 14, 1865, in San Francisco *Evening Bulletin*, July 12, 1865.

21. "Castine," Washington, May 22, 1865, in Sacramento *Union*, June 19, 1865.

22. Brooks to Edward McPherson, Washington, May 5, 1865, McPherson Papers, Lib. of Congress.

23. Brooks to Edward McPherson, Washington, May 19, 1865, McPherson Papers, Lib. of Congress.

24. *Annual Register of the U. S. Naval Academy*, 1865–66 (Washington, 1866), 3.

25. "Castine," Newport, R. I., June 8, 1865, in Sacramento *Union*, July 8, 1865. The Naval Academy was scheduled for return to Annapolis in Sept. 1865. N.Y. *Times*, June

6, 1865. The apprentices chosen for advancement to midshipmen were A. B. Fowler, W. F. Wood, Henry Monahan, Wm. P. Day, and Chas. Storms. N.Y. *Times*, July 10, 1865.

26. "Castine," Gettysburg, Pa., June 14, 1865, in Sacramento *Union*, July 14, 1865.

27. A. G. Henry to his wife, Washington, Apr. 19, 1865, copy in Lib. of Congress.

28. "Castine," Washington, June 28, 1865, in Sacramento *Union*, July 27, 1865.

29. San Francisco *Alta California*, July 26, 1865; N.Y. *Times*, Aug. 26, 1865.

30. *Official Register*, 1865, p. 14.

31. Brooks to Mrs. A. G. Henry, San Francisco, Aug. 13, 1865, Henry Papers, Ill. State Hist. Lib.

32. Mary Lincoln to A. G. Henry, Chicago, July 17, 1865, in Sandburg and Angle, *Mary Lincoln: Wife and Widow*, 234. Original letter owned by Justin G. Turner, Hollywood, Cal.

33. N.Y. *Times*, July 2, 1865; N.Y. *Herald*, June 30, 1865.

34. K. C. B., "Letters from the Sea," July 20, 1865, in Sacramento *Union*, July 27, 1865; Brooks to Mrs. A. G. Henry, San Francisco, Aug. 13, 1865, Henry Papers, Ill. State Hist. Lib.

35. K. C. B., "Letter from the Sea," July 20, 1865, in Sacramento *Union*, July 27, 1865; N.Y. *Times*, July 25, 26, 1865.

36. San Francisco *Alta California*, July 26, 1865. The Occidental was owned by Charles and Lewis Leland (who also operated the Metropolitan Hotel in New York) and had been in operation since about Jan. 1, 1863. N.Y. *Times*, Nov. 11, 1862; N.Y. *Herald*, Nov. 11, 1862.

37. San Francisco *Alta California*, July 26, 1865.

38. San Francisco *Bulletin*, July 26, 1865.

39. Brooks to Edward McPherson, San Francisco, Feb. 20, 1866, McPherson Papers, Lib. of Congress.

40. N.Y. *Herald*, Nov. 9, 1965.

41. *San Francisco Directory* (San Francisco, 1866), 95.

42. Register of Officers of the Customs, Treas. Dept. Records, National Archives.

43. Nathan Sargent to Brooks, Washington, July 27, 1865, Hatch Coll.

44. N.Y. *Herald*, Aug. 26, 1865; Brooks to Mrs. A. G. Henry, San Francisco, Aug. 13, 1865, Henry Papers, Ill. State Hist. Lib.

45. Capt. Thomas Buckley's report, Camp Lincoln, July 31, 1865, pub. in N.Y. *Herald*, Aug. 26, 1865. Capt. Buckley commanded the Sixth Infantry and was upon the scene of the disaster soon after the steamer sank. In vain he explored the beach for additional survivors. There were 112 passengers listed on the ship's records.

46. *San Francisco Directory*, 1866, p. 95.

47. Brooks to George Witherle, San Francisco, Sept. 20, 1866, Hatch Coll.

48. "Castine," Washington, Apr. 20, 1865, in Sacramento *Union*, May 19, 1865.

49. Mary Lincoln to Brooks, Chicago, Dec. 16, 1865, Hatch Coll. See also Francis Whiting Hatch, "Mary Lincoln Writes to Noah Brooks," *Jour. Ill. State. Hist. Soc.*, XLVIII, 45–51 (Spring, 1955).

50. N.Y. *Times*, June 10, 1865.

51. This was House Bill No. 35 and was immediately passed. *Congressional Globe*, 39th Cong., 1 Sess., pp. 59, 71, 172.

52. Brooks to Edward McPherson, San Francisco, Feb. 20, 1866, McPherson Papers, Lib. of Congress. John Hay wrote that the Jay Cooke fund "was never given to Mrs. L., but on the scandals of her last days at the White House becoming known was quietly restored to the donors, most of whom were Quakers." Dennett, ed., *Lincoln and the Civil War in the Diaries and Letters of John Hay*, 274.

53. Lincoln had wished to name Lyon consul to Havana in 1863, but he was not appointed. On February 2, 1864, the President appointed him governor of Idaho Territory and he was confirmed on Feb. 26. *The Collected Works of Abraham Lincoln*, VI, 195; VII, 1866.

54. Mary Lincoln to Brooks, Chicago, May 11, 1866, and stock certificates in Hatch Coll.; Mary Lincoln to A. G. Henry, Chicago, July 17, 1865, Justin G. Turner Coll., Hollywood, Cal.

55. Brooks, *Washington in Lincoln's Time*, 123.

56. San Francisco *Alta California*, Nov. 2, 1867. In his account of this stock, Brooks confused the number of shares in each company.

57. *Jour. of Executive Proceedings of the Senate*, 38th Cong., 2 Sess., vol. XIV, pt. 1, pp. 498, 506.

58. *Ibid.*, vol. XIV, pt. 2, pp. 558, 561.

59. Treas. Dept. Records, National Archives.

60. Brooks to Nathan Sargent, San Francisco, Apr. 5, 186, Treas. Dept. Records, National Archives.

61. Brooks to Nathan Sargent, San Francisco, June 1, 1866, Treas. Dept. Records, National Archives.

62. Brooks to Edward McPherson, San Francisco, Feb. 20, 1866, McPherson Papers, Lib. of Congress.

63. Treas. Dept. Records, National Archives.

64. Dated Washington, Aug. 21, 1866, in N.Y. *Herald*, Aug. 22, 1866.

65. Brooks to George Witherle, San Francisco, Sept. 20, 1866, Hatch Coll.

66. San Francisco *Call*, Aug. 25, 1866.

67. Marysville *Appeal*, Aug. 25, 1866.

68. Brooks to Edward McPherson, San Francisco, Feb. 20, 1866, McPherson Papers, Lib. of Congress.

69. J. W. S., N.Y., Aug. 23, 1866, in San Francisco *Evening Bulletin*, Sept. 17, 1866; Cornelius Cole to his wife, Washington, Aug. 6, 1866, Cole Papers, U.C.L.A. Lib.

70. *Memoirs of Cornelius Cole* (N.Y., 1903), 248–249.

71. "Castine," Washington, Apr. 28, 1865, in Sacramento *Union*, May 25, 1865.

72. Brooks to Edward McPherson, San Francisco, Jan. 9, 186[6], McPherson Papers, Lib. of Congress; J. W. Simonton to Cornelius Cole, N.Y., Dec. 24, 1866, Cole Papers, U.C.L.A. Lib.

73. Report from Los Angeles, Aug. 17, 1903, in N.Y. *Herald*, Aug. 18, 1903.

74. "Castine," Washington, Mar. 12, 1865, in Sacramento *Union*, Apr. 10, 1865.

75. "Castine," Washington, Apr. 24, 1865, in Sacramento *Union*, May 20, 1865.

76. Report from Washington, Feb. 1, 1867, in N.Y. *Herald*, Feb. 2, 1867.

77. *Jour. of Executive Proceedings of the Senate*, 39th Cong., 2 Sess., vol. XV, pt. 1, pp. 182, 281.

78. *Ibid.*, vol. XV, pt. 1, pp. 282, 332.

79. Report from San Francisco, Mar. 9, 1867, in N.Y. *Tribune*, Mar. 11, 1867.

80. *The Works of Hubert Howe Bancroft* (San Francisco, 1890), XXXVIII, 598.

81. Brooks to George Witherle, San Francisco, Sept. 20, 1866; N.Y., Mar. 13, [1867], Hatch Coll.

82. Sacramento *Daily Bee*, Oct. 23, 1866; Marysville *Appeal*, Oct. 2, 1866.

83. "Cosmopolitan," San Francisco, Oct. 26, 1866, in Marysville *Appeal*, Oct. 28, 1866.

84. Henry G. Langley, ed., *The Pacific Coast Business Directory for 1867* (San Francisco, 1867), 420; *San Francisco Directory, 1867*, p. 105; Brooks to George Witherle, San Francisco, Sept. 20, 1866, Hatch Coll.

85. Marysville *Appeal*, Sept. 7, 1866.

86. Brooks, *The Transition* (San Francisco, 1866), 14 pp.

87. Anna Lee Marston, ed., *Records of a California Family: Journals and Letters of Lewis C. Gunn and Elizabeth Le Brenton Gunn* (San Diego, 1928), 265.

88. Henry George, Jr., *The Life of Henry George* (N.Y., 1930_, 173–176. This book was first published in 1900 and Brooks supplied information for it.

89. Marysville *Appeal*, Nov. 8, 1866.

90. San Francisco *Times*, Nov. 15, 1866.

91. San Francisco *Bulletin*, Nov. 24, 1866. On this date, McClatchy was called "late editor of the Times."

92. Brooks, "Henry George in California," *The Century Magazine*, LVII, 549–552 (Feb., 1899).

93. N.Y. *Tribune*, Nov. 6, 1866.

94. Victor Rosewater, *History of Cooperative News-Gathering in the United States* (N.Y., 1930), 118–120, 147.

95. Brooks to George Witherle, N.Y., Mar. 13, [1867], Hatch Coll.

96. Rosewater, *History of Cooperative News-Gathering in the United States*, 147.

97. Brooks to George Witherle, N.Y., Mar. 13, [1867], Hatch Coll.

98. Brooks to Edward McPherson, N.Y., Apr. 1, 1867, McPherson Papers, Lib. of Congress.

99. Brooks to George Witherle, Boston, Apr. 6, 1867, Hatch Coll.

100. N.Y. *Tribune*, Apr. 12, 1867.

101. Brooks's statement in George, *The Life of Henry George*, 175–176.

102. Brooks, "Henry George in California," *The Century Magazine*, LVII, 550 (Feb., 1899).

103. *Ibid.*, LVII, 551–552 (Feb., 1899).

104. Brooks to George Witherle, N.Y., May 15, 1872, Hatch Coll.; Anon., "The Author of 'The Boy Emigrants,'" *St. Nicholas*, III, 525 (June, 1876).

105. Langley, ed., *The Pacific Coast Business Directory for 1867*, 420; *San Francisco Directory for 1868*, 111.

106. N.Y. *Herald*, Oct. 23, 1882.

107. John S. Hittell, *A History of the City of San Francisco* (San Francisco, 1878), 441–442.

108. San Francisco *Alta California*, June 19, 1869.

109. San Francisco *Call*, Apr. 10, 1897; Brooks to ed. of *Overland Monthly*, June 27, 1902, in *Overland Monthly*, XL, 225 (Sept., 1902).

110. Brooks, "Bret Harte in California," *The Century Magazine*, LVIII, 447 (July, 1899).

111. Brooks, "Mark Twain in California," *The Century Magazine*, LVII, 98 (Nov., 1899).

112. Albert Bigelow Paine, *Mark Twain: A Biography* (N.Y., 1912), I, 304–341.

113. Paine, ed., *Mark Twain's Autobiography* (N.Y., 1924), I, 243.

114. Samuel L. Clemens to Will Bowen, N.Y., June 7, 1867, in Theodore Hornberger, ed., *Mark Twain's Letters to Will Bowen* (Austin, 1941,) 15–16.

115. Brooks, "Mark Twain in California," *The Century Magazine*, LVII, 98 (Nov., 1898).

116. Brooks to ed. of *Overland Monthly*, June 2, 1902, in *Overland Monthly*, XL, 225 (Sept., 1902).

117. Paine, ed., *Mark Twain's Autobiography*, I, 245.

118. Brooks, "Mark Twain in California," *The Century Magazine*, LVII, 98 (Nov., 1898).

119. Paine, ed., *Mark Twain's Autobiography*, I, 244; Samuel L. Clemens to his mother, N.Y., Mar. 10, [1868], in Dixon Wecter, ed., *Mark Twain to Mrs. Fairbanks* (San Marino, 1949), 23.

120. Brooks, "Mark Twain in California," *The Century Magazine*, LVII, 99 (Nov., 1898).

121. Samuel L. Clemens to his mother, San Francisco, May 5, [1868], in Wecter, ed., *Mark Twain to Mrs. Fairbanks*, 26.

122. Mark Twain, *The Innocents Abroad* (Hartford, 1869); Paine, ed., *Mark Twain's Autobiography*, I, 245.

123. William Dean Howells, *My Mark Twain: Reminiscences and Criticisms* (N.Y., 1910), 36.

124. Brooks, "American Humorous Literature," MS. in Wright Coll.

125. Paine, *Mark Twain: A Biography*, IV, 1614–1615.

126. John P. Young, *Journalism in California* (San Francisco, 1915), 73.

127. Langley, ed., *San Francisco Directory for 1869*, 118.

128. Anon., "The Author of 'The Boy Emigrants,'" *St. Nicholas*, III, 525 (June, 1876); Upham *Genealogy and Family History of the Uphams*, 49, 51.

129. Brooks to George Witherle, San Francisco, Sept. 20, 1866, Hatch Coll.

130. "Record Book of Directors, Jan. 12, 1865 to June 10, 1875," 199, Y.M.C.A records of San Francisco; Mrs. B. R. Orth to the author, San Francisco, Oct. 19, 1950.

131. Certificate of Brooks's membership dated May 4, 1871, and issued to Brooks prior to his departure from California. Hatch Coll.

132. San Francisco *Call*, Apr. 10, 1897; Robert H. Fletcher, ed., *The Annals of the Bohemian Club from Its Beginning, 1872–87* (San Francisco, 1898), 2 vols.

133. Brooks, "Bret Harte," *Scribner's Monthly*, VI, 158 (June, 1873).

134. Brooks, "Harte's Early Days," *N.Y. Times Magazine*, May 24, 1902, p. 350.

135. Henry J. W. Dam, "A Morning with Bret Harte," *McClure's Magazine*, IV, 47 (Dec., 1894); Brooks, "Harte's Early Days," *N.Y. Times Magazine*, May 24, 1902, p. 350.

136. Brooks to eds. of *The Critic*, Newark, N.J., Aug. 20, 1892, in *The Critic*, XXI, 124 (Sept. 3, 1892).

137. "Castine," near Boonsboro, Md., July 12, 1863, in Sacramento *Union*, Aug. 10, 1863.

138. Anton Roman, "The Genesis of the Overland Monthly," *Overland Monthly*, XL, 220–221 (Sept., 1902), "The Beginnings of the Overland," *ibid.*, XXXII, 73–74 (July, 1898); W. C. Bartlett, "Overland Reminiscences," *ibid.*, XXXII 41 (July, 1898); Charles Warren Stoddard, *Exits and Entrances: A Book of Essays and Sketches* (Boston, 1903), 245–246; Brooks, "Bret Harte: A Biographical and Critical Sketch," *Overland Monthly*, XL, 202 (Sept., 1902).

139. Bret Harte to Charles Warren Stoddard, San Francisco, Mar. 22, 186[8], in Geoffrey Bret Harte, ed., *The Letters of Bret Harte* (Boston, 1926), 4–5.

140. Brooks, "Bret Harte in California," *The Century Magazine*, LVIII, 449 (July, 1899).

141. Brooks, "Mark Twain in California," *The Century Magazine*, LVII, 99 (Nov., 1898).

142. Brooks, "Bret Harte in California," *The Century Magazine*, LVIII, 449 (July, 1899).

143. Brooks, "Bret Harte: A Study and an Appreciation," *The Book Buyer*, XXIV, 360 (June, 1902).

144. George R. Stewart, Jr., *Bret Harte: Argonaut and Exile* (Boston, 1931), 156–157.

145. Brooks, "Harte's Early Days," *N.Y. Times Magazine*, May 24, 1902, p. 350.

146. Brooks, "Bret Harte: A Biographical and Critical Sketch," *Overland Monthly*, XL, 206 (Sept., 1902); "Etc." in *Overland Monthly*, IX, 284 (Sept., 1872).

147. Brooks, "Bret Harte in California," *The Century Magazine*, LVIII, 447 (July, 1899).

148. Brooks, "Bret Harte: A Biographical and Critical Sketch," *Overland Monthly*, XL, 202 (Sept., 1902).

149. Bartlett, "Reminiscences of a Co-Worker," *Overland Monthly*, XL, 231 (Sept., 1902).

150. Bret Harte to Fields, Osgood and Co., San Francisco, Apr. 23, 1869, in Harte, ed., *The Letters of Bret Harte*, 6.

151. Brooks, "Bret Harte in California," *The Century Magazine*, LVIII, 449 (July, 1899).

152. *Ibid.*; Brooks, "Bret Harte: A Biographical and Critical Sketch," *Overland Monthly*, XL, 202 (Sept., 1902).

153. Dam, "A Morning with Bret Harte," *McClure's Magazine*, IV, 45 (Dec., 1894).

154. Brooks, "Harte's Early Days," *N.Y. Times Magazine*, May 24, 1902, p. 350; Brooks, "Bret Harte," *The Book Buyer*, VII, 50 (Mar., 1890).

155. Brooks, "American Humorous Literature," MS. in Wright Coll.

156. "Overland Monthly: Account of Moneys Paid Contributors," MS. book in Univ. of Cal. Lib., Berkeley, Cal.

157. Brooks, "Early Days of 'The Overland,'" *Overland Monthly*, XXXII, 5 (July, 1898).

158. Bartlett, "Overland Reminiscences," *Overland Monthly*, XXXII, 42 (July, 1898).

159. Brooks, "Early Days of 'The Overland,'" *Overland Monthly*, XXXII, 7 (July, 1898).

160. When Brooks disguised the actual name of a person in his stories, he often substituted the name of one of his close friends. L. Barnard Ayer accompanied him to California and probably lent his name to the actual diamond maker.

161. *Overland Monthly*, I, 46–55 (July, 1868).

162. This is another instance in which Brooks chooses the name of a friend for one of his characters. He had a good friend in Boston by the name of Charles T. Wilder.

163. *Overland Monthly*, I, 254–263 (Sept., 1868).

164. *Ibid.*, I, 570–579 (Dec., 1868).

165. (N.Y., 1884), IV, 162–186.

166. Anon., "Noah Brooks," *The Book Buyer*, III, 272 (Aug., 1886).

167. The inspiration for Charlie Storrs was probably Brooks's brother-in-law, S. K. Upham, who did go to California in 1849 from Boston.

168. *Overland Monthly*, II, 57–63 (Jan., 1869).

169. *Ibid.*, II, 186–193 (Feb., 1869).

170. *Ibid.*, VI, cover (Feb., 1871).

171. Roman, "The Genesis of the *Overland Monthly*," *ibid.*, XL, 222 (Sept., 1902).

172. Harte, ed., *The Letters of Bret Harte*, 7.

173. Ella Sterling Cummins, *The Story of the Files: A Review of Californian Writers and Literature* (San Francisco, 1893), 145.

174. *Overland Monthly*, III, 30–37 (July, 1869).

175. "Old Lamps for New?" *Overland Monthly*, III, 559–566 (Dec., 1869).

176. "The Career of an American Princess," *Overland Monthly*, V, 41–469 (Nov., 1870).

177. San Francisco *Alta California*, Dec. 29, 1870.

178. Brooks, "Harte's Early Days," *N.Y. Times Magazine*, May 24, 1902, p. 350.

179. *Ibid.*; Brooks, "Bret Harte in California," *The Century Magazine*, LVIII, 451 (July, 1899); San Francisco *Alta California*, Feb. 2, 1871.

180. *Overland Monthly*, VI, 287 (Mar., 1871).

181. San Francisco *Alta California*, May 10, 1871.

182. Charles S. Greene, "Memories of an Editor," *Overland Monthly*, Xl, 264–265 (Sept., 1902).

Chapter IX. Night Editor in New York

1. Frederick Evans, "Noah Brooks," *The Lamp*, XXVII, 130 (Sept., 1903).

2. San Francisco *Alta California*, May 10, 1871; Dixon (Ill.) *Telegraph & Herald*, May 18, 1871.

3. N.Y. *Semi-Weekly Tribune*, May 19, 1871.

4. Brooks, *Washington in Lincoln's Time*, 60.

5. Fremont Rider, ed., *Rider's New York City and Vicinity* (N.Y., 1916), 8, 22.

6. *The New York Tribune: A Sketch of Its History* (N.Y., 1883), 7.

7. James Parton, *The Life of Horace Greeley* (Boston, 1872), 368–369; Charles T. Congdon, *Reminiscences of a Journalist* (Boston, 1880), 270.

8. William H. Rideing, *Many Celebrities and a Few Others* (Garden City, 1912), 43.

9. Joseph Bucklin Bishop, *Notes and Anecdotes of Many Years* (N.Y., 1925), 8.

10. Brooks to Thomas N. Rooker, N.Y., n.d., Misc. Papers, N.Y. Pub. Lib. A stone is a flat table where type is composed and a turtle is a curved plate which holds the type in a cylinder press.

11. Rideing, *Many Celebrities and a Few Others*, 44.

12. Parton, *The Life of Horace Greeley*, 361, 373, 376.

13. Brooks, "Horace Greeley," *The Youth's Companion*, LXXV, 400 (Aug. 15, 1901).

14. Brooks to George Witherle, N.Y., May 15, 1872, Hatch Coll.

15. Evans, "Noah Brooks," *The Lamp*, XXVII, 131 (Sept., 1903).

16. Brooks to George Witherle, N.Y., May 15, 1872, Hatch Coll.; Brooks's salary checks, Misc. Papers, N.Y. Pub. Lib.

17. Rideing, *Many Celebrities and a Few Others*, 48–49.

18. Brooks, "Harte's Early Days," *N.Y. Times Magazine*, May 24, 1902, 350.

19. Henry Holt, *Garrulities of an Octogenarian Editor* (Boston, 1923), 135.

20. William Roscoe Thayer, *The Life and Letters of John Hay* (Boston, 1915), I, 334.

21. *Harper's Weekly*, XV, 877 (Sept. 16, 1871).

22. Brander Matthews, *These Many Years: Recollections of a New Yorker* (N.Y., 1917).

23. Brooks, "Horace Greeley," *The Youth's Companion*, LXXV, 399 (Aug. 15, 1901).

24. William Winter, *Other Days* (N.Y., 1908), 170.

25. Octavius Brooks Frothingham, *Recollections and Impressions: 1822–1890* (N.Y., 1891), 227.

26. Holt, *Garrulities of an Octogenarian Editor*, 135.

27. Rideing, *Many Celebrities and a Few Others*, 40.

28. Dennett, ed., *Lincoln and the Civil War in the Diaries and Letters of John Hay*, 114, 138, 220.

29. Royal Cortissoz, "'W.R.': A Co-Worker's Impressions of William Reid as an Editor and Friend," *N.Y. Herald-Tribune*, Apr. 13, 1941.

30. Dennett, ed., *Lincoln and the Civil War in the Diaries and Letters of John Hay*, 328.

31. Paine, ed., *Mark Twain's Autobiography*, I, 233.

32. Rideing, *Many Celebrities and a Few Others*, 43.

33. Bishop, *Notes and Anecdotes of Many Years,* 171.

34. *Ibid.,* 53.

35. In December of 1875 Johnson retired from the managing editorship of *The Christian Union.* N.Y. *Tribune,* Nov. 15, 1875.

36. N.Y. *Tribune,* July 5, 1880; Frothingham, *George Ripley* (Boston, 1882), 203–205.

37. *The Writer,* II, 127 (May, 1888).

38. Bishop, *Notes and Anecdotes of Many Years,* 68–71; *The Critic,* III, 480 (Nov. 24, 1883).

39. *The Book Buyer,* XIII, 389–390 (Aug., 1896); Winter, *Other Days,* 169.

40. Laura Stedman and George M. Gould, *Life and Letters of Edmund Clarence Stedman* (N.Y., 1910), I, 479.

41. Lilian Whiting, *Louise Chandler Moulton: Poet and Friend* (Boston, 1910), 58, 107; *The Bookman,* XXVIII, 601–607 (Feb., 1909). Her *Tribune* articles were signed "L. C. M."

42. N.Y. *Tribune,* Apr. 28, 1871, Sept. 18, 1875, May 31, 1896.

43. Bertha Brooks Runkle Bash to author, Palo Alto, Cal., Aug. 22, 1953. Early in 1865, Greeley began his crusade by calling attention to the 173 "slaughter-houses, situated mainly in densely populated parts of the town." N.Y. *Tribune,* Jan. 9, 1865.

44. Bertha Brooks Runkle Bash to author, Palo Alto, Cal., Sept. 17, 1953; N.Y. *Tribune,* Nov. 29, 1875.

45. Brooks to Anna E. Dickinson, N.Y., July 14, 1872, Dec. 7, 1873, Dickinson Papers, Lib. of Congress.

46. Bertha Brooks Runkle Bash to author, Palo Alto, Cal., Aug. 22, 1953.

47. *Ibid.,* Sept. 1, 1853. About 1901 they moved to 328 W. 57th St.

48. *The Writer,* XIII, 111 (July, 1900); *The Book Buyer,* XX, 427 (July, 1900).

49. N.Y. *Tribune,* May 27, 1901. She married Louis H. Bash on Oct. 26, 1904, and also wrote *The Truth about Tolna* (1906), *The Scarlet Rider* (1913), *Straight Down the Crooked Lane* (1915), and *The Island* (1921).

50. The official list of the *Tribune* editors is found in *A Memorial of Horace Greeley* (N.Y., 1873), 160.

51. N.Y. *Tribune,* Apr. 9, 1897, June 7, 1898; *The Literary World,* XXVIII, 124 (Apr. 17, 1897).

52. N.Y. *Tribune,* Feb. 5, 1872.

53. Mrs. L. G. G. Runkle to Anna E. Dickinson, N.Y., Mar. 18, 1872, Dickinson Papers, Lib. of Congress.

54. Brooks to Anna E. Dickinson, N.Y., July 14, 1872, Dickinson Papers, Lib. of Congress.

55. Brooks to Anna E. Dickinson, N.Y., July 28, 1872, Dickinson Papers, Lib. of Congress. Long Branch was a favorite resort spot for New Yorkers, located on the New Jersey coast 32 miles from New York City. The New Jersey Southern R.R. had two ships, the *Jesse Hoyt* and the *Twilight,* which carried tourists from New York to their line. The entire trip took 1 hour and 35 minutes. N.Y. *Tribune,* May 27, 1875.

56. Anna E. Dickinson to Susan Dickinson, N.Y., Nov. 8, 1872; Brooks to Anna E. Dickinson, N.Y., Nov. 18, 1872; Dickinson Papers, Lib. of Congress.

57. Brooks to Anna E. Dickinson, N.Y., Apr. 7, 1873, Dickinson Papers, Lib. of Congress; Chicago *Inter-Ocean*, Dec. 27, 1873.

58. Brooks to Anna E. Dickinson, N.Y., Aug. 14, Sept. 17, 1872, Dickinson Papers, Lib. of Congress.

59. *A Memorial of Horace Greeley*, 23.

60. *The New York Tribune: A Sketch of Its History*, 15.

61. Brooks to Anna E. Dickinson, N.Y., Jan. 15, 1873, Dickinson Papers, Lib. of Congress.

62. *Scribner's Monthly*, VI, 506–507 (Aug., 1873).

63. N.Y. *Tribune*, July 27, 1874.

64. Brooks to Anna E. Dickinson, N.Y., July 31, Dec. 7, 1873, Dickinson Papers, Lib. of Congress.

65. Brooks to Anna E. Dickinson, N.Y., Jan. 17, 1874, Dickinson Papers, Lib. of Congress.

66. Stedman and Gould, *Life and Letters of Edmund Clarence Stedman*, I, 478.

67. N.Y. *Times*, July 30, 1893; Anon., "The Author of 'The Boy Emigrants,'" *St. Nicholas*, III, 525 (June, 1876).

68. Brooks to Anna E. Dickinson, N.Y., July 12 [1874], Dickinson Papers, Lib. of Congress.

69. Brooks to George Witherle, N.Y., Aug. 31, 1879, Hatch Coll.; Brooks to William Winter, N.Y. Aug. 18, 1879, Winter Papers, N.Y. Pub. Lib.

70. Foord resigned to take charge of the Brooklyn *Union-Argus*, a paper whose stock he inherited. *The Literary World*, XIV, 98 (Mar. 24, 1883).

71. Meyer Berger, *The Story of the New York Times 1851–1951* (N.Y., 1951), 5, 11.

72. N.Y. *Tribune*, Feb. 3, 1872.

73. *The Critic*, III, 374 (Sept. 22, 1883).

74. Brooks to William A. Seaver, N.Y., May 15, 1878, Ill. State Hist. Lib.

75. Brooks to Anna E. Dickinson, N.Y., Nov. 18, 1872, Dickinson Papers, Lib. of Congress.

76. Brooks to George Witherle, N.Y., Mar. 10, Oct. 28, 1882, Hatch Coll.; Brooks, "The Biography of Richard," *St. Nicholas*, XI, 916 (Oct., 1884).

77. Misc. Papers, N.Y. Pub. Lib.

78. Brooks to Louise Chandler Moulton, N.Y. (July 9, 1874), Moulton Papers, Lib. of Congress. Brooks invited Mrs. Moulton, but it is not known if she accepted.

79. Brooks to Anna E. Dickinson, N.Y., July 12, [1874], Dickinson Papers, Lib. of Congress.

80. N.Y. *Herald*, July 25, 26, 1874.

81. Brooks to George Witherle, N.Y., May 3, 1883, Hatch Coll.

82. Brooks to Anna E. Dickinson, N.Y., Nov. 9, 1874, Dickinson Papers, Lib. of Congress. For a sketch of Miss Cushman's life, see N.Y. *Semi-Weekly Tribune*, Feb. 22, 1876.

83. Brooks to Anna. E. Dickinson, N.Y., Nov. 9, 1874, Dickinson Papers, Lib. of Congress; N.Y. *Tribune*, Nov. 16, 1874.

84. N.Y. *Herald*, June 16, 1880.

85. Handbill in Misc. Papers, N.Y. Pub. Lib.; N.Y. *Tribune*, Oct. 30, Nov. 30, 1878.

86. N.Y. *Semi-Weekly Tribune*, Oct. 1, 1875.

87. Winkelreid Wolfgang Brown [Isaac H. Bromley], "The Horse-Car Poetry: Its True History," *Scribner's Monthly*, XI, 910–912 (Apr., 1876).

88. N.Y. *Semi-Weekly Tribune*, Sept. 28, 1875. It did not appear in the *Daily Tribune*.

89. The sheet music is reproduced in *Scribner's Monthly*, XI, 912 (Apr., 1876).

90. N.Y. *Tribune*, Jan. 10, 1876.

91. Mark Twain, "A Literary Nightmare," *Atlantic Monthly*, XXXVII, 167–169 (Feb., 1876).

92. Henry Holt recalled how popular the poem was, but passed it off as the work of either John Hay or Mark Twain. Holt, *Garrulities of an Octogenarian Editor*, 129.

93. "Anecdotes of Noah Brooks, Related by Newark Friends," Newark (N.J.) *Sunday News*, Aug. 23, 1903.

94. N.Y. *Semi-Weekly Tribune*, Nov. 19, 1875.

95. N.Y. *Tribune*, Dec. 9, 1875.

96. Oswald Garrison Villard, *Fighting Years: Memoirs of a Liberal Editor* (N.Y., 1939), 107; Richard N. Current, *The Typewriter and the Men Who Made It* (Urbana, Ill., 1954), 71–73, 115.

97. Brooks to George Witherle, N.Y., Apr. 29, 1879, Hatch Coll.

98. *Ibid.*; Brooks to William Winter, N.Y., Aug. 18, 1879, Winter Papers, N.Y. Pub. Lib.

99. *The Critic*, XIV, 286–287 (June 8, 1889); XIV, 300 (June 15, 1889).

100. *The Book Buyer*, X, 644 (Jan., 1894); *The Writer*, XI, 93 (June, 1898).

101. N.Y. *Tribune*, July 8, 1880.

102. Brooks to William Winter, Bar Harbor, Me., Aug. 21, 1880; Brooks to William Winter, N.Y., Sept. 1, 1889, Winter Papers, N.Y. Pub. Lib.

103. *The Critic*, XXXVIII, 74, 75–76 (Jan., 1901).

104. Jeanette Gilder continued to write for the Boston *Transcript* under the pen name of "Brunswick." *The Writer*, IV, 286 (Dec., 1890).

105. Rosamond Gilder, ed., *Letters of Richard Watson Gilder*, (Boston, 1916), 106.

106. George W. Cable to his wife, N.Y., Oct. 8, 1882, in Lucy L. C. Bikle, *George W. Cable: His Life and Letters* (N.Y., 1928), 83.

107. George Parsons Lathrop, "The Literary Movement in New York," *Harper's Magazine*, LXXIII, 832 (Nov., 1886).

108. *The Literary World*, XXIV, 62 (Feb. 25, 1893).

109. *The Critic*, IV, 113 (Mar. 22, 1884); IV, 169 (Apr. 12, 1884).

110. *Memoirs of Henry Villard: Journalist and Financier 1835–1900* (Boston, 1904), I, 339. He wrote for the N.Y. *Herald*, Cincinnati *Commercial* and Chicago *Tribune*.

111. N.Y. *Herald*, May 20, 1871.

112. Brooks to George Witherle, N.Y., May 3, 1883, Hatch Coll.

113. Brooks to Henry Villard, N.Y.., July 19, 1883, N.Y. Hist. Soc.

114. N.Y. *Tribune*, Aug. 28, 1883.

115. *Ibid.*, Aug. 30, 1883.

116. *Ibid.*, Sept. 2, 1883; Chicago *Tribune*, Sept. 1, 1883.

117. Chicago *Tribune*, Sept. 4, 1883; N.Y. *Tribune*, Sept. 4, 1883.

118. *Illinois State Journal* (Springfield), Sept. 3, 1883.

119. Chicago *Tribune*, Sept. 4, 1883.

120. N.Y. *Tribune*, Sept. 9, 1883.

121. *Ibid.*, Sept. 6, 1883.

122. *Ibid.*, Sept. 7, 1883.

123. Edward P. Mitchell, *Memoirs of an Editor: Fifty Years of American Journalism* (N.Y., 1924), 393.

124. N.Y. *Tribune*, Sept. 9, 1883.

125. *Illinois State Journal*, Sept. 12, 1883.

126. N.Y. *Tribune*, Sept. 18, 1883.

127. *Ibid.*, Sept. 28, 1883.

128. Bikle, *George W. Cable: His Life and Letters*, 121–122.

129. *The Critic*, IV, 163 (Apr. 5, 1884).

130. Hartford (Conn.) *Daily Courant*, Apr. 4, 1884.

131. Brooks to Mark Twain, N.Y., Mar. 31, [1884], Mark Twain Papers, Univ. of Cal. Lib., Berkley, Cal.

132. *The Critic*, IV, 32 (Jan. 19, 1884); Gilder, ed., *Letters of Richard Watson Gilder*, 112.

133. N.Y. *Tribune*, Apr. 29, 1885.

134. *Ibid.*, Apr. 30, 1885.

135. *The Book Buyer*, II, 128 (June, 1885).

136. N.Y. *Tribune*, Apr. 14, 1891.

137. Brooks to Edmund Clarence Stedman, Newark, N.J., Apr. 14, 1891, Stedman Papers, Columbia Univ. Lib.

138. Brooks to Anna E. Dickinson, N.Y., Mar. 11, 1873, Dickinson Papers, Lib. of Congress.

139. Brooks to Anna E. Dickinson, N.Y., Mar. 20, [1872], Dickinson Papers, Lib. of Congress.

140. *Scribner's Monthly*, III, 526–537 (Mar., 1872).

141. Anon., "Noah Brooks," *The Book Buyer*, III, 271–272 (Aug., 1886).

142. Brooks to Anna E. Dickinson, N.Y., Mar. 20, [1872], Dickinson Papers, Lib. of Congress.

143. "Awakened Japan," *Scribner's Monthly*, III, 669–672 (Apr., 1872).

144. "A Fan Study," *ibid.*, VI, 616–621 (Sept., 1873).

145. "Some Pictures from Japan," *ibid.*, XI, 177–193 (Dec., 1875).

146. Nautilus Island lies just outside the harbor of Castine. *Castine from Photographs by A. H. Folsom and Others* (Castine, 1893).

147. *Scribner's Monthly*, IV, 65–75 (May, 1872).

148. *Ibid.*, XVII, 76–86 (Nov., 1878).

149. Brooks to George Witherle, N.Y., Apr. 29, 1879, Hatch Coll.

150. *The Century Magazine*, XXIV, 587–597 (Aug., 1882).

151. "Bret Harte," *Scribner's Monthly*, VI, 158–161 (June, 1873).

152. Brooks to Anna E. Dickinson, N.Y., May 16, [1873], Dickinson Papers, Lib. of Congress.

153. "Personal Reminiscences of Lincoln," *Scribner's Monthly*, XV, 561–569, 673–681 (Feb., Mar., 1878); Lincoln's Imagination," *ibid.*, XVIII, 584–587 (Aug., 1879).

154. "An Old Town with a History," *The Century Magazine*, XXIV, 697–708 (Sept., 1882).

155. "The Baron de St. Castin," *Magazine of American History*, IX, 365–374 (May, 1883).

156. Brooks to George Witherle, N.Y., May 3, 1883, Hatch Coll.

157. N.Y. *Tribune*, Sept. 21, 1875.

158. *The Dial*, VII, 197 (Dec., 1886).

159. N.Y. *Semi-Weekly Tribune*, Apr. 13, 1875. The five magazines which *St. Nicholas* purchased were *The Little Corporal*, *The Schoolday Magazine*, *The Riverside Magazine*, *Our Young Folks*, and *The Children's Hour*.

160. *The Book Buyer*, III, 342 (Oct., 1886); *The Literary World*, XXI, 443 (Nov. 22, 1890).

161. Thomas W. Lamont, *My Boyhood in a Parsonage* (N.Y., 1946), 67.

162. *St. Nicholas*, I, 10–12 (Nov., 1873).

163. "Wrecked at Home," *ibid.*, I, 264–268, 349–353 (Mar.–Apr., 1874).

164. "A Century Ago," *ibid.*, IV, 802–805 (Oct., 1877).

165. *Ibid.*, I, 63–64 (Dec., 1873).

166. *Ibid.*, III, 427–429 (May, 1876).

167. "The Author of 'The Boy Emigrants,'" *ibid.*, III, 524 (June, 1876).

168. *Ibid.*, IV, 292 (Feb., 1877).

169. *Ibid.*, IV, 150 (Dec., 1876).

170. Jan. 12, 1877.

171. *Scribner's Monthly*, XIII, 424 (Jan., 1877).

172. *The Book Buyer*, VIII, 435 (Nov., 1891).

173. Royalty reports in the Wright Coll.

174. Brooks to George Witherle, N.Y., Aug. 31, 1879, Hatch Coll.

175. "How the Flag Was Saved," *St. Nicholas*, XXIII, 294–295 (Feb., 1896); "A Lesson in Patriotism," *ibid.*, XIV, 340–341 (Mar., 1887).

176. N.Y. *Herald*, Oct. 18, 1880.

177. *The Literary World*, XI, 441 (Dec. 4, 1880).

178. *St. Nicholas*, II, 162–168 (Jan., 1875).

179. "George the Third," *ibid.*, IV, 623–626 (July, 1877).

180. "A Noble Life," *ibid.*, IX, 59–61 (Nov., 1881).

181. "A Famous Sea-Fight," *ibid.*, IX, 714–716 (July, 1882).

182. "A Boy in the White House," *ibid.*, X, 57–65 (Nov., 1882).

183. *Overland Monthly*, IX, 105–114 (Aug., 1872).

184. Dispatch from San Francisco, Sept. 29, in N.Y. *Tribune*, Sept. 30, 1883.

185. *Overland Monthly*, I (2nd Ser.) 441–450 (May, 1883).

186. Anon., "Noah Brooks," *The Book Buyer*, III, 272 (Aug., 1886).

187. *The Californian*, IV, 365–374 (Nov., 1881).

Chapter X. A Club Man in New York

1. Francis Gerry Fairfield, *The Clubs of New York* (N.Y., 1873), 7.

2. "Necase," N.Y., Oct. 15, 1887, in San Francisco *Chronicle*, Nov. 27, 1887.

3. *The Century Association for the Year 1903* (N.Y., 1904), 34–35.

4. John Elderkin, *A Brief History of the Lotos Club* (N.Y., 1895), 10; C. B. Todd, "New York Clubs," *Lippincott's Magazine*, XXXII, 95 (July, 1883).

5. John Brougham and John Elderkin, eds., *Lotos Leaves: Original Stories, Essays, and Poems* (Boston, 1875), 321 n.

6. *The Literary World*, VIII, 213 (May, 1878).

7. N.Y. *Tribune*, Mar. 28, 1880.

8. Todd, "New York Clubs," *Lippincott's Magazine*, XXXII, 95 (July, 1883).

9. John Elderkin, Chester S. Lord, and Horatio N. Fraser, eds., *Speeches at the Lotos Club* (N.Y., 1901), xix, 34.

10. Elderkin, *A Brief History of the Lotos Club*, 12; Fairfield, *The Clubs of New York*, 200.

11. Chandos Fulton, "Legends of the Lotos," N.Y. *Dramatic Mirror*, Dec. 23, 1893.

12. Fairfield, *The Clubs of New York*, 234.

13. Clara Erskine Clement and Laurence Hutton, *Artists of the Nineteenth Century and Their Works* (Boston, 1884), I, 296.

14. Brooks to Roswell Smith, N.Y., Mar. 19, n.y., Illinois State Historical Library.

15. N.Y. *Herald*, Apr. 25, 1880.

16. *Ibid.*, Dec. 19, 1876; N.Y. *Times*, Apr. 2, 1879, Mar. 24, 1895; N.Y. *Tribune*, Dec. 16, 1884.

17. Royal Cortissoz, *The Life of Whitelaw Reid*, (N.Y., 1921), I, 235–236.

18. *Lotos Leaves: Original Stories, Essays, and Poems*, 205–220.

19. *The Literary World*, V, 94 (Nov., 1874).

20. N.Y. *Tribune*, Mar. 20, 1876.

21. N.Y. *Herald*, Apr. 19, 1876; N.Y. *Semi-Weekly Tribune*, Apr. 21, 1876.

22. Printed invitation dated Nov. 22, 1876, Misc. Papers, N.Y. Pub. Lib.

23. N.Y. *Herald*, Mar. 19, 1877.

24. Elderkin, *A Brief History of the Lotos Club*, 42, 53; N.Y. *Tribune*, Jan. 13, 1879; *The Works of E. P. Roe: He Fell in Love with His Wife* (N.Y., n.d.), 453.

25. Brooks to Mark Twain, N.Y., May 12, 1879, Mark Twain Papers, Univ. of Cal. Lib., Berkeley.

26. This street number was later changed to 149 Fifth Avenue.

27. N.Y. *Tribune*, May 21, 1877.

28. Todd, "New York Clubs," *Lippincott's Magazine*, XXXII, 96–97 (July, 1883). Knox died at his Lotos Club quarters on Jan. 6, 1896. *The Dial*, XX, 53 (Jan. 16, 1896).

29. Brooks to George Witherle, N.Y. Apr. 29, 1879, Hatch Coll.

30. Brooks, "The Biography of Richard," *St. Nicholas*, XI, 912–916 (Oct., 1884).

31. George Parsons Lathrop, "The Literary Movement in New York," *Harper's Magazine*, LXXIII, 830 (Nov., 1886).

32. N.Y. *Tribune*, Nov. 10, 1879.

33. *Ibid.*, Dec. 2, 1878.

34. N.Y. *Herald*, Apr. 15, 1883.

35. *Ibid.*, Nov. 21, 1880.

36. Dixon Wecter, ed., *The Love Letters of Mark Twain* (N.Y., 1949), 244, 268.

37. Winter, *The Poems of William Winter* (N.Y., 1909), 123–124. Winter also wrote a poem for the Lotos Club entitled "Comrades." N.Y. *Tribune*, Nov. 10, 1875.

38. N.Y. *Tribune*, Mar. 28, 1880.

39. *Ibid.*, June 8, 1880.

40. In Brooks's personal photograph album there is a picture of Brougham inscribed "To Noah Brooks from his friend John Brougham," Hatch Coll.

41. N.Y. *Semi-Weekly Tribune*, Nov. 9, 1877.

42. *The Autobiography of Joseph Jefferson* (N.Y., 1889), 338–340.

43. Nathaniel H. Belden, known on the stage as N. B. Clarke, was one of the many actors buried there. His funeral was on Apr. 16, 1872. N.Y. *Tribune*, Apr. 17, 1872.

44. The other pallbearers were Judge John R. Brady, S. L. N. Barlow, Edwin Booth, F. C. Bangs, William Winter, Dr. Charles Phelps, and John W. Carroll. N.Y. *Tribune*, Apr. 17, 1872.

45. Brooks to William Winter, N.Y., July 19, 1880, Winter Papers, N.Y. Pub. Lib.

46. Brooks to William Winter, Bar Harbor, Me., Aug. 21, 1880, Winter Papers, N.Y. Pub. Lib.

47. Brooks to William Winter, N.Y., Sept. 1, 1880, Winter Papers, N.Y. Pub. Lib.

48. Winter, ed., *Life, Stories, and Poems of John Brougham* (Boston, 1881), 147–154.

49. *The Critic*, I (2nd ser.), 6 (Jan. 16, 1881).

50. N.Y. *Herald*, Mar. 23, 1890.

51. N.Y. *Tribune*, July 2, 1892; Theodore F. Wolfe, *Literary Haunts & Homes: American Authors* (Philadelphia, 1899), 84.

52. Handbook of the Lotos Club.

53. Todd, "New York Clubs," *Lippincott's Magazine*, XXXII, 91 (July, 1883).

54. *The Century Association Reports* for 1899 (N.Y., 1900), 123.

55. "The Century Club," written by a N.Y. correspondent for the Chicago *Tribune* and reprinted in *Illinois State Register* (Springfield), July 4, 1884.

56. Todd, "New York Clubs," *Lippincott's Magazine*, XXXII, 94 (July, 1883).

57. Raphael Pumpelly, *My Reminiscences* (N.Y., 1918), II, 582.

58. Max O'Rell, *A Frenchman in America: Recollections of Men and Things* (N.Y., 1891), 256.

59. George Augustus Sala, *America Revisited* (London, 1882), I, 41. A "whisky skin" is a slang term for a drink containing whiskey.

60. James Herbert Morse Diary, entry of Apr. 27, 1884. MS. owned by William Gibbons Morse, N.Y.

61. Holt, *Garrulities of an Octogenarian Editor*, 129.

62. Brooks to E. C. Stedman, N.Y., [1896], Columbia Univ. Lib.

63. *The Century Association Reports* for 1891 (N.Y., 1892), 13; for 1898 (N.Y., 1899), 12; for 1903 (N.Y., 1904), 10.

64. Richard Henry Stoddard willed 1,000 volumes to the club. Fielding H. Garrison, ed., *John Shaw Billings: A Memoir* (N.Y., 1915), 309.

65. *The Century Association Reports* for 1903 (N.Y., 1904), 34.

66. James Grant Wilson, *The Life and Letters of Fitz-Greene Halleck* (N.Y., 1869), 400.

67. N.Y. *Tribune*, Feb. 24, 1864.

68. *Ibid.*, Mar. 1, 1893.

69. Charles de Kay, "Reminiscences of the Authors Club," MS. owned by Mrs. Phyllis de Kay Wheelock, N.Y.; N.Y. *Tribune*, Mar. 1, 1893; George Cary Eggleston, *Recollections of a Varied Life* (N.Y., 1910), 272–273; Bikle, *George W. Cable: His Life and Letters*, 86; Gilder, ed., *Letters of Richard Watson Gilder*, 119–120; *The Authors Club* (N.Y., 1891), 3–7; Brander Matthews, *These Many Years: Recollections of a New Yorker* (N.Y., 1917), 220.

70. Eggleston, *Recollections of a Varied Life*, 272–273; Matthews, *These Many Years*, 220–221; Stedman and Gould, eds., *Life and Letters of Edmund Clarence Stedman*, II, 464–465.

71. Rossiter Johnson, "The Authors Club," *The Critic*, XXX, 315 (May 8, 1897).

72. *The Literary World*, XX, 112 (Mar. 30, 1889).

73. *Ibid.*, XX, 129 (Apr. 13, 1889).

74. *The Authors Club*, 1891, pp. 5, 24; 1892, p. 5; "Minutes of the Executive Council," I (1888–1895), MS. records of Authors Club, N.Y.

75. *The Literary World*, XIII, 426–427 (Dec. 2, 1882); *The Critic*, II, 328–329 (Dec. 2, 1882); *The Book Buyer*, IX, 110 (Apr., 1892).

76. L. Frank Tooker, *The Joys and Tribulations of an Editor* (N.Y., 1923), 152.

77. *The Literary World*, XX, 112 (Mar. 30, 1889).

78. Eggleston, *Recollections of a Varied Life*, 177.

79. *The Literary World*, XVII, 65 (Feb. 20, 1886).

80. Todd, "New York Clubs," *Lippincott's Magazine*, XXXII, 100 (July, 1883).

81. *The Literary World*, XXIII, 147 (Apr. 23, 1892); Matthews, *These Many Years*, 224–225.

82. Matthews, *These Many Years*, 221; *The Critic*, IV, 168 (Apr. 12, 1884).

83. Stedman and Gould, eds., *Life and Letters of Edmund Clarence Stedman*, II, 464; *The Literary World*, XIX, 347 (Oct. 13, 1888).

84. Eggleston, *Recollections of a Varied Life*, 279.

85. *The Critic*, IV, 113 (Mar. 8, 1884); James Herbert Morse Diary, Mar. 2, 1884; N.Y. *Tribune*, Feb. 29, 1884.

86. James Herbert Morse Diary, Apr. 25, 1884.

87. *Ibid.*, May 31, 1884; *The Critic*, IV, 275 (June 7, 1884).

88. Lathrop, "The Literary Movement in New York," *Harper's Magazine*, LXXIII, 830–831 (Nov., 1886); James Herbert Morse Diary, Mar. 21, 1886; *The Literary World*, XVI, 448 (Nov. 28, 1885).

89. *The Literary World*, XVIII, 104 (Apr. 2, 1887); XX, 112–113 (Mar. 30, 1889).

90. Photo of this group, in *Harper's Magazine*, LXXIII, 812 (Nov., 1886).

91. James Herbert Morse Diary, Sept. 30, 1886.

92. Frederic Harrison, *Autobiographic Memoirs* (London, 1911), II, 207–209.

93. *The Literary World*, XXV, 254 (Aug. 11, 1894).

94. Johnson, "The Authors Club," *The Critic*, XXX, 315–317 (May 8, 1897).

95. *The Dial*, XVIII, 221 (Apr. 1, 1895).

96. N.Y. *Tribune*, Apr. 23, 1886; *The Literary World*, XVII, 152 (May 1, 1886); James Herbert Morse Diary, Apr. 23, 1886. Roe was an inveterate gardener who lived at Cornwall-on-the-Hudson, N.Y. He wrote *Play and Profit in My Garden* (N.Y., 1886).

97. De Kay, "Reminiscences of the Authors Club," MS. owned by Mrs. Phyllis de Kay Wheelock, N.Y.

98. *The Critic*, XVI, 28 (Jan. 18, 1890).

99. *Ibid.*, XVI, 189 (Apr. 12, 1890); *The Literary World*, XXI, 131 (Apr. 12, 1890).

100. *The Literary World*, XXIII, 478 (Dec. 17, 1892); *The Critic*, XXX, 315–317 (May 8, 1897).

101. *The Literary World*, XXIII, 146 (Apr. 23, 1892).

102. Eggleston, *Recollections of a Varied Life*, 285.

103. *The Literary World*, XXIII 132 (Apr. 9, 1892).

104. *Ibid.*, XXIII, 478 (Dec. 17, 1892).

105. *The Critic*, XXIV, 8 (Jan. 6, 1894).

106. Eggleston, *Recollections of a Varied Life*, 285–286.

107. Brooks, "The Books of an Old Boy," *Liber Scriptorum* (N.Y., 1893), 66–72.

108. N.Y. *Tribune*, Mar. 1, 1893; *The Literary World*, XXIV, 72–73 (Mar. 11, 1893); James Herbert Morse Diary, Feb. 28, 1893.

109. James Herbert Morse Diary, Feb. 18, Apr. 13, 1894.

110. *The Dial*, XVII, 301 (Nov. 16, 1894); *The Literary World*, XXV, 428 (Dec. 1, 1894); N.Y. *Herald*, Jan. 27, 1895.

111. *The Literary World*, XXVI, 447 (Dec. 28, 1895).

112. *The Dial*, XVI, 120 (Feb. 16, 1894).

113. *The Writer*, III, 238 (Oct., 1889).

114. *The Book Buyer*, XIII, 221 (May, 1896).

115. *Current Literature*, XVIII, 475 (Dec., 1895).

116. Holt, *Garrulities of an Octogenarian Editor*, 113.

117. *The Bookman*, III, 112 (Apr., 1896).

118. N.Y. *Herald*, Mar. 26, 1897.

119. *The Lamp*, XXVI, 408 (June, 1903). Stoddard was a noted poet and after serving as literary editor on such papers as the N.Y. *World* and N.Y. *Evening Express*, he

accepted a similar position on the N.Y. *Evening Mail* in 1880. *Good Literature* (N.Y.), Nov. 27, 1880.

120. N.Y. *Tribune*, Mar. 4, 1898.

121. James Herbert Morse Diary, Feb. 27, 1898.

122. *Ibid.*, Dec. 24, 1919.

123. *Collections and Proceedings of the Maine Historical Society* (Portland, 1891), II (2nd ser.), 167–168.

124. Records of the New Eng. Soc. in the N.Y. Pub. Lib.

125. Although Brooks went west in 1859, Twain did not go until 1861. Brooks, however, always confused this point and thought that both he and Twain had journeyed westward in the same year. Brooks, "Mark Twain in California," *The Century Magazine*, LVII, 97 (Nov., 1898). Perhaps this blunder of Brooks's was the cause of Twain's saying that Brooks was "a good historian where facts were not essential." Paine, ed., *Mark Twain Autobiography*, I, 245.

126. Brooks to Mark Twain, N.Y., Apr. 27, 1882, Mark Twain Papers, Univ. of Cal. Lib., Berkeley. This letter is typewritten.

127. N.Y. *Tribune*, Dec. 23, 1882.

Chapter XI. *The Fruitful Years*

1. N.Y. *Herald*, Apr. 28, 1884.

2. *The Critic*, IV, 215 (May 3, 1884).

3. *Ibid.*, IV, 288 (June 21, 1884).

4. Brooks to George Witherle, N.Y., May 26, 1884, Hatch Coll.

5. "Necase," N.Y., Oct. 15, 1887, in San Francisco *Chronicle*, Nov. 27, 1887.

6. *The Literary World*, XV, 447 (Dec. 13, 1884).

7. Brooks to William Winter, Newark, N.J., Jan. 11, 1893, Winter Papers, N.Y. Pub. Lib.

8. *The Book Buyer*, III, 513 (Dec., 1886).

9. Brooks to George Witherle, N.Y., May 26, 1884, Hatch Coll.

10. "Necase," N.Y., Oct. 15, 1887, in San Francisco *Chronicle*, Nov. 27, 1887; Lathrop, "The Literary Movement in New York," *Harper's Magazine*, LXXIII, 824.

11. N.Y. *Social Register* for Aug., 1893 (N.Y., 1893), 33.

12. Brooks to George Witherle, Newark, N.J., Mar. 9, 1891, Hatch Coll.

13. Brooks to Edmund Clarence Stedman, Newark, N.J., Mar. 8, 10, 22, 1894, Columbia Univ. Lib.

14. Newark *Evening News*, Aug. 18, 1903.

15. *Club Men of New York 1895–97* (N.Y., 1896), 14, 107. Brooks dropped his membership in the Essex Club and the Essex County Country Club about 1900.

16. Newark *Sunday News*, Aug. 23, 1903.

17. Bertha Brooks Runkle Bash to author, Palo Alto, Cal., Aug. 22, 1953.

18. Newark *Sunday News*, Aug. 23, 1903.

19. Brooks to Edmund Clarence Stedman, Newark, N.J., Nov. 14, 1891, Columbia Univ. Lib.

20. Newark *Evening News*, Aug. 18, 1903.

21. Doane was born at Boston in 1830, the son of a Protestant Episcopal bishop, but in 1855 he became a Roman Catholic. In 1880 he was given the title of Right Reverend Monsignor and was the Vicar General of the Newark Diocese. At times Doane visited with Brooks in Castine. N.Y. *Herald*, Mar. 29, 1880; Newark *Daily Advertiser*, Aug. 18, 1903.

22. *The Writer*, V, 191 (Sept., 1891); Fabyan House, known at the time of this writing as Fabyan-Bretton Woods, is a famous resort in the Presidential Range of mountains.

23. Brooks to George Witherle, Newark, N.J., Mar. 9, 1891, Hatch Coll.

24. *Collections and Proceedings of the Maine Hist. Soc.* (Portland, 1891), II (2nd ser.), 124.

25. Mitchell, *Memoirs of an Editor*, 434–437.

26. *The Literary World*, XVII, 370 (Oct. 30, 1886).

27. "Necase," N.Y., Oct. 15, 1887, in San Francisco *Chronicle*, Nov. 2, 1887.

28. *St. Nicholas*, XI, 912–916 (Oct., 1884).

29. *Ibid.*, XIV, 340–341 (Mar., 1887).

30. *Ibid.*, XV, 525–529 (May, 1888).

31. *Ibid.*, XVI, 246–256 (Feb., 1889); *The Literary World*, XIX, 391–392 (Nov. 10, 1888).

32. *St. Nicholas*, XVI, 883–886 (Oct., 1889).

33. This story ran in *St. Nicholas* from Nov. 1890 until June 1891.

34. *The Book Buyer*, VIII, 291 (Aug., 1891).

35. *The Dial*, XII, 287 (Dec., 1891).

36. *The Book Buyer*, VIII, 435 (Nov., 1891).

37. *Overland Monthly*, VIII (2nd ser.), 337–347 (Oct., 1886).

38. *The Critic*, V, 98–99 (Aug. 30, 1884); XXI, 124–125 (Sept. 3, 1892).

39. "The Newspaper of the Future," *The Forum*, IX, 569–578 (July, 1890).

40. *The Book Buyer*, VI, 437–458 (Dec., 1889).

41. *Ibid.*, VII, 49–51 (Mar., 1890).

42. *Ibid.*, VII, 511–539 (Dec., 1890).

43. *Ibid.*, IX, 545–573 (Dec., 1892).

44. *Ibid.*, X, 497–531 (Dec., 1893).

45. *The Literary World*, XVII, 217 (June 26, 1886).

46. Brooks to W. H. Knight, Newark, N.J., Nov. 2, 1886, U.C.L.A. Lib.

47. *The Book Buyer*, V, 235 (July, 1888); *The Literary World*, XIX, 199 (June 23, 1888); *Magazine of American History*, XX, 86 (July, 1888).

48. William E. Barton, *Abraham Lincoln and His Books* (Chicago, 1920), 74.

49. *The Book Buyer*, V, 60 (Mar., 1888); *The Writer*, II, 100 (Apr., 1888).

50. Newark *Evening News*, Aug. 18, 1903.

51. N.Y. *Times*, July 30, 1893.

52. *The Lamp*, XXVII, 131 (Sept., 1903).

53. *The Critic*, XXIII, 79 (July 29, 1893).

54. *The Literary World*, XXIV, 255 (Aug. 12, 1893).

55. Brooks to William Winter, Newark, N.J., Oct. 3, 1893, Winter Papers, N.Y. Pub. Lib.

56. *The Book Buyer*, X, 405 (Nov., 1893).

57. *Ibid.*, XI, 589–623 (Dec., 1894); XIII, 787–828 (Dec., 1896); XVII, 443–481 (Dec., 1898).

58. *Ibid.*, XXIV, 358–362 (June, 1902). It was entitled "Bret Harte: A Study and an Appreciation."

59. *Harper's Weekly*, XXXVII, 1147 (Dec. 2, 1893); XXXVIII, 198 (Mar. 3, 1894).

60. Brooks to R.W. Gilder, Newark, N.J., Feb. 3, 1894, Century Coll., N.Y. Pub. Lib.

61. *Abraham Lincoln: A History* ran serially from Nov. 1886 until Feb. 1890 and then was published in ten volumes.

62. Frank H. Scott to Brooks, N.Y., Feb. 17, 1894, Hatch Coll.

63. Brooks to R.W. Gilder, Newark, N.J., Feb. 28, 1894, Century Coll., N.Y. Pub. Lib.

64. Frank H. Scott to Brooks, N.Y., Mar. 6, 1894, Hatch Coll.

65. Frank H. Scott to Brooks, N.Y., Mar. 8, 1894, Hatch Coll.

66. *The Critic*, XXIII, 301 (May 5, 1894); *The Writer*, VII, 78 (May, 1894).

67. Brooks to George Witherle, San Francisco, Sept. 20, 1866; N.Y., May 15, 1872; Newark, N.J., Mar. 9, 1891, Hatch Coll.

68. *Annual Report of the Town Officers of Castine, Maine* (Ellsworth, 1895), 9; Wheeler, *Castine Past and Present* (Boston, 1896), 85; Newark *Sunday News*, Aug. 23, 1903; unidentified newspaper clipping in author's collection entitled "Noah Brooks in His Castine Home."

69. Noah Brooks Hooper to author, Castine, Me., Oct. 13, 1950, Nov. 26, 1952.

70. Mrs. Thomas A. Hall to author, San Francisco, Apr. 11, 1953.

71. Mary D. Devereux to author, Castine, Me., Sept. 19, 1953; Noah Brooks Harper to author, Castine, Me., Nov. 26, 1952.

72. Brooks to George Witherle, N.Y., Oct. 25, 1880; Newark, N.J., Mar. 9, 1891, Hatch Coll.

73. *Annual Report of the Town Officers of Castine, Maine*, 1896, 30–32. The Castine Library was established in 1855.

74. *Ibid.*, 1900, 2.

75. These stories are "Pansy Pegg," "The Apparition of Jo Murch," "The Phantom Sailor," "The Waif of Nautilus Island," "The Hereditary Barn," "A Century Ago," and "The Honor of a Family."

76. *The Literary World*, XXV, 174 (June 2, 1894); *The Dial*, XVI, 372 (June 16, 1894).

77. *The Literary World*, XXV, 231 (July 28, 1894).

78. *Ibid.*, XXVI, 9 (Jan. 12, 1895).

79. Brooks, *Washington in Lincoln's Time*, 1.

80. "Washington in Lincoln's Time," *The Century Magazine*, XLIX, 140–149 (Nov., 1894); "Glimpses of Lincoln in War Time," *ibid.*, XLIX, 457–467 (Jan., 1895); "Lincoln, Chase, and Grant," *ibid.*, XLIX, 607–619 (Feb., 1895); "Two War-Time Conventions," *ibid.*, XLIX, 723–736 (Mar., 1895); "Lincoln's Reelection," *ibid.*, XLIX, 865–872 (Apr., 1895); "The Close of Lincoln's Career," *ibid.*, L, 18–27 (May, 1895).

81. Contract of May 14, 1895, in files of Appleton-Century-Crofts, N.Y.

82. *The Book Buyer*, XII, 678 (Dec., 1895).

83. *American Historical Review*, I, 377 (Jan., 1896).

84. *The Literary Digest*, X, 447 (Feb. 9, 1895); X, 717–718 (Apr. 13, 1895).

85. Brooks, "Prohibition Does Not Prohibit," N.Y. *Times*, Jan. 14, 1898.

86. *The Writer*, VII, 163 (Nov., 1894).

87. N.Y. *Social Register* for Nov., 1894, 43.

88. Theodore F. Wolfe, *Literary Haunts & Homes: American Authors* (Philadelphia, 1899), 92–94. Davis lived here from about 1892 until 1899. Charles Belmont Davis, ed., *Adventures and Letters of Richard Harding Davis* (N.Y., 1917), 59.

89. *Club Men of New York 1901-2*, 136.

90. Newark *Daily Advertiser*, Aug. 18, 1903; William Webster Ellsworth, *A Golden Age of Authors: A Publisher Recollection* (Boston, 1919), 58–59.

91. N.Y. *Tribune*, Dec. 8, 1894; N.Y. *Herald*, Dec. 8, 1894; *The Literary World*, XXV, 456 (Dec. 15, 1894).

92. "The Beginnings of American Parties," *Scribner's Magazine*, XVII, 48–64 (Jan., 1895); "The Passing of the Whigs," *ibid.*, XVII, 199–213 (Feb., 1895); and "When Slavery Went Out of Politics," *ibid.*, XVII, 338–352 (Mar., 1895).

93. It is a small book, containing 205 pages.

94. *The Bookman*, I, 200 (Apr., 1895).

95. Brooks to George Witherle, Chelsea, Mass., May 13, [1851], Hatch Coll.

96. Edmund Clarence Stedman went to Europe in 1882. *The Critic*, II, 129 (May 6, 1882). In 1894 William Winter, Mark Twain, and William Dean Howells toured Europe. *The Writer*, VII, 94, 95 (June, 1894); VII, 111 (July, 1894).

97. N.Y. *Herald*, Jan. 29, 1895; *The Critic*, XXVI, 114 (Feb. 9, 1895). Brooks's companion cannot be identified from the passenger list.

98. Brooks, "Madeira and the Azores," N.Y. *Times*, Feb. 24, 1895.

99. Brooks, "Gibraltar and Algiers," *ibid.*, Mar. 10, 1895.

100. Brooks, "Superb Genoa and Nice," *ibid.*, Mar. 24, 1895.

101. Brooks, "Island of the Knights," *ibid.*, Mar. 17, 1895.

102. Brooks, "Land of the Pharaohs," *ibid.*, Apr. 7, 1895.

103. Brooks, "The Sphinx's Stony Gaze," *ibid.*, Apr. 14, 1895.

104. Brooks, "Pilgrims to Jerusalem," *ibid.*, Apr. 21, 1895.

105. Brooks, "Gem of Athens's Crown," *ibid.*, Apr. 28, 1895.

106. Brooks, "Christians in Turkey," *ibid.*, May 5, 1895.

107. Brooks, "Night in Mid-Ramazan," *ibid.*, May 12, 1895.

108. The *Fürst Bismarck* sailed from Naples on Mar. 23 and reached New York on Apr. 5. N.Y. *Herald*, Apr. 6, 1895.

109. Brooks, "Naples, Rome, and Milan," *ibid.*, June 2, 1895.

110. *The Writer*, VIII, 27 (Feb., 1895).

111. Edmund Clarence Stedman had also written a guide to Europe after his trip. *The Critic*, III, 222 (May 12, 1883).

112. Brooks, *The Mediterranean Trip: A Short Guide to the Principal Points on the Shores of the Western Mediterranean and the Levant* (N.Y., 1895).

113. *The Literary World*, XXVI, 472 (Dec. 28, 1895); *The Book Buyer*, XII, 831 (Jan., 1896).

114. Brooks, "The Rector's Hat," *Scribner's Magazine*, XVIII, 202–212 (Aug., 1895).

115. It was issued at New York about May of 1895.

116. *The Book Buyer*, XII, 240–241 (May, 1895). See also *The Literary World*, 167 (June 1, 1895) and *The Cyclopedic Review of Current History*, V, 489 (Apr. 1-June 20, 1895).

117. Newark *Sunday News*, Aug. 23, 1903.

118. Records of the Grafton County Probate Court, Woodsville, N.H. Most of Wilder's fortune was left to Dartmouth College. *The Dartmouth*, XIX, 10 (1897).

119. The other two books are *Short Studies in Party Politics* and *How the Republic Is Governed*.

120. E. L. Burlingame to Brooks, N.Y., July 9, 1895, Wright Coll.

121. Chapt. XVII, p. 435.

122. E. L. Burlingame to Brooks, N.Y., Nov. 19, 1895, Wright Coll.

123. Brooks to Frank R. Dixon, Castine, Me., Feb. 21, 1896, George C. Dixon Coll.; N.Y. *Social Register* for July, 1896, 34.

124. Brooks, "How the Flag Was Saved," *St. Nicholas*, XXIII, 294–295 (Feb., 1896).

125. *St. Nicholas*, XXIII, 640–647; 739–744; 858–861; 954–959; 998–1003; XXIV, 65–67; 137–139; 242–245; 341–343; 425–429; 509–513 (June, 1896-Apr., 1897).

126. *Ser Marco Polo, The Venetian* (London, 1871).

127. *The Bookman*, VIII, 394 (Dec., 1898); *The Literary World*, XXIX, 375–376 (Nov. 12, 1898).

128. Brooks, "The Coming and Going of Pete," *St. Nicholas*, XXXI, 583–586 (May, 1904).

129. *Annual Report of the Town Officers of Castine, Maine*, 1896, 33–35.

130. *The Critic*, XXIX, 369 (Dec. 5, 1896).

131. Los Angeles *Times*, Dec. 14, 1896.

132. Edith Upham Boyers to author, Los Angeles, Aug. 4, 1951.

133. Brooks, "In Southern California," N.Y. *Times*, Jan. 31, 1897.

134. San Francisco *Call*, Apr. 10, 11, 1897.

135. Sarah Brooks Gay was the daughter of Benjamin D. Gay and Phebe Perkins Brooks; she was born on Apr. 16, 1851 and died on Apr. 25, 1911.

136. Noah Brooks Hooper to author, Castine, Me., Oct. 13, 1950.

137. G. H. Putnam to Brooks, N.Y., Dec. 4, 1897, Wright Coll.

138. Brooks, "American Interest in American History," *N.Y. Times Saturday Review of Books and Art*, Dec. 11, 1897; "Prohibition Does Not Prohibit," N.Y. *Times*, Jan. 14, 1898; "California's Golden Jubilee," *ibid.*, Jan. 24, 1898; "The Final Estimate of Lincoln," *ibid.*, Feb. 13, 1898.

139. G.P. Putnam's Sons to Brooks, N.Y., Feb. 12, 1898, Wright Coll.

140. Brooks, *Henry Knox: A Soldier of the Revolution* (N.Y., 1900), v. In 1910 the Knox Papers were deposited in the Mass. Hist. Soc.

141. Stedman and Gould, *Life and Letters of Edmund Clarence Stedman*, II, 471; Brooks to Edmund Clarence Stedman, N.Y., Mar. 12, 1898, Columbia Univ. Lib.; Laura Stedman, "Confession of an Album," *The Bookman*, XXXVII, 268 (May, 1913).

142. *Overland Monthly*, XXXII, 3–11 (July, 1898).

143. Brooks to R. W. Gilder, Castine, Me., Aug. 15, 1898, Century Coll., N.Y. Pub. Lib. Brooks meant that he would write articles on Mark Twain, Bret Harte, and Henry George.

144. Brooks to R. W. Gilder, Castine, Me., Aug. 26, 1898, Century Coll., N.Y. Pub. Lib.

145. Brooks to R. W. Gilder, Castine, Me., Aug. 22, 1898, Century Coll., N.Y. Pub. Lib.

146. Brooks, "Mark Twain in California," *The Century Magazine*, LVII, 97–99 (Nov., 1898).

147. *The Literary World*, XXIX, 438 (Dec. 10, 1898).

148. Royalty reports from Charles Scribner's Sons, Hatch Coll.

149. Brooks to Maine Hist. Soc., Castine, Me., Oct. 4, 1898, Collections and Proceedings of the Maine Hist. Soc. (Portland, 1899), X (2nd ser.), 110–111.

150. Brooks to Henry George Jr., National Home for Disabled Soldiers, Cal., Jan. 3, 1899, Henry George Papers, N.Y. Pub. Lib.

151. Brooks, "Henry George in California," *The Century Magazine*, LVII, 549–552 (Feb., 1899).

152. Brooks, "Bret Harte in California," *ibid.*, LVIII, 447–451 (July, 1899).

153. G. H. Putman to Brooks, N.Y., Mar. 15, 1899, Wright Coll.

154. Brooks to R. W. Gilder, N.Y., Apr. 7, [1899], Century Coll. N.Y. Pub. Lib.

155. Brooks to R. U. Johnson, N.Y., [1899], Century Coll., N.Y. Pub. Lib.

156. G. H. Putnam to Brooks, N.Y., July 19, 1899, Wright Coll.

157. G. H. Putnam to Brooks, N.Y., July 20, 1899, Wright Coll.

158. Brooks, *Henry Knox*, vi.

159. Brooks himself explained this matter in a letter to the Maine Hist. Soc. on Oct. 4, 1898. Collections and Proceedings of the Maine Hist. Soc., X (2nd ser.), 110–111.

160. *The Literary World*, XXXI, 151 (Aug. 1, 1900); *American Historical Review*, VI, 367–368 (Jan., 1901).

161. Elbridge S. Brooks to Brooks, Boston, Jan. 2, 1899, Wright Coll.

162. Dana Estes & Co. to Brooks, Boston, Sept. 25, 1899, Wright Coll.

163. This set was published by James T. White & Co. of N.Y. Brooks served from the first issue in 1891 until his death.

164. Charles Eugene Hamlin, *The Life and Times of Hannibal Hamlin* (Cambridge, 1899).

165. Adams, *Castine Sixty Years Ago* (Boston, 1900), 3.

166. *The New-Eng. Hist. and Geneal. Reg.*, LV, xxxv.

167. Brooks to R. W. Gilder, Castine, Me., Nov. 29, 1900 Century Coll., N.Y. Pub. Lib.

168. Various letters and envelopes in the Wright Coll.

169. *History of the Expedition under the Command of Lewis and Clark* (N.Y., 1893).

170. *The Book Buyer*, XXIII, 433–434 (Dec., 1901).

171. Jan. 2, 1902. Brooks received clipping service from The Authors' Clipping Bureau of Boston and the National Press Intelligence Co. of N.Y. Wright Coll.

172. *The Book Buyer*, XXI, 535–537 (Jan., 1901).

173. Brooks, "Horace Greeley," *The Youth's Companion*, LXXV, 399–400 (Aug. 15, 1901).

174. Brooks, "Mrs. Thankful's Charge," *The Century Magazine*, LXII, 563–580 (Aug., 1901).

175. *The Book Buyer*, XXIII, 437 (Dec., 1901).

176. *Lem* sold well in both England and the U.S. Royalty reports in Wright Coll.

177. Brooks to R. W. Gilder, Castine, Me., Nov. 19, 1901, Century Coll., N.Y. Pub. Lib.

178. Brooks to R. U. Johnson, Castine, Me., Nov. 30, 1901, Century Coll., N.Y. Pub. Lib.

179. *The Century Magazine*, LXIII, 803–820 (Apr., 1902).

180. Knickerbocker Pub. Co. to Brooks, N.Y., Feb. 21, 1902, Wright Coll.

181. Knickerbocker Pub. Co. to Brooks, N.Y., Apr. 25, 1902, Wright Coll.

182. "Harte's Early Days," *N.Y. Times Magazine*, May 24, 1902, p. 350; "Bret Harte: A Study and an Appreciation," *The Book Buyer*, XXIV, 358–362 (June, 1902), a condensation of which appeared as "An Appreciation by an Old Friend" in *Booklovers Magazine*, II, 30–31 (July, 1903); "Bret Harte: A Biographical and Critical Sketch," *Overland Monthly*, XL, 201–207 (Sept., 1902).

183. Francis W. Halsey to Brooks, N.Y., July 25, 1902, Hatch Coll.

184. Francis W. Halsey to Brooks, N.Y., Aug. 12, 1902, Wright Coll.

185. Edith Upham Boyers to author, Los Angeles, Aug. 4, 1941.

186. "Lincoln Reminiscences," *N.Y. Times Saturday Review of Books and Art*, Oct. 18, 1902, p. 715. The article is dated Castine, Oct. 10, 1902.

187. Charles Scribner to Brooks, N.Y., Dec. 17, 1902, Wright Coll.

188. Statement of George Hobart Doane, Newark *Daily Advertiser*, Aug. 18, 1903.

189. Newark *Evening News*, Aug. 18, 1903.

190. Obituary notices state that he had been in California about eight months before he died.

191. Newark *Sunday News*, Aug. 23, 1903.

192. "How We Bought the Great West," *Scribner's Magazine*, XXXIV, 561–569 (Nov., 1903); "The Coming and Going of Pete," *St. Nicholas*, XXXI, 583–586 (May, 1904).

193. Newark *Evening News*, Aug. 18, 1903.

194. Pasadena *Daily News*, Aug. 17, 1903; Edith Upham Boyers to author, Los Angeles, Aug. 4, 1951.

195. Death certificates in the Dept. of Health, Pasadena; records of Ives & Warren Co., 100 N. Hill Ave., Pasadena.

196. Pasadena *Evening Star*, Aug. 17, 1903.

197. Edith Upham Boyers to author, Los Angeles, Aug. 14, 1951.

198. *The Writer*, XVI, 27 (Feb., 1903).

199. Bangor *Daily News*, Aug. 27, 1903.

200. C. H. C. Wright to author, Paris, Me., July 27, 1951.

201. Adams, *An Address at the Funeral of Noah Brooks, Castine, Maine*, August 26, 1903 (Boston, n.d.)

202. Howard Clinton Dickinson, of Essex Fells, N.J., composed a poem to the memory of Brooks and published it in the Newark *Sunday News*, Aug. 23, 1903. It was reprinted in *The Lamp*, XXVIII, 117–118 (Mar., 1904).

Editors' Acknowledgments

THE EDITORS ARE GRATEFUL for the assistance of Ai Miller, a notably faithful student assistant, for help with the management of the archival and editorial aspects of this project. The Knox College Library once again provided ready assistance, with Jeff Douglas, Laurie Sauer, and Sharon Clayton deserving particular mention. All of our editorial projects have benefited from the assistance and advice of John M. Hoffman of the University of Illinois Library, James Cornelius of the Abraham Lincoln Presidential Library, and Michelle Knowles of the Library of Congress. Steven Rogstad was particularly helpful in this project. Perhaps the oldest ally of the Lincoln Studies Center, Michael Burlingame, was a very active supporter of this project from the time of its inception, and we are especially grateful for his informative Introduction. We are pleased to acknowledge the steadfast encouragement and support of another early ally, Lewis Lehrman. Finally, we gratefully acknowledge the indispensable cooperation and assistance of Wayne C. Temple.

Index